THE
VESTRY BOOK

OF

PETSWORTH PARISH

GLOUCESTER COUNTY, VIRGINIA

1677-1793

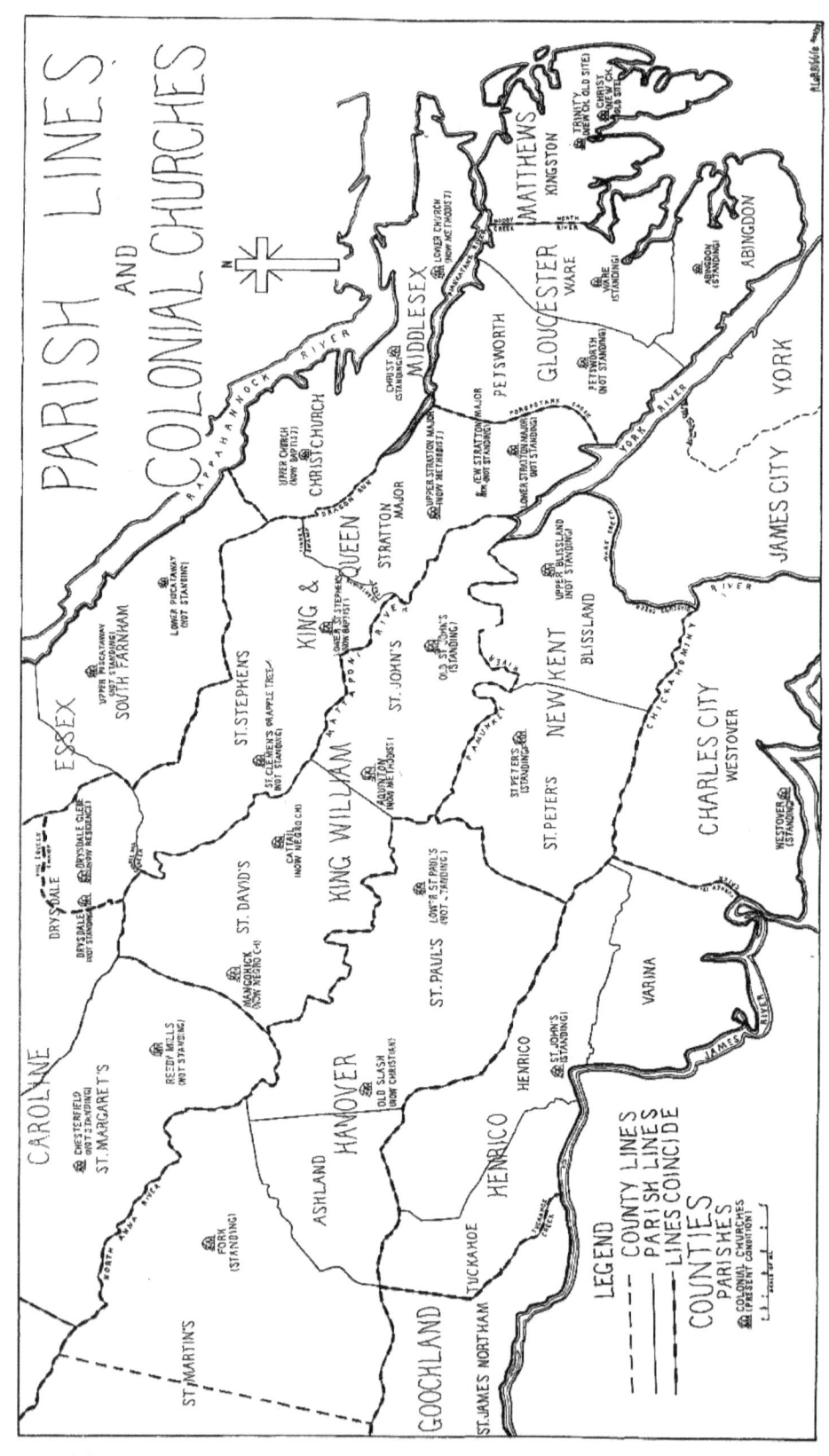

THE VESTRY BOOK

OF

PETSWORTH PARISH

GLOUCESTER COUNTY, VIRGINIA

1677-1793

TRANSCRIBED, ANNOTATED AND INDEXED
BY
C. G. CHAMBERLAYNE

Southern Historical Press, Inc.
Greenville, South Carolina

This volume was reproduced from
A personal copy located in the
Publisher's private Library

All rights reserved. No part of this publication may be reproduced,
stored in a retrieval system, transmitted in any form, posted
on to the web in any form or by any means without
the prior written permission of the publisher.

Please direct all correspondence and orders to:

www.southernhistoricalpress.com
or
SOUTHERN HISTORICAL PRESS, Inc.
PO BOX 1267
375 West Broad Street
Greenville, SC   29601
southernhistoricalpress@gmail.com

Originally published: Richmond, VA. 1933
ISBN #0-89308-244-9
All rights Reserved.
Printed in the United States of America

Introductory Note

With the publication of the present volume Dr. Churchill Gibson Chamberlayne again comes forward with a most valuable contribution to the church history of Colonial Virginia. His former volume published by the Library Board was "The Vestry Book of Stratton-Major Parish, King and Queen County, Virginia, 1729-1783." He had already published at his own expense "The Vestry Book and Register of Bristol Parish, Virginia, 1720-1789," "The Vestry Book of Christ Church Parish, Middlesex County, Virginia, 1663-1767," and "The Vestry Book of Kingston Parish, Mathews County, Virginia, 1679-1796."

The present volume is as carefully edited as the Stratton Major volume or the three volumes published by Dr. Chamberlayne at his own expense. This is praise indeed, since those volumes have established Dr. Chamberlayne's reputation as a careful and accurate scholar, and one in love with the records of his church and the history of the Colony and State of Virginia. Without remuneration from the State he gives his time to this important work, as does Mr. Landon C. Bell, the editor of the immediately preceding volume in this church records series, "Charles Parish, York County, Virginia, History and Registers, 1648-1789."

Both these gentlemen intend to continue their work. The Library Board is most fortunate, as are the people of Virginia, that two such scholarly and painstaking workers are willing to engage in this very exacting work without hope of monetary reward, but simply because they recognize the importance of it and because they wish to make worthy contributions to the printed historical documents of their State. Surely the General Assembly of Virginia will make adequate appropriations for the continuance of the work.

A very valuable feature of the present volume is the map, prepared by the Rev. A. LeB. Ribble, of Herndon, Va., giving not only the bounds of Petsworth Parish but those also of neighboring parishes—in fact, of most of the colonial parishes of Tidewater Virginia between the Rappahannock and the James. The map will be very useful to one wishing to locate the old colonial churches in that region and to know their present status. When the vestry books and registers of other parishes are printed, the map may be used again. The thanks of the Library Board are extended to Mr. Ribble for his aid.

H. R. McILWAINE,
State Librarian.

Richmond, September 22, 1933.

Preface

The MS. volume hereinafter reproduced embodies the earliest consecutive records of Petsworth (or Petsoe) Parish, Gloucester County, Virginia, known to be in existence. However, the parish can be traced back to the year 1666 (see page ix), and was possibly established as early as 1656 (see page xi). This old volume is one of the many vestry books that Bishop Meade used as sources when writing his *Old Churches, Ministers and Families of Virginia*. It is now in the possession of the vestries of Abingdon and Ware parishes, Gloucester County, Virginia.

The MS. Vestry Book is a folio measuring 11½ by 7½ inches. It consists of 205 leaves (410 pages) of laid paper, showing the "Puritan hat" water mark (2½ by 2½ inches), and covers the period from January 23, 1677, to July 11, 1793. Referring to this old volume Bishop Meade (*Old Churches*, Vol. I, page 321) says: "This book contains, with a slight exception, the records of the vestry-meetings from the year 1677 to 1793. When commenced and closed, its torn condition permits us not to discover." From the foregoing one would naturally infer that Bishop Meade thought that the Vestry Book was incomplete at both ends; *i. e.*, that pages were missing in the front and at the back of the MS. In this opinion the present editor does not concur with the Bishop, and for the following reasons:

1. When one examines the last leaf of the book (pages 409 and 410), he discovers on page 409 a complete entry; namely, that of a vestry meeting held July 11, 1793. The next page, which affords space sufficient to hold the full record of any ordinary vestry meeting, is entirely blank, except for some idle scribblings written in a hand other than that of the writing on the preceding page. The inference is obvious either that the vestry discontinued the recording of minutes after July 11, 1793, or that they then began to use another book.

2. Turning to the first leaf of the book as it is at present, we note (a) that the record begins not with the continuation of

something begun on a preceding page but with the words regularly used at the beginning of the minutes of a vestry meeting; and (b) that the date of this first entry is January 23, 167[7].

Now (a) is only negative (and hence inconclusive) evidence that no pages had once preceded the present page 1. (b), too, while evidence to the same effect, is also merely negative evidence and hence inconclusive, but it is weightier when considered in the light of certain well established facts:

1. 1676 was the year of Bacon's Rebellion.

2. Gloucester County was one of the chief centers of the disturbance; and it is to be noted (a) that it was at the house of a Mr. or Dr. Pate in Gloucester County that Bacon the Rebel is said to have died, and (b) that in 1677 a Major Thomas Pate was one of the church wardens of Petsworth Parish.

3. Only one of the thirty or more extant colonial vestry books antedates Bacon's Rebellion; and in this one case it is to be noted (a) that all that part of the MS. dealing with events prior to November 20, 1701, was transcribed from a still older MS. (long since lost) between that date and May 4, 1702 (*The Vestry Book of Christ Church Parish, Middlesex County, Virginia,* 1663-1767, pages 92 and 93), and (b) that there is a transcriber's note appearing just before the entry dated May 8, 1677, to the following effect:

"M° Some of the Former Vestrys were Defaced in the old Booke and Some were wanting, But from hence forward all are perfect &c." (*Ibid,* page 24.)

In view of the foregoing, it seems to the present editor more than probable that at least in those parishes directly and fundamentally affected by Bacon's Rebellion it was found advisable the year following the Rebellion (1677) to destroy the existing vestry records or at least to render illegible some part of those records. At any rate, what little evidence there is, negative as well as positive, leads to that conclusion.

Summing up the matter, the present editor is of the opinion that the MS. Vestry Book of Petsworth Parish reproduced in the following pages is the original book whole and entire (except where indicated) and with no single page missing.

The continuous history of Petsworth Parish begins with the date January 23, 1677, but the parish can be traced back to February 16, 1665/6 (Virginia Land Office, *Patent Book No. 5*, page 573) and it is probable that it was established some years earlier than that. However in order to arrive at the most likely date for the establishment of the parish, it is necessary first to determine as nearly as possible the date of the establishment of Gloucester County, which preceded the former by at least several yars.

On April 18, 1644, war broke out in Virginia between the colonists and the Indians, led by the hundred years old Opechancanough. This war was ended October 5, 1646, by a treaty of peace between the colonists and the Indian king, Necotowance, the successor of Opechancanough. The second article of this treaty states:

"That it shall be free for the said Necotowance and his people, to inhabit and hunt on the north-side of Yorke River, without any interruption from the English. *Provided* that if hereafter, It shall be thought fitt by the Governor and Council to permitt any English to inhabitt from Poropotanke [the present boundary line between Gloucester and King and Queen counties] downewards [*i. e.,* in what are now Gloucester and Mathews counties], that first Necotowance be acquainted therewith." (*Hening*, Vol. I, page 323.) Two years later, in October, 1648, it was enacted that the inhabitants might remove and settle on the north side of Charles River (York River) and Rappahannock River after the first of the following September. (*Hening,* Vol. I, page 353.) Accordingly what is now Gloucester County was opened to settlement September 1, 1649. However, the first reference to the county by name found by the present editor is under the date Jan. 9, 1651 (which, of course, may mean 1652) or the date May 21, 1651. (Virginia Land Office, *Patent Book No. 2*, pages 353 and 319.)

Up to the present time the Act establishing Gloucester County —if it was established by particular Act—has not come to light, and until it does, or until further investigations carry the county still farther back, May 21, 1651 (or possibly January 9, 1651), can be taken as the earliest date for Gloucester County.

In explanation of our ignorance in regard to the exact date of the establishment of Gloucester County, it may be well to call attention here to the disturbed state of affairs in Virginia between January 30, 1649, when King Charles I was beheaded, and March 12, 1652, when Virginia was surrendered to the Commonwealth of England. During these three years but one Grand Assembly was held, on October 10, 1649, and at this Assembly only four acts apparently were passed, none of which makes any reference to Gloucester County. When the next Grand Assembly met (April 26, 1652), Gloucester County was represented by two Burgesses, Mr. Hugh Guinne and Mr. Fra. Willis.

The beginnings of Petsworth Parish, like those of Gloucester County, are obscure, and the exact date of its establishment impossible at present to determine—the same thing being true of the other three parishes, Kingston, Abingdon, and Ware, lying within the limits of *old* Gloucester County (*i. e.,* Gloucester County before Mathews County was carved out of it), for in the case of no one of these parishes has an Act specifically establishing it been found. The reason for this failure, probably, though not certainly, is that no such Act was ever passed, and that these parishes came into being under the provisions of Act IX of the session of the Assembly beginning March 10, 1655/6, which reads as follows:

"That all countys not yet laid out into parishes shall be divided into parishes the next county court after publication hereof." (*Hening*, Vol. I, page 400)—or of Act LXXV of the next session beginning March 13, 1657/8, which states:

"Bee it enacted by this Grand Assembly, That it shall be lawfull for the comissioners of the several counties not yet laid out into parishes, with consent of the inhabitants thereof to devide their counties into parishes as by the major part of the said counties shall be agreed." (*Hening*, Vol. I, page 469. See also *Hening*, Vol. I, page 478, where, as Act *CI*, Act *IX* of the previous session was reenacted practically word for word.)

Taking into consideration, then, the facts: (1) that during the period between March 12, 1652 (the date of the surrender of the Colony to the Commonwealth) and March 13, 1659/60 (the opening date of the last Grand Assembly held before the Restoration) we find in the records *before* March 10, 1655/6, Acts specifically establishing the parishes of Ocquhanocke, Marston, and Stratton Major; (2) that between March 10, 1655/6, and March 13, 1659/60, we find only one Act for the establishment of a parish (Middletowne, which was formed April 1, 1658, by *uniting into one parish two long-established parishes*); (3) and that on March 10, 1655/6, a general Act was passed (and reenacted two years later) requiring the county courts to divide into parishes all counties not yet laid out into parishes; and (4) that from the records it appears that Kingston Parish (one of the four parishes in old Gloucester County) was in existence on March 15, 1657 (or 8) (Virginia Land Office, *Patent Book No. 4*, page 304)—we may perhaps assume that Petsworth Parish was established by county court action following the passage of Act *IX* of the Assembly of March 10, 1655/6. If the above conclusion be correct, then it follows as a strong probability at least that the four parishes in old Gloucester County were established at one and the same time and at a date between March 10, 1655/6, and March 15, 1657 (or 8).

Of definite facts in connection with the history of Petsworth Parish prior to January 23, 1677, there are but two to recount. These two are the following:

1. Petsoe Parish is mentioned in a Land Patent, to Wm Thornton for 164 acres, dated Feb. 16, 1665/6. (Virginia Land Office, *Patent Book No. 5, page 573.*)

2. "Mr. Thomas Vicars Clk" was granted 650 acres of land in Gloucester County (name of parish not given) on Feb. 16, 1665/6, the same date as above, (Virginia Land Office, *Patent Book No. 5, page 574.*) Mr. Vicars (or Vicaris) was minister of Petsworth Parish in 1677.

When Petsworth Parish ceased to exist it is impossible for the present editor to say. He believes, however, that it must have ceased to function shortly after July 11, 1793; for had it flourished after that date, the indefatigable Bishop Meade would doubtless have been able to unearth some facts in connection with its subsequent history, and having done so would have recorded them in his book—which is completely silent on the subject.

The sketch map of that portion of Tidewater Virginia extending from the Rappahannock to the James which accompanies this volume and which is to be found inserted as a frontispiece, was drawn for this publication by the Rev. A. LeB. Ribble, of Herndon, Va. The editor wishes here to make grateful acknowledgment of his indebtedness to Mr. Ribble in this connection. He also wishes to thank the Rev. Arthur P. Gray, of West Point, Va., for his invaluable assistance in locating the sites of several churches and in defining various parish boundary lines, and the Rev. Dr. G. MacLaren Brydon for many helpful suggestions made in connection with the map and for his courtesy in reading and criticizing this preface.

In a former publication in this series, *The Vestry Book of Stratton Major Parish, King and Queen County, Virginia*, 1729-1783, the editor listed, on pages XIII to XVIII, the MS. parish record books known to be in existence. In that list he inadvertently made a regrettable mistake by listing among the yet *unpublished* records *The Reverend John Cameron's Registers*,

1784-1815. These records were published in 1930 by Landon C. Bell, Ph. B., M. A., LL.B., in his monumental work, *Cumberland Parish, Lunenburg County, Virginia*, 1746-1816. The editor is glad of the opportunity here given him to correct his error and to present his public apologies to Mr. Bell. Including, then, the Cameron Registers and Mr. Bell's later work, *Charles Parish, York County, Virginia, History and Registers*, 1618-1789 (published by the Library Board in 1932), the list of published parish records includes sixteen titles (Vestry Books and Registers); there still remain thirty-two parish records that have never been put into print.

In the MS. Vestry Book the parish is always styled "Petsoe" until the year 1714 (Feb. 12), when the name "Petsworth" appears (page 126) for the first and only time in 37 years. Then on Oct. 1, 1729, "Petsworth" occurs again (page 218); and for some years after this latter date the two names are used more or less interchangeably. Finally "Petsoe" appears to have been dropped entirely and "Petsworth" is uniformly used.

With regard to the origin of the names "Petsoe" and "Petsworth" as applied to this Virginia parish the editor knows nothing. However, in this connection reference may well be made to the old town of Petworth, in Sussex County, England, 55 miles S. S. W. from London. Possibly "Petsworth" is a corruption of "Petworth," but that is a mere guess and one entirely unsupported by any evidence in the editor's possession.

A glance at the map in this volume will be sufficient to give the main geographical features of Petsworth Parish. As will be seen, the parish is bounded on the west and north-west by King and Queen County, on the north by Middlesex County (from which it is separated by Piankatank River and the Dragon Run), on the east and south-east by Ware Parish and Abingdon Parish, and on the south and south-west by York River. Petsworth parish is entirely rural in character; it contains no towns at all and few villages of any considerable size. Its many creeks flow into the Piankatank or into York River.

Between pages 314 and 315 of the MS. Vestry Book there is a page which was never numbered and which is closely covered with sermon notes written in a microscopic hand. The editor did not include this page in his transcript, as he did not consider it in any sense a part of the official vestry record.

The four-line heading to page 1 of this volume is, of course, not a part of the original record. The MS. record begins with the words:

"Att a vestry held for Petsoe parish y^e: 23^d: Jan^{ry}: 167[]"

The facsimile pages of the MS. used to illustrate the volume are from photographs of the origin pages. Wherever in the MS. the word "Seal," or the impression of a seal in wax, occurs, the printed volume shows the word "Seal" in parentheses. Blanks in the MS. which were left by the Clerk to be filled in later, but were never filled in, are indicated in the printed volume by blank spaces. Gaps in the MS. resulting from tearing, rubbing, or other kinds of intentional or unintentional mutilation are indicated by blank spaces enclosed in brackets. Unintentional omissions in the MS. and all mistakes of whatever kind are, as far as was found possible, reproduced in the printed volume as made. Pages in the MS. are indicated in the printed volume by Arabic numerals enclosed in brackets. In the indexes the number of times a name or a topic occurs on a page is indicated by a small Arabic numeral above, and to the right of, the numeral indicating the number of the page.

The editor has read the proof sheets of the present volume several times, each time using the original MS. as his guide, but he is well aware of the fact that in work of this kind some mistakes are bound to occur, and he can only hope that the number of mistakes (whether of judgment or of oversight) in the volume is small. In this connection he would refer the reader to the list of probable errata to be found in the Appendix. Any one wishing to check up on the editor in his work can do so by comparing the printed volume with the original MS. (in the custody of the Clerk of the Circuit Court, Gloucester, Va.) or with the photostat copy of the original on file in the Archives Department of the Virginia State Library in Richmond.

C. G. CHAMBERLAYNE.

Richmond, Va.,
September 20, 1933.

The Vestry Book
... of ...
Petsworth Parish

Gloucester County, Virginia, 1677-1793

Att a vestry held for Pettsoe parish y^e: 23^d: of Jan^{ry}: 167[ ]

m^r. Thomas vicaris minister

present m^r. John Buckner ⎫ m^r. W^m. Thorntone ⎫
        m^r. Robt. Lee   ⎬ m^r. W^m. Pritchett ⎬
        m^r. Tho: Roystone ⎭
        m^r. Phill: Lightfoot & maj^r. Tho: Pate Church: wardens

    Parish deb^{tr}.

To m^r. Vicaris: & caske	12000
To m^r. Lightfoote for 33 Cedar posts and cariage by 6 oxen and fouer men	02150
To Robt. warner for officiatinge as clerke	0500
To Tho: Hide for keepinge a Bastard Child	1000
To Bartholemew Austine for keepinge Rumball	1000
To m^{rs}: Thorntone	0500
To m^r. Lightfoote for Comunion wine	0100
To m^r. Buckner for a cast accon at ye suite of wisdom for which he gave y^e: parish Credit Last year	050
To him for Exon v^s: Evans	015
To m^{rs}: moodie for her husbands takeinge the subscriptions for buildinge ye church at poplar Springe	500
	17815
To caske at 80 ℔^{r} 1000	01440
	19255

₱ʳ. Conᵗʳ: Cʳ:
By mʳ. Barnards Bill as security for his maids fine   545

The Churchwardens are hereby Impowered to Collect of Every Tythable in this parish 43 pounds of tobo per poll, and upon their refusall of payment to make distreſse for yᵉ same, and pay Each parish Creditor his due

[2]   Upon yᵉ: request of Tho: Hide to yᵉ. vestry, they have bound unto him a Bastard child borne of Thomas wisdoms servᵗ. woman, named Edward Grabige untill he come to yᵉ: age of twenty and one yeares, and he yᵉ: said Hide to be allowed five hundred lb: tobo and caske for keeping of yᵉ: said child next yeare, without any further charge to yᵉ: parish

Att a vestry held for pettsoe parish June yᵉ: 14ᵗʰ. 1677

mʳ Thom: vicaris ministʳ

present majʳ. Thom: Pate
        mʳ. John Buckner   mʳ. Robᵗ. Lee
        mʳ. Wᵐ. Thorntone   mʳ. Jnᵒ. Throckmortone

In obedience to an order of Court beareinge date may yᵉ: 16ᵗʰ. 1677 for makeing good yᵉ: worke of such persons as are gone out in this p͠nt Expedition agˢᵗ yᵉ: Indians, by which yᵉ: vestry of each parish is Impoured to levy & proportione yᵉ: same: And accordinge to yᵉ. number of tythables in this parish there is 36 to make good one man's worke dureing yᵉ. time of his being out in yᵉ. service: It is therefor ordered by this p͠nt vestry that each housekeeper or master of a family in whose house any of yᵉ: aforesaid persons did reside, give nottice to soe many of yᵉ: next Inhabitants as amounts to yᵉ: number of 36, to appoint or prefix a day or dayes for yᵉ. paymᵗ of yᵉ: said worke *at *yᵉ *time *appointed: And if any person shall refuse or faile to send his worke at yᵉ. time appointed

*Note! These four words are scratched through with a pen in the original MS., but are distinctly legible.—C. G. C.

he or they soe faileing or refuseinge to be fined at y^e. Courts discretione.

And whereas y^e: vestry are Ignorant w^t. person are prest out in y^e: p̄nt service. The respective Constables are hereby desired & entreated to proportione y^e. said worke amongst y^e. Inhabitants in their severall precincts

[3] Att a vestry held for Pettsoe parish 8^{br} y^e: 4th 1677

present   m^r Thom: vicaris minister

m^r. John Buckner	Capt. Tho Ramsey	⎫
m^r. John Ascough	m^r. Thom: Miller	⎪
m^r. W^m. Thornton Senr:	m^r. Rich: Barnard	⎬ vestry men
m^r. Robt. Lee	m^r. Thom: Roystone	⎪
m^r. W^m. Hansford		⎭

m^r. Phill: Lightfoote	⎫
maj^r. Thomas Pate	⎬ Church wardens
m^r. John Throckmorton	⎭

It is ordered, by this p̄nt vestry, that y^e: inside worke of y^e: Church now in Buildinge at poplare Springe, bee done in manner as followeth vizt: the walls and ceilinge over head to be substantially Lathed, daubed & plastered; the Chancell to be 15 foote and a Scrime to be runn a Croſse y^e: Church wth: ballisters; a Communione table 6 foote & ½ to be inclosed on three sides at 3 foote distance, to be done wth. ballisters, 2 wainscoate double pews one of each side of y^e. Chancell, Joyninge to ye Scrime with ballisters suitable to y^e: said Scrime. 1: double pew above y^e: pulpitt & deske Joyninge to ye Scrime, all y^e: rest of y^e: pews of both sides of y^e: said church to be double, and all to be done wth: wainscoate Backs, the pulpit to be of wainscoate 4 foote diameter, & made with 6 sides, 6 foot allowed for y^e: reading desks & paſsag[e] into y^e: pulpitt: y^e: ministers pew to be under y^e: pulpitt, & raised 18 Inches and y^e: readers deske under it, the two uppermost pews in y^e: Body of y^e: Church & y^e: two pews in y^e: Chancell to have doores.

And it is further order'd that ye: Church wardens doe in behalfe of ye: parish bargaine and agree wth. good sufficient workmen for ye: doeing & finishinge of ye: said worke.

Ordered that Daniel dickinson be Surveyor of ye: highwayes for ye: Lower parte of ye: parish.

Ordered that John Swabbsone be Surveyor of ye: highwayes for ye: middle parte of ye: parish

Ordered that mr. Robt. Carter and Fran: Smithing be Surveyors of ye: highwayes for ye: upper parte of ye: parish

Ordered by this p̄nt vestry that mr. Ralph Greene Senr be Churchwarden for ye: Lower parte of ye: parish, and to continue in ye: said office dureing ye: terme of two yeares next Ensueing accordinge to a former order of this vestry.

Ordered that a vestry be held for this parish on ye: 6th of november next.

[4] Att a vestry held for Pettsoe parish at poplare Springe 9br: 13th: 77.

present   mr. Thomas vicaris minister

Capt Thom: Ramsey	mr. Robert Lee	
mr. John Buckner	mr: Rich: Barnett	
mr. Ralph Greene	mr: Thom. Miller	vestry men
mr. Wm. Thorntone	mr. Wm. Pritchett	

mr. Phill: Lightfoote
majr. Thomas Pate } Church wardens

The Parish debtr. 9br: 1677

	lb: Tob: & caske
To mr. Thom: vicaris for officiateing as minister	12000
To Thom: Hide for keepeing a Bastard child	00500
To Rowland Thomas for keepeing a bastard 4 moneths	00400
to mrs. Thorne for Looking after ye church as sexton	00500

To Rob\ufeff^t. warner for officiateinge as Clerke	01000
To Sam: Duninge for Building y^e: Church at poplare Springe	04000
To Lewis Day for Timber to Build y^e. Church	01000
To m^r. Lightfoote for glaſse, Bookes, nailes & other neceſsaries	03200
To Barth: Austine for keepeing of Rumball	01000
To John oakes for keepeing a Bastard Child	00500
To m^r. Buckner clerk for Fees	00072
	24172
To caske	02417
	26589

To Samuell duninge for Building y^e: Church in money as p^r: agreement   lb: s: d. 43:00:00

$$D^r: 43:00:00$$
$$C^r: 43:06:08$$

$$00:06:08$$

43 || 00 || 00
43 || 06 || 08

00 06 08

[5]   The Parish C^r.

	lb: tobo.		lb: tobo.
By m^r: Vicaris	1200	By Peter Lawd	0050
By maj^r. Lewis	0500	By Abra: Good	0050
By m^{rs}. Morgan	0500	By Thom: Hide	0050
By m^r. Miller	0200	By Dun: Drumond	0050
By m^r. Pritchett	0200	By Edw: Clare	0050

By Edw. Simons	0050	By Rich: Hubbard	0100
By Shep: Johnson	0050	By Thom: wisdome	0050
By Rich: Ireland	0200	By Jnº. Blaſsinghame	0050
By Thom: Loraigne	0050	By wid: Moore	0050
By John Booth	0100	By willm: Hurst	0050
By Tho: Lawrence	0050	By Sam: Conaway Se- curity for his womans fine	0500
By Robt. Warner	0100		
By Hump. Evans	0150		
	———	By Tho: Shedd for Ann willetts fine	0500
	3350		
			1550
		By Robt. Hoggsdone	0050
			———
			1600
			3350
			———
			4950

Dr: 26589
Cr: 04950

which sume of 21639: divided by 438 ye: number of tyth-abes in this parish Comes to 50lb: tobo pr polle.

Cr: in money

	lb : s : d
By Coll. John Smith	10 : 00 : 00
By majr Tho: Pate	05 : 00 : 00
By mr. Carter	05 : 00 : 00
By Coll. Warner	10 : 00 : 00
By mr. Lightfoote	05 : 00 : 00
By mr. Ascough	06 : 06 : 08
By mr. Barnard	02 : 00 : 00
	43 : 06 : 08

Ordered that yᵉ Church-wardens levy & collect of every tythable persone in this parish 50ˡᵇ: tobo per pole, and in case any person shall refuse to make payment of yᵉ: said sume, to make distreſe for yᵉ sumes and pay each parish Credʳ his due.

Upon yᵉ: request of mʳ. wᵐ. Crimes to this vestry, It is ordered that a Bastard Child named Hannah Cocke daughter of Mary Cocke dec whoe was late servant to yᵉ: said Crimes, be bound unto yᵉ said Crimes untill she shall attaine to yᵉ age of one and twenty yeares

Ordered that mʳ. Robᵗ. Carter be added to yᵉ vestry.

Ordered that mʳ Ralph Greene Senʳ: be dismist from being church warden, he being by reason of his age unfitt to discharge yᵗ. office & that mʳ. Ralph Greene Junʳ: be added to yᵉ: vestry, and is hereby appointed Churchwarden for these two yeares next ensueing for yᵉ: lower part of yᵉ: parish and that he collect yᵉ: levy for this present yeare.

[6]
This day majʳ. Thomas Pate, in Consideratione of yᵉ: sume of eight thousand pounds of tobo and caske to be paid by yᵉ: parish, did undertake to plaister, Lath & white wash yᵉ: church at poplar Springe, and to prepare oyster shells for Lime & all other things neceſsary for yᵉ: Compleating & furnishing yᵉ: yᵉ: said plaister worke, wᵗʰ.out any manner of further Charge to yᵉ. parish.

Ordered that Sam: duninge put croſse beames to every small rafter & fitt yᵉ: small peeces for yᵉ: plaister worke, as allsoe amend and rectifie all & every yᵉ: defects & faults in yᵉ: covering & weather boards of yᵉ: Church at poplar Spring, & in consideration of his paines therein to be paid five hundred pounds of tobo and caske next yeare by yᵉ: parish.

Att a vestry holden for pettsoe parish at poplar springe 8ᵇʳ: yᵉ. 30ᵗʰ 1678 & continued till november yᵉ: 3ᵈ: 1678

pn.ᵗ m.ʳ Thomas vicaris minister
m.ʳ John Buckner   m.ʳ Rich: Barnard   ⎫
m.ʳ John Throckmorton   m.ʳ Will: pritchet   ⎬ vestry men
m.ʳ W.ᵐ Thorntone Sen.ʳ   m.ʳ Thom: Royston   ⎭
m.ʳ W.ᵐ Hansford   m.ʳ Phill: Lightfoote ⎫
m.ʳ Thom: miller   Co.ˡˡ Thom: Pate   ⎬ Chur: wardens

	lb tob & caske
The parish d.ʳ: 78	
To m.ʳ: vicaris for officiating as minister	12000
To Co.ˡˡ pate for y.ᵉ: plaister worke of y.ᵉ Church	08000
To y.ᵉ: Joyners for y.ᵉ: inside worke by agreem.ᵗ	06000
To m.ʳˢ Thorntone as sexton	00500
To Barth: Austine for keeping Rumball	01000
To Thom Hide for keeping a Bastard	01000
To Rob.ᵗ warner for officiatinge as clerke	01000
To Samuel duninge by ord.ʳ vestry last yeare	00500
To Geo: Hogg for Sawyers work being 6262 foote at 700.ˡᵇ tobo p.ʳ M.	04387
To y.ᵉ: Glasier	00500
To m.ʳ Lightfoote p.ʳ: Interest of his money & severall other particulares as p.ʳ: acco.ᵗ	01700
To Co.ˡˡ pate for bringinge y.ᵉ timber & planks & other neceſsaryes for y.ᵉ Church	03000
To Co.ˡˡ Lewis for a lock to y.ᵉ church doore	00050
	39637
C.ʳ	01100
	38537
To caske at 80 p.ʳ: thousand	02780
Totall	41317

41317.ˡᵇ ᵗᵒᵇᵒ (87.ˡᵇ: p.ʳ pole
Tythables 475

[7]

The parish dʳ. in money	Cʳ by gifts given by	
lb s. d.		lb. s. d
To mʳ. Lightfoote	majʳ. Robᵗ. Beverley	05:00:00
for yᵉ. Cushone	mʳ. Jnº. Buckner	03:00:00
comunion table	mʳ. Tho: Royston	02:10:00
cloaths and ap-	mʳ. Ed: Hoile	01:10:00
purtinances 17:04:00	Jacob warner	01:00:00
	mʳ. Wᵐ. Crimes	00:10:00
	Tho: Dudley	01:00:00
lb s d.	David Monorgan	01:00:00
dʳ. — 17:04:00	Robᵗ. Littefeild	01:00:00
Cʳ. — 21:10:00	nich: Francklin	01:00:00
	Wᵐ. Shirley	01:00:00
04:06:00 allowed	Wᵐ. Fuller	01:00:00
for the trouble in collectinge	Sam: Sallis	01:00:00
& for wᵗ: cannot be payd.	Paul Spinke	01:00:00
		21:10:00

Ordered by this p̄nt vestry that yᵉ: persons abovenamed, pay the severall respective sūmes according to their severall engagements unto the abovenamed mʳ. Phillip Lightfoote whose receipt shal[] be their sufficient discharge.

	Contʳ. Cʳ. 1678	lb: tobo
By wᵐ. Collanes woman servᵗˢ fine		0500
By Coˡˡ. pates servants fine		0500
By wᵐ. Stannums gift		0100
		1100.

Ordered that yᵉ: respective Churwardens in their severall precincts, doe collect, this p̄nt yeare, of every tythable person in this parish eighty seven pounds of tobacco per pole, & in case of faillour to make distreſse for yᵉ. same: & that they yᵉ: said Churchwardens pay Each parish Creditor his Just due.

ordered that yᵉ: present Churchwardens continue in yᵉ said office till Easter next.

Ordered that John Mackwilliams be sexton to both churches for yᵉ: future

Ordered that Thomas Powell be allowed in yᵉ: levy next yeare the sũme of five hundred pounds of tobo and caske to be paid by the parishe.

This day John Breemer (as marrying yᵉ: relict & Exoʳ of James Clarke ded:) did, according to yᵉ said Clarks will, deliver to yᵉ. vestry, to yᵉ. use of yᵉ. parishe a flowred Crimson velvett pulpit cloath bequeath by the sd Clarke to yᵉ: use aforesaid: for which yᵉ said B[ ]mer did disburſs 1000ˡᵇ of tobo & caske and [ ] pounds seventeen shill ster: money.

[8]
Ordered that mʳ. Rich: Barnet be surveyoʳ. of yᵉ: High wayes for yᵉ midle parts, and mʳ wᵐ Howard Junʳ: for yᵉ: Lower parts of yᵉ parish, for this pnt yeare. & yᵗ. mʳ. Robᵗ. Carter & Francis Smithing surveyors for yᵉ. upper parts be for this yeare Continued in yᵉ: said office

Att a Veſtry held for yᵉ piſh of Petſoe 9ᵇᵉʳ yᵉ. 13ᵗʰ. 1679

Prnᵗ.   mʳ. Tho: Vicaris Miniſter
   Capᵗ. Tho Ramſey   mʳ. Wᵐ. Hansford
   mʳ. Jnᵒ. Buckner   mʳ. Wᵐ. Thornton Senʳ
   mʳ. Robᵗ. Carter   mʳ. Ralph Green Senʳ   Veſtry
   mʳ. Tho: Royston   mʳ. Ralph Green Junʳ   men
   mʳ. Tho: Miller   mʳ. Cha: Roan
   mʳ. Roger Shacleford
         Coˡ Tho: Pate—Churchwarden

The piſh Dbr. 1679

	lb tob.
To Robt. Draper for making ye frame on which ye King's armes are drawen	00500
To Rich Sinkoe as Clarke	01000
To ye Sexton	00500
To Tho: Powell for draweing ye Cherubin	00500
To Jno. Augur ℔ Ironwork ℔ ordr of Court & coſt	00853
To Col Pate for Painting ye Church	01500
To Tho: Jones out of Charity	00500
To majr. Lightfoot ℔ Comunion wine Nayles, & Tarr	00475
To Col Pate for Comunion wine & nayles	00120
To ye keeping of Rumball	01000
To mr. Jno. Buckner, & Samll: Sallis for paling ye Church yard	02000
To mr. Vicaris for officiating as Miniſter	12000
To mr. Vicaris on arrears	00100
To Phil: May	00500
	21548
*To *Caſk	02000
	19548
To Casſk	01560
	21108

Per Contr Cr

By Rich Coxe's fine ℔ his woman Servt.	00500
By Wm. Faulkner's Fine, & Servts.	01000
by Rich Minor's fine ℔ his wom: ſervt.	00500
	02000

---

*Note! These two words are scratched through with a pen in the original MS., but are distinctly legible.—C. G. C.

[9]
    Petſoe piſh further Dbr. 1679 upon ye Souldrs. accots

	lb tob
To Coll Tho: Pate ℔ Horſe, & man 5 moneths according to Act	1400
To 5 Bush Corne, & 2 bush meale	0140
To 1lb. powder, & 3lb Shott	0020
	1560
To mr. Tho: Royston ℔ Ditto	1560
To mr. Cha: Roan ℔ ditto	1560
To mr. Robt. Carter ℔ ditto	1560
To mr. Tho: Vicaris ℔ Ditto	1560
To mr. Jno. Buckner ℔ Ditto	1560
To majr Lightfoot ℔ ditto	1560
To mr. Wm. Hanſford ℔ Ditto	1560
To mr. Jno: Throckmorton ℔ Ditto	1560
	14040
To Guilb: macrary ℔ 20lb Bacon at 3lb ℔ lb	0060
To mr. Thornton ℔ 18lb½ Ditto	0052
To Capt. Ramſey ℔ 11lb Ditto	0033
To Wm Thornton Junr. ℔ 4lb Ditto	0012
To mr. Shacleford ℔ 3lb½ Ditto	0010
To mr. Ralph Green Junr. ℔ 32lb Ditto	0096
To Jno Evans ℔ 14lb dryed meat	0042
To mr. Wm. Howard Senr. ℔ 16lb Bacon	0048
To mr. Wm. Handsford ℔ 14lb Ditto	0042
To mr. Ralph Green Senr. 16lb Ditto	0048
To Rich Pearſe ℔ 7lb Ditto	0021
To mr. Jno. Throckmorton ℔ 26lb Dryed meat	0078
To Cha Roan ℔ 50lb Bacon	0150
To mr. Royſton ℔ 80lb Ditto	0240
To majr Lightfoot ℔ 80lb Ditto	0240

To mr. Jno. Buckner ⅌ 80{lb} Ditto	0240
To mr Carter, mr Vicaris, & Col Pate ⅌ 337{lb} beef at 1{lb}½ ⅌ lb	0506
	1918
	14040
	15958
To Caſke	1280
To Sallary	1360

	lb tob		
The piſh Charge is	43 ⅌ pole	Sold{rs} charge	18598
The Soldiers Charge is	39 ⅌ pole	Pariſh Charge	21108
The whole is	82 ⅌ pole		39706

Tithables 480

[10]

Ordered That Co{ll} Thomas Pate one of the Church wardens of this piſh; doe collect this prnt yeare of every Tithable perſon in this piſh Eighty two pounds of Tobb{o}. ⅌ pole, and in Caſe of Failure to make diſtreſs for ye. Same; And that the Said Col Tho: Pate doe therewith defray, & pay of Every piſh Credito{r}. to his juſt Due, with all poſsible speed, & conveniency

This prnt Veſtry at ye. humble requeſt of George Hogg have given to ye. S{d}. Hogg all ye Sawen Timber belonging to ye piſh, & lying in Morgan's neck; & doe hereby impower ye S{d} Hogg to diſpoſe of it, for his own uſe; & intereſt.

Att a Vestry held for Petſoe piſh Febry. yᵉ 2ᵈ 167 9/80

Prnt Capt. Tho: Ramſey
    mr. Jnᵒ. Buckner
    mr. Robt. Carter
    mr. Wm. Thornton Senr
    mr. Tho Miller
    mr. Robt. Colles
    mr. Tho: Royſton
    mr. Cha: Rhoan
    mr. Ralph Green Junr.
    mr. Wm. Thornton Junr.
    Coll Tho: Pate Churchwarden

Ordered That mr. Robt. Colles, & mr. Wm. Thornton Junr. be added to yᵉ Veſtrye.

Ordered That mr. Tho: Vicaris yᵉ prñt miniſter of this piſh, be continued in his Said place, & exerciſe his Miniſterial Function, until yᵉ next Shipping, on likeing, & hopes of his future amendment, he Declaring his willingneſs then to leave the place, if not approved of by the piſh, and Veſtrye.

It is the opinion of this Veſtry That Five ſhillings, or Fifty weight of Tobbᵒ. is but a reaſonable reward, or paymt. for yᵉ Clerk, or Reader, for publiſhing Banns of matrimonye.

mr. Robt. Colles having promiſed, & obliged himſelfe to maintain yᵉ Orpht. Child of Owen Caley for one whole yeare, from this day,—It is ordered That the Said mr. Colles shall be allowed, or paid for yᵉ Same Five Hundred pounds of Tobbᵒ. & caſke yᵉ next yeare by the piſh.

[11]

Att a Vestry held for Petso piſh 8ber yᵉ 14ᵗʰ. 1680

Prſent   mr. Tho Vicaris miniſter
    mr Jnᵒ. Buckner   Lt Coll Lightfoot
    mr Robt Carter   mr Roger Shacleford
    mr Wm Hanſford   mr Tho: Miller
    mr Wm Thornton Senr   mr Charles Roan
    mr. Wm. Thornton Junr.
        Coll Tho: Pate Churchwarden

Petʃoe piʃh is Dʳ. Anº. Dni 1680

To mʳ. Vicaris as miniſter	12000
To Richd Simco as his Clerk	01000
To yᵉ Sexton	01000
To Rumball	01000
To Capᵗ. Colles ⅌ Caleys orphᵗ.	00500
To Thomas Taunton in charity	01000
To Coll Lightfoot ⅌ hooks & Hinges	00070
To idm̃ ⅌ Comunion wine	00050
To idm̃ ⅌ Tarring yᵉ Church	00400
To Coll Pate ⅌ Com̃union wine	00100

Souldier's Charge

To mʳ. Vicaris ⅌ Horſe & man three monethes	00840
To mʳ. Jnº. Buckner for yᵉ Same	00840
To mʳ. Carter ⅌ Horſe & man ⅌ 7 mº.	01960
To Coll Pate ⅌ yᵉ Same	01960
To Coll Lightfoot ⅌ yᵉ Same	01960
To mʳ. Tho: Royston ⅌ yᵉ Same	01960
To mʳ. Wᵐ Hanſford ⅌ yᵉ Same	01960
To mʳ. Roan ⅌ his horſe 7 mº.	00560
To mʳˢ. Throckomorton ⅌ Horſe & man 7 mº.	01960
To mʳ. Buckner ⅌ Fees	00180
To Coll Lightfoot } ⅌ 5 Caſk at 5ˡᵇ Tobº ⅌ Caſk To mʳ Buckner	00125
To Phil May ⅌ Services	00500
	31925
To Caſk at 8 ⅌ Cent	2552
	34477

Per Contʳ.   Cʳ.

By 561 Tithables at 62ˡᵇ. Tobº ⅌ pole } 7 being deducted ⅌ mʳ. Vicaris	34477

Ordered That mʳ. Roger Shacleford be Churchwarden this next Enſuing yeare for the upper part of this piſh, mʳ. Wᵐ. Thornton for yᵉ midle part, & mʳ. Wᵐ. Hanſford for the lower pᵗ of yᵉ piſh

[12]

Ordered That yᵉ pʳſent Church wardens doe within their Severall pʳcincts Leavy & Collect of every Tithable pson Sixty two pounds of Tob p pole and therewith pay of and defray every piſh Creditor his juſt due, with all poſsible Speed & conveniencye.

Whereas mʳ Robᵗ Lee by his laſt will & Testament did give ten pounds Sterl to the poor of this piſh of Petſo

It is ordered by this pʳſent Veſtry That mʳ. Edward Porteus who married the Execʳˣ of yᵉ Sayd Lee Doe pay and diſtribute the Said Sum̃ of ten pounds Sterl to the Sevˡˡ psons hereafter named, and in Such ℔porcons as is herein Expreſsed. vizᵗ

	l	s
To Jnᵒ Mackwilliams	1	10
To Tho Jones	1	10
To Richd Holloway	1	10
To Jnᵒ Davyes	1	10
To Jnᵒ Whittamore	1	10
To Richd Bennett	1	10
To Wᵐ Pemberton	1	00
	10	00

And Farther that yᵉ Said mʳ. Edward Porteus take their Severall receipts for yᵉ Same, & produce the Same to the next Veſtry, & then he shall be diſcharged of yᵉ Same.

Ordered That the pʳſent Churchwardens doe wᵗʰ all poſsible Speed & conveniencye well & Sufficiently cover the Church with good Shingles, and that they allſo Erect &

Build a good & Substantiall Porch to yᵉ Church at Poplar Spring, of Such dimenſions as they shall think convenient; & correſpondent to yᵉ Church.

Whereas at a Veſtry held for this piſh Feb^ry. yᵉ 2ᵈ 1679/80 It was then ordered & appoynted That mʳ Tho: Vicaris Should be continued miniſter of this piſh until this pʳſent Shipping, on likeing, and this veſtry with the Inhabitants of yᵉ. Sᵈ. piſh well approving of his prſent life & converſacon doe order & appoynt that he be Still continued in his pʳſent place & office, and Exerciſe his miniſteriall Function in the ſᵈ piſh as formerly.

[13]
Att a Vestry held for Petſo piſh October yᵉ 11ᵗʰ. Anᵒ Dni 1681

Preſent   mʳ. Tho: vicaris minister

Capᵗ Thomas Ramſey ⎫ mʳ. Wᵐ. Thornton Senʳ. ⎫
Collᵒ. Tho: Pate   ⎬ mʳ. Edward Porteus   ⎬ Vestry men
mʳ. John Buckner   ⎭ mʳ. Ralph Green Senʳ. ⎭

    mʳ. Roger Shacleford ⎫
    mʳ. Wᵐ. Hansford   ⎬ Church wardens
    mʳ. Wᵐ. Thornton junʳ ⎭

	Petso piſh is Dʳ. 1681	lb tobᵒ
To mʳ. Tho: Vicaris as minister		12000
To mʳ. Richd Simco his Clerk		1000
To Jnᵒ. Mackwilliams Sexton		500
To Ditto in Charity		500
To Rumball		1000
To Collᵒ. Pate, ℔ pᵈ. to Oakes for keeping a bastard		200
To Tho: Taunton a Criple formerly ſerᵗ to mʳ Bernard		1000
To Elizᵃ. Lawrence for maintaining George yᵉ Currier an year in meat Drink & Cloathes ℔ agreement with the Churchwarden		1000

To Robᵗ. Hogsden In Charity	500
To Capᵗ. Robᵗ. Colles ℔ Caley's orphants maintenance	500
To mʳ. Shacleford ℔ maintaining Swans Child	1000
To idm̃ ℔ maintaining mʳ. Dudley's wenches bastard 1 year, he promiſeing to repay wᵗ is Due if the Child Dyes	1000
To Thomas Jones in Charity	500
To John Mead in charity	500
To Richd Bennett in charity	500
To mʳ. vicaris on arrears	62
To Coll Pate for Coll Warners overcharge anno 1679	435
To mʳ. Mann ℔ 16 Tithables not allowed	00400
To Phil May as Clerk of yᵉ vestry	500
	22697
To Cask	1816
	*24816

Pʳ Contra is Cʳ.

By 590 Tithables at 42ˡᵇ tobᵒ. ℔ pole 6 being allowed mʳ. vicaris   †24816

[14]

Ordered That yᵉ preſent Churchwardens Doe Collect 42ˡᵇ of tobᵒ. of every Tithable pſon in this piſh and in caſe of refuſall of payment of yᵉ ſd Sum̃ by any pſon, That they make Distreſs for yᵉ same, and therewith pay of all piſh Creditoʳˢ. their just Dues with all poſsible speed & conveniencye

Mʳ Edward Porteus moveing this vestry that he might be diſcharged from yᵉ legacye of ten pounds given by mʳ Robert Lee to yᵉ poor inhabitants of this piſh, he averring that he hath payᵈ yᵉ same according to the Direccons of the last vestry, but not produceing yᵉ recpts of yᵉ Severall

---
*Peculiar addition. †Peculiar multiplication.—C. G. C.

pſons to whome the money is payd, It is therefore Ordered That Phil May Clerk of this vestry Doe in yᵉ name, & on yᵉ behalfe of yᵉ vestrye Signe a Diſcharge to yᵉ Said mʳ. Porteus, upon yᵉ receiveing of the Said recpᵗˢ from yᵉ ſd. mʳ. Porteus.

Forasmuch as there are yearly Sundry & great Charges brought on this piſh by reason of Entertayning of impotent & Sick people in the houſes of Divers yᵉ Inhabitants of this piſh, It is therefore Ordered by this vestrye That noe pſon inhabiting in this piſh Doe pʳſume to Entertayne any Forreigner or pſons of another piſh in their houſes, wᵗʰout giveing preſent notice thereof to yᵉ next Church-warden to yᵉ End That noe pſon may pretend to a lawfull ſettlement here, under the penalty of maintaining yᵉ sᵈ. pſons themſelves, and Ord That the Clerk of yᵉ vestry Doe transcribe this our Ordʳ. & Deliver it to mʳ vicaris to publish yᵉ Same to yᵉ intent noe pſon may pʳtend ignorance herein.

[15]
Att at Vestry held for Petſo piſh October yᵉ 24ᵗʰ. Anᵒ. 1682

mʳ. Tho: Vicaris miniſter.

Prnt mʳ John Buckner ⎫ mʳ. Robᵗ Carter ⎫
mʳ. Wᵐ. Thornton Senʳ. ⎬ Capᵗ Robᵗ Colles ⎬ Veſtrymen
mʳ. Tho: Royſton ⎭ mʳ Wᵐ Crimes ⎭

mʳ. Wᵐ Hansford ⎫
mʳ. Wᵐ. Thornton junʳ. ⎬ Churchwardens
mʳ. Roger Shacleford ⎭

Petſo piſh is Dʳ. 1682

To mʳ. Vicaris as miniſter	12000
To Richd Simco as Clerk	1000
To yᵉ Sexton	1000
To Phil May as Clerk of yᵉ Veſtry	500
To mʳ Shacleford overchargd 5 Tithables at 42 ℔	
℔ole is	0210

To idm for keeping mr Dudley's wenches Baſtard 3 monethes	0250
To mr. Hansford for keeping a baſtard 9 mo.	0800
To Capt. Colles ⅌ keeping Caleys Orphant	0500
To Rumball	1000
To Tho: Taunton	1000
To mr. Buckner Clerks Fees	0198
To mr. Clunies for Sherr Fees	0060
	18518
To Cask at 8 ⅌ Cent	1480
	19998
To Collection of ye Sum & Cask	1080
	21078

Contr is Credr.

By 518 Tithables at 41 ⅌ pole—mr Vicaris being allowd 6 Tithables is 21078

[16]

It is Ordered by this preſent veſtry That for the future the Church Wardens of this piſh may putt the piſh Debts into ye Sheriffs hands to Collect & allow him 5 ⅌ Cent for Collecting ye Same, & ye Sayd allowance shall be levyed for him, provided That they & every of them take Caution of the Sheriff for the well paying every piſh Creditor in the piſh as Tobbo. Shall arriſe. and if they doe not agree with the Sheriff That the Church wardens for ye time being or who elſe they Doe Employ Shall be allowd the Said Sallary for Collecting ye Same.

Ordered That Ellenor Hogsden be Sexton for the upper Church at Poplar Spring, & John Litey for ye Lower Church in this piſh and that Each of them be pay 500lb tob & Cask ℔ annū on the pformance of their Duty in that office.

This Veſtry having duly conſidered yᵉ Severall wills of John Mackwilliams decᵈ. & Isabella his wife. & that their Orphants & Eſtate by their wills are left to yᵉ Tuition of Francis Linford by the ſd. wills, It is therefore Ordered That the Sayd Lynford keep the Sayd Mackwilliams's plantacon the Space of three yeares next Enſuing, & he hath liberty given him to take in one Freeman & noe more on yᵉ Sayd Plantacon; and That the Small Eſtate given them by their Decᵈ Parents Remain in his hand, during the time aforeſᵈ.

Phil May Clerk of the Veſtry is impowered and Ordered by this Veſtry to Signe Indentures for thirteen yeares Service of John Mackwilliams unto mʳ Francis Iremonger and alſo for Five yeares Service of Elizᵃ Mackwilliams unto Coll Phil Lightfoot

Ordered That Francis Linford Give Bond & good Security to yᵉ piſh for yᵉ paymᵗ & delivery of yᵉ Eſtate of yᵉ orph Mackwilliams Children unto them when they come of age, or are Free.

[17]
The Church wardens or any two of them are hereby impow[ ] & Ordered to agree wᵗʰ: mʳ. John Baynton or any other [   ] bound for Briſtoll for Tho Taunton's paſsage into England, and what Bargain the Sayd Churchwardens Doe make this Veſtry will Confirm & pay, and in the mean time who ever Shall maintain & accomodate the Sayd Taunton Shall be payd & allowed by this Veſtry as formerly.

Ordered That the Churchwardens Do with all poſsible Speed new Cover Poplar-Spring Church, and repayr yᵉ old Church with all ſuch needfull reperacons as the Churchwarden's of the midle & lower ptes of the piſh Shall adjudge to be needfull & neſceſsary.

mʳ Wᵐ Crimes mʳ John Delawood, mʳ John Evans, mʳ Edwᵈ Greenley & mʳ James Dudley are added to yᵉ Vestry of this piſh

Ordered That Capᵗ. Robᵗ. Colles be Churchwarden this next Enſuing year for the upper pt of this piſh, mʳ Edwᵈ Porteus for the midle pte, & mʳ John Evans for the lower part.

Ordered That yᵉ pʳſent Church-wardens Collect Forty [   ] ℔ounds of Tobacco of Every Tithable pſon in this [   ] & therewith pay of Each piſh Creditoʳ their juſt Due.

[18]
Att a Veſtry held for Petſo piſh the 24ᵗʰ of Septembʳ. 1683

mʳ Tho: Vicaris miniſter

Prnt mʳ Wᵐ. Thorton Senʳ.
mʳ Robᵗ. Carter
mʳ Wᵐ Hansford
mʳ James Dudley
mʳ. Roger Shacleford
mʳ Tho: Miller
mʳ Wm Crimes
} Veſtrymen

mʳ Ed Porteus
mʳ Robᵗ: Colles
mʳ Jnᵒ. Evans
} Church-wardens

Petſo parish is Dʳ. Anᵒ 1683

To mʳ Vicaris as miniſter	12000
To Richd Simco as Cler	1000
To yᵉ Sextons'	1000
To Rumball	1000
To Taunton	1000

To mʳ Porteus for maintenance of a Baſtard Child one whole year	900
To mʳ. Colles ⅌ Kelley	500
To Coll Lightfoot for Comunion wine	0100
To mʳ Evans for poſting & Covering yᵉ old Church	2000
To mʳ. Hansford for keeping a Baſtard 3 mᵒ.	0200
To mʳ. Colles ⅌ 60 gall Tarr at 10ˡᵇ ᵗᵒᵇ p Gall	0600
To Idm ⅌ 15000 nayles at 4ˢ ⅌ m. in tobᵒ.	0600
To Phil May Cler of yᵉ Veſtry	0500
To Clerks fees	0108
	21608
To mʳ. Colles for Severall Tithables not found	410
	22018
To Caſk at 8 ⅌ C	1760
	23778
Sallary 5 ⅌ Cent	1238
	25016

Cʳ

By 520 Tithables at 48 ⅌ pole 6 being deducted for mʳ. Vicaris — 25016

[19]

Ordered That yᵉ pʳſent Church-wardens continue in their places this Enſuing year.

Ordered That mʳ Tho: Dawkins be added to yᵉ Vestry, and he is hereby Declared a member of yᵉ Vestry of this piſh

Ordered That the Church-wardens of this piſh Doe in their Severall precincts Collect yᵉ Sum̃ of forty Eight pounds of Tobᵒ. of Every Tithable pſon, & upon failure of payment to make Diſtreſs for yᵉ Same. & therewith pay Every piſh Creditoʳ their juſt Due.

[20]

Att a Vestry held for Petſo piſh the 9ᵗʰ. of 7bʳ. 1684

mʳ Tho: Vicaris minister

Prnt Collº. Tho: Pate   mʳ. Cha: Roan
mʳ. John Buckner   mʳ. Roger Shacleford
mʳ. Tho: Miller   mʳ. Cha: Roan
mʳ. Wm. Crymes   mʳ. James Dudley } Vestrymen.

mʳ. Ed: Porteus
mʳ. Robᵗ. Colles
mʳ. Jnº. Evans } Churchwardens

Ditto piſh is Dʳ. 1684 vizᵗ.

	lb tobº.
To mʳ. vicaris as minister	12000
To Richard Simco as Cler	01000
To John Litey as Sexton	00500
To Ellenor Hogsden as ſexton	00500
To Rumball	01000
To Tho: Taunton	01000
To Capᵗ. Colles for Kelley's Orphant	00500
To Comunion wine 2 yʳˢ. Given by mʳ Porteus	
To mʳ Ed: Porteus for Timber & nayles for the old Church, Surplice &cª. as p accoᵗᵗ.	04348
To Collº. Lightfoot on arrears for Comunion wine	00100
To mʳ. Buckner for Clerks fees	00286
To Phil May as Cler: of yᵉ Vestry	00500
	18734
	3000
	15734
To Cask at 8 ℔ Cᵗ.	1256
To Sallary at 5 ℔ Cᵗ.	0999
	17989

[21]

Ditto piſh is Cr	lb tobo.
By Wm. Anderson ⅌ his womans fine	0500
By mr. Carter for his womans fine	0500
By mr. Porteus for his womans fine	0500
By Dr. Crymes for his womans fine	0500
By Wm. Richardſon to be pd. by Tho: Stendham	0500
By John Smith for his womans fine	0500
	3000
By mr Iremonger for David Gooſetrees piſh Levyes 1683	0048
By 525 Tithables (6 being allowed mr. Vicaris out of yᵉ List) at 34 ⅌ pole is	17989

[22]

His Excellency the Governr. haveing Given to this Church One large Bible, One Booke of Comon Prayer, One Booke of Homilyes, the 39 Articles, & Booke of Cannons of the Church of England. It is Ordered That yᵉ Clerk of the Vestry Enter yᵉ Same in the Regiſter to the End his Lordship's Soe pious a Gift may be gratefully remembered.

Ordered That yᵉ Clerk Enter into yᵉ Regiſter of this piſh the Generous & pious Gift of the Hon'ble Collo. Augustine Warner decd. to this Church, vizt One Silver Flaggon, two Silver Bowles, and two Silver Plates, which though long Since Given hath not yet been Entered.

Ordered That for yᵉ future there be an addition of Five hundred pounds of tobaccoes & Cask to the yearly Sallary of yᵉ piſh Clerk, and that it be leavyed for & payd him over & above his p'ſent Sallary.

Ordered That for yᵉ. future there be an Adittion of Five hundred pounds of tobo. & Csk to yᵉ Clerk of yᵉ Vestry's yearly Sallary.

m^r. Roger Shacleford is by this Veſtry impowered & requested to agree with Some maſter of a Ship bound for Bristoll, for ye paſsage of W^m. Pemberton, and what the Sayd Shacleford Shall undertake, he shall be reimburſed the next Levye.

This Veſtry Doe impower m^r. Robt. Colles to appear & ℘ſecute Martin Butler at ye Suit of the piſh in an accon of ye Caſe for breach of Articles.

[23] It being repreſented to this Veſtry by Some members thereof That ye Sum̃ of One thousand pounds of tobacco & Cask p annũ allowed Thomas Taunton for his maintenance is too little to give him a Competent Subſiſtence for that by reaſon of his lameneſs & miſerable weake Condicon he can doe nothing for the getting any thing to cloath himſelfe, & y^e ſ^d. 1000 tob^o. will hardly gett him accomodacons of victualls & lodgeings It is therefore Ordered That for ye future he be allowed Five hundred pounds of tob^o. & Cask once in two years towards his Cloathing, untill it Shall pleaſe God to recover his health.

Ordered That ye Church-wardens of this piſh Doe the next Court bring their Informacon agn^t thoſe pſons who have concealed their Tithables.

Ordered That m^r. Charles Roan be Church-warden for ye upper part, & m^r John Buckner [*] for the midle & lower pte of this piſh. And that they or their Side-men (whome they are hereby impowered to Nominate & appoynt) Doe Collect of Every Tithable pſon in this piſh this p^rſent year ye Sum of thirty Four pounds of tob^o. & therewith pay of the Severall piſh Debts to whome the Same is ℘porconed or in Caſe of failure or refuſall to make diſtreſs for ye Same.

---

*Illegible word or abbreviation.—C. G. C.

[24]

Att a Vestry held September y° 22ᵈ. 1684

Prñt   mʳ Tho: Vicaris minʳ.

Collº. Tho: Pate	mʳ. Wᵐ. Crymes
mʳ. Ed: Porteus	mʳ. Rogʳ. Shacleford.
mʳ. Wᵐ. Thornton Senʳ.	mʳ. Thornton junʳ.
Capᵗ. Robᵗ. Colles	mʳ R Green junʳ
	mʳ Jnº. Evans.

} Vestrmen

mʳ. Jnº. Buckner
mʳ Cha: Roan   } Church-wardens

Whereas Att ye laſt Vestry held for this piſh the 9ᵗʰ. Instant for the laying of the Leavy, there was Credit given the Sᵈ. piſh for Five hundred pounds of tobaccoes & Cask to be Collected of Jnº. Smith for his woman Serᵗˢ. Fine which in right ought not to be pᵈ. untill yᵉ next year, Soe that the Leavye of thirty Fower pounds of tobº. p pole will not be Sufficient to Sattisfy yᵉ piſh Debts by 178 lb tobº. It is therefore Ordered That the Churchwardens Collect yᵉ Suñ of thirty Five pounds of tobº. p pole of Every Tithable pſon this piſh for yᵉ defraying the piſh debts. &c

This Veſtry takeing into their Conſideracon the great neſceſsity of new Covering, or Shingling the Church at Poplar Spring, It is put to yᵉ Vote whether the Sᵈ. Church Shall be new Covered with riv'd boards or Shingled? It is voted by yᵉ majʳ pte That it is beſt & moſt convenient that yᵉ Sᵈ. Church be Covered wᵗʰ Boards, & therefore Ordered That yᵉ Church-Wardens take care that it be forthwith effectually done accordingly.

[25]   Contra is Cʳ.

By mʳ. Vicaris	00800
By R: Simco	00700
	01500
Dʳ.	24814
Cʳ.	1500

rest	23314
Caſk	01864
Paccage	01165
Dᵗ. in all	26343

Cʳ. by 545 Tithables at 48½ p pole.

It is Ordered by this pʳſent vestry That mʳ James Dudley be diſmiſt from his office of Churchwarden in the upper part of this piſh & mʳ. Wᵐ. Crymes is Ordered to officiate in his roome. & mʳ Robert Carter is continued in yᵉ Same office for yᵉ lower ptes, & Ordered that they & Every of them Doe forthwith Collect of Every Tithable pſon in this piſh the Sum̃ of 48½ lb of tobᵒ. & therewᵗʰ pay of the piſh Credʳˢ with all poſsible Speed & Conveniencye.

[26]
Att a Meeting of yᵉ Inhabitants of Petſoe piſh the 12ᵗʰ. Day of June 1690 for makeing Choyce of a Select Veſtrye for yᵉ Sᵈ piſh

The Gent here under written were by the majority of voyces of yᵉ Sᵈ Inhabitants, choſen & Elected for Vestry men

Vizᵗ.	Capᵗ Phil Lightfoot	⎫
⅌ yᵉ midle pte	mʳ Ed: Porteus	⎬
	mʳ Jnᵒ. Buckner	
	mʳ. Robᵗ. Carter	⎭
⅌ yᵉ upper pte.	mʳ. Tho: Royston	⎫
	mʳ Robᵗ. Yard	⎬
	mʳ Ja: Dudley	
	mʳ. Conquest Wyatt	⎭
⅌ yᵉ lower pte.	mʳ. Tho: Green	⎫
	mʳ Wᵐ. Thornton Senʳ	⎬
	mʳ. Wᵐ. Thornton junʳ.	
	mʳ Ralph Green	⎭

[27]
Att a Vestry held on Tuesday yᵉ 22ᵈ. of September 1690.

pʳſent   mʳ. Tho: Vicaris miniſter
- mʳ. Ed: Porteus   mʳ. Tho: Green   ⎫
- mʳ. Tho: Royston   mʳ. Robᵗ. Yard   ⎬ Vestry men
- mʳ. Ja: Dudley   ⎭
  - mʳ. Wᵐ. Crymes.   ⎫
  - mʳ. Robᵗ. Carter   ⎬ Church-wardens

It is Ordered That for yᵉ Future there be a Vestry held annually on the first Tuesday in October for the laying of the piſh Leavye.

Ordered That mʳ. Thomas Green, & mʳ. Robᵗ. Yard be Churchwardens for the two next enſuing yeares for this piſh.

[28]
Att a Veſtry held for Petſoe piſh ye 1ˢᵗ. of Octobʳ. 1690

Preſent   mʳ. Thomas Vicaris miniſter
- Capᵗ. Phil Lightfoot   mʳ James Dudley   ⎫ Vestry
- mʳ. Robᵗ. Carter   mʳ. Wᵐ. Thornton   ⎬ men
-         mʳ. Tho: Green Church-Warden

piſh Charge. Petſoe piſh is Dʳ.	lb tobᵒ.
To mʳ. Vicaris as Miniſter	12000
To Richard Simco Clarke	01500
To Rumball	01000
To Widdow Hogsden Sexton	00500
To Jnᵒ. Litey Sexton	00500
To Phil May Cler: of yᵉ Veſtry	01000
To Doctoʳ Crymes on accoᵗᵗ. for Severall poore & impotent pſons	00675
To mʳ Samˡˡ. Iremonger for bringing tarr to yᵉ Church	00080
To Capᵗ. Lightfoot for bringing tarr for the Church	00280
To Tho: Powell for plaiſtering yᵉ Church	03000

To Stephen Hall for a baſtard Childs maintenance 6 monethes	00500
To Richard Simcoe for a ball laſt years acco^{tt}.	00062
To m^r. Thornton jun^r. for repayring ye old Church	00200
	21297
Package at 5 p Cent	1065
	22362
Caske at 8 p Cent	01789
	24151

C^r.

By 540 Tithables at 45 p pole (6 being deducted for m^r. Vicaris) res^t. 536 is   24151

[29]

Ordered by this p^rſent Veſtry That m^r. Thomas Green & m^r. Robert Yard Church-wardens of this piſh Doe Collect & Gather from every Tithable pſon in this piſh the Sum of 45^{lb}. tob^o. p pole the S^d. Sum being this p^rſent yeares piſh Leavy and that therewith they pay of & diſcharge all the piſh Credito^{rs}., & in caſe of delay or refuſall of ye Leavye aforeſ^d. They ye Sayd Church-wardens & Every of them & their Collecto^{rs}. are hereby impowered to make diſtreſs for ye Same.

Ord. that Phillip. May Clerk of the. vestry ſeale and: deliver. unter Steven. Hall.; an Indenture. for Thomas Mampus. the. ſon of Thomas Mampus late of Gloſt^r. County; having Long ſince. departed: the County. without makeing any p^rviſion for his Education & bringing up: That the. ſaid. Thomas Mampus Junr. ſarve ſeven years: to ye above. ſaid Steven Hall. he alowing him ſuffitient Neſceſsry apparrell: Lodging waſhing and Dyatt

[30]
Att a Veſtry held October. the. 19ᵗʰ. 1691

        mʳ. Thomas. Vicares. Miniſter
Preſent. Mʳ. Edw. Porteus   Mʳ. Jnº. Buckner
       Mʳ. Robᵗ. Carter   Mʳ. James. Dudley
       Mʳ. Wᵐ. Thornton: junʳ.   Mʳ. Will. Thornton Senʳ.
       Mʳ. Robᵗ. Yard   ⎫
       Mʳ. Tho: Green ⎬ Churchwardens

        Petſoe, Pariſh. is Debᵗʳ.

pariſh. Charge	Tobacco
To mʳ. Thomas Vicares. Miniſter	12000
To: Richᵈ. Simcoe. Clerke	01500
To: Phillip. May Clerk of yᵉ Veſtry	01000
To: widd: Hogsdon. ſexton	00500
To: Jnº. Lightys tobacco to be paid. Jnº. Roſe. for nine. munths. for yᵉ uſe of his Children. and. the. Remainder to Steven: Hall.	00500
To: Jnº. Rumball	01000
To: mʳ. Edw. Lewis. one. barrell of Corn. for old Lennard	00150
To: m. Tho: Green. for Richᵈ. Panters Cure	01500
To: mʳˢ. Grinly for his accomodacons: 3: Mounths	00200
To: Henry Bray for keeping a poor woman & child	00100
To: Steven. Hall. for keeping a baſtard. Child. 9: mounths	00750
To: mʳ. Robᵗ. yard. on accᵗ old Lennard: & a poor woman	00253
To: Richd. Simco. for ſhooes & ſtockings for ſam: Maſtin	00050
To: mʳ. Brookin. for meat: for old. Lennard	00200
To: Richᵈ. Simco. accᵗ. for old. Lennard	00333
To Jnº. Brocks. 2: Levies. & Robᵗ. Eltons. 1: not fown'd	00135
To: mʳ. Jnº. Buckner for Clerks. fees	00070

To: mʳ. Edw. Maylin for. 2: jurneys from James Town 00400
To: widd. Hogſdun. for keeping a baſtard Child of }
   mʳ. wᵐ. Thorntons woman ſarvᵗ.   } 00100

                                                     20741
To: Packing of yᵉ Sᵈ. ſum. 5 : ℔ Cent   01037
To. Caſk. at   8 : ℔ Cent   01725

                                                     23503
By 527. Tithables. out of wʰ. 6. being deducted: for }
   mʳ. Vicares — — 521: Reſᵗ. due. at 45: p pole } 23503
   is   }

[31]

Order by this preſent Veſtry. haveing taken into there Conſideracon yᵉ poor & mean Eſtate of Jnᵒ. Gront and his ſickly family Doe in Charity. appoynt that Docʳ. Alexſander in Conſideracon. of his Effecting a Cure on the. wife. of yᵉ ſayd Gront. Shall be alowed twelve. hundred. pounds of tobb. and. Caſk. to be. payd. when Levied. yᵉ next yeare. out of which mʳ. Edw. Porteus hath. aſſumed. & promiſed to pay. twenty ſhillings; mʳ. Thomas Vicares ten ſhillings; mʳ. Robᵗ. yard ten ſhillings; mʳ. Robᵗ. Carter. ten ſhillings:

Ordered by this Veſtry that Henry Bray be payd after yᵉ Rate. of one. thouſand. pounds of tobacco and Caſk. p annum. for yᵉ maintenance. of Alice Peirſons Child.

Ordʳ. that mʳ. Robᵗ. yard. and. Doʳ. Thomas. Green. Church wardins. are. to Collect of Everey tythable. parſon of this pariſh. 45:ˡᵇ tobb. ℔ Pole and therewith to pay yᵉ parſʰ Charges. and in Caſe. any Shall Refuſe to pay yᵉ a bove ſᵈ pariſh Leavye, to Ether of them or ther Collectʳ. Are hearby Impowered. to make. diſstres for the. ſame.

Ordered. that Dʳ. Alexſander be payd. 1500ˡᵇ of tobb. & Caſk the next year: in Conſideracon of his Cureing Samˡˡ. Maſtin of the. diſtemper. he. now Labours under memᵈ. yᵗ. mʳ. Robᵗ. Carter Doth this Day. att a full Vestry held for this parish. aſsumed & promiſed to keep and maintaine. a malatto baſtard. Child. which his woman Sarvant Dorothy Roſum Lately had; soe. that it ſhall not for yᵉ future. be troubleſome. or Chargeable. to the. ſaid pariſh

[32]
At a Veſtry held. Octobʳ. yᵉ. 5ᵗʰ 1692:

     mʳ. Thomas Vicares. Miniſter
Preſent mʳ. John. Buckner. ſenʳ mʳ. Robᵗ. yard
    mʳ. James. Dudley   mʳ. Tho: Green
    mʳ will: Thornton: ſenʳ.
    mʳ. wᵐ. Thornton. Junʳ. ⎫
    mʳ. Conquist. Wyatt   ⎬ Church wardins

Petſoe. pariſh Dʳ.
To: mʳ. Thomas. Vicares. Miniſter	12000
To: Richᵈ. ſimco. Clerk	01500
To: widd: Hogſdon. ſexton	00500
To: Steven. Hall. ſexton	00500
To: Jnᵒ. Rumball.	01000
To: Docᵗʳ. Tho: Blake. pʳ. Thomas Elcock	01500
To: mʳ. Robᵗ. yard. pʳ. Elcocks Accomodations. five months and. diſburſtmᵗ. pʳ. a pariſh. Child. & old Lennard	00820
To: mʳ. Vicares. pʳ: a barrell. of tare. & bringing to yᵉ Church:	00220
To: Docᵗʳ. Green. pʳ. Elizbeth. Vinſon.	01000
To: mʳ. Jnᵒ. Buckner. pʳ. Clarkes fees.	00196
To: Richᵈ. ſimco. pʳ. tobb. under. Levid. Ano. 90: & 91 And. one Levie Over Charg'd Capᵗ. Page.	00224
To: Docᵗʳ. Alexſandʳ. pʳ. expence. of means. and ſeaverall jurneys. made. Endevering yᵉ Cure of Samˡˡ Maſtin now. decᵈ	01000
To: Henry Bray pʳ. keeping a pariſh. Child of George Peirſons decᵈ.	01000

To: mʳ. David Allexſander. pʳ. Cureing Jnº. Gronts wife	00700
To: Job. Hopkins. pʳ. keeping a baſtard. Child: 8: monethes	00750
To: will. ſmith. pʳ. keeping wᵐ. Allins Child) ten monthes at the. Rate. of a hundred. pʳ. month by agreemᵗ.	01000
To: Tho: Cook. pʳ. mending yᵉ old Church.	00600
To: Richᵈ. ſimco. Clark of yᵉ veſtry	00500
To: ſallary & Caſk. att. 5. and. 8. pʳ. cent	02315
	27815
To. ball. due. from yᵉ Church wardins next year to be accountable. for. being Over Levied	317
	28132

By: 547: tythables out of which: 6: being deducted. for mʳ. vicares. 541: Reſts due

52: pds. tobb. pʳ. pole. to be Recᵈ of 541 tythbls is   28132

[33]   By this pʳſent veſtry

Tis Order'd that mʳ. Wᵐ. Thornton. Junʳ. and. mʳ. Conquis[ ] Wyatt. Church wardins of this Pariſh. Doe. Collect & get from Everey tythable, parſon. of this Pariſh. the ſum of 52ˡᵇ. of tobb. pʳ. pole. the ſaid ſum. being this pʳſent years Pariſ Levie: and that thay therewith pay of and Discharge. all yᵉ pariſh. Credᵗʳˢ. And, in Caſe. of delay or refuſall: of the Levie a fore. ſd, thay yᵉ ſaid: Church wardins & Everey of them. and. their Collectʳˢ. are hear. by impowered. to make. diſstreſs for yᵉ ſame.

   memᵈ. Ther being a fraccon of three. hundred. and ſeventine pounds of tobb. in this years. Levie. due. by ballᵉ to yᵉ pariſh wᶜʰ. yᵉ Church. wardins are to be Accountable. for yᵉ next year.

By yᵉ Conſent of this pʳſent Veſtry Capᵗ. Jnᵒ. Smith is made. Choyſe on for a vestryman. in Capᵗ Lightfoo[ ] Roome. for this pariſh.

Whare. as. George Peirſon yᵉ ſon of George Peirſon decᵗ.) has. bin ſum time paſt a burden to yᵉ pariſh Henry Bray proforing to Eaſe. yᵉ pariſh & take the. ſaid Child off. (from being any Charge. for. the. fueture.) Order is by this pʳſent veſtry that the Church Wardins bind him to Henry Bray till he. Come. to the. age. of one. & twenty years

By the Conſent of this vistry Richᵈ. ſimco is maid Clerk of the veſtry

[34]
At A veſtry held for yᵉ pariſh of Petſoe.—Octobʳ. yᵉ. 29ᵗʰ. Ano: 1693

Mʳ. Thomas Vicares. Miniſter

Preſent. mʳ Edward Porteus   ⎡mʳ. Thomas. Royſton.
    mʳ. will. Thornton, ſenʳ.   ⎨mʳ. Thomas Green.
    mʳ. Robᵗ. Yard.   ⎣mʳ. James. Dudley
    Mʳ. Conquiſt wyat. Church Wardin:

Petſoe, Pariſh is Debᵗʳ. to Pariſh Charge.	
mʳ. Thomas. Vicares	12000
Richᵈ. ſimco. ſimco Clerk	02000
Widd. Hogſdon. ſexton	00500
Steven Hall. ſexton	00500
Jnᵒ. Rumball	01000
Jnᵒ. Chapman. for keeping wᵐ. Allins Child	01000
Steven Hall for keeping a baſtard Child	00550
Jobb Hopkins for keeping yᵉ ſame. Child	00450
mʳ. wyat for Tho. Elcocks. Maintiᵉᵉ. =5= months	00600
mʳ. wyat for ſarah Mathis Cure & maintinᵉᵉ.	00535
mʳ. Buckners Clerks fees	00029
Debᵗʳ.	19164
Credᵗʳ.	00817

Reſt due.	18347
Caſk at 8. pʳ. Ct.	1468
Sallary at. 5. pʳ. Cᵗ.	0915
Debᵗʳ. in all	20730

Credᵗʳ.

By 499 Tythables ſix being deducted for mʳ. vicares And one for Richard Ierland. Reſts 492=at 42 pʳ Pole. is 20730. with yᵉ fracktion of 66. pounds of tobb due. to yᵉ Church. wardins next year.

[35]

Conᵗʳ.		Credᵗʳ.
By mʳ. James whitlock for Eliz. walkers fine		500
By the ballance of Laſt years pariſh Levie		317
		817

It is ordered by this preſent veſtry that mʳ. wᵐ. Thornton. Junʳ. And mʳ Conquiſt wyat Church wardins of this pariſh: due forthwith Collect of Every tythable. parſon in this pariſh. the Sume of forty two pounds of tobacco pʳ pole. It being this pſent years pariſh Levie—And that therewith thay pay of and Diſcharge—all yᵉ pariſh Credᵗʳ. And in Caſe any Refuſe paymᵗ. of the: A fore. ſayd Levie Thay the Sᵈ. Church wardins and Every of them And ther Collectʳ. Are hearby impoward to make Difſtres for the Same.

It is ordered by this preſent veſtry that Richᵈ. Ierland. pay no pariſh Levie this year. nor for the future. He haveing maid his Complaint of being much afflictted with Sicknes—very Anttiant and paſt his Labor.

[36]

At a Vestry held for yᵉ Pariſh of Petſoe. Septbʳ. yᵉ 6ᵗʰ: Ano: 1694

Preſent.   mʳ. Thomas Vicares Miniſtʳ.
    mʳ. Edw Porteus   mʳ. William Thornton Senʳ
    Capᵗ. Jnᵒ. Smith   mʳ. Tho: Royſton
    mʳ. Robᵗ. Carter   mʳ. James Dudley
    mʳ. Robᵗ. Yard
      Mʳ William Thornton. Junʳ. Chrʰ wardⁿ.

In obediance to an Order of Cort; the vestry have thought fitt. to devide the Pariſh into Saverall percinks. In Order to the perſestioning the Severall tracts of land therein; According to law. as followeth

1: ═ from yᵉ Lower bounds of the pariſh. to Mʳ Thomas ℞.ʳcinks Cooks; and ſoe to yᵉ mouth of Bennits Creek....yᵉ
    firſt pʳ.cinks

2: ═ from yᵉ mouth of Bennits Creek to yᵉ mouth of Jones ℞.ʳcinks Creek. from thence to yᵉ mill; and up yᵉ Branches of
    Said Creek

3: ═ from mouth of Jones Creek to yᵉ mouth of Totopot-℞ʳcinks tomoys Creek. and ſoe up yᵉ branches thereof.

4: ═ from yᵉ. mouth of Totopottomoys Creek. to yᵉ mouth ℞ʳ.cinks of Eaſtermas Creek. and ſoe up yᵉ ſwamp to Coll
    Thomas Pates—quartʳ.; from thence direct to Mʳ. Tho: Royſtons. and ſoe to yᵉ brierry branch to Edw Simmons. And from thence to yᵉ head of popler ſpring branch

5: ═ from Eaſtermas Creeks mouth to parradice brige ℞.ʳcinks ſwamp. and ſoe to Iſack Olyvers. from thence to Mʳ
    W.ᵐ Crimes. Ending at Mʳ. Tho: Roystons.

6: ═ from Paradice bridg ſwamp. along yᵉ Rode on yᵉ left ℞ʳ.cenks hand to yᵉ Draggon brige

[37]

7: ═ from yᵉ Draggon bridg Rode. to yᵉ Richlans ſwamp ℞ʳcinks rode to yᵉ ferry

8: = from yᵉ Richland Swamp rode down to yᵉ extent of ℔cinks the remaining part of yᵉ pariſh

Order is by this preſent veſtrey: yᵗ the overſears. of yᵉ highways. whoſe percinks. belongs to Coll: Tho Pates Mill Dam —doe forthwith make a good Sofitiant bridge for foot and hors men Over yᵉ Runn=and all Overſears of yᵉ highways. belonging to this Pariſh doe forthwith. Clear and amend yᵉ highways belonging to thire ſeverall ℔ercinks

By yᵉ Conſent of this preſent veſtry mʳ. Richard Myner is made Choyſe on for a veſtreyman. for yᵉ Lower ℔ercinks of this pariſh. In yᵉ place of mʳ. Ralph Green Junʳ. decᵗ.

[38]

at a veſtry held. for yᵉ pariſh of Petſoe. Octobʳ. yᵉ: 12ᵗʰ: 1694

mʳ. Thomas Vicares Miniſter

mʳ. Edw Porteus	mʳ. Robᵗ. Yard
mʳ. Jnᵒ. Buckner	mʳ. Tho: Royſton
mʳ. Robᵗ. Carter	mʳ. Tho: Green
Captᵗ. Joⁿ. Smith	mʳ. James Dudley
Preſent. mʳ. will Thornton. ſenʳ.	mʳ. Richard Myner

mʳ. Will Thornton Junʳ. and mʳ. Conquist Wyat Church Wardins

	yᵉ pariſh is dʳ.	tobacco
mʳ. Tho. Vicares		12000
Richard Simco Clarke		2000
Jnᵒ. Rumballs. maintinance		1000
Widd Hogſdon. ſexton		500
Steven Hall ſexton		500
Jnᵒ. Cobſon for pailing in yᵉ Church yard and finding timbʳ and nails		2000
Jnᵒ. Berrey for keeping a baſtard. Child: 3: months		250
Steven Hall. for keeping a baſtard Child: 6: months		500
mʳ. Wᵐ. Collawn. for keeping James jenkins: 9: months		750

mͬ. Jnᵒ. Cant diſburſtmᵗ. for James jenkins	150
To ſallary & Caſk	2554

$$22204$$

By: 529 tythables 6. being deductted out for mͬ. vicares Remains to be Lev[y]'d on 523 wᶜʰ. of Everey tythable parſon at 42:½ᵇ ℔ᵣ. pole. Recᵈ. a mounts. to 22204

Order is by this preſent veſtrey: finding yᵉ Lower Church of this pariſh being ſo decayed and Rotten that it is paſt Repare. = It is put to yᵉ vote whether a new Church Shall be built in the Saime place (to which the whole veſtrey excepting mͬ. Robᵗ. yard mͬ. James Dudley—voteted A Church Should be built in the Saime place.

[39]
It is Ordͬ [*is] by this preſent veſtrey that yᵉ new Church now to be built in the Lower part of this pariſh—Is to be in bredth between yᵉ walls. twenty foot: and forty foot in lanth between yᵉ walls/yᵉ walls to be brick thirtine foot pitch with brick geable ends. (an engliſh fraim'd Roofe, and Covered with ſhingles (and therfore ordered that yᵉ preſent Church wardins take Care that it be forthwith efecttualy done Accordingly/with all yᵉ expedition as may be.

It is Ordͬ [*is] by this preſent veſtrey, that it alſo be put to yᵉ vote. whether there ſhall be a Chappill built in the upper part of this pariſh (all yᵉ whole veſtrey voteted: there ſhould be noe Chappill built: mͬ. Robᵗ yard and mͬ. James Dudley voteted there ſhould be but one Church in yᵉ Pariſh

It is Ordͬ. [*is] by this preſent vestrey that mͬ william Thornton Jun[] and mͬ. Conquist wyat be diſmiſt from there office of Church wardin: And Capᵗ. Jnᵒ. ſmith and mͬ. Thomas

---

*Note! These words are scratched through in the MS., but are still legible.—C. G. C.

Royſton is ordered to officiate yᵉ office of Church wardins for yᵉ two next enſuing years for this pariſh. and that they doe geather and Collect from everey tythable parſon of this pariſh forty two pounds and a half of tobb. ℔ʳ.pole. the ſayd ſume being this preſen years pariſh Levie: And that therewith thay pay of and diſcharg all yᵉ pariſh Credᵗʳˢ and in caſe of delay or Refuſall of yᵉ Levie afore ſᵈ thay yᵉ ſayd Church wardins and every of them and there Collectʳˢ. are hearby impowered to make diſtreſs for yᵉ faime

[40]
    at A vestrey held yᵉ 7ᵗʰ. of deſembʳ. 1694
      for yᵉ pariſh of Petſoe.

     mʳ Thomas Vicares. Minister
Preſent. mʳ. Edw. Porteus. mʳ. Robᵗ. yard
    mʳ. Jnº. Buckner.   mʳ. Wᵐ. Thornton Junʳ
    mʳ. Robᵗ. Carter   mʳ. Conquiſt Wyat.
    mʳ. william Thornton: ſenʳ. mʳ. Richᵈ. Myner
    mʳ. Tho: Green
  Capᵗ. Jnº. Smith. and Mʳ. Tho: Royſton Church Wardins

It is orderᵈ by this preſent veſtrey. that yᵉ execūt of an order of veſtrey held for this pariſh yᵉ 12ᵗʰ. day of octobʳ. Ano 1694 for yᵉ building of a brick Church in the lower part of this pariſh be ſuſspended untill yᵉ meeting of yᵉ freeholders and houſekeepers of this pariſh. wᶜʰ. meeting is Opoyntted to be on yᵉ 8ᵗʰ day of Jan.ʳʸ next. at popler ſpring Church.

It is orderᵈ by this pʳſent veſtrey. that publycation be made that all freehoulders and houſe keepers of this pariſh. be Requeſted to meet yᵉ veſtrey yᵉ. 8ᵗʰ day of Jenʳʸ next at popler ſpring Church. to give there votes Concarning yᵉ rebuilding of yᵉ old Church in yᵉ lower part of yᵉ pariſh.

It is ordered by this preſent veſtrey. that yᵉ Gentᵐ. thereunto belonging doe meet yᵉ Inhabitance of the pariſh [ ] yᵉ

8th. day of Jenry next. Concarning ye Rebuilding of ye old Church. in the lower part of the parish.

[41]

at a vestry held for petso parish. octobr. ye 7th. 1695

present   mr. Tho. Vicares ministr.
    mr. Edw Porteus.   mr Tho. Green
    mr. Robt. yard   mr Rich Miner
    mr. Wm. Thornton. Junr.
       Capt. Jno. Smith } Church wardins
       mr. Tho: Royston }

	Tobacco
The parish is Dr.	
mr. Tho. Vicares as minist'	12000
Richd. Simco. ⅌. Clarke of ye Church. and vestry	2000
Jno. Rumball	1000
widd: Hogsdon. sexton	500
Steven. Hall sexton	500
Wm. Ivers ⅌ 4 months keeping Robt. Mathews from ye 18th. day of may last to this day	332
Wm Ivers. ⅌ a Rugg	030
Jeff Austin ⅌ 3. months keeping Grace. Blackman from ye 29th. of June. last to this day	250
Jerr: Darnill senr. ⅌ keeping Jno. Dawson three. months from June. ye 15th. to this day	250
mary Hogsdon ⅌r keeping Jane. Benson. 5. months from. Aprell ye 27th. last to this day	415
By: agreemt. of mr. Royston Church wardin an Consent of ye vestry—have added. to make up six months pay on ye acc of ye above Benson. to mary Hogsdon	85
mr. Edw Porteus. pr. goods ⅌ ye parish use	208
Capt. Jno. Smith. ⅌r. James jenkings maintinance	500
Robt. Pryer ⅌ posting ye Church	600
Robt. Pryer ⅌r. making a hors Block	060

Margery Darnill ⅌ keeping of Margery Steward 5: weeke	100
mr. Jno. Smith. ⅌ a. 11. poſts for ye Church	110
Summ	18940
Sallary. at 5: ⅌ Cent	945
Caſk at. 8 ⅌ cent	1584
Totall	21469

By: 532 tythables—6: being deducted out for mr. vicares Remains to be levied on 526=wch of Everey tythable parſon. 41. Recd. amouts to: 21469

[42]

Whareas it was made manifeſt to this preſent veſtry that Thomas Grindy of this pariſh haveing Contrary to a former order of this *pariſh veſtry octobr. ye 11th. Ano. 1681 entertained Margrit Steward and ſhe bigg with Child ſo long time that ſhe became an inhabitant of this pariſh. doth promiſe and agree with this preſent veſtry. to alow ye Said Margrit Steward an Child She goeth with ſofficiant maintinance. diatt waſhing an lodging for one. whole yeare. and on ye true ⅌formance therof: this veſtrey have ordered that ye next inſuing yeare. he ſhall be allowed five hundred pounds of tobacco and Caſk.

It is ordered by this Preſent veſtry that Capt. Jno. Smith and mr. Tho: Royston Church Wardins. for petſoe pariſh due forthwith collect of everey tythable parſon of this pariſh forty one pounds of tobacco ⅌ pole to diſcharge ye pariſh Credt. and in Caſe any refuſe paymt. to make disstress for the Saime.

*Note! This word has been scratched through in the MS. and the word "vestry" written above it.—C. G. C.

at a veſtry held for petſo pariſh octobr. ye 14th. 1695

Order is that Capt. Jno. Smith. and mr. Thomas Royſton. be diſcharg'd of being Church wardins and mr. Thomas Buckner and mr. Wm. Barnard is opoynted Church wardins in there Roome for ye two next inſuing years.

Order is by this preſent veſtry that mr. Nicholas Smith. and mr. william Carver. be Overſeyears of the high ways this next inſuing year. for ye upper part of petſoe pariſh. in ther Severall ℔r.cincts. as this veſtry have thought fit to ye beſt of ther jugment. in ye deviding the Saime.

[43]

at a veſtry held for petſoe: pariſh octbr. ye 14th. Ano 1696

mr. Tho. vicares miniſtr

Preſent Capt. Jno. Smith   mr. James Dudley
mr. Robt. yard   mr. Conquiſt Wyat
mr. Robt. Carter   mr. Richd. Miner
mr. Tho: Royſton

mr. Tho. Buckner }
mr. willm. Barnard } Church wardins

Petſoe. pariſh is Dr.	Tobacco
To: mr. Tho. vicares	12000
To: Richd. Simcoe. Clark of ye Church and veſtrey	02000
To: Widdow Hogsdon. Sexton of popler Spring Church	00500
To: Steven Hall. Sexton. of purton Church	00500
To: Jno. Rumball	01000
To: Margery Darnill ℔r. Keeping Jno. Dawſon	00800
To: Margery Darnill for keeping Margrit Steward: from ye. 28th. of mar.ch till this Day	00542
To: widdow Darnill is alowed ℔ goods She Spar.d Margrit Steward in her neſſissity	00100
To: Jo. Smith. for keeping Grace Blackman two months.	00166

To: Robt. Humphris for keeping Grace Blackman. seven Months	00584
To: Capt. Jno. Smith for goods to grace Blackman	00155
To: widdow Hogsdon for keeping Two women. one yeare	01000
To: mr. Tho. Royſton. ℔r. Edw Row.	00150
To: margrit Steward, preſent relefe leved	00200
	19697
Sallary at 5 an 8 ℔. ſent	2561
Totall	22258

This pariſh liſt being this year 532 tythables. 6 being deductted out as a cuſtamerry alowance ℔r. mr. vicares Remains 526 wch Comes to 42 lb of tobb. ℔r. pole

The fracktion is a 166 pounds of tobb to be payd ye Church Wardins next year } mr Buckner & mr Barnard

[44]

Where as ye former Overſeyer of ye upper part of petſo parish have made Complant to this preſent veſtry. that ye upper part of this pariſh is to great and trublefume for one Overſeyer to Clear ye Rodes and mend the bridges. tis therfore ordered by this preſent veſtry that two Overſeyers be apoyntted to Clear and mend the Saime. according to ther Severall precincts. as hearafter is nominated;

Order is by this veſtry that mr. nicholas Smith be overſeyer of ye highwas this preſent year and for his precincts tis ordered that he Clear ye Kings highways and mend the bridges. that are in ye upper part of petſoe pariſh. between popler Spring rode. the Turck ferry. and Kink and Quine County

Order is by this veſtry that mr. wm. Carver be overſeyer of ye high-ways this preſent year. and for his precincts. tis ordered that he begin at popler Spring. and ſo along the rode. to yᵉ turcks ferry. and that he Clear al Rodes and mend the bridges belonging to yᵉ Kings Highways in yᵉ pariſh of petſo. between yᵉ above Sayd rode and ware. pariſh

order is by this preſent vestry that mʳ. Thomas Buckner and mʳ. wᵐ. Barnard Church wardins for petſoe pariſh this preſent year. due forthwith Collect and gether from everey tythable parſon of this pariſh 42¹ of tobacco ℔ pole. it being this preſent years pariſh Levie. and that therwith thay pay of an diſcharge all yᵉ pariſh Cred.ᵗʳˢ and in Caſe any Shall refuſe paymᵗ of yᵉ ſaime. that yᵉ Church wardins or ether of them or ther Collectrs are hearby impowerd to make diſſtreſs for y.ᵉ ſaime

[45]

Deſemb.ʳ yᵉ 14ᵗʰ theſe oathes taken by yᵉ Gentlemen of this veſtry Anᵒ 1696

Oathes Enjoyned by Act of Parlament to be taken in Stead of the oathes of Allegeance and Supremacy

I. A. B. doe Sincerely promiſe and Sware that I will be faithfull and bare true Allegiance to his majestey King* William George

So help mee God.

I. A. B. Do Swear that I doe from my heart abhore Deteſt and abjure as Impious and hereticall that Damnable Doctrine and Position that Princes Excommunicated or deprived by yᵉ Pope or any authority of the See of Roome. may be depoſed or Murdered by there Subjects or any other whatſoever. and I doe declare that noe forreign Prince. Perſon prelate State or Potentate hath or ought to have any Juridiction power

---

*Note! The word "William" has been scratched through with a pen, and the word "George" substituted for it. The word "George" is written in the same hand and the same ink as that of page [121] of the MS.—C. G. C.

Superiority preeminince or Authority Eccleſiasticall or Spirituall within this Realme.

So help mee God

The Teſt

Wee whoſe names are under written doe hear [ ] teſtify and declare that wee doe not believe yᵗ there is any Transubstantiation of the Elements of bread and wine in yᵉ Sacrament of yᵉ lords Supper at or after the Conſecration thereof by any perſon whatſoever

Thomas Vicaris

Thomas Buckner	Joⁿ: Smith
Will. Thornton: Junʳ	Conqᵗ Wyatt
James Dudley	Robᵗ Yard
Will: Bernard	Tho: Greene
Conqᵗ Wyatt	Will: Thornton
Da: Alexander	Thomas Royston
Robᵗ: Porteus	Robert Carter
Augᵗⁿ Smith	Walt Waters

Aprill ye 10ᵗʰ 1704
Wᵐ Upſhaw

Aprill yᵉ 29ᵗʰ 1708
John Royſton
Albion Throckmorton

Thomas May Cleark of yᵉ Veſtery Octoᵇʳ yᵉ: 6ᵗʰ: 1708

J W: Pratt
Jnᵒ Coleman
Richard Bayley

[46]
*This *othath This following oath taken by the Gentlemen

---

*Note! These words are scratched through with a pen in the MS.—C. G. C.

who have Signed the Teſt as the oaath of a Veſtrymen as followeth

you Shall Sware that as a veſtryman of petſoe parish you will act & doe in all things relateing to that offis justly & truly to yᵉ beſt of yoʳ. judgmᵗ.

So help me God

Order is by this veſtry. that all who Shall heare after be made choyse on as vestrey men for this pariſh. Shall take yᵉ oaths. as before is under written by yᵉ Severrall Gentlemen of this parish. as also the above oath. of a veſtryman

Whareas this day the Gentlemen of the vestry mett Concarning the Rebuilding of the old Church that was gon to ruin. whether their Should be a nother built in the Saime place. or not. (thay haveing well Considdered the great Charges the whole pariſh would be at. And the remotenes of the inhabitants. of yᵉ upper parts of this pariſh. to a Church built in the place whare the old Church Stood.—

It is ordered by this preſent veſtry that ther Shall be no other Church in the pariſh. but popler Spring Church. And that alwas to be kept in good repare.

At A Vestey held for Pettſo pariſh Jenʳʸ Anº 1696/7

Perſent

   Capᵗ. Jnº. Smith   mʳ. Conquiſt Wyat
   mʳ. Wᵐ. Thornton Sen.ʳ mʳ. Tho: Royſton
   mʳ. Robᵗ. yard   mʳ. Wᵐ. Thornton Junʳ
   mʳ. Robᵗ. Carter   mʳ. Tho: Green
   mʳ. James Dudley
    mʳ. Tho: Buckner ⎫
    mʳ. Wᵐ. Barnard ⎭ Church Wardins

[47]

Jen'y 25ᵗʰ At a vestry held for petſoe pariſh Jen'y 25ᵗʰ
1696/7

It is ordered by thes preſent. veſtry. haveing agreed with mʳ. Josiph Hoult. Miniſter of Straten majʳ. pariſh to aficiat as ther Miniſter once a fortnight. at Popler Spring Church. And to have half yᵉ Sallary mʳ Vicares formarly had proportionably for yᵉ time he afiſiats.

And it is farther ordered yᵗ if mʳˢ vicares Can procure. mʳ. James Clack to preach at popler Spring Church yᵉ Other Sundays that mʳ. Joſiph Hoult doth not aficiate. the remaindʳ. of this years Sallary then Shall be alowed to mʳˢ. vicares; but if She cannot procure him. It is ordered yᵗ if mʳ. Joſiph Hoult will undertake to preach everey Sunday & adminisʳ. yᵉ Sacremᵗ. at yᵉ usuall times. then he to have the full ſallary proportionably for yᵉ time hee officiats.

Order is by this Preſent vestry. that for yᵉ beter encourigemᵗ. and Accomodation of a minister yᵗ Shall hearafter offer himſelf to oficiate in this pariſh there be a gleeb of land Containing two or three hundred Acrees provided as Soon as poſsible it may be purchised conveniant in the pariſh. haveing never yett bin at any Such Charges which the law Injoyns us to provide. the veſtry being deſirus no longer to be deſtitute of Such a conveniance. hath ordered that this to give notis. be publiſhed and put up at yᵉ Church. if any perſon in yᵉ pariſh hath a tract of land to disspoſe of as above: thay give notis to yᵉ Church Wardins. and thay Call a Vestry to agree for the Saime

[48]

At a vestry held for petſoe pariſh octobʳ. yᵉ 13 Anº 1697
Preſent Capᵗ. Joⁿ. Smith. mʳ. Robᵗ yard
mʳ. Robᵗ. Carter. mʳ James. Dudley
mʳ. Tho: Royſton. mʳ. Wᵐ. Thornton, Junʳ.
mʳ. will. Barnard Church wardin

Petſoe. Pariſh. is Dʳ.

To: mʳ. Josiph. Hoult. Minniſtʳ.	9000
To: Mʳˢ. Dorrathy Vicares. pʳ. 3 months. due Mʳ. vicares	3000
To: Richᵈ. Simcoe. Clark of yᵉ pariſh and veſtry	2000
To: Rumball-a Criple	1000
To: widdow Hogsdon. as ſexton	500
To: mʳ. Wᵐ. Barnard pʳ. a poore woman; for tar and. Carting. anl last years. ballance	406
To: mʳ. David Allexſander. ℔ accᵗ. phiſick	90
To: mʳ. Wᵐ. Brookins Keeping Grace Blackburn: 10 months	900
To: widd Darnill pʳ. Keeping Margritt Steward one year	[1]000
To: widd Darnill pʳ. Phiſick of mʳ. Crimes. pʳ. ditto	150
To: Robᵗ. Pryer. for Tarring yᵉ Church. and other worke	450
To Caſk & ſallary at 5 & 8 pʳ Cent.	2339

	Debᵗʳ.	20835
To mʳ. fowlers Judgmᵗ.	Credᵗʳ.	500

yᵉ parish Charg in all is 20335

20475 pounds of tobacco being Levied on 525 tythables this years. parish Liſt, Comes. to. 39 lb. of tobbacco ℔ʳ. Pole. with yᵉ fracktion of 140 ˡᵇ of tobacco. wᶜʰ. yᵉ Church. wardins are. to be accountable for next year. to yᵉ Pariſh

Order is by this veſtry that mʳ. wᵐ. Barnard finding Tarr to finniſh yᵉ Church. with. what begun. Shall be allowed

Sixty pounds of tobb out of yᵉ above fracktion and yᵉ Remaindʳ. to be alowed. yᵉ widdow Darnill

It is Ordered by this preſent veſtry that mʳ. Tho: Buckner and mʳ. william Barnard Church wardins of this pariſh or eather of them preſent to yᵉ Cort mʳ. william Crimes and mʳ. Richᵈ. Bayley Overſears. of yᵉ highways. for yᵉ upper part of yᵉ pariſh And mʳ. william Thornton Junʳ and mʳ. Peter Smith for yᵉ Lower part: of

[49]

Order is by this preſent veſtry that mʳ. Thomas. Buckner And mʳ. Wᵐ. Barnard Church wardins of this parish. for this pʳſent year doe. forthwith. demand. and gether. together. 39 pounds of tobacco of everry tythable parſon in yᵉ pariſh of petſoe. it being this yea[rs] pariſh Levie. And if any freehouldʳ. houſe Keepʳ. or freeman refueſe to pay yᵉ Saime. yᵉ Church wardins or ther Colletʳ. to make diſtreſs for yᵉ Saim.. it being Levied to pay and diſcharg the Sume of 20475 pounds of tobacco: to Severall Credᵗʳˢ. as on the Other Side; yᵉ pariſh is indebted.

Rich Ierland. was. by Conſent of mʳ. Tho: Buckner & mʳ. willᵐ Barnard. Church wardins. & Sum other of yᵉ. Gentlemen of yᵉ veſtry Enter tain'd to be Sexton of popler Spring Church. yᵉ. 17: day of Aprell 1698

at a veſtry held for petſoe pariſh July yᵉ 1ᵗʰ. 1698

preſᵗ mʳ. Robᵗ. yard. mʳ. James dudley
mʳ. Wᵐ. Thornton. Senʳ mʳ. Rich Miner
mʳ. Tho: Buckner: } Church wardins
mʳ. Wᵐ. Barnard.

Ordʳ. is by this veſtry that mʳ. Wᵐ. Miller nicholas Smith and mʳ. Tho: Cook. be added to yᵉ veſtry and they have. hearby declared. members of yᵉ veſtry of this pariſh

At a veſtry held for petſo pariſh Octob'. y® 24th.
An°. 1698

m'. Tho: Buckner and m'. william. Barnard Are deſcharged from being Church wardins haveing made up ther acc'. with y® veſtry and Geatherd y® Leves. the two years laſt paſt m'. william Miller and m'. Nicholas Smith are made Church wardins in there roome

[50]

At a veſtry held for petſoe. pariſh Octob'. y® 24th. An°. 1698

Preſent m'. Conquiſt Wyatt   m'. W^m. Thornton. Jun'
    m'. Tho: Buckner   m'. W^m. Barnard.
    m' Tho: Royſton   m' Wm Brookin.
    m'. James Dudley   m'. Tho: Cook.
      m'. Nicholas Smith ⎫ Church
      m'. W^m. Miller   ⎭ wardins

Petſoe. pariſh is D'.	Tobacco
To m'. Joſiph Hoult Mininſt'.	16000
To: Jn°. Rumball. a Cripple	1000
To: m^rs. Doruthy vicares p'. acc^t.	58
To Rich^d. Ierland. Sexton. p'. half year	250
To: m^rs. Mary Smith p'. Keeping A baſtard Child: 4: months.	320
To m' Ralph. Baker. p'. two Sick women be had in Cure	3000
To Jn°. Brown. p'. Keeping Job Hopkins Child 5 months	250
To Jn°. Brown. p'. Keeping Jn°. Berrys Child=3= months.	250
To: Tho: watters Carreing a Sick woman	20
To: m'. W^m. Barnards acc'. for y® releefe of ſeverall Sick people	[]09
To: m'. W^m. Barnard p'. Keeping Jn°. Berrys Child :3: Months. & 20 days.	305

To: Major Beverly pr. Clarkes fees	113
To: mr. Tho: Buckners acct.	75
To: Robt. Pryer. pr. forms made.	60
To: Sherr: fees.	10
To: Steven Johnſon pr. keeping a poore woman.	383
To: widd Darnill pr. Margt. Steward	350
To: mr. Wm. Brookin. pr. 10: Months Keeping Grace Blackman	830
To: Richd. Simcoe. Clarke. of ye Church & veſtry	2000
	2698[ ]
To Sallary & Caſk of 10948. pounds of tobacco at 13. pr. cent is	140[ ]
To: Sallary of mr. Joſiph Hoults tobacco. 16000. At: 5: pr. cent is	800
In all	28[ ]84

[51]

Order is by this preſent veſtry wee haveing mad[ ] an Agreemt. with mr. Joſiph Hoult ye Miniſtr of Stratton Major parish. in ye County of Kin[ ] and Quine; that he preach. a Sarmon everey Lords day in ye afternoone at popler. Spring Church. in this Pariſh. And then. and thare. & at all times elce what ever belongs to his Offiss. wee deſire may be truely perform'd. by him as Our. Continnued: Miniſter: untill Sume Other Miniſtr. offers. Or wee provide Our ſelves. Otherways. Order is therefore by this preſent veſtry. that mr. Josiph Hoult. be alowed at ye rate. of Sixtine thouſand pounds of tobb. pr. yeare. for ye time he offeciates in our pariſh. and al ye perquiſits therunto blonging; being juſtly due Shal be payd.

528: tythables. with adition of 56lb of tobb.. a Mounts to 55lb of tobb. pr. pole: ye 56: being over and a bove ye pariſh Charge. tis Ordered ye Church wardins pay ye Same to Rich Ierland. Sexton.

The Gent^n. whoſe names are: und^r. writen took ye Oathes Enjoined by Act. of parlament. to be taken in Stid of ye Oathes of Allegence & Supremacy. Signed to ye teſt and took ye Oathes of a veſtryman

1706 Aprile y^e: 23^d   Robt Porteus   William Miller
                        Jno Pate   Nicho: Smith.
                                             W^m. WB Brookin.

Order is m^r. Richd Bayly. be continnew. Overſeare of y^e highways. he was. laſt yeare: m^r. Robt. yard. in m^r. W^m. Crimes. roome. next unto King & Quine County.==m^r. Tho: Buckner & m^r. W^m. Thornton Junr. Overſears for y^e Lower p^r.cinks. of this pariſh

[52]

Order is by this veſtry that Richd Ierland Shall be allowed at y^e Rate of Six hundred pounds of tobb. and Cake p^r. year for being Sexton of popler Spring Church.

Order is by this preſent veſtry that m^r. W^m. Miller & m^r. Nicholas Smith Church wardins of this pariſh due geather of Everey tythable perſon 55 pounds of tobb. p^r. pole. to pay of and diſcharge. ye pariſh debts. and if any Shall refuſe to pay ye Same. to make d[ ]stress

feby ye 9th 1698/9 at a vestry held for petso. par^h.

Preſent m^r. W^m. Thornton. Senr.   M^r. w^m. Thornton. Junr.
         m^r. Tho: Buckner   M^r W^m. Barnard
         m^r. Robt. yard   m^r. Tho. Cook
              m^r. nicholas Smith } Church. wardins.
              m^r. W^m. Miller   }

Order is by this preſent veſtry that m^r Thomas Buckner and m^r. W^m. Miller. dispoſe as they See Conveniant of ye ten pounds Left to ye poore of ye pariſh. by Capt. Jno. Smith deceſt; after the [ ] poore people as followeth. have had there parts thereof.

widdᵂ. Davis: Rich Bradshaw widd Smith: widd Wiſdum: & Law. Pattrick: if eather of theſe named have recᵈ of mʳ. John Pritchett any part of ten pounds Soe Left to yᵉ poore of yᵉ. pariſh by Capᵗ. Robᵗ. Thurſton. deceſt. tis ordered that thay diſſpoſe. of Capᵗ. Smiths to Sume Other of yᵉ *pariſh poore. According to there discretion

[53]

At a veſtry held for petſoe pariſh Octoʳ. yᵉ 4ᵗʰ. 1699

Preſent: mʳ. Joſiph Hoult. Minister
  mʳ. Wᵐ. Thornton. Senʳ.   mʳ. Tho: Cook
  mʳ Conquist Wyatt.   mʳ. Wᵐ. Brookin
  Capᵗ. Tho: Buckner   mʳ. David Allexsander
  mʳ. Wᵐ. Barnard
    mʳ. Nicholas Smith } Church Wardins
    mʳ. Wᵐ. Miller   }

Petſoe parish Dʳ.	Tobacco
To: mʳ. Joſiph Hoult. Minister	16000
To: mʳ. Wᵐ. Humphryes: 7: Months Clarke	875
To: mʳ. Joſiph Ocaine: 5: Months Clarke	625
To: Richᵈ. Simcoe. Clarke. of yᵉ vestry	500
To: Richᵈ. Ierland. Sexton	1000
To: mʳ. Conquist Wyatt. pʳ. Accᵗ. 5: Months Keeping of Jnº. Rumball. & his fuenarall	415
To: mʳ. Wᵐ. Millers Accᵗ.	830
To: mʳ. David Allexsanders. Accᵗ.	400
To: Jnº. Cobson. pʳ. reparing yᵉ. Church yard Pails. hors. Blocks. & puting up Benches.	350
To: mʳˢ. Mary Cary for Keeping Berrys Child: 3: months. and one. weeke.	270
To: Tho: Watters. for Charls Taylor. 2: weeks	42

*Note! The word parish is scratched through in the MS, but is still legible.—C. G. C.

To: Dockter Backer. Keeping Margritt Steward three months. &: 3: week: at 83 pr. month	312
To: Jnº. Brown. for: 6: weeks Keeping Children	100
To: mr. Tho: Powell plaſtering. & white washing yᵉ Chu.	1500
To: Maddm. Smith Keeping. a parish Child	1000
To: Natt Mills. Keeping. Nicho Lewis Child: 6: Months	500
To: alowance. for Shirts & frocks. pr yᵉ Child	40
To: mr. Tho: Powell: for writing yᵉ vers. on yᵉ Guarder. in yᵉ Church. Requesᵗ of mr. Hoults	40
	24799
To: Sallary: of 24799 at 5 pr. Cᵗ	1237
To: Caſk of 8759 at 8 pr. Cᵗ:	700
	26736

557: at 48. pr. pole a mount to yᵉ Sume. of 26736. pounds of tobb.

[54]

Octobr. yᵉ. 4ᵗʰ. 1699: Petſoe parish.

At this preſent veſtry mr. Conquist wyat & mr. david Allexsander. tooke yᵉ Oathes. enJoned by Act of parlament. to bee taken. in Stid of yᵉ Oathes of alegence. & Supremacy. and yᵉ Oathe of Veſtry men. and have. Signed to yᵉ teſt.

At a veſtry held for this parish yᵉ day and date above. it was Ordered that mr. wm. Thornton. Junr. be Continewed Overſeare. of yᵉ highways. for yᵉ Lower parts of this parish. as he was Laſt yeare: And mr. Rich. Bayly for yᵉ upper. part. thay haveing not perform'd ther offiss thare unto belonging. yᵉ year Past. mr. wm. Barnard. is Opoynted Overſear of yᵉ highways. for part of yᵉ Lower percinks of this parish in Capᵗ. Tho: Buckners. roome: and mr. wm upshaw pr. yᵉ upper parts in mr. Robᵗ. yards roome thay haveing each pr.form'd there Charge in there Severall precinks. According to Order of vestry.

Order is by this vestry that Rich Simcoe make Endentures between Henry Morris of Straten Major in yᵉ County of King and Quine. and Necholas Lewis, a fatherlis and motherlis Child of this Parish. and that he Sarve yᵉ Sayd Morris till he Come to yᵉ age of one and twenty: yᵉ Endentures to be Signed by yᵉ now Church wardins. and thay See all articles perform'd in wrighting as was, declare'd to this vestry. and yᵉ Said Morris obliges himſelf for to Learn yᵉ ſaid orphant yᵉ art of Coopery

Order is by this present vestry that mʳ. wᵐ Miller and mʳ. Nicholas Smith Church wardins due demand of everey tythable. Parson of this parish. forty Eight pounds of tobb. pʳ. pole. and if any refuſe to pay. to make diſſtress. it being to pay yᵉ parih debts

[55]
Septuageſima Sunday January yᵉ 28ᵗʰ. 1 699/700 it then being the Last Sermont Preached by mʳ Joseph Hoult

At A vestrey Held for Pettſoe Parrish on the *5ᵗʰ Day of †[ ]ebruary 1 699/700

Pʳſent mʳ Joseph Hoult Minister⎫
    mʳ William Thornton Seʳ. ⎪ mʳ David Alexander
    mʳ Robert Yard   ⎬ mʳ William Bernard
    Captain Tho Buckner   ⎭ mʳ Thomas Cooke

This Veſtrey Called for yᵉ Ellection of a Clarke and Mett then Moving to Samuell Hope Conſidering his poverty for to Continue in His Clarkſhip a month Longer for a further tryall of His aproving himſelf; the which Proffer he Refuſed; upon which the Miniſter with yᵉ Veſtrey thought fitt to make tryall of mʳ Underwood and mʳ Daniell Poole in Reading and Singing Pſalms which was accord-

---

*Note! Above "5th" is written "first" †Note! "[]ebruary" is scratched through in the MS, and "Janua" is written to the left and in place of it.—C. G. C.

ingly Done and after Such Tryall made it is the opinion of this Veſtrey that Hugh Macktyer be Entertained as Clark of the Church and Veſtrey Paying him His Sallary as acuſtomed

James City January yᵉ 26ᵗʰ 1 699/700

Sirs I receaved yours on the 6ᵗʰ of this inſtant from Doctor Alexander and I had given you an anſwear ſooner but I was then Daily in hopes that Some Clergymen would arive, who now I thank god are ſo according to your pious Deſire of having a Miniſter, I have ordered you one the Reverend mʳ George young who is ſent by the Right Reverend father, in god Henry Lord Biſhop of London in whoſe Dioceſe Virginia and his Lordſhip hath given him all the neſſeſary Inſtruments whereby he is qualified to Exerciſe his miniſteriall function in this His Majesties antient and great Collony and Dominion of Virginia according to his Majesties Royall Inſtructions and Comands to him who is your Afectionat friend

Franches Nicholſon

To the gentlemen of yᵉ veſtrey in
Pettſoe Parriſh Glouestʳ

[56]

At A vestrey Held for Pettſoe Parriſh ffebruary yᵉ 5ᵗʰ 1 699/700

Preſent
   mʳ William Thornton Senior Captain Thomaſ Buckner
   mʳ Robert yard   mʳ James Doodley
   mʳ William Thornton Junior mʳ William Berrnard
        mʳ William Miller Churchwarden

It is ordered by this preſent Veſtrey that mʳ George young is Entertained as Minister in this our Parrish of Pettſoe untill the first weddensday of occtober next as alſo to be allowed His Sallary according to Law with all other Perquiſites he the Said mʳ George young well performing his office in his Ministeriall function

ordered by this Veſtrey that yᵉ Clark of the Church be paid half a crown or thirty pounds of Tobbo for Pubblishing the Banns of Matrimony.

At A veſtrey Held for Pettſoe Parriſh Aprill yᵉ 24ᵗʰ: 1700

Preſent
    William Thornton Senior   mʳ William Thornton Jun
    Captain Thomas Buckner   mʳ David Alexander
    mʳ James Duddly   mʳ William Berrnard
        mʳ Nicholas Smith Churchwarden

[57]

It is ordered by this Vestrey that Hugh Macktyer Clarke of the Vestrey Doe in the name and behalfe of the Vestrey and Church wardens Sign and Deliver unto mʳ William Berrnard an Indenture for Richard Allen the Sonn of Suſsanna Allen a father Leſs Child he being now at the Age of fouer years fouer Months and the Said orphant to Serve the Said Bernard untill he comes to the Age of one and twenty years, mʳ William Bernard by Aſumption to the Vestrey Doth oblige himſelf for to give the Sᵈ Richard allen three years ſcooleing; & upon which Conſideration the Veſtrey granted to pay unto mʳ William Berrnard Six Hundred Pounds of Tobbo and Caſk to be paid him in the next Collection

It is allſo ordered by this Vestrey that Hugh Macktyer Clerk of the Vestrey Doe in the name and behalfe of the Vestrey and Church wardens Sign and Deliver unto James Haſe and indenture for James the Sonn of Nicholas Lewis father Leſs and Mother leſs and to Serve him the Said James Haſe untill he comes to Age according to Law as alſo the Said James Haſe is hear obliged for to give the Said orphan James Lewis three years Scooleing; he being now at the Age of five years old on the ninth Day of this next Month and it is further ordered that James Haſe Shall give good Suffitient Security for to Keep and Save the Said orphant for the future to be in any wayes burdenſome to the Pariſh untill the tearm and Space of his indenture be fully Compleated

Att a veſtrey Held for Pettſoe Parriſh Septemb' ye 10th 1700

Preſentt   m' George young Miniſter
   m' Conquist wyatt   m' David Allexander
   Cap Tho Buckner   m' William Berrnard
   m' Robert yard
     m' Nicholas Smith
     m' William Miller   Church wardens

Itt is conſidered by this preſent Vestrey y° Low and mean Condition of Samuell Hope and five Helpleſs Children and wife all wch are unkapable to gett their Living; therfore we Doe think it fitt to Sett Him Levey free During the time of His Poverty

[58]

This indenture made y° 4th day of Aprill in y° twelfth year of our Sovereign William King of England Scott Land france and Ierland Defender of y° faith annoqz Domini one Thouſand Seven Hundred

I Nicholas Smith and William Miller Church wardens for y° Parrish of Pettſoe and County of Gloucester Doe in the name and behalfe of the vestrey Sign and Deliver unto m' william Bernard an indenture for Richard Allen the Son of Richard Allen according to an order of Veſtrey and by the free conſent of His Mother Suſsana Allen we

Doe Bind unto mʳ william Berrnard yᵉ above named Richard Allen for to Serve him the Said Berrnard his Heirs Executors or Aſigns untill he comes to yᵉ age of twenty and one yeares and in all Such Service or imploy as he yᵉ Said maſter Shall or will imploy him about as alſo yᵉ Said maſter by this indenture, promiſe and oblige himſelf for to give unto the above Bound Richard Allen three years Scooleing and he to be ſent to Scoole at yᵉ years of twelfe or thereabouts and yᵉ Said master Doe covenant and agree to and with Nicholas Smith and william Miller churchwardens for to find and alow yᵉ Said Richard allen Suffitient aparrell meat Drink waſhing and Lodging During yᵉ Said Tearm of time and yᵉ Said master for to pay unto yᵉ above Bound Richard Allen all Such neceſsary allowancess as is to him Due according to the Cuſtome of this countrey in wittnes whereof yᵉ Parties above Have interchangeably Sett their Hands and Seales yᵉ Day and year above written

      Signed by mʳ William Berrnard
 Signed Sealed and Delivered
in the Preſence of us   (Seal)
 Hugh Macktyer Clarke of yᵉ Veſtrey
 Conqueſt Wyatt

[59]

THIS INDENTURE made yᵉ 4ᵗʰ: Day of Aprill in yᵉ twelfth year of our Sovereign William King of Ingland Scotland france and Ierland Defender of the faith annoqz Domini one Thouſand Seven Hundred

I Nicholas Smith and William Miller Church wardens for yᵉ Parrish of Pettſoe and County of Gloucester Doe in yᵉ name and behalfe of yᵉ Vestrey Bind unto Hennery Morriſh an orphant Boy by name Nicholas Lewis unto him His heirs and Aſigns untill he comes to yᵉ Age of twenty and one yeares and yᵉ Said orphant to Serve him yᵉ

Said Morriſh in all Such Service or imploy as he yᵉ Said Maſter Shall or will imploy him about. as alſo yᵉ Said hennery Morriſh Doe covenant and Agree to and with yᵉ above named Church wardens for to instrucht and Learne yᵉ Said nicholas Lewis yᵉ true art and Skill of a Cooper as alſo to find him Suffitient aparrall meat Drink washing and Lodging and to be Kindly uſed and at yᵉ End of yᵉ Said Tearm of time for to pay unto Nicholas yᵉ above bound one broad Cloth *Sute Shute two shirts Hatt Shooſe and stocking, in wittneſs whereof yᵉ parties Mentioned have to theſe indentures interchangeably Sett their Hands and Seales yᵉ Day and year first above written

```
                                           his
Signed Sealed and Delivered     Henery HM Morriſh
   in yᵉ Preſence of us                    mark
   Hugh Macktyer Clarke of yᵉ Vestrey              (Seal)
   John Macktyer
```

[60]

This Indenture Made on yᵉ 24ᵗʰ Day of Aprill in yᵉ twelfth year of yᵉ Reign of our Sovereign Lord William King of England Scottland france and Eirland anno Domini Seventeen Hundred

I Nicholas Smith and William Miller both Church wardens for yᵉ Parriſh of Pettſoe in yᵉ county of Gloucester Doe in yᵉ name and behalfe of yᵉ vestrey Bind unto James Hayes by this indenture an olphant Boy by name James Lewis unto him his heirs or Aſigns untill he comes to yᵉ age of one and twentee years, and by an aſumption made by the above named Hayes in open vestrey that he will give yᵉ Said olphant three years Scooleing and that to be given when yᵉ Said Olphant is capable to receave Such Education he therefore yᵉ Said Hayes Doe hearin bind him-

---

*Note! The word Sute in the MS. has been scratched through, but is still legible.—C. G. C.

ſelf and his heirs et cetra; for to fullfill and perform yᵉ above promiſe made unto yᵉ Said olphant as alſo we yᵉ above named Church wardens Doe by this indenture order that yᵉ above bound James Lewis olphant shall Serve yᵉ above named James Hayes untill he comes of Age and in all Such Service or imploy as he yᵉ Said master shall or will imploy him about, yᵉ above named Hayes Doe covenant and agree to and with Nicholas Smith and William Miller Church wardens for to find and alow yᵉ above bound James Lewis olphan Suffitent aparell meat Drink washing and Lodging Dureing yᵉ tearm of time above Spetified as alſo yᵉ Said James Hayes Doe hearby oblige himſelf his heirs and Aſigns for to Keep yᵉ above bound James Lewis from being in any wayes burdonſome unto yᵉ Parrish untill yᵉ expiration of yᵉ tearm of time above mentioned and at yᵉ end of yᵉ Tearm yᵉ above named James Hayes for to pay unto yᵉ above bound James Lewis all such neceſsary allowances according to yᵉ cuſtome of this country in wittneſs wherof the Parties above mentioned have interchangeably Sett their hands and Seales yᵉ Day and year above written

Signed Sealed and Delivered
  in yᵉ preſence of us   Signum
  Henry Bolton   Signed by James: A. Hayes   (Seal)
  Richard Cooke

                  Hugh Macktyer Clarke of yᵉ Vestrey
                  Looke back and you will find his Age

[61]

Att a vestrey Held for Pettſoe Parrish occtober yᵉ 2ᵗʰ 1700

    mʳ George young Minister

Preſent
  mʳ William Thornton Senior mʳ William Berrnard
  mʳ Conquest Wyatt mʳ William Miller
  Captⁿ Thomas Buckner mʳ Nicholas Smith
  mʳ James Duddley mʳ William Brooken
  mʳ Thomas Cooke

mʳ David Alexander and mʳ Thomas Cooke church wardens

Parrish is Dettʳ

To mʳ George young Minister—*Mr Thomas nealle Sherriff: 70	10821
To mʳ Joseph Hoult minister	5179
To Hugh Macktyer clark of yᵉ church and vestrey	1183
To mʳ William Berrnard for eaſing yᵉ Parrish of an olphan Child	600
To Nathaniell Mills for Keeping Nicholas Lewis olphan child	1000
To Samuell Hope for eleven weeks being clarke	317
To Samuell Hope by a gift from yᵉ Parrish	400
To Richard Eirland Sexton	1000
To Major Petter Beverley for clarkes fees	137
To mʳ William Miller for his expenches over yᵉ River to his exellentee	90
To Colloˡˡ: Mathew Page for being twice charged 3 levies: in 98 at 42: pʳ pole	126
To Lawrance Patrick in charity	600
To Madam Mary Smith for Keeping a bastard child provided Shee clears yᵉ Parrish from yᵉ child being any further trouble	1000
	22523

 *Note! This word is hard to make out. It may be "Mo" rather than "Mr"—C. G. C.

Parrish Creditt Pʳ Supra		Parrish Creditt	960
By mʳ walter watters	500		21563
By mʳ Robert yard	250	To Sallary of 21563: at 5ʳ cent is	1078
By mʳ Nicholas Smith	150	To cask for 5563 at: 8 pʳ cent is	0445
By mʳ willᵐ: Berrnard	060		
	960		23086

587: Tythables at 39: pʳ pole
amount to 23086 pounds Tobbo

Itt is ordered by this vestrey that mʳ Nicholas Smith and mʳ William Miller be Discharged from being church wardens they having made up their accots wᵗʰ: yᵉ vestrey and collected yᵉ Levies the two year Last past and paid Each Parrish Creditor his Due

Itt is alſo ordered that mʳ David Allexander and mʳ Thomas Cooke be made Church wardens in their Roome for yᵉ two next Inſuing years

By a fraction in this Division: 115 lb of Tobbo Due to the Church wardens

[62]

Itt is ordered by this preſent vestrey that mʳ David Allexander and mʳ Thomas Cooke church wardens of this Parrish for this preſent year Doe forth with demand and Collect together 39: pounds of Tobaccos of every Tythable perſon in yᵉ Parrish of Pettſoe it being this years Parrish Leavie and if any free houlder houſe Keeper or freeman Doe or offer to refuſe to pay yᵉ Same, the Church wardens or their collecters are by this vestrey impowered to make Diſtreſs for yᵉ Same: it being Levied for to pay and Discarge yᵉ Sum of 23086: pounds of Tobbo to Severall creditors as on yᵉ other Side which yᵉ Parrish is indebted to

Itt is ordered that mʳ Robert Nettleſs be Surveyor for yᵉ

uper part of this Parifh this prefent year in the Roome of mʳ William upfhaw and that he be Discharged from his office

Itt is alfo ordered that mʳ William Fleming be overfeer of the High wayes in yᵉ midle perchinks in yᵉ Roome of mʳ william Berrnard and that yᵉ Said Berrnard be Discharged from his office

The above order of Fleming as overfheer is forbiden

Itt is ordered by the Said Vestrey that mʳ William Berrnard be Discharged this prefent year from His office as being overfeer of yᵉ High wayes, and yᵗ mʳ John Stubbs *Senior Junior is by this Vestrey ordered to take place for yᵉ midle percinks and there to well offitiate untill he be Dismist by this Vestrey

[63]

At a vestrey Held for Pettfoe Parrish on yᵉ 28ᵗʰ of octobʳ: 1700

Prefent

Itt is ordered by this prefent Vestrey that mʳ Emanuell Jones Minister be Intertained as our Minister for Pettsoe Parrish from yᵉ Date Heareof untill the first weddnesday of occtober next as allfo to be allowed this Sallary at the Rate of Sixteen Thoufand Pounds of Tobaco; with all other perquisits Due to him shall be Justly Paid as alfo yᵉ Said mʳ Emanuell Jones minister well behaving and perrforming himfelfe in His ministeriall function upon all occations.

    Emanuel Jones Minister of Pettsoe
    William Thornton   Da: Alexander. Ch: Ward
    Thomas Buckner   Tho. Cooke Ch: w
    Robᵗ Yard
    Will: Bernard
    Will: Thornton: Junʳ

---

*Note! This word is scratched through in the MS but is still legible.—C. G. C.

Nicho Smith
Will: Miller

[64]

This Indenture

Made on yᵉ Sixt Day of November and in yᵉ twelfth year of yᵉ Reign of our Sovereign Lord William King of England Scottland france and Eirland Deffender of yᵉ faith anno Domini Seventeen Hundred

David Alexander and Thomas Cooke Church wardens of Pettſoe Parrish in yᵉ County of Gloucestʳ Doe in yᵉ name and behalfe of yᵉ Vestrey Therof by this Indenture Bind unto Nathaniell Mills an orphant Boy named John Lewis untill He comes to yᵉ Age of one and twenty years In all Such Service as the Said Mills will Imploy him about he yᵉ Said Mills obligeing himſelf by this this Indenture to give unto yᵉ Sd orphant John Lewis two years Scooleing and yᵗ to be given at nine years years of Age and not before he comes to yᵉ afore Said Age as Alſo for to find and alow yᵉ Said Lewis Suffitient aparrell Meat Drink waſhing and Lodging Dureing yᵉ afore Said term of time as Alſo to Pay unto yᵉ above Bound John Lewis all Such Neceſsary Alowancheſs as is to him Due according to the Cuſtome of this Countrey, In wittneſs whereof yᵉ Partieſs above mentioned have Interchangably Sett their Hands and Seales yᵉ Day and year above written

               Signum

Theſt   Nathaniell NM Mills
 Hugh Macktyer
 Ric Hill

[65]

THIS INDENTURE Made on yᵉ Sixteenth Day of June and in yᵉ thirteenth year of yᵉ Reign of our Sovereign Lord William King of England et Cetra annoqz Domini Seventeen hundred and one; I david Alexander and Thomas Cook Church wardens for yᵉ parrish of Pettſo in the County

of Gloceſter, we Doe firmly in yᵉ name and behalfe of yᵉ
Vestrey Bind unto mʳ Phillip Smith Executor to Madam
Mary Smith by this Indenture unto him one orphant Girll
by name Elliſabeth Carter unto him yᵉ Said Smith his
hears Executors addministerators; untill Shee cometh to
yᵉ full age as yᵉ Law Directs; and She faithfully to Serve
him her Said Maſter his hears et Cettra in all Service or
imploy as he or they Shall Sett her about and the Said
Phillip Smith Doe covenant and agree to and with David
Alexander and Thomas Cook Church wardens; for to carefully instruct Learn Educate yᵉ Said orphan in all such
wayes that she may be Capable after her Indented time
is expired for to gett her own Living; and to allow her
Suffitient meat Drink washing good aparrel untill yᵉ expiration of her indented time, and at yᵉ end of the Said
tearm for to pay unto her Elliſsabeth Carter, Double
aparrel with all other such neceſsary allowancheſs as yᵉ
Law Directs unto bound orphants; as allſo yᵉ above maſter
Phillip Smith Doe hearby by theſe Indentures oblige himself his hears et Cettra for to Keep and Save yᵉ above
bound Elliſsabeth Carter from being in any wayes Bur-
Donſome to yᵉ parriſh untill this indenture is expired; and
if the above Bound Eliſsabeth Carter, should within yᵉ
space of time above mentioned in any Case become burdonſome to this parriſh; that then the Said Phillip Smith
his hears et Cettra Doe and Shall forfitt unto this parrish
*two *thouſhand pounds of good Tobbo and Cask to be
paid in the parrish and County aforeſaid upon the breatch
without fraud or Deceitt in witneſs hearof yᵉ parties above
named have Interchangeably Sett their Hands and Seales
yᵉ yᵉ Day and year above written Signed Sealed and Delivered in yᵉ preſence of us; ye above bound being at yᵉ
age of fower yeares upon yᵉ ninth Day of May Laſt paſt
                   Phill Smith

---

*Note! These two words are scratched through in the MS, but are still fairly legible.—C. G. C.

[66]

Att A veſtrey Held for Pettſo: Parish July yᵉ 24ᵗʰ 1701
mʳ Emanuell Jones minister

Preſent

mʳ William Thornton Seʳ
Captain Thomas Buckner
mʳ James Duddley
mʳ William Thornton Juʳ

mʳ William Berrnard
mʳ Nicholas Smith
mʳ William Brooken

mʳ David Allexander
mʳ Thomas Cooke

Church Wardens

Itt is ordered that mʳ David Allexander and mʳ Thomas Cooke church wardens are hereby ordered and impowered in the name and behalfe of this vestry to bargain conclude and agree to and with mʳ Larken Chew for the enlargening of the popullor Spring church that is to Say the back worke on the north Side to be built in Length five and twenty foot and the inſide twenty foot clear work from wall to wall

Itt is ordered by this veſtrey that William fallkoner be overſeer of the High wayes for the midle perchinks for this next enſuing year in the Roome of mʳ John Stubbs and he carefully and Diligently See and cauſe all Roades and bridges well Cleared and mended in his perchinks untill Such time as he be Diſmist by the Veſtrey

Hugh Macktyer Cv

[67]

Att A veſtry Held for Pettſoe Parrish occtober yᵉ 1ᵗʰ 1701

Preſent mʳ Robert yard
Capᵗ: Tho: Buckner
mʳ William Berrnard

mʳ William Miller
mʳ Nicholas Smith

mʳ David Alexander
mʳ Thomas Cooke

Church wardens

Parrish Dett[r]	Tobacco
To m[r] Emanuell Jones Minister	1600
To Nathaniell Mills for Keeping of John Lewis orphant	1000
To Mills for keeping Margrett Stantton 3 Months and burying hr	350
To m[r] David alexander for his Service and Charge in y[e] Parrish buſineſs and Mediccens to Margrett Stanton	965
To nicholas oliver for keeping Elliſſabeth Starrs Child: 6: months	500
To m[r] Robert Porteus for caſements for y[e] Church windowes	300
To Richard Ireland Sexton	1000
To m[r] John Heſter for worke about y[e] Church	600
To m[r] Tho: Cooke for a ſedar pale 2: stooles a pewter baſon	120
To m[r] William Miller for a regiſter booke Connon prayer B:	550
To Hugh Macktyer Clarke Ch: Vestry	1500
To Robert Enies in Charity	600
To m[r] Larken Chew for Inlargening y[e] Church	12000
To towards purchaſeing a gleeb	10000
To Samuell fowler for Doing y[e] glaſs windows of y[e] Ch	200
	45685
To Sallary at 5 p[r] Cent is	2284
To Caſk for 29685: at 8 p[r] Cent is	2374
In all	50343
599 Tythableſs att 84 p[r] pole amount to	50316
Remains Due to y[e] Church wardens for Robert Ennies Levie given by the vestry	84
by a fracction in y[e] above acco[t]:	27
	111

Itt is ordered by this preſent veſtry that mʳ David Alexander and mʳ Thomas Cooke Church wardens Doe forth Collect 84: pounds of Tobaco of Every tythable perſon in this parrish it being this years Levie and if *I any free houlder houſekeep or free man Doe or offer to refuſe to pay the Same, then the Church wardens or their collectors are heare impowered to make Diſtreſs for yᵉ Same and it being Levied for to pay the above Sum which yᵉ Parrish is indebted to

    Hugh Macktyer Clarke Veſtrey

[68]

    occtoʳ yᵉ 1: 1701

By a legacee Left by Madam Mary Smith of five Pounds in the hands of mʳ Philip Smith Executoʳ to the said Mary Smith Diceaſed to be Diſtributed amongst the poor of this parriſh mʳ Philip Smith moving to the veſtry the Said Legacie he being now ready to pay the Said Debt and So be Diſscharged, upon which the veſtry orders the Said Smith Executoʳ: to pay the Said five. pounds unto thoſe perſons whoſe names are under written proportionably, and take their receits

    Robert Enies
    William Edwards
    Richard Ireland
    Iſack oliver
    Widdow †Gregory

[69]

This Indenture made the eight day of Novembʳ 1701. & the fourtenth year of our ſoveraigne Lord William of Great Brittain ffrance & Ireland King Witneſseth That Wee Thomas Cooke & David Alexander Church Wardens of Petsoe pariſh In yᵉ County of Gloſter Doe firmly in the

---

 *Note! This word is scratched through in the MS, but is still legible.—C. G. C.

 †Note! This name in the MS. is hard to read. I may have read it wrong.—C. G. C.

name & behalfe of yᵉ Veſtry of yᵉ ſd pariſh bind unto Mr
Jnº. Day of yᵉ forſᵈ. pariſh one Orphan boye called James
Luis of yᵉ age of seven yeares (who was formerly bound
unto James Hayes now deceaſt & now takne from his
widow for want of maintinance) unto the ſᵈ Day his heires
exors &c: untill he arrive att the full age as the law directs to ſerve him & them in all mañer of service & imploy
that he or they shall ſett him about And yᵉ ſᵈ Jnº. Day
does obildge himselfe his heires exors &c: to Give him
yᵉ ſᵈ Orphan three yeares shooling & to carefully inſtruct
learn & educate the ſd Orphan in all ſuch wayes that he
may able after his indented tyme expyre to gett his own
living & to allow him ſufficient meat Drink lodging & ap-
parele untill the expyration of ye ſd tyme, & after the finiſhing of the ſame To pay unto the ſd James Luis Double
apparell wᵗ all other ſuch allowances neceſsary as the law
Directs in ſuch caſes As alſo to keep the afoſd parish
During the aforſd intented tyme from all manner of charges
or being any wayes burdenſome to the ſd pariſh & the
abovenamᵈ Church Wardens Doe obildge themſelves in
quality aforſd to have allowed to the ſd Day five hundred
lb: tob, att the nixt levie In conſideration of his three
yeares schooling In witnes whereof both yᵉ ſd parties
have heerunto ſett their hands & seals Day & year firſt
above written.

John Day

Hugh Macktyer
    Clarke of Veſtry

[70]

    Att a Vestry held for Petso Parish *Mart. 12ᵗʰ. 1701.
        Mr Emanuell Jones Ministʳ.

₱sent   Mr William Thornton   }   Mr William Bernard
        Capᵗ Thomas Buckner   }   Mr Tho: Cooke
        Mr William Thornton Juʳ }   David Alexander

*Note! This word in the MS is hard to make out. I may have read it wrong.—C. G. C.

It is ordered That Mr Thomas Cooke & David Alexander Church Wardens doe take & receave of Mr Godfrey Van †Ittoon bills of Exch: for the money Due upon yᵉ Acct of tob: raiſed in this parish for the purchaſing of a gleeb & conſigne it in the name of the vestry of ye forſd parish into the hands of Mr Micajah Perry & Comp

    Att the forsaid Vestry

It is ordered That Thomas Potts be Clerke of yᵉ Church And that he have one thousand pounds of Tob: & caske yearly During his service

[71]

 Att a Veſtry Held for Pettſo Parrish Octoʳ: yᵉ 26ᵗʰ:

170[ ]

	Mʳ Emanuell Joneſ Meniſtʳ.
Pſent	Mᵗ William Miller
Mʳ Conqueſt Wyatt	Mʳ Nichᵒ: Smith
Capᵗ. Thomas Buckner	Mʳ William Brooking
Mʳ James Dudley	William Bernard

  Capᵗ David Alexander Church Warden

    Petſo Parriſh is Dʳ: Tobacoe

To Mʳ Emanuell Joneſ Meniſtʳ	16000
To Mʳ Larkin Chew for the Remaindʳ Due to him for the Adition of the Church	08000
To Isaac Oliver for Keeping & burying Elizabeth Starks Child	00275
To John Day for James Lewis Orfant	00500
To Doᵒᵗʳ Ralph Baker for Eliz: Carter Cuer	01000
To Capᵗ. David Alexander for Rouling 14 hodds of Tobacoe	00422

 †Note! This word in the MS is hard to make out. I may have read it wrong.—C. G. C.

To Majo'. Peter Beverley for Clarks fees	00326
To m' Tho'. Cook for Laſt Years Ballance	00027
To M' Hugh Macktyer for 4 months Salary for being Clark of the Church	00500
To Rob' Ennis Charity	01000
To Tho': Potts for being Clark of the Church	00600
To Richard Ireland Sexton	01000
To m' Tho'. Cook for Rouling Tobb and ap' of Blancots	00415
To Doct'. Ralph Baker for Looking aft' Rob' Ennis	01600
To Richard Burnitt for Goeing to Joſeph Colemans	00050
To Tho'. Neale for Shriefs fees	00040
To Mary Wright for Keeping and Burying Tho'. Garnet	00100
To M' Jones meniſt'. for want of a Gleeb	02000
	33855
To Salary for 33855^{lb} of Tobb	1692
To Caſke for 17855 of Tobb	1428
	36975

It is ordred by this p'sent Veſtry that Cap' David Alexander and m' Tho' Cook be Diſcharged from being Church Wardens they having made up their Acco'". with the Veſtry and Collected the Levies the two Laſt Years paſt: and paid Each parriſh Creditour his Due

It is alſo ordred by this preſent Veſtry that m' William Brooking & William Bernard be Apoynted Church Wardens In their Roome for the two next Inſuing Years

[72]

By a fraction in ye Deviſion of 36975^{lb} ^{Tobb} is 93^{lb} of Tobacoe Due to ye Church Wardens m' William Brooking and William Bernard which is to be paid them Next Year

Order is by this p'sent Vestry that mr William Brooking and William Bernard Church Wardens for this p'sent Year: Doe forthwith Demand and Colleckt together 54 pounds of Tobacoe of Every tithable person in ye Parrish of Petso: it being this Years parrish Leivie and if any freeholder house Keeper or free man Doe or offer to Refuse to pay the Same; the Church Wardens or their Collectors are by this p'sent Vestry Impowred to make Distress for the Same; it being Levied for to pay and Discharge the Sum of 36975 pounds of Tobb To Severall Creditors as on ye other Side which ye parrish is Indebted To

It is ordred that Mr John Royston be Surveyor for ye Lower part of ye uper precincts of Petso parrish this present Year In ye Room of mr Richard Bailey and that he be Discharged from his office

It is also ordred by this p'sent Vestry that mr John Stubs Junor: be Surveyor of the high Ways for ye Midle precints of Petso parrish this p'sent Year In ye Room of mr William Falkner and that he be Discharged from his office

It is ordred that mr William Brooking & William Bernard Church Wardens for this p'sent Year Draw Conditions with mr John Clark for the Repairing the Walls of Popular Spring Church

[73]

At a Vestry held at William Bernards ye 28th June 170[ ]

P'sent

mr Robt Yard	mr Thos Cook
mr Wm Miller	Capt David Alexander
mr Nicho: Smith	

William Bernard Church Warden

It is ordr by This p'sent Vestry that William Bernard Church Wardn Doe forthwith Agree with Some Workmen for ye Building & Ereckting of a Gleeb houſe upon ye Gleeb plantation; Six & thirty foot Long & twenty foot wide with two Outſide Chemneys two 8 foot Square Cloſsetts planckt above & below, with two Chambers above Staires and ye Staires to Goe up in ye midst of ye houſe with 3 Large Glaſs windows Below Stair[] Each to have 3 Double Lights in y^m with a Glaſs window in Each Chamber above Staires Each to have 3 Lights in y^m & Each Cloſsett to have a window in it and Each window to have 3 Lights

This Indenture Wittneſseth y^t margrett Goodwin with ye Conſent of her huſband Abraham Goodwin, she being mother & neareſt friend to George Syms Malatto of Petſo Parriſh & County of Glouceſter, in Conſideration and Regard y^t ye S^d Margrett Goodwin is Very poor and Indigent & not able to provide & maintaine ye S^d George Syms, doth Bind & put him out as a Servt to John Steer of ye parriſh and County afore S^d and him after ye manner of a Servt To Serve from ye Date of theſe p^{r}sents untill ye S^d Georg[] Syms Malatto Shall attaine to Lawfull age, Dureing wch Time ye S^d Geo: Syms Shall faithfully & Duely Serve ye s^d Steer and his wife their heirs Execut^{r}s Adminiſtr or aſsignes in all manner of Services or Serviſes while hee By him her or Either of y^m Shall be Imployed or put about & Shall faithfully & Deligently Obſerve & Obey all ye Lawfull Commands of his S^d Maſter or Miſtriſs and be Subjeckt to and Demean himself towards y^m; in all poynts as a Servt Ought to Doe and not upon any pretence Whatſoever Abſent himſelf from their Service During ye sd Time without Leave or Licence of one or Either of them

In Conſideration of wch Service to be Duely performed by ye Said george Syms Malatto, ye S^d John Steer Doth hereby bind and oblige himſelf his heirs Exec^{rs} Adminiſt^r or aſignes to find and allow ye S^d George Syms During his Service Good Suffitie[ ] Apparrell meat Drink Waſhing & Lodgin[ ] [74] and all other Neceſaryes Sutiable for a Servt: in his Degre and to Learn ye S^d George Syms to Reade in ye time of his Service to ye True performance of ye above Covenants and Agreements Each party bindeth y^m Selves to ye other firmly by Theſe p'sents in Witteneſs whereof they have Inter Changably Sett Their hands & Seals this 20th of Aprill 1703

Sind Sealed & Delivered   Her mark
in p'sent of us   Margrit M Goodwin (Seal)
   W^m: Bernard C-W
   Rich^d: Cordell   John Steer (Seal)

[75]

Att a Veſtry Held for Pettso Pariſh Octob^r. y^e. 26th. 1703

Preſ^t

Capt: Thom^s Buckner ⎫ Mr Robt Yard
Capt: David Alexander ⎪ Mr William Miller
Mr Willm. Thornton Senr. ⎬ Mr Thomas Cooke
Mr William Thornton Junr ⎭ Mr Nicholas Smith

   Mr William Bernard ⎫
   Mr William Upshaw ⎬ Churchwardens

The Parriſh of Pettso is D^r.   Tobacco

To Mr Emanuell Jones Miniſt^r:	16000
To Thomas Potts Clarke of ye Church	01000
To Nathaniell Mills in parte of pay for a gleebe	05000
To ye Widdow Ireland Sextone	01000
To Robt: Ennis Charity	00600
To John Eaſter for paeling in ye Church	02000
To John Mackwilliams	00083
To William Bernard for ye ball of laſt years *account levis and to Maj^r: Beverly	00189
To Maj^r Beverly Clarks fees this year	00043

*Note! This word is scratched through in the MS. but is still legible.—C. G. C.

To Richard Cordle for Sherife fees	00020
To William Upshaw	00100
	26035
To Caſke for 10035 at 8 ℔ʳ Sent	00802
To Sallʳ: for 26035 at 5 ℔ʳ: Sent	01301
	28138

[76]

It is ordered by this preſt Veſtry yᵗ Mʳ William Bernard and Mʳ William Upshaw Churchwardens for this preſᵗ year, Do forthwith Demand and Collect together 41½ pounds of Tobacco of every tythable perſon in the Pariſh of Pettso it being this years Pariſh levie and if any freehoulder houſekeeper or freeman do or offer to Refuſe to pay yᵉ Same yᵉ Churchwardens or their Collectors are by this preſᵗ Veſtry Impowred to make Diſtreſs for yᵉ Same it being Levie for to pay and Diſcharge yᵉ Sum of 28138 pounds of Tobacco to Severall Creditours as on yᵉ other Side wᶜʰ: yᵉ Pariſh is indebted. And it is farther ordered yᵗ if Mʳ Emanuell Jones Do not Come and officiate as formerly then to be pᵈ. proportionably for yᵉ time he did officiate in yᵉ Pariſh aforeSaid

It is ordered yᵗ fifty Shillings be received of John Gilbord by yᵉ Churchwardens and an account be returned to yᵉ veſtry

It is allso ordered yᵗ Robert Nettles and John Royston be preſented to Next Court for not Sufficiently repairing yᵉ highwayes: by yᵉ Churchwardens

It is allso ordered by this preſᵗ Veſtry yᵗ if any of *Them yᵉ Genᵗ: of yᵉ veſtry Do not meet at yᵉ Day appointed when a veſtry is Called they Shall pay ten Shillings to yᵉ Churchwardens and yᵉ Same to be Diſtributed to yᵉ poor of yᵉ Pariſh

*Note! This word is scratched through in the M.S. and above it has been written, "yᵉ Genᵗ of yᵉ vestry."—C. G. C.

Except it pleaſe God to afflict them with Sickneſs or lameneſs. then to Send a note to yᵉ reſt of yᵉ gentlemen of of yᵉ Veſtry which are preſᵗ and they are Excuſable

[77]

At a veſtry held for Pettſo Pariſh Febʳ yᵉ 10ᵗʰ 170 3/4

Preſᵗ

Capᵗ Thoˢ: Buckner ⎱ Mʳ Willᵐ: Bernard ⎱ Churchward[ ]
Capᵗ David Allexander ⎰ Mʳ Willᵐ: Upshaw ⎰ *wardens

Abſent

Mʳ Conqueſt Wyatt   Mʳ Willᵐ Miller
Mʳ Nicolas Smith   Mʳ James Dudly
Mʳ Willᵐ Thornton: Junʳ: Mʳ Thoˢ Cooke

On Consideration of the Laws of Virginia proviſion being made by yᵉ act intituled Church to be built or Chappell of Eaſe for yᵉ building a Church in Each pariſh, and by yᵉ act intituled miniſters to be inducted yᵗ Miniſters of Each pariſh Shall be inducted on yᵉ preſentation of yᵉ pariſhioners and yᵉ Churchwardens being by yᵃ act intituled Churchwardens to keep yᵉ Chur[ ] in repaire and provide Ornamᵗˢ, to Collect the Miniſters Dues, and by yᵉ act for yᵉ better Support and maintenance of the Clergy proviſion *being being made for yᵉ Miniſters of the pariſhes, and by the Sᵈ act for Inducting Miniſters the Governour being to Induct yᵉ Ministers to be preſented and thereby he being Constituted Ordinary and as Biſhop of yᵉ Plantation and with a power to puniſh Miniſters preaching Contrary to yᵉ Law, I am of Oppinion yᵉ Advewson and right of preſentation to yᵉ Churches is Subject to yᵉ Lawes of England (there being no expreſs Law of yᵗ Plantatⁿ made further Concerning the Same) therefore when the pariſhioners preſᵗ. their Clerk, and he is inducted by the Governour (who is to and muſt

---

*Note! These words are scratched through in the MS., but are still legible.—C. G. C.

Induct on the preſentation of the pariſhners) The incumbent is in for his Life and Cannot be Diſplaced by the pariſhners: If yᵉ veſtry do not preſᵗ A miniſter to yᵉ Governour within Six Monthes after any Church Shall become void, yᵉ Governour as ordinary Shall and may Collate a clerk to Such a church by laps, and his Collatee Shall hold yᵉ Church for his Life: If yᵉ Pariſhners have never preſented, they have a reaſonable time to preſᵗ a miniſter but if they will not preſᵗ being required So to Do, the Governour may also in their Default Collate a miniſter: In inducting Miniſte[] by the Governour on yᵉ Preſentation of the pariſhes or on his own Collation he is to Se the Miniſters be qualified according as that act for Inducting Miniſters requires in Caſe of the avoydance of any Church the [78] Governour as Ordinary of the plantation is according to the Statute of 28 H 8 Cap 11ᵗʰ Sect 5ᵗʰ to appoint A miniſtʳ to officiate till yᵉ pariſh Shall preſt one or the Six Monthes be Lapsed, and Such person appointed to officiate in the vacancy is to be paid for his Service out of Profitts thereof from the time the Church becomes void: By the Law above Sᵈ Stated in this Caſe no Miniſter is to afficiate as Such till he hath Shewed to the Governour he is quallified according *to as the Said Act for Induction Directs if the veſtry do not Levy the Tobacco for the Miniſter the Courts there Muſt Decree the Same to be Levied

Edw Northey
July yᵉ 29 1703

At a Council held at williamsburgh the 3ᵈ day of March 1703

Preſent

his Excellency in Councill

Upon reading at this Board Sʳ Edward Northey Knᵗ her majesties Attorney Genˡˡ: his Opinion upon yᵉ act of Aſsembly

---

*Note! The word "to" is scratched through in the MS and the word "as" has been written above it.—C. G. C.

of this Colony relating to the Church and particularly Concerning Induction of Miniſtrs

His Excellency in Councill is pleaſed to order that a Coppy of Sr Edward Northey his opinion be Sent to ye Churchwardens of Each pariſh with in this Colony Requiring them upon receipt thereof forthwith to Call a veſtry, and there to cauſe the Same to be read and entered into the veſtry book to the intent the Sd veſtry may offer to his Excellency what they think proper thereupon

Wil Robertson Cl Con

ffr Nicholson

[79]

At A veſtry held for Pettso Pariſh Aprill ye 10th 1704

Preſt.

For preſentatn:	Contra
Mr Robt Yard	Capt: Thos Buckner
Mr Conqt Wyat	Mr Willm Thornton
Mr James Dudly	Mr Nicolas Smith
Capt David Alexander	Mr Willm Miller
Mr Thos Cooke	

Mr Willm Bernard
Mr Willm Upshaw } Churchwardens

Williamsburgh
Aprill ye 18th 1704

Gentlemen

I understand yt you have had a veſtry laſt week but you have not Sent me ye reſult of it in writing as other veſtrys have done, and therefore I would have you Call an other veſtry and Let me have ye Determination of it under yor hands, yt I may Send it to England by this Shipping. I hear yt an other pariſh has given a preſentation of their living to Mr Emanuell Jones yor Miniſter. So yt I would know wht reaſons you had in refuſing him ye Same favour, and what particular objections

yᵒ have againſt him. Either as to his life or doctrine. and whether you are willing to part wᵗʰ him or no: A speedy anſwer to this is Expected by him who is
    yoʳ moſt affectionate Friend
          ffr Nicholſon

To yᵉ Churchwardens &
Veſtry of pettso pariſh in
Glowceſtʳ County

[80] At a veſtry held for pettso Pariſh Aprill yᵉ 24ᵗʰ 1704

      preſt

for preſentation	Contra
Mʳ Conqᵗ. Wyat	Capᵗ Thoˢ Buckner
Capᵗ David Allexander	Mʳ Wᵐ Miller
Mʳ James Dudly	Mʳ Wᵐ: Thornton Juʳ:
Mʳ Thoˢ Cooke	
Mʳ Wᵐ: Bernard } Chwardens	
Mʳ Wᵐ Upshaw }	

Memorandum yᵗ we yᵉ Subſcribʳˢ were at pettso pariſh Church on Sunday yᵉ 2ⁿᵈ of July 1704 and did then hear yᵉ Reverend Mʳ Emanuell Jones rector of yᵉ Sᵈ pariſh) read yᵉ thirty nine articles During yᵉ time of Common prayer and declare his unfeigned aſsent and Conſent to all the *things therein Contained, & afterwards did read his Certificate from yᵉ Biſhop of London & his Subſcription to yᵉ Decliration following & at yᵉ Same read yᵉ Decleration it Self in yᵉ Church before yᵉ Congregation there aſsembled. In theſe words I Emanuell Jones rector of Pettso Do declare yᵗ it is not Lawfull upon any pretence whatsoever to take armes againſt yᵉ Queen & that I Do abhor yᵗ trayterous Poſition of taking armes by her authority againſt her perſon or againſt thoſe yᵗ are Com̃iſionated by her & yᵗ I will Conforme to yᵉ Liturgy of yᵉ

---

*Note! Above this word is written, in the same hand "matters &."—C. G. C.

Church of England as it now Eſtabliſhed to wᶜʰ *to we Subſcribe our names

      Robᵗ Yard
      Thoˢ Buckner
      David Allexander
      Thoˢ Potts

[81]

Memorandum yᵗ upon Sunday yᵉ 30ᵗʰ Day of July in yᵉ year of our Lord 1704 yᵗ yᵉ Reverend Mʳ Emanuell Jones Rector of Pettso in yᵉ County of Glowceſter in Virginia did read Comon Prayer in yᵉ Said Pariſh Church of Pettso, both in yᵉ forenoon & afternoon of yᵉ Same day according to yᵉ form and order preſcribed & Directed by yᵉ book entituled yᵉ book of Comon prayer & adminiſtration of yᵉ Sacraments, & other rites & Ceremonies of yᵉ Church, according to yᵉ use of yᵉ Church of England, together wᵗʰ yᵉ PSalter or PSalmes of David appointed as they are to be Song or Sᵈ in yᵉ Churches & yᵉ form or manner of Making, ordaining, & Conſecrating of Biſhops Prieſts & Deacons. & immediately after reading yᵉ Same made a declaration of his unfeigned Assent & Conſent to all the matters & things therein Containᵈ in yᵉ form & words above written. In testimonie whereof we SubScribe our names.

      Robᵗ Pourteeſ
      John Peat
      Thoˢ Cooke
      John Royston
      Thoˢ Potts Cl V:

---

*Note! This word is scratched through in the MS., but is still legible.—C. G. C.

[82]

At a veſtry held for Pettso pariſh Octobʳ yᵉ 4ᵗʰ: 1704

Preſᵗ:

Mʳ EManuell Jones Miniſtʳ.

Capᵗ Thoˢ Buckner ⎫ ⎧ Capᵗ David Allexander
Mʳ Conqᵗ Wyatt ⎬ ⎨ Mʳ James Dudly
Mʳ Willᵐ Thornton ⎭ ⎩ Mʳ Willᵐ Miller

	Tobacco
The Pariſh of Pettso is Dʳ	
To Mʳ EManuell Jones Miniſtʳ	16000
To Thoˢ Potts Cl: Ch: V:	01500
To Widdow Ireland Sexton	01000
To Robᵗ Whitehead for yᵉ Cure of Robᵗ Ennis	02000
To Charles Tomkies for yᵉ Cure of Elᵇ Carter	01800
To Elizᵇ: Brumbly for keeping Wid: Writes Child from yᵉ last Day of March at yᵉ rate of 1000ˡᵇ tobᶜᵒ ℔ year & for Coffin & buring	00600
To Thoˢ Cooke for Robᵗ Ennis Levie	00084
To Capᵗ David Allexander for keeping Abigall Hurts Child a year	01000
To Nathaniell Mills in part of paymᵗ of a gleeb	05000
To John Clark for repairing yᵉ Church	04000
	32984
To Sallery of 32984 at 5 ℔ C is	1649
To Caſk of 16984 at 8 ℔ C is	1358
In all	35991

630 tythables at 57 ℔ pole amount to 35991

[83]

It is ordered by this preſt Veſtry yᵗ Mʳ Conqᵗ Wyat & Mʳ Willᵐ Thornton Junʳ: Churchwardens for this preſt year Do forthwith Demand & Collect together 57 pounds of tobᶜᵒ of Every tythable peſton In yᵉ Pariſh of Pettso it being this years

Pari∫h levie and is any freehoulder hou∫keeper or free man Do or offer to Refu∫e to pay y⁰ Same y⁰ Churchwardens or their Collectʳˢ are by this pre∫t ve∫try are Impowred to make Di∫tre∫s for y⁰ Same It being levie for to Di∫charge y⁰ Sum of 35991 pounds of tob⁰⁰: to Severall Creditours as on y⁰ other Side wᶜʰ y⁰ Pari∫h is Indebted to:

It is ordered yᵗ Mʳ Wᵐ Thur∫ton be Surveyor for y⁰ upper part of this pari∫h this pre∫t year in y⁰ roome of Mʳ Robᵗ Nettles and that he be Discharged from his office

*Order is by this Ve∫try yᵗ Thoˢ Potts make Indenture

It is ordered by this pre∫ᵗ ve∫try yᵗ Mʳ Conque∫t Wyatt and Mʳ William Thornton Junior Churchwardens Do in y⁰ name and behalf of y⁰ ve∫try Sign and deliver unto William Fiffe an Indenture for ffrancis Wright fatherle∫s and motherle∫s and to Serve him y⁰ Sᵈ ffiffe untill he Comes to y⁰ age of one and twenty yeares and allso y⁰ Sᵈ ffiffe is here obligded to Learn y⁰ Sᵈ orphant to read any Chapter in y⁰ bible. and to find him Such nece∫ary allowances as is to him Due acording to y⁰ Cu∫tome of this Country

[84]

This Indenture made on y⁰ Sixteenth Day of Novembʳ in y⁰ third year of y⁰ reign of our Sovereign lady anne Queen of England Scotland france & Ireland Defender of y⁰ faith anno Domi Seventeen hundred and four

I Conque∫t Wyatt and William Thornton Junior Churchwardens of Pettso pari∫h in y⁰ County of Glowe∫ter Do in y⁰ name and behalf of y⁰ ve∫try there of by this Indenture bind unto William Fiffe an orphant boy named Francis Wright untill he Comes to y⁰ age of one and twenty in all Such Lawfull Service as y⁰ Sᵈ ffiffe will Imploy him in or about he y⁰ Sᵈ ffiffe obligding him Self by this Indenture to learn y⁰ Sᵈ orphant

---

*Note! This entire line is scratched through in the MS, but is still legible.—C. G. C.

Francis Wright to read any Chapter in yͤ bible. as allso to find [ ]nd allow yͤ Sᵈ Wright Sufficient apparell meat Drink waſhing and lodging Dureing yͤ above Sᵈ term of time and allso to pay unto yͤ above named Francis Wright all Such neceſſary allowances as is to him Due according to yͤ Cuſtome of this Countrey in wittneſs whereof yͤ parties above mentioned have Interchangeably Set their hand and Seal ye Day and year above written

           Signum
Signed See and Delivered William X Fiffe
in yͤ preſence of us
 Thoˢ Cooke
 Thoˢ Potts

[85]

Att a veſtry held for Pettso pariſh Nvembʳ yͤ 12ᵗʰ 1704

      preſt
Capᵗ Thomas Buckner Mʳ Willᵐ: Miller
Capᵗ David Alexander Mʳ Thoˢ Cooke
Mʳ James Dudly
  Mʳ Conquest Wyatt } Churchwᵈˢ:
  Mʳ Willᵐ Thornton

It is agreed by this veſtry that the *that Church wardens Draw Conditions wᵗʰ Ezra Cotten for yͤ building of a gleebhouſe & a kitchen yͤ Sᵈ houſe to be of yͤ Same Dementions as Mʳ Robᵗ Pourtees. & to be framed on Good white oak Sills and to Stand upon blocks & to be lathᵈ. wᵗʰ Goo[ ] oak lathes and Shingled wᵗʰ Good Siprus Shingles The Sᵈ houſe to be 36 foot in Length & 20 foot wide, yͤ Roof to be 18 Inches Jet and to have two outSide Chimnies and two Cloſets adjoyning to them, and all things Ells pertaining according to yͤ Dementions of yͤ above Sᵈ Robᵗ Pourtees houſe, Viz, yͤ above Sᵈ Kitchin to be foot Long & foot wide

---
 *Note! This word is scratched through in the MS but is still legible.—C. G. C.

[86]

Att A veſtry held for pettſo pariſh Octobr yᵉ 3ᵈ 1705

Preſᵗ
Mr Emanuell Jones Miniſtr

Mr Robt yard	Mr Nicholas Smith
Capt Thoˢ Buckner	Mr William Miller
Mr James Dudley	Mr William Upshaw
Capt David Alexandr:	
Mr Conqueſt Wyatt } Churchwardˢ	
Mr William Thornton Jur }	

The Parish of Pettſo is Dr:	Tobᶜᶜ
To Mr Emanuell Jones Miniſtr	16000
To Thoˢ Potts Clark Ch V	1500
To Widdow Ireland Sexton for 12 weeks	231
To Widdow Forgiſson Sexton	769
To Widdow Mills For keeping of Wᵐ Hanford 3ᴹ: 3 ʷᵉ.	307
To Capt Thoˢ Buckner for Carting timber for yᵉ Gleebhouſe	450
To Will Thornton Jur for two new Shirts for Wᵐ Hanfᵈ	60
To Will Miller for a levy over Charged year	57
To Doctr Will Crimes for keeping Sarah Peacocks baſtard Child Six Months	500
To Doctr Allexander for physick & attendance for Wᵐ Hanford	1105
To Mr Ezra Cottle for building yᵉ Gleebhouſe	3000
To Mr Ezra Cottle for Extraordinary Service	1000
To Doctr Ralph Baker by agreemt Wm Upshaw	800
To Mr Conqueſt Wyatt & Mr Wᵐ Thornton Jur	81
To yᵉ Estate of Nathaniell Mills Deceaſᵈ	5000
To George Mitchell for Charity	700
lb tobᶜᶜ	31560

To Salery for 31560 at 5 ⅌ C is   1578
To Cafk for 15360 at 8 ⅌ C is   1244
                                    ─────
                                    34382

650 Tythab⁰ˢ at 52 ⅌ pole amᵗ to 34382 ᴵᵇ tob⁰⁰

[87]

It is ordered by this preſt veſtry yᵗ Mʳ Conqueſt Wyatt & Mʳ William Thornton Junʳ Churchwardens for this preſt year Do forthwith Demᵈ & Collect together 52ᴵᵇ of tob⁰⁰ of Every Tythable person In yᵉ Pariſh of Pettso it being this years pariſh Levie, and if any freehoulder houſkeeper or freeman Do or after refuse to pay yᵉ Same yᵉ Churchwardens or their Collectʳ are by this preſt veſtry Impowered to Make Diſtreſs for yᵉ Same it being Levied for to Diſcharge yᵉ Sum of 34382ᴵᵇ tob⁰⁰ to Severall Creditoʳˢ as on the other Side wᶜʰ yᵉ pariſh is Indebted to

It is ordered by this preſt veſtry yᵗ Timothy Hay be over Seer of yᵉ highwayes for yᵉ upper percints in yᵉ room of Willᵐ Thurſton and yᵗ he be Diſcharged from his office.

It is ordered by this preſt veſtry yᵗ Samˡˡ Bernard be overſeer of yᵉ highwayes for yᵉ middle percᵗˢ In yᵉ room of Mʳ John Stubbs and yᵗ he be Diſcharged from his office

By yᵉ Conſᵗ of this preſᵗ veſtry Mr John Pate is made Choiſe of for a veſtry man for the   percints of this pariſh In yᵉ place of Mʳ Willᵐ Bernard Decᵈ

It is ordered by this preſᵗ veſtry yᵗ John Clark be pᵈ 4000ᴵᵇ tob⁰⁰: on Demand ⅌ yᵉ Chrchwardens of this pariſh of Pettso. it being for yᵉ repairing yᵉ Church

[88]

Att a Vestry held for petso parish Aprill y^e: 23^d: 1706

Psent

Mr Emanuell Jones Rect^r

Capt Thomas Buckner
Mr James Dudly
Mr Nicholas Smith
William Miller

Capt David Alexander
Mr Thomas Cooke
Mr John Pate

Mr William Thornton Ju^r Churchwarden

Mr William Thornton Senr Desiring to have a quoetus It is ordered by this P^rsent vestry that Mr Robert Porteus be a vestryman in his stead

Allsoe Joseph Ledford is appoynted Clerke of the Church and Vestry (on Condition William Miller will supply the Clerke of the Vestry Office) and that he the sayd Ledford have fifteen hundred pounds of tobacco and Cask yearly During his servis

[89]

Att a Vestry held October y^e: 9th: 1706 for petsoe parish

P^rsent   Mr Emanuell Jones minist^r

Mr Robt yard   Capt Tho: Buckner
Mr Nicholas Smith   Capt David Alexander
M^r W^m: Upshaw   Mr Tho: Cooke
                          Wm Miller

Mr William Thornton Junr
Mr Conq: Wyatt
} Church wardens

	tob^o
The Parish of petsoe is D^r	
to m^r Emanuell Jones minister	16000
to Joseph Ledford Clark of Church & vestry for Six months	00750
to mary Fergoson Sextoniss	01000

to Do^r w^m Crymes for keeping Sarah Peacocks Child	01000
to mad^d margerett Porteus for keeping a baſtord Child Eight munths and a halfe	00708
to John Shackelford for keeping a baſtord Child seventeen months	01415
to Tho: Neale for Clarks & Shreiffs fees	00053
to Richard Candel for Shreiffs fees	00040
to Wm Thornton Junr for Curing & keeping John Dickſon Six mounths	00570
to Larance Patrick for Charity	00800
to George Stitchell for Chaarity	00800
to Humphry Bell Adm^{rs} of nathanell mills Dec^d for loſs of weights in his tobaccoes	01099
to Robt Pryer for setting up new benches and horſe blocks	00400
	24635
to Sallery of 24635 ^{lbs tobo}: at 5 ℔ Cent is	01231
to Caſk for 08635 at 8 ℔ Cent is	00690
	26556
726 Tythables at 37 ℔ pole is 26862 ^{lbs tobo}: & there remains Due to the pariſh	00306
	26862

Itt is ordered by this ℔ſent veſtry that m^r William Thornton [ ] be Diſmiſt from his office of Church-wardin & m^r Conqueſt Wyatt & m^r Robt Porteus is ordered to officiate the office of Churchwardins for this next Enſueing year for this ℔ariſh and that thay Doe geather & Collect from Every Tythable perſon of this Pariſh thirty seven pounds of tobacco ℔ pole the S^d Sum̃ being this ℔ſent years Pariſh Levie and that there wth thay Pay & Diſcharge all the pariſh Credit and in Caſe of Delay or refuſall of the Levie afore S^d thay the S^d Church wardens and every of them and their Collect[rs] are hereby Impowered [90] Impowered to make Diſtreſs for the Same

Itt is ordered by this ℘ſent Veſtry that m[r] John Royſton Shall be a Veſtry man in the Stead of m[r] John Pate decd

allſoe it is ordered that Mary ffergeſon keep Sarah Peacock Child this next Enſueing year and to be payd for the Same at the rate of one thouſand pounds of tob[o] ℘ year

[91]   Att a veſtry held for petſoe pariſh Octo[br] y[e]: 1[d]: 1707

℘ſent   M[r] Emannuell Jones Miniſt[r]

M[r] Rob[t] yard
M[r] James Dudley
M[r] W[m] Thornton Ju[r]
M[r] Conq[t] Wyatt
M[r] Nicho[s] Smith

Cap[t] Tho: Buckner
Cap[t] David Alexander
M[r] Tho: Cooke
M[r] Rob[t] Porteus

M[r] W[m] Upſhaw and m[r] Walter Waters Church-wardens

Petſoe Pariſh is D[tr]	tob[o]
To m[r] Emannuell Jones Miniſt[r]	16000
To m[r] Joſeph Ledford C C & V	01500
To Mary Fargaſon Sextonis	01000
To John Shackelford for a baſterd Child	00585
To mdd margrett Porteus for keeping Tho: mathewis Child	00917
To ſeven Tythables returned by m[r] Rob[t] Porteus	00251
To mary Fergaſon for keeping a baſtard Child	01000
To m[r] W[m] Fleming one Levie over charg[d]	00037
To Cap[t] David Alexand	00225
To m[r] Rob[t] Pryer for Shingling the Church	06000
To George Stichell for Charitey	00800
To Laurance Patrick for Charitey	00800
To ſam[ll] Whiteſeed for Charitey	00600

To two Levies returned by m' Wyatt	00074
To m' Emannuel Jones for roling of tob°	00150
	29939
To Sallery of 29939 ᵗᵒᵇᵒ att 5 ⅌ Cent is	01496
To Caſk of 13939 lbs of tob° at 8 ⅌ Cent is	01115
	32550

Cʳ

⅌ 710 Tythables att 45ˡᵇ of tob° ⅌ pole is	31950
Due to the Churchwardens	00600
	32550

Itts ordered by this preſent veſtry that the Church-wardens doe bind out Richard Auſtin unto Richard Hill & the Sᵈ Hill is to give the Sᵈ Auſtin three years Scooling

Itt is allſoe ordered by the Sᵈ veſtry that the Church-wardens doe bind out mary Peacock a pariſh Child unto Daniell Brown and he the Sᵈ Brown is to give the Sᵈ Peacock three years Scooling & to have five hundred pounds of tob° the next year in Conſideration of the ſame

m' walter waters is Elected a veſtry man & hath taken the Oaths

[92]

Itt is ordered by this ⅌ſent Veſtry that m' Conqueſt Wyatt and m' Robert Porteus be Diſcharged from being Church-wardens, and itt Is ordered that m' William Upſhaw & m' Walter waters be Church-wardens for this next Enſueing year in this pariſh and That thay doe geather & Collect from Every Tythable perſon of this pariſh forty five pounds of tobacco ⅌ pole the Sᵈ Sum̃ being this pſent years pariſh Levie & that therewith thay pay and diſcharge all the pariſh Debts

& in Cafe of delay or Refufall of the Levie aforeſᵈ thay the Sᵈ Church-wardens & Every of them or their Collectors are here by Impowred to make Diſtreſs for the Same

Itt is allſoe ordered by the aforeſᵈ Veſtry that mʳ Robᵗ Pryer give the Church-wardens good Security for the Shingling of the Church according to bargain before thay pay him any tobaccoe

[93]

This Indenture made on the Seventeen Day of Novemᵇʳ in the Sveth year of the reign of our Sovereign Lady Anne Queen of England Scotland France and Ireland Queen Defender of the faith Anno Dom̃ Seventeen hundred and Seven ....Witneſseth that I William Upſhaw & walter waters Church-wardens of petſo pariſh in the County of Gloucſᵗʳ doe in the name & behalfe of the Veſtry there of by this Indenture bind unto Daniell Brown & his heirs a pariſh Garll named mary Peacock untill She Comes to the full age as the Law derects to Serve him or them in all manner of Lawfull Servis or imploymᵗ that he or thay Shall ſett her a bout & the Sᵈ Daniell Brown bind & obledge him ſelfe his heirs &c to give her the ſaid mary Peacock three years Scooling & to Carefully inſtruct learn & Educate the Sᵈ Peacock in all Such wayes that She may be able after her Indented tyme is Expyred to gett her own Leiving & to allow her ſufficent meat drink lodging & apparrell untill the Expyration of the Sᵈ tyme & after the finiſhing of the ſame to pay unto the Sᵈ mary Peacock all Such allowances as the Law Derects in Such Caſes as allſoe to keep the aforeſᵈ pariſh During the aforeſᵈ intended tyme from all manner of Charges or being any wayes burdenſum to the Said pariſh & the above named Church-wardens doe obledge themſelves in quallitey aforeſᵈ to have allowed to the Sᵈ Brown five hundred pounds of tobᵒ & Caſk at the next Levie in Conſideration of her three years Scooling

in witneſs whereof both the pᵣtyes have hereunto ſet their hands
& ſeals Day & year above written
Will: Miller for
Joſeph Ledford Clarke
of the Veſtry

[94]

Att a Veſtry held for petſoe pariſh Aprill yᵉ: 29ᵗʰ: 1708

Preſent Mʳ Emanuell Jones Miniſtʳ
  Mʳ James Dudly Capᵗ Tho: Buckner
  Mʳ Wᵐ Thornton Capᵗ David Alexander
  Mʳ Conqᵗ Wyatt Mʳ Robᵗ Porteus
Mʳ William Upſhaw & Mʳ Walter Waters Church-wardens

Mʳ Robᵗ Yard being Diſabled with the Gout & not able to attend as a Veſtry man has Deſired to be releaſt: and by the Conſent of this preſent Veſtry mʳ John Royſton is made Choyſe off in his Stead & hath taken the Oaths

Likewiſe it is ordered by the fore-ſᵈ Veſtry that the Church-wardens Doe bind out to mʳ John Shackelford a pariſh Child named Sarah Bellfure

[95]

Att a Veſtry held for petſoe pariſh Sepᵇʳ yᵉ: 13ᵗʰ: 1708

℔ſent Mʳ Emanuiell Jones Miniſtr
  Mʳ Conqᵗ Wyatt Capᵗ. Tho: Buckner
  Mʳ Wᵐ Thornton Capᵗ David Alexander
  mʳ Nicholas Smith mʳ John Royſton
  mʳ Robᵗ Porteus Wᵐ Miller
  mʳ Tho: Cooke
  Mʳ William Upſhaw Church-warden

    Petſoe Pariſh is Dʳ Tobᵒ
To mʳ Emannuel Jones Miniſter 16000
to Joseph Ledford C C & V 1500

to mary fforgeſon Sextonnis	1000
to Coll Peter Beverley Clarks fees	0405
to Larrance Patrick for Charitey	0800
to mrs Suſanah waters for Dyett of George ſtitchel 3 munths	0200
to mrs Suſanah waters for keeping John Di[ ]kſon 80 dayes at the rate of a thouſand ℔ yeare	0219
to mrs Suſanah waters for keeping John Dickſon in his ſickneſs wth wine ſhugur & Rum & funirall Charges	0300
to Capt David Alexander acct for phiſick for John Dickſon	1300
to mr Robt Pryer by agreemt	4000
to mr Wm Upſhaw accot	0480
to Daniell Brow by agreemt for keeping a pariſh Garl	0500
to mr Wm Thornton for keeping George ſtitchel 5 munths at the rate of 800 ℔ year	0333
	27037
pariſh Cr is	2936
to Sallery of	24101
at 5 ℔ C is	01205
to Caſke for 8101 at 8 ℔ C	00648
	25954

℔ pariſh Crt	Tobo
By mr Conqt Wyatt	500 & Cake
By Tho: matthews Bond	853 & Caſke
By John Coopers & Bernards bond	250 & Caſk
By mr John Pratt note: 6lb: 13ˢ: 4d in tobo at 10 ℔ C is	1333
	2936

725 Tythables at 36 ℔ p amounts to 26100 ᵗᵒᵇᵒ
and there remains Due to the pariſh   146

           25954
        Caried over

[96]

By the Conſent of This Veſtry mʳ Robᵗ Porteus has relinquiſᵈ his office of being a Veſtry man & he is Diſchargᵈ

And mʳ John Royſton is appoynted Church-warden in the roome of mʳ Wᵐ Upſhaw & he is Diſchargᵈ from that Office

And it is ordered by This ℘ſent Veſtry that mʳ Emannuell Jones doe Collect this Enſuing pariſh Levie in the lower perſinks of the Sᵈ pariſh it being 36 p pole & in Caſe any refuſes paymᵗ to make Deſtreſs for the ſame

*And it is Likewiſe by yᵉ Veſtry aforeſᵈ that

And it is ordered by the Veſtry aforeſᵈ that mʳ John Pratt and mʳ John Smith be ſummonᵈ to meat the ſᵈ veſtry at the uſeall place on the firſt wedneſday in October

And it is ordered by this ℘ſent Veſtry that the Church-warden of the upper ℘ſinks of the ſᵈ pariſh Collects of Every Tythable perſon in his perſinks of the ſᵈ pariſh 36ᵗᵇ of Tobᵒ ℔ pole to Defray the pariſh Charge & in Caſe any refuſe paymᵗ to make Deſstreſs for the ſame.

[97]

Att a veſtry held for Petſoe pariſh October yᵉ: 6ᵗʰ: 1708

Preſent   Mʳ Emanuel Joanes miniſtʳ
         Capᵗ Tho: Buckner   mʳ Tho: Cooke
         Capᵗ David Alexander   mʳ Wᵐ Upſhaw
         mʳ James Dudley   Wᵐ Miller
         mʳ Wᵐ Thornton
              mʳ John Royſton Church-warden

---

*Note! This whole line has been scratched through in the MS. but is still fairly legible.—C. G. C.

It is Ordered by this ꝑſent veſtry that mʳ John Pratt & mʳ John Coleman be Veſtry men & thay have taken the Oaths perſcribed & ſined to the Teſt

Allſoe it is ordered that mʳ John Coleman be Church-warden for this Enſuing yeare in the Lower perſincks of the Sᵈ pariſh

and it is ordered by the Veſtry aforeſaid that there ſhall be Levied for the uſe & releaſe of George Stitchel Eight hundred pounds of Tobacco & Caſke at the laying of the next pariſh Levie

merandam that mʳ John Royſton has got mʳ John Pratts note for Six pounds thirteen ſhillings & foure pence and mʳ Emanuell Joanes has gott Tho: matthews bond for ſeventeen hundred & fifty three pounds of Tobacco & Caſke and mʳ Cooper & Bernards bond

[98]

Att A Veſtry Held For Petſo Parriſh The 6ᵗʰ: of Aprill Anno 1709

Pſent   Mʳ Emmanᵉˡˡ Jones Meniſtʳ
     Mʳ James Dudley   Mʳ Wᵐ Thornton
     Capᵗ Thoˢ: Buckner   Mʳ Wᵐ Upſhaw
     Mʳ Nichᵒ. Smith   Mʳ Jnᵒ. Pratt
                          Wᵐ Miller

Mʳ Jnᵒ. Royſton & Mʳ Jnᵒ. Coleman Church wardens

In Obedience to an order of Glouceſter County Court Bearing Date The 16ᵗʰ: of March 1708 wch Said ordʳ was Delivered to the Veſtry on the 6ᵗʰ day of this Inſtant & In purſuance of the Sᵈ. order The Veſtry did Devide The Parriſh Into Tenn precincts as followeth Vizᵗ.—

1   Beginning at yᵉ Lower End of the Sᵈ parriſh at Clay Bank Creek thence up The Sᵈ parriſh to Bennits Creek & So Croſs to ware Parriſh for the firſt precinct

2   From thence to Jones Creek & up yᵉ Sᵈ Creek & Swamp & Croſs to ware parriſh for the Second precinct

3   From thence to attopotomoys Swamp & up the Sᵈ Swamp to ware Parriſh for the Third precinct

4   From thence to Collᵒ pates Mill & So up the mill Swamp to Sampſons Quarter & from thence to mʳ Simons Quarter for the fourth precinct

5   And from Collᵒ Pates Mill up The Sᵈ parriſh on the Left hand of The Dragon Road to Doctʳ Bakers & Down poropotank Swamp for the fifth precinct

6   and from Doctʳ Baker on the Left hand The Dragon Road To The Dragon bridge for the Sixth Pʳſinct

7   And from Collᵒ pates mill Swamp on the Right hand of the dragon Rode to Doctʳ Bakers & from thence to the head of the Rich Land Swamp & down the Sᵈ Swamp to the Turks ferry Road & So to Mʳ Simons Quarter for the Seventh precinct

8   And from Doctʳ Bakers on the Right hand of the Dragon Road to Peanketank River & down the Sᵈ River to the mouth of the Rich Land Swamp & up the Sᵈ Swamp to the ferry Road by mʳ Collawn's for the Eight Precinct

9   And from mʳ Simons Quarter to mʳ Pages Quarter & from thence to Chiſtake mill & the Rich Land Swamp for the Ninth precinct

10   And from mʳ Pages Quarter Down to mʳ Balyes & up peanketank River to Chiſtake mill for the tenth Precinct

[99]

Att A Veſtry Held for Petſo Parriſh Aprill yᵉ 6: 1709

It is ord'd by the Sᵈ Veſtry that mʳ Albion Throckmorton & mʳ Thomas Dickeſon Doe Begin on the 13ᵗʰ: Day of this Instant Aprill & See the Lands within the firſt & Lower precinct of the Sᵈ parriſh Proceſsioned & make a Returne of their proceedings to The Church Wardens of the Sᵈ parriſh by the Last day of June next Beginning at Claybank Creek to proceſsion thence up the Sᵈ parriſh to Bennits Creek & So Croſs to Ware parriſh

At a Veſtry Held for Petſo parriſh apʳⁱˡˡ. yᵉ 6: 1709

ordered that mʳ Ambroſe Berry & mʳ Tho. Green Doe Begin on the 13ᵗʰ: day of this Inſtant aprill & See the Lands within yᵉ 2 precinct of the Sᵈ parriſh proceſsioned & make a Return of their procedings to the Churchwardens of the Sᵈ parriſh by the Laſt day of June next Beginning at Bennitts Creek to proceſsion & from thence to Jones Creek & up the Sᵈ Creek & Swamp & Croſs to ware parriſh

At a Veſtry Held for Petſo Parriſh aprill yᵉ 6ᵗʰ: 1709

order'd that mʳ Jnᵒ Stubbs & mʳ Thoˢ. May Doe begin on the 13ᵗʰ day of this Inſtant aprill & See the Lands within the third precinct of the Sᵈ parriſh proceſsioned & make a Return of their procedings to the Churchwardens of the Sᵈ parriſh by the Laſt day of June next, Beginning at Jones Creek to proceſsion & from thence to attopotomoys Swamp & up the Sᵈ Swamp to ware parriſh

At a Veſtry Held for Petſo Parriſh Aprill yᵉ 6ᵗʰ: 1709

ord'd that mʳ Jnᵒ Day & mʳ Richᵈ Crittenden do begin on yᵉ 13ᵗʰ day of this Inſtant aprill & ſee the Lands wth in the fourth precinct proceſsion'd & make a Returne of their proceding to the Churchwardens of the Sᵈ parriſh by the Laſt day of June next Beginning at attopotomoys Swamp & from thence to Collᵒ pates mill & So up the mill Swamp to Sampſons quarter & from thence to mʳ Simons Quarter

[100]

5: Ordered that m^r Richard Hubbard & m^r Robt Carter doe begin on the 13th: day of this inſtant aprill & See the lands within the fifth precinct of the ſaid pariſh proceſsioned and make a return of their procedings to the Church-wardens of the ſaid pariſh by the laſt Day of June next: beginning at Cor^{ll} Pates mill thence up the Said pariſh on the left hand of the Draggon road to Doc^r Beakers and Down potopotank Swamp

6: Ordered that m^r William Roan & m^r Robt Hall doe begin on the 13th: Day of this inſtant aprill and ſee the lands with the ſixth precinct of the ſaid pariſh proceſsioned and make a return of their procedings to the Church-warden of the ſaid pariſh by the laſt day of June next. beginning at Doc^{tr} Beakers to proceſsion & from thence all on the left hand of the Draggon road to the Draggon bridg

7: Ordered that m^r Ralph Beaker & m^r William Collawn doe begin on the 13th Day of this inſtant aprill and ſee the lands within the ſeventh precinct of the ſaid pariſh proceſsioned and make a return of their procedings to the Church-wardens of the ſaid pariſh by the laſt Day of June next. beginning at Cor^{ll} Pates mill Swamp on the right hand of the Draggon road to proceſsion thence up to Doc^r Beakers thence to the head of the richland ſwamp & Down the ſaid ſwamp to the turcks ferry road & Soe to m^r Simmons quarter

8 Ordered that m^r James Rannalds & m^r John Pritchett doe begin on the 13th Day of this inſtant aprill and ſee the Lands within the Eight precinct of the ſaid pariſh proceſsioned and make a return of their procedings to the Churchwarden of the ſaid pariſh by the laſt Day of June next. beginning at Doc^r Beakers to proceſsion thence on the right hand of the Draggon road to peanketank River & Down the ſ^d river to the mouth of the richland Swamp and up the ſ^d Swamp to the ferry road by m^r Collawns

[101]

9: Ordered that mr John Amis & mr Tho: ſwepſon doe begin on the 13th Day of this inſtant aprill and ſee the Lands within the Ninth precinct of the ſaid pariſh proceſsioned and make a return of their procedings to the Church-wardens of the ſaid pariſh by the laſt Day of June next Beginning at mr Simmons quarter to proceſsion thence to mr Pages Quarter & from thence to Chiſcak mill & the richland ſwamp

10: Ordered that mr Auguſtin Smith & mr John Harper Doe begin on the 13th Day of this inſtant Aprill and ſee the lands within the tenth precinct of the ſaid pariſh proceſsioned and make a Return of their procedings to the Church-wardens of the ſaid Pariſh by the laſt Day of June next. Beginning at mr Pages Quarter thence Down to mr Bayleys & up peanketank river to Chiſcake mill

And it is Ordered by this pr ſent Veſtry that the Gentm appoynted to ſee the ſeverall precincts within this pariſh proceſsioned whoſe Names are under writt begins on the 13th Day of this Inſtant aprill to proceſsion the Lands within their reſpective precincts and make a return of their procedings to the Churchwardens by the laſt Day of June next—

And it is allſoe ordered that the miniſter of the ſaid pariſh give pubblick notice of this at the Church on Sunday next that all the freeholders may have notice thereof.

1: mr Albin Throckmorton & mr Thomas Dickeſon is appoynted to ſee the lands within the first precinct of this pariſh proceſsioned

2: and mr Ambroſe Berry & mr Thomas Green is appoynted to ſee the lands within the ſecond precinct of this pariſh proceſsioned

3: and mʳ John Stubbs & mʳ Thomas May is appoynted to ſee the lands within the third precinct of this pariſh proceſsioned

4: and mʳ John Day & mʳ Richard Crittenden is appoynted to ſee the Lands within the forth precinct of this pariſh proceſsioned

5: and mʳ Richard Hubbard & mʳ Robᵗ Carter is appoynted to ſee the Lands within the fifth precinct of this pariſh proceſsioned

6: and mʳ William Roan & mʳ Robᵗ Hall is appoynted to ſee the Lands within the ſixth precinct of this pariſh proceſsioned

7 and mʳ Ralph Beaker & mʳ William Collawn is appoynted to ſee the Lands within the ſeventh precinct of this pariſh proceſsioned

8 and mʳ James Rannalds & mʳ John Pritchett is appoynted to ſee the lan[ ] within the Eighth precinct of this pariſh proceſsioned

[102]
9: and mʳ John Amis & mʳ Thomas Swepſon is appoynted to ſee the Lands within the ninth precinct of this pariſh proceſsioned

10: and mʳ Augustin Smith & mʳ John Harper is appoynted to ſee the Lands within the tenth precinct of this pariſh proceſsioned

[103]
Att a Veſtry held for Petſoe pariſh October yᵉ: 5ᵗʰ: 1709

   Preſent mʳ Emanuell Jones Miniſᵗʳ
 Mʳ Wᵐ Thornton Capᵗ David Alexander
 Mʳ Nicho Smith Wᵐ Miller
 mʳ Tho: Cooke
Mʳ John Royſton & Mʳ John Coleman Church-wardens

	Petſoe Pariſh is Dʳ	tobᵒ
to mʳ Emanuell Jones miniſᵗʳ		16000
to Joſeph Ledford Clarke		1500
to Mary Fargeſon Sextonnis		1000
to George Stitchell for his mentaynance		0800
to Larrance Patrick for Charitey		0800
to Richard Hill for keeping Elizabeth Fowler 7 munths at the rate of a 1000 ℔ year		0586
to Tho: neals accoᵗ		0060
to Ann Bray for keeping Tho: Wright one munth		0084
to John Crockford for keeping Sarah Alling 5 munths		0400
to mʳ John Coleman accoᵗ		0704
		21934
the pariſh Cʳ is		1996
		19938

℔ Pariſh Cʳ	tobᵒ	
by the laſt years ball Due from the Church-wardens	146	
by mʳ yards bill	500	
by Tho: Matthews bond	850	
by mʳ Robᵗ Porteus for mary Hooks fine	500	
	1996	
to Sallery at 5 ℔ Cᵗ for 19938 pounds of tobᵒ is		0996
to Caſke for 3938 pounds of tobᵒ at 8: ℔ Cᵗ is		0315
		21249
713 tythables at 30 ℔ pole amounts to	21390	
and their remains Due to the pariſh	00141	
	21249	

Caried over

[104]

and it is ordered by this pſent Veſtry that mʳ John Royſton & mʳ John Coleman Church-wardens of this pariſh Doe
Collect and geather from every tythable perſon of this pariſh the
Sum of thirty pounds of tobacco ℔ʳ pole the ſaid Sum being this
pſent years pariſh Levie and that thay therewith pay and Diſcharge all the ſaid pariſh Debts and in Caſe of Delay or refuſall
of the Levie aforeſaid thay the ſaid Church-wardens & every of
them and their Collectors are hereby Impowered to make Deſtreſs for the Same

And it is ordered by this ℔ſent Veſtry that Patrick Bugg
Shall be Levie free the next year

[105]

Att A veſtry held for petſoe pariſh October yᵉ: 4ᵗʰ: 1710

Preſent   Mʳ Emmanuel Jones Miniſter
    mʳ James Dudley   Capᵗ David Alexander
    mʳ Nicho: Smith   mʳ Wᵐ: Upſhaw
    mʳ Tho: Cooke   Wᵐ miller
        mʳ John Royſton Church-warden

	Petſoe Pariſh is Dʳ	Tobᵒ
To	mʳ Emmanuel Jones miniſᵗʳ	16000
To	Joſeph Ledford Clarke	1500
To	yᵉ Sextonˢ Mary Roberts	1000
To	part of mʳ wᵐ Thornton accoᵗ	0300
To	Capᵗ David Alexander accoᵗ	0745
To	Doctʳ Charles Tomkies for Doyle Quorrels	1000
To	John Crockford for keeping Sarah Allin	0800
To	Richard Hill for keeping Eliſabeth Fowler	1000
To	Hanah Hope for keeping Robᵗ Woods Child 5 munths	0415
To	Suſanah Waters for keeping George ſtitchell	0800

To mr John Royſton for keeping James Bellfure 9 munths 0720
To Larrance Patrick for Charetey   0800

                                                          25080
                                    Deduct   191

                                                          24889

        ℔ Cr   Tob°
    by laſt years ball   141
    by part of matthews bond   050

                                    191
To Sall for 24889 pounds of Tob° at :5: ℔ Cent is   01244
To Caſke for 8889 pounds of Tob° at :8: ℔ Cent is   00711

                                                          26844

                    Cr   Tob°
By 701 Tythables at 38lbs ℔ pole is   26638
and their remains Due to the Churchwardens 00206

                                                           26844

Order that if Doctr Charles Tomkies ſalivates Doyle Quorrells again & uſes his utmoſt indevour to Cure him he is to be payd 1000 pounds of Tobacco the next year

Order that the Church-wardens buies neſsaries for Doyle Quorrells

Order that the Churchwardens bind ſarah Bellfure to Richard Timberlack tell ſhe Come to Lawfull age

[106]

Att a Veſtry held for Petſoe pariſh October yᵉ: 18ᵗʰ: 1710

Preſent   mʳ Emmanuel Jones Miniſter
    mʳ James Dudley   Capᵗ David Alexander
    mʳ Nicholas Smith   mʳ Tho: Cooke
    mʳ Wᵐ: Upſhaw   william Miller
      mʳ John Royſton Church-warden

Order that mʳ John Royſton be Diſmiſt from the office of Church-warden and majʳ Richard Bayley is appoynted Church-warden in his Stead

Order that mʳ Albin Throckmorton be a Veſtry-man and Church-warden for the Lower perſinct of the Sᵈ pariſh

And it is ordered that the ſaid Church-wardens Doe Collect 38 pounds of Tobacco of every Tythable perſon in this pariſh and in Caſe of refuſall of payment of the ſaid Sum̃ by any perſon that thay make Diſtreſs for the Same and therewith pay of all pariſh Creditors their juſt dues with all poſsible Speed & Conveniancye

Att a Veſtry held for petſoe pariſh Novemᵇʳ yᵉ: 9ᵗʰ: 1710

Preſent   mʳ Emmanuel Jones miniſtʳ
    mʳ James Dudley   Capᵗ Tho: Buckner
    mʳ Wᵐ: Thornton   Capᵗ David Alexander
    mʳ John Pratt   mʳ Tho: Cooke
                  Wᵐ miller
  Majoʳ Richard Bayley & mʳ Albon Throckmorton Church-wardens

It is ordered by the Sᵈ Veſtry that the Church-wardens Shall agree wᵗʰ a workman as ſoon as poſsible thay Can to mend the Chamber Chimbley of the Gleib-houſe and build an outſide Chimbley to the Citching & playſter the Same

[107]

Att a Veſtry held for petſoe pariſh July yᵉ: 7ᵗʰ: 1711

Preſent Mʳ Emannuel Jones Mineſᵗʳ
  Mʳ James Dudley Capᵗ David Alexander
  Mʳ Wᵐ. Thornton Mʳ John Royſton
  Mʳ Tho: Cooke Wᵐ: miller
   Mʳ Albon Throckmorton Church-warden

whereas it has bin repreſented this Day to this preſent veſtry that George Stickel wᵐ Bowels & Sarah Michell have bin on this pariſh is able to mentayn themſelves It is therefore ordered by this preſent veſtry that the Church-warden Doe give them preſent notice to provid themſelves for the pariſh will allow noe further mentanence

and it is ordered by this veſtry that from this Day their Shall be noe more allowed for Sarah Allins mentaynence then four hundred pounds of Tobᵒ ℔ year and that the Church-warden give John Crockford preſent notice thereof

It is allſoe ordered by this veſtry that mʳ John Royſton Deliver tenn pounds unto mʳ Albin Throckmorton Church-warden wᶜʰ he received for the fine of Catherine Lagg

It is allſoe ordered that mʳ Auguſtin Smith be added to the veſtry in the roome of mʳ Richard Bayley decd and Sworn by the firſt opperteunitey

Att a Veſtry held for petſoe pariſh Sepᵇʳ yᵉ: 18ᵗʰ: 1711

Preſent mʳ Emmanuel Jones miniſtʳ
  mʳ James Dudley Capᵗ David Alexander
  Capᵗ Tho: Buckner mʳ wᵐ: Upſhaw
  mʳ Nicho Smith mʳ Tho: Cooke
  mʳ John Pratt mʳ John Royſton
        wᵐ miller
   mʳ Albon Throckmorton Church-warden

Itt is ordered by this ℘sent vestry that mᵣ Augustin Smith Smith Shall officeate the office of a Church-warden this next Ensueing year in the upper presencts of this parish.

Itt is allsoe ordered that the Clarke of the vestrey get a Copy of the list of Tythables for this ℘sent year by the next wednesday

[108]

Att a Vestry held for petsoe parish Sepᵇʳ yᵉ: 26ᵗʰ: 1711

Present   mʳ Emmanuel Jones minisᵗʳ
    mʳ James Dudley   mʳ Wᵐ Upshaw
    Capᵗ David Alexander   mʳ John Royston
    mʳ Tho: Cooke   *mʳ Wᵐ Miller
  mʳ Albon Throckmorton & mʳ Augustin Smith
              Church-wardens

	Petsoe parish is Dᵗʳ	Tobᵒ
To mʳ Emmanuel Jones minisᵗʳ		16000
To Joseph Ledford Clarke		1500
To mary Roberts Sextonis		1000
To the last ball		0206
To Tho: Ballard & Edw: Musgrove over Chargd the last year		0076
To Capᵗ Tho: Buckner for Keeping masdrye Sandiland bastard Child ten munths at the rate of 1000 ℘ year		0832
To mʳ Emmanuel Jones for the Copy of the last year list of Tythables		0020
To mʳˢ ann Coleman accoᵗ for keeping Wᵐ Bowels & 3 quᵗ of Clarrit		1319
To John Crockford for Keeping Sarah Allin		0664
To John Pass for Keeping James Belfeire one year		1000

Note! This word is scratched through in the MS, but is still fairly legible.—C. G. C.

To Suſanah waters for Keeping George ſtichel 6 munths	0400
To George Stichels own mentaynance 2 munths	0133
To mary Hill for Keeping Eliſabeth Fowler one year	1000
To Afreca Hope for Keeping Chariety woods one year	1000
To Co^{ll} Beverleys acco^{t}	0048
To John Pratt for Keeping ſarah Michel Eight munths	0266
To James Forſith for setting up two horſe block and findin planck & nales	0100
To Joſeph Ledford for mending the Church Doores	0030
	25594
Deduct	1500
	24094
To Sallery at 5 ꝑ C for 24094	01204
To Caſk for 8094 at 8 ꝑ C	00647
	25945

Pr Pariſh C^{tr}	Tob
By Robt Brookins bill	500
By w^{m} Andersons bill	500
By Albon Throckmorton	500
	1500
670 Tythables at 39: ꝑ pole is	26130
and their remains Due to the pariſh	185
	25945

[109]

Tis ordered by this preſent Veſtry that m^{r} Albon Throckmorton an[] m^{r} Auguſtin Smith Church-wardens of this parish doe Collect and geather from every Tythable person in this parish the Sum of Thirty nine pounds of Tobacco ℔ pole the Said Sum being this present years parish Levie and that they therewith pay & Discharge all the parish Debts and in Case of Delay or refusall of the Levie aforesaid they the said Church-wardens & every of them & their Collectors are hereby impowered to make Distress for the Same.

and it is allsoe ordered that the Said Church-wardens *Repaire the Said Church & Keep the ballance of this accompt & the fifty five Shillings & ten pence in their hands till further order

1. and it is ordered that mʳ John Pratt & mʳ Albon Throckmorton Se[] the Lands within the first precinct of this parish processioned between the last day of this Instant September & the last day of march next.

2. and it is ordered that Capᵗ Robᵗ Porteus & mʳ Philip Smith See the Lands within the Second precinct of this parish processioned between the last Day of this Instant September & the last day of march next

3. and it is ordered that Capᵗ Thomas Buckner & Capᵗ John Smith See the Lands within the third precinct of this parish processioned between the last day of this Instant September & the last day of March next

4. and it is ordered that Capᵗ David Alexander & william miller See the Lands within the fourth precinct of this parish processioned between the last day of this Instant September & the last day of march next

and it ordered that mʳ Nicholas Smith & mʳ Robert Carter See the Lands wᵗʰi[] the fifth precinct of this

---

*Note! This word was hard to make out. It may be that I have read it wrong.—C. G. C.

5 pariſh proceſsioned between the laſt Day of this inſtant September & the laſt day of march next

and it is ordered that mʳ william upſhaw & mʳ william Roan See the land[ ] within the Sixth precinct of
6 this parish proceſsioned between the laſ[ ] Day of this inſtant September & the laſt Day of march next

and it is ordered that mʳ James Dudley & mʳ william Collawn See the Lands within the Seventh precinct of
7 this pariſh proceſsioned between the laſt Day of this inſtant September & the laſt Day of march next

[110]
and it is ordered that mʳ James Reanalds & mʳ John Pritchett See the Lands within the Eight precinct of this
8 parish proceſsioned between the laſt day of this inſtant September & the laſt Day of march next

and it is ordered that mʳ John Royſton & mʳ Francis Wyatt See the lands within the Ninth precinct of this
9 pariſh proceſsioned between the laſt day of this inſtant September & the laſt Day of march next

and it is ordered that mʳ Auguſtin Smith & mʳ Richard Seaton See the lands within the tenth precinct of this
10 pariſh proceſsioned between the laſt day of this Inſtant September & the laſt Day of march next

Att a Veſtry held for petſoe pariſh November yᵉ: 3ᵗʰ: 1711

Preſent   mʳ Emmanuel Jones miniſᵗʳ
        mʳ Wᵐ Thornton   Capᵗ Tho: Buckner
        mʳ James Dudley   Capᵗ David Alexander
        mʳ Nichol Smith   Wᵐ Miller
        mʳ John Royſton

Order that Capᵗ Thomas Buckner & Capᵗ John Smith begin & See the Lands wᵗʰin the third precinct of this pariſh proceſsioned on the twenty Sixth Day of this Inſtant November according to Glouceſtr Courts order

Order that Capt David Alexander & wm miller begin on the third Day of December next & ſee the lands wthin the fourth precinct of this pariſh proceſsioned according to Glouceſtr Courts order

Order that mr John Royſton & mr Francis Wyatt begin on the Second munday in December next & ſee the lands wthin the ninth precinct *proceſsioned of this pariſh proceſsioned according to Glouceſtr Courts order

Order that mr James Dudley & wm Collawn begin on the thirty first Day of December next & ſee the lands wthin the ſeventh precinct of this Prſh proceſsioned according to Glouceſtr Courts order

order that mr Nicholas ſmith & mr Robt Carter begin on the Seventh Day of Janry next & ſee the lands wthin the fifth precinct of this pariſh proceſsioned according to Glouceſtr Courts order

[111]
†Order that mr Wm Upshaw & mr Wm. Roan begin on the fourteenth Day of Janry next & ſee the lands wthin the ſixth precinct proceſsioned according to Glouceſtr Courts order

Order that mr Wm Upshaw & mr Wm. Roan begin on the fourteenth Day of Janry next & ſee the lands wthin the Sixth precinct of this pariſh proceſsioned according to Glouceſtr Courts order

Order that mr James Rennalds & mr John Prichard begin on the twenty first Day of Janry next & ſee the lands wthin

---

*Note! This word is scratched through in the MS, but is still legible.—C. G. C.

†Note! This entire entry is scratched through in the MS, but is still legible.—C. G. C.

the Eight precinct of this parish processioned according to Gloucest' Courts order

Order that m'r Augustin Smith & m'r Richard Seaton begin on the twenty Eight Day of Jan'y next & see the lands w'thin the tenth precinct of this parish processioned according to Gloucest' Courts order

Order that m'r John Pratt & m'r Albin Throckmorton begin on the fourth Day of Feb'y next & see the lands w'thin the first precinct of this parish processioned according to Gloucest' Courts order

Order that Cap't Rob't Porteus & m'r Philip Smith begin on the Eliventh Day of Feb'y next & see the lands w'thin the second precinct of this parish processioned according to Gloucest' Courts order

Order that m'r Emmanuel Jones send to England for a surplis on the parish acco't

Order that the Churchwardens get all the lawes Relating to the poor of the parish & vestry & thay to be Kept w'th [ ] Vestry Book

[112]
Att a Vestry held for petsoe parish March y'e 22'th: 1711

Present M'r James Dudley   Cap't David Alexander
       Cap't Tho: Buckner   M'r W'm Upshaw
       M'r Nicho Smith   W'm Miller
       m'r John Royston

M'r Albin Throckmorton & m'r Augustin Smith Churchwardens

Order that Ezekiel Smith be allowed Eight hundred pounds of Tob'o and Cask at the laying of the next levie for keeping & Scooling Jane Holloway

Order that the Church-wardens do fourthwith get the law relating to the procefsioning lands & the law for binding Orphens

Order that the Church-wardens agree wth: a Workman to repair the playftring of the Church

[113]

This Indenture made this twenty fecond Day of march In the Year of our Lord go[ ] one thoufand feven hundred & Eliven & in the tenth year of the Reign of our Soveraing Lady Anne of Great brittain France & Ireland Queen Defender of the faith &c. witnefseth that we Albin Throckmorton & Auguftin Smith Church-warde[ ] of petfoe parifh in the County of Gloucefter Doe firmley in the name & behalfe of the veftry of the said parifh bind unto Ezekiel Smith of the aforefaid parifh [ ] orphen Girl Called Jane Holloway of the age of two years untill she arrives at age as the law directs to ferve him the faid Ezekiel Smith & his wife in all manner of lawfull fevifses & imploym^t that he or fhe fhall fet her about and the faid Ezekiel Smith does bind & oblidge himfelfe his heirs &c to give the faid orphen two year[ ] fcooling & to Carefully inftruct her afterwards that she may read well in any part of the Bible & alfo to inftruct & learn her the faid orphen fuch lawfu[ ] way or wayes that fhe may be able after her Indented time is Expyred to get her own living and to allow her fufficient meat Drink lodging & appar[ ] untill the Expyration of the faid time and after the finifhing of the fame to pay unto the faid Jane Holloway all fuch allowances as the law Directs in fuch Cafes as alfoe to keep the aforefaid parifh during the aforefaid Indented time from all manner of Charges or being any wayes burdensom[ ] to the faid parifh. In witnefs whereof the parties above named have hereunto Interchangably ſet their hands & ſeals the Day and year above written

       Ezekiel Smith
        ſignum
      Mary U ſmith

Seald In Preſence
 Will: Miller
 Joseph Ledford
 Seth Thornton

[114]

Att a Vestry held for petſo parriſh October yᵉ 1ˢᵗ: 1712

Preſent mʳ Emanuel Jones Miniſter
  mʳ Wᵐ Thornton   { mʳ John Royſton
  Capᵗ: Tho Buckner { mʳ Wᵐ Miller
  Capᵗ Daᵈ: Alexander {
 Mʳ Albion Throckmorton & Mʳ Augⁿ: Smith Church
      wardens

Petſo Parrish	is Dʳ
To Mʳ Emaˡˡ: Jones Minʳ:	16000
To Joſeph Ledford Clark of Church & Veſtry	1500
To Mary Robberts Sextonis for 8 months Service	666
To Africa Hope for being Sextonis 3 months	334
To Africa Hope for Keeping Robᵗ Woods Child	1000
To Mary hill for keeping a parriſh Woman 8 months	666
To Capᵗ: Thoˢ: Buckners acᵗ:	1000
To Coˡˡ Beverleys acᵗ:	182
To Mʳ Wᵐ Thornton for Corne to Doyle Quarrills	300
To mʳ John Royſton for Glaſs	200
To Stephen Johſons acᵗ	150
To Capᵗ Allexanders acᵗ: for Phiſick	100
To Mʳ Augᵗ Smiths acᵗ.	100
To Mʳ Emanˡˡ: Jones acᵗ: for lime for mending yᵉ Gleib Chimneys	200

To Cap⁺ John Smiths Eſsᵗ for keeping Wᵐ Bowells 9 months	747
To Capᵗ Davᵈ Allexander for 4 Tythables laſt yeare Over Charg'd	156
To Joſeph Ledford for Mending the Benches	50
To Mʳ Albion Throckmortons Acᵗ:	44
To Joſeph Ledford for Extrodinary Charges	500
	23895
Creditt Deducted	1585
	22310
To Sallʳʸ of 22310 att 5 pʳ Cᵗ	1115
To Caſk for 6310 att 8 pʳ Cᵗ	504
	23929

Pʳ Conʳ Cʳ

By Mʳ: Augⁿ Smiths	900	
By Wᵐ Miller	500	
By Mʳ: Smiths Laſt year Ballᶜᵉ	185	
	1585	
673 Tythables att 36 ℔ʳ: pole is		24228
& Theire Remains Due to yᵉ parriſh		299
		23929

[115]

And itt is ordered that Capᵗ Tho Buckner be Church Warden in Mʳ Throckmortons Roome

Memᵈ Thos May waſs this day Elected and Sworne Cleark of the Veſtry & is to be allowed 1000ˡᵇ pound of tobᵒ & Caſk pʳ yeare

A True Entry Test Thoˢ: May C V P P

Att A Vestery held in petso Parrish Septemb': y° 22ᵈ: 1713

Present   Mʳ: Emmˡˡ Jones Miniʳ:
  Mʳ Wᵐ Thorton   { Mʳ Thoˢ: Cook
  Capᵗ David Allexander { Mʳ Wᵐ Miller
  Mʳ Wᵐ Upshaw   { Mʳ James Dudley
   Capᵗ: Thoˢ: Buckner Church Warden

This present Vestry desiers mʳ Emmˡˡ: Jones Minister to agree with Charles Hansford for 200 Acres of Land Joyning on the Gleib
    A True Entry Test Thoˢ: May C V P P

Att A Vestry held for petso parrish Octobʳ the 7ᵗʰ: 1713

Present mʳ Emanuell Jones Minister
  Capᵗ David Allexander Mʳ: Thoˢ: Cooke
  Mʳ James Dudley   Mʳ: Wᵐ Upshaw
  Mʳ Wᵐ Thorton   Mʳ John Royſton
  Mʳ Nichoˢ: Smith
   Capᵗ: Thoˢ: Buckner Church Warden

Petso Parrish is Dʳ: 1713	
To Mʳ Emanuell Jones Minister	16000
To Thoˢ May Cleark of Church & Vestry	2000
To Africa Hope Sextonis	1000
To Wᵐ Thornton for Keeping George Stichell 12 months	800
To Ezekiell Smith for keeping & Schooleing Jane Holloway	800
Carried Over	20600
[116] Brought Over	20600ˡᵇ
To Wᵐ Anderson for Keeping & Schooleing Mary Saunlings	500

To Joseph Ledford for makeing 2 horſe Blocks	200
For the purchaſeing a peice of Land to yᵉ Gleib	6000
	27300
Cʳ deducted	299
	27001
To the Sallery of 27001ˡᵇ Tobᵒ at 5 pʳ Cᵗ	1350
To cask of 11001ˡᵇ Tobᵒ at 8 pʳ Ct	880
	29231

    Pʳ Conʳ Cʳ
by mʳ Jones Last Years Ballance 299

Pʳ   Conʳ   Cʳ
By 680 Tythables at 43ˡᵇ tobᵒ pʳ pole is 29240
              29231

Ballance due to the parrish   00009

Also it is ordered by this present Vestry that Thos: May Cleark of the Vestry make Indentures to bind Orphin Children and Sign the Same in behalf of the Sᵈ Vestry

It is ordered by this present Vestry That Thoˢ: Grindly pay no more parrish Levy for the futer he having made his Complaint of being Very Antient and past his Labour

and it is ordered by this Vestry that Wᵐ Miller be church wardin in mʳ Augᵗ: Smiths roome for the Upper persinks

It is ordered by this Vestry that Capᵗ: Thos. Buckner & mʳ. Wᵐ Miller Church Wardens of this parrish Collect and gather from Every Tythable in this parrish forty Three pound of tobᵒ: to defray the parrish Charge and in caſe any refuse payment to make diſstreſs for the Same

[117]

Memorand^m: that Mr Aug^t: Smith has got Nicholas Browns bill for 500^lb of tob^o:

A True Entry   Test Thos: May C V p p

Att A Vestry held for petso parrish Aprill y^e: 10th: 1714

Present   M^r: Ema^ll Jones Minist^r:
   Capt: David Allexander   M^r: Thos: Cooke
   M^r: Aug^t: Smith   M^r: Nicho^s: Smith
   M^r: Willm: Thornton   M^r: James Dudley
   Capt: Thos: Buckner & M^r: Willm: Miller Church
                  Wardens

Order'd by this present Vestry that the Cleark of y^e: Vestry give notes (to y^e: Sever^ll: people whose names are as followeth Viz: widdo Oliver Widd^o: Simkins Widd^o: Shillerd Widd^o: Hill Widd^o: Sweptson Widd^o: Shurrud Isaac Oliver Thos: Ballerd) on m^r: Aug^t: Smith for £1:17:6 apeice and that he take in theire notes with theire receipts for the Same

Ordered by this present Vestry y^t: y^e: Church Wardens bring Suit against m^r Bayleys Execut^rs: for a Legacie of £20 given to ye pore of petso parrish by y^e: S^d Bayley Dec^d

Ordered by this present Vestry that ye Church wardens Imploy workmen to repaire ye Gleib Houſe

or^d: by this pres^t: Vestry that Thos: Dudley pay no more parrish Levy for y^e: futer he having made his Complaint of being very antient and past his Labour

Order^d: by this pres^t: Vestry that ye Church Wardens Imploy a workman to pale ye Church yard in

Memor^dum: That Nicho^s: Browns bill for 500^£ of tobac[ ] is Lodge'd in ye Vestry Book
   a True Entry Test Thos: May Cl V p p

Memo^dm: that Ap^ll: y^e: 14 1714 *that I gave Elianer Shillerd a note to M^r: Aug^t: Smith for £1:17:6 according to ye above order of Vestry
    Car^d Over
[118]   Brought Over
mem^dum: that Ap^ll: y^e: 17th: 1714 I gave Isaac Oliver a note on M^r: Aug^t: Smith for £1:17:6 According to Order of Vestry on ye other Side
    Thos: May C pp V

mem^dm: that Ap^ll: y^e: 17th: 1714 I gave Jane Swepston a Note on M^r: Aug^t: Smith for £1:17:6 According to Order of Vestry on ye other Side
    Thos: May Cl pp V

mem^dm: that Ap^ll: y^e: 17: 1714 I gave Mary Shurrud a Note on M^r: Aug^t: Smith for £1:17:6 According to Order of Vestry on ye other Side
    Thos: May Cl pp V

mem^d. that may ye 2^d 1714 I gave Wid^o: Oliver a Note on M^r: Aug^t: Smith for £1:17:6 According to ye Order of Vestry on ye Other Side
    Thos: May Cl pp V

Mem^dm: that July the 29th: 1714 I gave the Wid^o. Simkins a Note on Mr Aug^t: Smith for £1:17:6 According to ye Order of Vestry on ye Other Side
    Thos: May Cl pp V

†Att a Vestry held for Parris

---

*Note! This word is erased in the MS, but is still legible.—C. G. C.
†Note! This whole line is scratched through in the MS, but is still legible.—C. G. C.

Att a Vestry held for Petso Parrish Octob': 8th: 1714

P'ſt   Mr: Emll: Jones Ministr:
   Capt: David Allexander   Mr John Royston
   Mr Augt Smith   Mr Nichs: Smith
 Capt: Thos: Buckner & Mr Wm Miller Church Wardens

Petso Parrish Dr 1714	
To Mr Emll Jones Minisr:	16000
To Thos: May Cl: of Church & Vestry	2000
To Affrica Hope Sexton	1000
To Mr Frans: Whiteing for paileing the Church Yard in	1500
Card: Up	20500

[119]

Brought Up	20500
To Coll Peter Beverly for Cleark fees 304 yo 10 pr Ct being deducted is due to him	274
To Thos: Harris for plaistering the Church	1000
To John Day for diet & attendance plasterer	650
To Thos: Scott for lime for ye: Church	360
To Thos: Swepson for 2 bushlls ½ haire	25
To Henry Singleton for plaistering ye gleib House	1000
To Mary Smith for keeping Jno: Hues child from ye 3d: of March till ye 8th: Octobr	581
To Mr Read for 1 gll: Rum & 1 gll: Molases to fowler	80
To Jno: Mackwilliams for Bief to Do	39
To Thos: Boulton lime for ye Glieb	468
To Thos: Scott lime for ye glieb	280
To Do f 5 bushells White wash	45
To Thos: Easter for carring ye chain for ye glieb	50
To Thos: Scott for a Tubb	25
To Madm: Portues a barrll: corne to ye Glasier	100
To Mr Wm Thornton for Keeping George Stichell	800

To Mr Thos: Cook for Surveying ye glieb land	500
To Mr Charles Tomkies acct	2800
To Mr Wm Millers acct	2970
To Mr Augt. Smiths act	125
To Thos. Mays act.	400
To Mr Emll: Jones act:	517
To 4 tythables returnd by Emll. Jones	172
To Mr Nichs: Smiths tythable overchd last year	43
	33804
Cr by mr Emll: Jones	9
	33795
To cask for 17795lb tobo	761
671 tythables att 51½ is	34556

*and there remains due to ye par
               Card Over
[120]   Brough Over

Memdm that the Vote was put to this Vestry whether ye pubblick Should be alow'd Cask for this yeare or no; Capt Dad: Allexander Mr Augt: Smith & Mr Nicho: Smith Voted not; Capt: Thos Buckner Mr Wm Miller & Mr John Royston Voted it ought to be allowed and was carried by Mr Emll Jones Ministr:

Ordered by this prſt Vestry that Mr John Pratt be Church Warden in Capt: Thos: Buckners roome & that he be discharged from his Churchwardenship and that mr Wm Miller be Continued Church Wardin for the Ensuing year

also this Vestry doth appoint 3 days for Each church warden to make up the accts with the parrish

---

*Note! This whole line has been scratched through in the MS, but is still legible.—C. G. C.

It is ordered by this Vestry that John Staples Edwd Musgrove & Samll: Whiteseed pay no more parrish Levies they being Old and past their Labours

Also it is agreed on by this Vestry that Totopomoy Swamp be the dividing between the Uper and lower percints of this parr{h}

  a True Entry Test Thos: Mays Cl P p V

[121]

This Indenture made this Twenty fifth day of Jan{ry} in ye year of our Lord God one thousand Seven hundred & fourteen & in ye: first yeare of ye Reign of our Sovereign Lord George off great brittane France and Ireland King defender of ye faith &c

Witneseth that I Thos: May Clark of ye Vestry of petso parrish in ye County of Gloster do firmly in ye name and behalf of ye Vestry of ye S{d} parrish bind unto Affrica Hope of ye S{d}: parrish one orphin Girll Nam'd Charity Wood of ye age of five yeares old the Nineteenth day of ye Above Nam'd Month allredy past untill She arrives at the age as the Law directs to Serve hir ye S{d} Affrica Hope hir hers &c: in all manner of Lawfull Services & Imploym{ts}: that Shee Shall Sett hir about & ye S{d} Affrica Hope doth bind and Oblidge hir Self hir heirs &c: to Learne the S{d} orphin to Read & to carefully Instruct hir afterward yt Shee may read well in any part of ye Bible and also to Instruct and learne hir ye S{d} orphin Such Lawfull way or ways yt: Shee may be able after hir Indented time is Expired to gitt hir own Liveing & to allow hir Sufficient Meat drink Lodgeing & apparill until ye: Expiration of ye S{d} time and after ye finishing of ye S{d} time to pay to ye S{d} Charity Wood all such allowances as ye Law directs in Such cases as Also to keep ye aforeeS{d} parrish dureing the aforeS{d} Indented time from all maner of Charges or being any ways burdensome to ye. S{d} parrish In Witnefs whereof I have hereunto Sett my hand and Seale the day and yeare Above Written

Signm

Seal'd in presenc Affrica ⋃ Hope (Seal)
  of   Jane May
    S Sarah Simcoe

[122]

At a Vestry held for Pettso Parish Feb^{ry}: y^e: 5th: 1714

Prs^t: M^r: Em^{ll}: Jones Minis^r:
  Capt: Thos: Buckner ⎰ m^r Aug^t: Smith
  Capt: Dav^d: Allexander ⎱ m^r Albion Throckmorton
E∫sq^{re}: Robt: Portues & m^r Wm Miller Church Wardins

By this p^{rst} Vestry E∫s^{re} Robt: Portues is Elected a Vestryman and has taken y^e: oath of a Vestry man and also is chose Church Warden for y^e: Lower percint in the roome of m^r John Pratt

This p^{rst} Vestry hath Chose m^r John Reade m^r Richd Seaton m^r Fran^s: Wyatt and m^r Phill Smith as Vestry men in ye roome of m^r James Dudley m^r Wm Upshaw m^r Nich^s: Smith and m^r Wm Thornton

Order^d: by this p^{rst}: Vestry that Thos: May C^l: Vestry Git y^e: addition^{ll}: Tob^o: Law & a copia of that Oath y^e: Vestry took at the Last Court

  A True Entry   Test Thos: May C^l P P V

Att A Vestry held for Petso Parish Feb^{ry}: y^e: 12th: 1714

Present M^r Em^{ll}: Jones Minis^{tr}:
    Capt: David Allexander Mr Phill Smith
    M^r: Aug^t: Smith   Mr Richd Seaton
    M^r: John Royston   Mr Fran^s: Wyatt
  Robt Portues E∫sq^{re} & Mr Wm Miller Church Wardens

This day m^r Phillip Smith m^r John Royston m^r Richd Seaton & m^r Fran^s: Wyatt hath taken y^e: Oaths of Alleagens & Supremacy ye Oath of Abjuration & ye Oath of Vestrimen

also this day the Church wardens gave Bonds to y^e: Vestry for ye payment all such Agents Notes as Shall come into theire hands upon y^e: Acc^t: of y^e: parish Levies

[123]

Also this Pres^t: Vestry hath Ordered that y^e: Cleark Enter ye Oaths of Alleagence Supremacy Abjuration & y^e: Oath of a Vestryman in y^e: Vestry Book
      A True Entry   Test Thos: May Cl P P V

[124]

THIS INDENTURE made the Twelveth day of Febuary in y^e: yeare of our Lord God one Thousand Seven hundred & fourteen & in y^e: first year of our Sovereign Lord George of Great Brittain France & Ireland King defender of ye faith &c: WITNESETH that I Thos: May Clerke of y^e: Vestry of petso parish in the County of Gloster do firmly in ye name & behalf of y^e: Vestry of y^e: afore S^d: parish bind unto m^r Phillip Smith of y^e: S^d parish & County one Orphin Boy Named James Belfure of y^e: age of Six years old ye first day of Last July — untill he arives at ye age as ye Law Directs to Serve him y^e: S^d Phillip Smith his heirs &c: in al maner of Lawfull Services & Imployments that he shall sett him about and y^e: S^d Phillip Smith doth bind & Oblidge himself his heirs &c: to give y^e: S^d orphin Three years Schooleing & to carefully Instruct him afterwards that he may read well in any part of the Bible also to Instruct & learn him y^e: Said Orphin such Lawfull way or ways that he may be Able after his Indented time Expire'd to git his own Liveing &: to alow him Sufficient Meat drink washing & apparill untill Expiration of yᵉ Said time & after yᵉ: finishing of yᵉ: Sᵈ time to pay yᵉ: Sᵈ James Belfure all such Alowances as yᵉ Law directs in such Cases as also to keep yᵉ: aforeSᵈ: parish dureing yᵉ: aforesaid Indented time from al maner of Charges or being any ways Burdensom to yᵉ: Sᵈ parish in WITNEſS whereof I have hereunto Set my hand & Seale the day & yeare above Written

Phill Smith (Seal)

Sign & Seal'd in
the p'sents of
    Fr Wyatt
    Richᵈ Seaton
      1714

[125]

I A B do ſincerely promise & Swear that I will be faithfull & bear a True allegiance to his Majesty King George
So help me God &ᶜ:

I A B do Sweare that I do from my heart Abhor detest & abjure as impious & Hereticall that damnable Doctrine and poſsition that Princes Excommunicated or deprived by yᵉ pope or any Authority of yᵉ: See of Roome may be deposed or Murthered by theire Subjects or any other whatsoever; & I do declare that no Forreign Prince Person Prelate State or Potentate hath or ought to have any Juriſdiction Power Superiority Preeminence or Authority Ecclesiasticall or Spirituall whitin this Realm
So help Mee God &ᶜ:

I A B do truly & Sincerely acknoledge profeſs Testifie and declare in my concience before God & yᵉ: world that our Sovereign Lord King George is Lawfull & rightfull King of this Realm & of all other his Majesties Dominions and Countrys thereunto belonging And I do Solemnly and

Sincerely declare that I do believe in my Concience that the Person pretended to be the Prince of Whales dureing the life of ye late King James & Since his decease pretending to be & takeing upon himself y^e: Stile & title of King of England by ye name of James y^e: third; hath not any right or title whatsoever to y^e: Crown of this Realm or any other y^e: dominions thereto belonging And I do renounce refuse & abjure any Alleagiance or Obedience to him & I do Sweare that I will beare faith and true Alleagenc to his Majestie King George & him will defend to the Utmost of my power against all Traiterous conspiraces and attempts whatsoever which shall be made against his Person Crown or dignity And I will do my Utmost Endeavour to disclose & make knowne to his Majestie & his Succefsors all Treasons & Traitorous Conspiraces which I Shall know to be against him or any of them And I do faithfully Promise to y^e: Utmost of my power to Support Maintaine & defend the Succefsion of y^e: Crown against him ye Said James & all other persons whatsoever as the same by an Act Entituled an Act for y^e: further Limitation of y^e: Crown & better fecureing the rights & liberties of y^e: Subject is and [126] Stands limitted to the Princefs Sophia Electrefs & Dutchefs Dowager of hannover and the heirs of hir body being protestants And all these things I do plainly and Sincerely Acknowledge and Sweare According to y^e: Exprefs words by me Spoken & according to y^e: plain & Common Sence and Understanding of the Same words with out any Equivocation mentall evation or Secret refervation whatsoever And I do make this recognition ascknowledgment abjuration renunciation & promife heartily willingly & truly upon y^e: true faith of a Christian

      So help mee God &^c

The Test

I A. B. Do ſincearly promis and Swear that I will *in *all *Things True and faithfully Serve As A Vestry man for the Parish of †Petsworth According to the best of my Judgment. So help me God

[127] The Test

Wee whoſe names are Under Written do hereby Testify & Declare that we do not believe that theire is any Transubstantiation of yᵉ: Elements of Bread & Wine in yᵉ: Sacrament of yᵉ: Lords Supper att or after yᵉ Conſecration thereof by any Person Whatsoever

    ‡John Royſton
    Phill Smith
    Richᵈ Seaton
    Fran: Wyatt
    §John Read
    Henry Willis
    Thomas Greene
    Fra: Thornton
    ¶———————
    Samˡ Buckner
    Thomas Booth Junior
    Bayley Seaton
    Thoˢ Stubbs

[128]

Att A Vestry held for Petso Parish May yᵉ: 14ᵗʰ: 1715

---

*Note! These words are scratched through in the MS., but are still legible.—C. G. C.

†Note! This is the first appearance of the word "Petsworth" in the MS.—C. G. C.

‡Note! This signature and the twelve signatures following are evidently autographs.—C. G. C.

§Note! This signature has been scratched through in the MS but is still legible.—C. G. C.

¶Note! This signature has been almost completely blotted out in the MS. and is not legible.—C. G. C.

Present   M^r: Em^{ll}: Jones Minis^r:
   Mr John Royston   { Capt: Dav^d: Allexander
   M Augt Smith   }
Robt Portues E$\int$sq^r: and M^r: W^m: Miller Church Wardens

It is Ordered by this Vestry that y^e: Clark of y^e: $\int^d$ Vestry give notes (to y^e Seve^{ll}: people Whou$\int$e names are a$\int$s followeth Viz Mary Ballard John B[ ]rton James Ward Jane Swep$\int$on Sam^{ll}: Whiteseed John Simcoe Mary Hill Elianor Shillerd) on M^r W^m: Miller Church Warden for £1:5^s apeice and that he take in theire notes with theire receipts [ ] y^e Same also it is Ordered that Mary Ballerd John Burton Jane Swepson John Simcoe and Elianer Shillerd have notes on y^e: Above S^d: nam'd Church Warden for a bar^{ll}: of Corne apiece

Robt: Porteus E$\int$sq^{re}: Church warden having Inform'd this p^{r}sent Vestry that he has foure Delinquents in his precint Viz (Edwd Carter 1: Rich^d: Wright 1: Edwd: Griffith 2:) y^e: S^d Vestry has Order'd that he shall be Allowe'd them at y^e: Laying of y^e: next parish Levy also John Pagget not having any thing to pay his Levy y^e: S^d Church Warden is desiered to git his Bond wth: Security if he can but if not to be allowed for him at y^e Laying of the next parish Levie

Memo^{dm}: that this day m^r Aug^t: Smith hath Comply'd with y^e: order of Vestry dated Ap^{ll}: 10th: 1714

A True Entry Test Thos: May Cl P P V

[129]

Att A Vestry held for Petso Parish: Septeb^r. y^e: 14: 1715

Pr$\int$ent   Mr Em^{ll} Jones Minis^r:
   Capt: Dav^d: Allexander ⎡ Mr Phillip Smith
   Mr John Royston   ⎨ Mr Rich^d: Seaton
   Mr Aug^t: Smith   ⎣
         M^r W^m: Miller Church Warden

Orderd by this Prest Vestry y^t: y^e: Cleark of y^e: Vestry Record all y^e: Returns of Jurys from y^e: Court Concerning Procefsioning of Land in this Parish which has bin Return'd by y^e: Church Wardins or hereafter Shall be return'd

1

In Obedience to an Order of Gloster Court dated the 28 day of July Laft this Present Vestry has Ordered that Mr Albion Throckmorton & M^r Jno: Pryor See ye Lands within y^e: first Precinct of this Parish Procefsioned Begining on y^e: tenth day of October Next att Mr John Pratts ye S^d: Precinct Extending Crofs y^e: Parish as far as ye Branch between M^r: Hansfords & y^e: S^d John Pryors

2

In Obedience to an Order of Gloster Court dated y^e: 28 Day of July Last This Present Vestry has Ordered that Mr Fran^s: Thornton & Mr Thos: Green begin att Mr Willm Thorntons on y^e: Seventeenth Day of Octob^r: Next to See ye Lands within y^e: Second Precinct of this Parish Procefsioned, y^e: S^d Precinct begining at y^e: branch between Jno: Pryors & Mr Hansfords & So up y^e: Parish to Mr Thorntons Mill Swamp

3

In Obedience to an Order of Gloster Court dated ye 28 day of July Last this Present Vestry has Ordered y^t: Mr John Stubs & Mr Wm Fleming begin on y^e: Twenty fourth day of October Next att Capt: Allexanders quarter in the Neck to See y^e: Lands within y^e: Third Precinct of this Parish Procefsioned y^e: S^d: Precint Containing all the Lands between m^r Thorntons Mill Swamp & Populer Spring Swamp

Carried Over

4

In Obedience to an Order of Gloster Court dated ye 28 day of July Last This Present Vestry has ordered that m^r W^m

Miller & mʳ John Carter begin on yᵉ: Thirty first day of Octobʳ Next att mʳ Wᵐ: Millers to See yᵉ: Lands within yᵉ: fourth Precinct of this Parish Proceſsioned yᵉ: Sᵈ Precinct Containing all yᵉ: Lands between Populer Spring Swamp Mʳ Pates Mill Swamp & Bryery Branch aſs far aſs Stephen Johnſons

5

In Obedience to an Order of Gloster Court dated yᵉ. 28 day of July Last This Present Vestry has Ordered that mʳ Robᵗ. Carter & Mʳ .... Walford begin on yᵉ Seventh day of November Next att mʳ Richᵈ: Hubbards to See yᵉ. Lands within yᵉ. fifth Precinct of this Parish Proceſsioned; yᵉ: Sᵈ Precinct Containing all yᵉ: Lands from Mʳ Pates Mill Swamp to Docʳ: Bakers Swamp takeing in Mʳ James Dudleys & Doʳ: Crymes Land

6

In Obedience to an Order of Gloster Court dated yᵉ: 28 day of July Last This Present Vestry has ordered that mʳ James Amis & mʳ Wᵐ: Brookin begin on yᵉ: fourteenth day of November Next att mʳ Wᵐ: Brookins to See yᵉ: Lands within yᵉ: Sixth Precinct of this Parish Proceſsioned yᵉ Sᵈ: Precinct Containing yᵉ: Lands on yᵉ: Left hand of yᵉ: road to yᵉ: Dragon Bridge

7

In Obedience to an Order of Gloster Court dated yᵉ 28 day of July Last this Present Vestry has ordered that mʳ Seth Thurston & mʳ John Hayns begin on yᵉ: Twenty first day of November Next att mʳ Seth Thurstons to See yᵉ Lands within yᵉ: Seventh Precinct of this Parish Proceſsioned yᵉ: Sᵈ: Precinct Containing all yᵉ: Lands from Bakers Swamp on yᵉ: right hand of the Dragon road too yᵉ: Bridge & ſo croſs the Parish to yᵉ: Richland Swamp

[131]   8

In Obedience to an Order of Gloster Court dated y⁰. 28 day of July Last This p'sent Vestry has ordered that m' John Read & m' Wᵐ Collawne begin on the Twenty Eight day of November Next att M' Augustine Smiths to See y⁰ Lands within y⁰: Eight Precinct of this Parish Proceſsioned y⁰: Sᵈ Precinct Containing all y⁰: Lands from y⁰: Sᵈ Smiths to Stephen Johnsons & Croſs y⁰: Parish from y⁰: Richland Swamp to Co¹¹: John Lewis Mill Swamp

9

In Obedience to an Order of Gloster Court dated y⁰ 28 day of July Last This Present Vestry has ordered that M' Franˢ: Wyatt & M' Jn⁰: Harper begin on y⁰: fifth day of December Next att m' Franˢ: Wyatts to See y⁰ Lands within y⁰: Ninth Precinct of this Parish Proceſsioned y⁰: Sᵈ Precinct Containing all y⁰ Lands from Co¹¹: John Lewis Mill to y⁰: out Side of y⁰ Parish

A True Entry Test Thoˢ: May Cl p p V

Att A Vestry held for petso parish Octobʳ: y⁰: 5ᵗʰ 1715

Prst: M' Em¹¹: Jones Minister
         Capᵗ: Davᵈ: Allexander   M' Franˢ: Wyatt
         M' Thoˢ: Cooke   M' Phillip Smith
         M' John Royston   M' John Read
         M' Augᵗ. Smith
    M' Wᵐ Miller & Robᵗ Portues Eſsqʳᵉ. Church Wardens

Petso Parish is	Dʳ: 1715
To M' Em̃¹¹: Jones Minʳ:	16000
To Thoˢ. May Cl of Church & Vestry	2000
To Affrica Hope Sextonis	1000
To Robᵗ Portues Eſsqʳᵉ. Accᵗˢ.	1799½
To Madⁿ. Margrett Portues accᵗ	361

To Capt: Allexander for a rug to Fowler	100
To two Levies Overch^d. to Doc^r. Crymes E$\int\int^t$. Last yeare	103
Car^d: Over	2136[ ]
[132] Brought Over	21363½
To 1 Levy Overch^d Benjn: Read Last yeare	51½
To John Lewis for two bottles Wine	30
To W^m: Miller for Last yeares Colletion	612
To Mr Charles Tomkies Ac^{ts}	2769
To Robt Portues for this years Collex^n.	600
To Mr Wm Thornton for George Stichell	800
To Wm Upshaw for corn to Fowler	100
To Mr Augt. Smiths ac^t	180
To Ezekiell Smith for Keeping Hues Child 1 yeare	1000
To Co^{ll}: Beverley for Cl fees	104½
To John Willcocks Sheriffs fees	18
To Henry Purcill for Christian Roo$\int$s Child	582
To Richd Seaton for this yeares Collex^n.	600
To Mr Ema^{ll}. Jones ac^t	401
	29211½
parsh C^r	
by 665 Tythables att 44^{lb} of Tob^o p^r pole is	29260
and theire remains due to y^e parish	48½
	29211½
	29260

It is or^d. by this p'st Vestry that Richd Seaton be Church Warden in m^r W^m. millers roome for y^e upper Precinct

Also this Vestry has agreed with Robt Porteus E$\int$q^{re}. to Deliver at y^e. Church 7000 Shingles to Shingle y^e. Church &

he to be payd att yᵉ Laying yᵉ. Next Parish Levie 1000 pound of Tob°

a True Entry Test Tho May Cl p p V

At a Vestry held for Petso parish May yᵉ 5ᵗʰ 1716

Pʳſᵗ

Mʳ. Em͞nˡˡ: Jones Minisʳ:
Capᵗ. Thoˢ. Buckner   Mʳ Franˢ: Wyatt
Mʳ Wᵐ. Miller   Mʳ Phill. Smith
Mʳ Jn°. Royston   Mʳ Jn°. Reade
Mʳ Augᵗ: Smith
    Mʳ Richᵈ Seaton Church Warden

Order'd by this pʳst Vestry yᵗ. Mʳ Wᵐ. Miller be discharged from Celia Mackcartees fine he produceing Receipts that he has payd it to yᵉ. poore of yᵉ. parish according to yᵉ order of Vestry dated May yᵉ: 14: 1715

Ordered by this prsᵗ. Vestry that Mʳ Wᵐ Miller be discharged from paying yᵉ: five Barills of corne to yᵉ. pore of yᵉ parish that he was to pay by an order of Vestry dated May yᵉ. 14ᵗʰ: 1715 Nichˢ. Brown faileing to pay it to yᵉ. Sᵈ Miller, & he yᵉ Sᵈ. Miller has return'd yᵉ. Sᵈ: Browns Bill for five hundred pounds of Tob°: & cask to mʳ Richᵈ. Seaton Ch Wardin of petso parish

Ordered by this pʳst Vestry yᵗ. yᵉ: Clark of the Vestry record yᵉ returns of yᵉ: proceſsioners in yᵉ. record Book kept for yᵗ: purpose

Car: Over

Brought Over

This prst Vestry has also Lodge'd Mʳ Wᵐ Millers Bill for 500ˡᵇ Tob°: & Cask in yᵉ Cleark of yᵉ Vestry hands

Upon yᵉ. Petition of Jn°. Simcoe that he is Very Old & past his Labour this Vestry has ordered that he pay no more parish Levies for yᵉ futer

Upon yͤ Petition of Isaac Oliver that he is Very Old & past his Labour this prst Vestry has Ordered that he pay no more pariſh Levies for yͤ. futer

   A True Copy Test Thoˢ: May Cl P P V

[135]

  A Vestry held for Petso Parish Octobʳ. yͤ 3ᵈ: 1716

    Present Mʳ Em̃ˡˡ: Jones Minʳ:
 Capᵗ. Thoˢ. Buckner { Mʳ Augᵗ. Smith
 Mʳ Wᵐ Miller
 Mʳ Jnᵒ. Royston   { Mʳ Phillip "
  Mʳ. Richᵈ. Seaton Church Wardin

Petso Parish	Dʳ 1716
To Mʳ Em̃ˡˡ Jones Minʳ	ˡᵇ 16000
To Thoˢ May Cl Church & Vestry	02000
To Affrica Hope Sextonis	01000
To Mʳ Wᵐ. Thornton for keeping George Stichell	00800
To Joseph Ledford for Shingling yͤ Church makeing five forms finding plank for them and ye ridgeing yͤ Church & nailes for yͤ Same	01500
To Coˡˡ. Beverleys Fees	00095
To Sheriff Willcocks fees	00009
To Cap Allexander for Phiseck to Mary Portegees	00310
To Mʳ Wᵐ. Miller for paying Mʳ Read for fowler	00080
To Mʳ Em̃ˡˡ Jones accᵗ for a Surplice & Wine	00816
To Thoˢ Davis for keeping Jnᵒ. Ballerd	00050
To Mʳ Richᵈ. Seatons accᵗ for Wine	00092
To Ezʳ. Smith for keeping Jnᵒ. Hues Child 12 months	01000
To Henry Purcill for keeping Christian Roſs Child	00800
To Samˡˡ. Whiteseed for yͤ. releife of his Wife & Self	01000
To yͤ. Church Wardins for this years Collextion	01200
To Robᵗ. Portues Eſqʳᵉ. for Shingles for yͤ Church	01000

            27752

P' Con'	C'
by y°. Church Wardins	48½

	27703½
by 661 Tythables at 42¹ᵇ Tob°. pʳ pole is	27762
Due to y°. Parish	58[ ]
	277[ ]

[136]

Brought Over

It is ordered by this p'sent Vestry that Mʳ Phillip Smith be Church Wardin in Robᵗ. Porteues Eſqʳᵉ. Roome for yᵉ. Lower Precinct

   A True Entry Test Thoˢ. May Cl p p V
   *True Entry Test Thoˢ May P

[137]

This Indenture made yᵉ: Thirtieth day of octobʳ: in yᵉ Yeare of our Lord God one Thousand Seven Hundred & Sixteen & in yᵉ Second yeare of our Sovereign Lord George of Great Brittain France & Ireland Defender of yᵉ faith &ᶜ Wittneſseth that I Thoˢ. May Cleark of Petso Parish In Gloster County do firmly in yᵉ. name and behalf of yᵉ Vestry of yᵉ Parish abov Sᵈ: Bind unto Ralph Bevis of yᵉ Sᵈ Parish & County a Molatto Boy Named George Petsworth of yᵉ age of two yeares old yᵉ. Sixth day of March Next Insuing yᵉ Date of theſe p'sents untill he arives att yᵉ Age as yᵉ Law Directs to Serve him yᵉ Sᵈ Ralph Bevis his heirs &ᶜ: in all maner of Lawfull Services & Imployments yᵗ. he Shall Sett him about and yᵉ Sᵈ Ralph Bevis doth Bind & Oblidge himself his heirs &ᶜ: to give yᵉ. Sᵈ. Molatto Boy Three years Schooleing & to Carefully Instruct him afterwards that he May read well

*Note! This line is in a different handwriting from that of the rest of the page.—C. G. C.

in any part of yͤ Bible also to Instruct & Leare him yͤ. Sͩ. Molatto Boy Such Lawfull way or ways that he may be able after his Indented time Expiared to gitt his own Liveing & to alow him Sufficient Meat Drink washing & Apparrill untill yͤ: Expiration of yͤ. Sͩ. time & after yͤ. finishing of yͤ. Sͩ. time to pay yͤ Sͩ George Petsworth all such alowances as yͤ Law Directs in Such Cases as also to keep yͤ. afore Sͩ Parish Dureing yͤ. aforesͩ: Indented time from all maner of Charges or being any way Burdensome to yͤ Sͩ. Parish in Witneſs Whareof I have hereunto Sett my hand & Seale yͤ. Day & yeare above written

Sign'd & Seald in   Ralph Beves
yͤ P'sts of
 Jane May
  hir
 Ann X Higgins
  marke

[138]

Att a Vestry held for Petso Parish May yͤ 21 1717

Pͬˢᵗ Mͬ Em̃ᵘ. Jones Minͬ
Capͭ Thoˢ. Buckner   Mͬ Augᵗ. Smith
Mͬ Wͫ. Miller   Mͬ Franˢ. Wyatt
Mͬ Thoˢ. Cook   Mͬ. Jn° Read
Mͬ Jn°. Royston
Mͬ Phill Smith & Mͬ Richͩ. Seaton Church Wardins

order'd by this Vestry that Mͬ Portues pay yͤ Poore of this Parish five pound it being for Christian Roſs fine

ordered by this Vestry that Mͬ Phillip Smith Recei[]e of Mͬ Robᵗ. Portues fifty Shillings it being part of Christian Roſs fine Mͬ Emᵘ. Jones Having Aſsured yͤ. payment of yͤ. other fifty Shillings it being yͤ remaining part of yͤ Sͩ Roſs fine and also five Shillings More for one Jn°. Berrys Sweareing which he y[e]. S[d] Porteus has Re[d] for y[e] Uſe of y[e]. Poore of this Parish

This Day Nich[s] Brown has payd to this Vestry 233 pounds of Tob[o]. in part of his Wifes fine & M[r] Phillip Smith Chh Wardin is ordered by this Vestry to Sell y[e] S[d] Tobacco to y[e] Merchant at M[r] Thorntons at Twenty five Shillings p[r]. Hundred and to take up goods (as he Sells them at y[e] first cost) & to pay y[e] S[d] goods to y[e] following people Namly Jn[o]. Simcoe £1:15[s] Mary Hill 10[s]/ to Isaac Oliver 13[s]/3[d] also it is []dered that y[e]. Cleark of y[e]. Vestry give notes to y[e] above []am'd persons on M[r] Phillip Smith Ch Wardin for y[e] aforeſ[d]. Sum and take in y[e] Notes with theire recepts and produce them to y[e] Next Vestry

[139]

Att this Vestry M[r] Jn[o]. Pratt has Made a prsent of five pounds to y[e] poore of this pariſh and is to be Diſstributed as followeth (by order of this Vestry) to y[e]. W[do]. Oliver £1: to y[e]. Wid[o]. Swepson £1: to y[e]. Wid[o]. Shellerd £1: 10[s] & to Margret Lacey £1: 10[s] and it is order'd that y[e] Clark of y[e] Vestry give Notes on M[r] Jn[o]. Pratt to y[e] above persons for y[e]. above S[d]. Sums

Ordered by this Vestry that M[r] Emm[ll]. Jones Minis[r]. pay to y[e]. wid[o]. Ballard and Mary Shurrad y[e]. fifty five Shillings he aſsum'd to pay for M[r] Rob[t] Portues aſs followeth Vz to y[e] Wid[o]. Ballard £1: 15[s]. to Mary Shurard £1: and it is ordered by this Vestry that y[e]. Clark of y[e] S[d]. Vestry give Notes on M[r] Emm[ll]. Jones to y[e]. Above Nam'd Persons for y[e] afore Mentioned Sums and that he take in the Notes with theire recp[ts]. and produce them to y[e] Next Vestry

And it is ordered by this Vestry that when M[r]. Phillip Smith Ch. Wardin has rec[d]. y[e]. fifty Shillings in M[r] Robert Portues Hands & M[r] Rich[d]. Seaton Church Wardin y[e]. two pound

Nineteen Shillings in Nichoᵒ. Browns Hands that they give Notice to yᵉ. Cl of yᵉ. Vestry that he may give Notes on them *for to yᵉ following people for 12ˢ 1ᵈ apeice Namly to yᵉ. widᵒ. Oliver widᵒ. Ballard Widᵒ. Shellerd widᵒ. Swepson Jnᵒ. Simcoe widᵒ. Hill Mary Shurrard Margret Losey & Isaac Oliver and that they yᵉ. Sᵈ. Ch. Wardins Take in all Such Notes with theire receipts and produce them to yᵉ. Next Vestry after Such payments

Upon yᵉ Petition of Thoˢ. West to this Vestry that he is Very old & past his Labour this present Vestry has ordered that he pay no more pariſh Levies for yᵉ future

Ordered by this Vestry that yᵉ Cl of yᵉ Vestry Deliver to Mʳ Wᵐ. Miller his bill for 500ˡᵇ of Tobacco that was taken on acc.ᵗ of Christian Roſse fine

A True Entry Test Thoˢ. May Cl P P V

[140]

Att a Vestry held for petso parrish Octobʳ. yᵉ 2. 1717

Prſent Mʳ Emmᵘˡˡ. Jones Minʳ
Capᵗ. Thoˢ. Buckner   Mʳ Albion Throckmorton
Mʳ Wᵐ. Miller   Mʳ Robᵗ. Portues
Mʳ. Jnᵒ. Royston   Mʳ Jnᵒ. Read
Mʳ Augᵗ. Smith   Capᵗ Henry Willis
Mʳ Phillip Smith & Mʳ Richᵈ. Seaton Church Wardins

This day Capᵗ Henry Willis was Elected and Sworn a Vestry Man in Capᵗ David Alexanders Roome

a True Entry Test Thoˢ May Cl P P V

---

*Note! This word is scratched through in the MS, but is still legible.—C. G. C.

Att A Vestry held for Petso Parish November the 25th 1717

Present Mr Emll Jones Minr

Capt. Thos. Buckner	Mr Augt. Smith
Mr Wilm. Miller	Mr Robt. Portues
Mr Thos. Cooke	Mr Frans. Wyatt
Mr Jno. Royston	Capt. Henry Willis

Mr Phillip Smith & Mr Richd. Seaton Church Wardins

Petsoe Parifh	Dr lb
To Mr Emll Jones Mr	16000
To Jos. Ledford Cl Church	01000
To Affrica Hope Sexton	01000
To Thos May Cl Vestry	01000
To Mr Charles Tomkies for Cureing Margret Forgas	02000
To Jno. Crockford for keeping Eli: Gipson 13 Months & 23 days	00900
To Mr Wm Thornton for keeping George Stichell 12 Months	00800
To Jno. Whitehorne for Bording Margret Forgas	00255
To Henry Pucill for keeping Christian Rofs Child 13 Months & 17 days	00090
To Arthur Pryor for Thos. Levitts Levie when gon to Carolina	00044
To Jno. Wilson for Punches Levie when gon to Carolina	00044
Card Up	23943
[141] Brought over	23943
To Mr Augt. Smith for Mr Phillip Smiths acct of 11 Bottles wine at 27/6 in Tobo at 2d pr lb	00165
To Mr Augt Smith for Mr Emll. Jones acct for Repaireing ye. Gleib Chimleys at 30/in Tobo. at 2d pr lb	00180
To Samll Whitseed for his Releife	00300

To Mʳ Seaton for Jnº. Carnills *Last *years Levie run away	00044
	24632
Creᵈ. by Last years Ballance due from yᵉ Church Wardins	59½
	24572½
To yᵉ 5 pr Cᵗ. of 24572ˡᵇ Tobº.	01228
To yᵉ 8 pʳ Cᵗ of 8572ˡᵇ Tobº.	00685
	26485½
Creᵈ	
673 Tythables at 39½ˡᵇ Tobº. pʳ pole is	26583
Rests Due to yᵉ Pariſh	00098
	26485

Order'd by this prst. Vestry that yᵉ. Church Wardins Receive of Every Tythable person in this parrish teen pounds of Tobacco or one Shilling in Currant Money for the Repaireing the Gleib house which comes to 6730ˡᵇ of Tobacco or Thirty Three pound Thirteen Shillings in money and upon yᵉ. Refusall of yᵉ. payment of the Same yᵉ. Church Wardins are hereby Required to make Diſstreſs and that yᵉ. Church Wardins are to be alowed 5 pʳ Ct: for Receiveing yᵉ. above Sᵈ. Tobº. or Mony

Order'd by this Vestry that mʳ Franˢ. Wyatt be Church Wardin for yᵉ. upper precints of this parish in mʳ Richᵈ Seatons Roome & that he be Discharged from his Church-wardinſhip.

---

*Note! These two words are scratched through in the MS., but are still legible.—C. G. C.

[142]

Att a Vestry held for Petſo Parish Octo^r: y^e: 6th: 1718

P^{r}ſent   M^r Em^{ll}: Jones Mini^r
Capt Thos Buckner   Robt Pourtus Eſq^r
Mr Willm Miller   Mr Aug^{ust} Smith
Mr Thos: Cooke   Mr Richd Seaton
Mr John Royston   M^r Jno: Read
Mr Phillip Smith & Mr Francis Wyatt Church Wardins

	Petso Parish is D^r	lb
To	Mr Em^{ll} Jones Mini^r	16000
To	Joseph Ledford Clarke of the Church	01000
To	Elianah Shellard Sextonis	01000
To	Jane May	00500
To	Mr Francis Thornton for Keeping Go: Stichalls	00800
To	Co^{ll}: Peter Beverlyes Acco^t	00040
To	Mr James Candill for Curing Mary Yates	01360
To	Capt Dav'd Allexander for Keeping Marther Thomases Baſterd Child five Month	00333¾
To	Mr Em^{ll} Jones Acco^t of Thos: Grindlyes and Willm Greenwoods Leiveis not payd the Laſt year	00084
To	Mr Francis Wyatts Acco^t	00858
To	Mr Francis Wyatts Acco^t for £3:1^s:6^d Cash at 2^d p lb	00369
To	Mr Thos: Green one Leivie over Charg'd ye Last year	00039½
To	Mr Phillip Smith one Leivie over Charged	00039½
		22423¾
To	Sall^y: of 22423^{lb} Tob^o at 5 p C^t: is	01121
To	Caske for 4742^{lb} Tob^o at 8 p C^t is	00379
		23923¾

By C'ʳ Due from yᵉ Church Wardins yᵉ Laſt years Leivies	00098
Carid Vup	23825¾
[143] Brought Vup	23825¾
By Cʳ of 698 Tythables at 34½ pʳ pole is	24081
Rest Due to yᵉ Parish	00255¼
	23825¾

Itt is Ordred by this Pʳsent Vestory that yᵉ Church Wardins Recive of every Tythable Parson In this Parish Thirty Pounds of Tobᵒ: or Three Shillˢ Current Money for Reparing the Gleib house Which Comes to 20940ˡᵇ of Tobᵒ: or one hundred and foore Pounds fourteen Shillˢ: in money and upon yᵉ Refusall of the Paymᵗ of the Same, yᵉ Church Wardins are hereby Required to Make Distreſs and that yᵉ Church Wardins are to be Allowed 5 pʳCᵗ for Receiveing yᵉ above Said Tobᵒ. or money

Ordered that yᵉ Clarke of yᵉ Vestry Sine Indentures to Bind Christians Roſses Child to Jnᵒ. Crockford Allso to Sine Indentures to Willᵐ Anderson for Mary Sandling [] Child

Ordred by this Pʳsent Vestry that Jnᵒ Acre is Sett Leivie free from yᵉ Parish and that yᵉ Clarke of the Vestry give him a Sertifficte of the Same

Ordred by this Pʳsent Vestry that Mʳ Thoˢ Cooke be Church Wardin in the Room of Mʳ Phillip Smith in the Lower Precinct of this Parish and that Mʳ Phillip Smith be Discharged from his Church Warden Ship

Ordred that John Day have After yᵉ Ratte of Two hundred pounds of Tobᵒ. an Acere for Church Land and that he is to be paid out of the Tobᵒ: Due to yᵉ Parish this year Two hundred pounds of Tobᵒ: for one Acer of Land

*Ordred that Jnº Carter be Sworne Cl of the Vestry

     Carid Over
[144]   Brought Over
Itt is Ordred by this Pʳsent Vestry that Jnº Carter be Sworne Clarke of the Vestry of this Parish befor Some Justices of Peace and that he gett a Sertificate of yᵉ Same

    True Entry Teſt Jnº Carter Cl P P V

At A Vestry held for Petso Parish Feb͞ʳʸ: yᵉ 21ᵗʰ 1718/9

   Pʳsent Mʳ Emˡˡ Jones Miniſtʳ
 Capᵗ: Thoˢ: Buckner Mʳ Augsᵗ: Smith
 Mʳ: Willᵐ Miller   Mʳ Richd Seaton
 Mʳ Jnº: Royston   Mʳ Jnº Read
 Collº Robᵗ Pourtus Capᵗ Hen͞ʳʸ Willis
        Mʳ Jnº Washington
Mʳ Fra: Wyatt and Mʳ Thoˢ Cooke Church Wardins

Att This Pʳsent Vestry Mʳ John Washington was Elected and Chosen Vestry Man in Mʳ Throckmorteons Rume Decesed

Att this Pʳsent Vestry Ann Tryplow was Elected & Chosen Sextonis

Att this Pʳsent Vestry Willᵐ Grumley was Elected and Chosen Clarke of yᵉ Church and that he is Not to Officeate tell yᵉ fall, and In Case that any Person offers himselfe that is more fetten †then †he for yᵉ Place then he, then this Pʳsent Vestry has ordʳ that yᵉ Pʳson that offers him Selfe Shall be Voted for

---

 *Note! This line is scratched through in the MS., but is still legible.—C. G. C.
 †Note! These two words are scratched through in the MS., but are still legible.—C. G. C.

Ordered by this P'sent Vestry that ẙ Clarke of ẙ Vestry Sine Indentures to bind Willm Duglace to Jane Miner

True Entry Teſtis Jn° Carter Cl p p V

[145]

This Indenture made ẙ Six day of July In ẙ Yeare of our Lord God one thousand Seven hundred and nineteen and In ẙ fifth Yeare of our Soverane Lord George of Gratt Brittiane France and Ireland King defender of ẙ faith &c Witneſseth that I John Carter Clearke of petso parish Vestry In Glocester County do firmly in ẙ Name and bhalf of ẙ parish above S^d bind unto John Crockford of ẙ Same parish and County one orphin Boy Named Edward Carter of ẙ age of   years old ẙ   Day of   untell he arive at ẙ age as ẙ Law Dericts to Serve him ẙ Said John Crockford his heires and &c: In all maner of Lawfull Servies and Imployments y^t he Shall Sett him about And ẙ S^d John Crockford doth Bind and oblidge him Selfe his heires &c to give ẙ S^d orphin Three years Scooling and Carefully to Instruct him afterward that he my Read well in any part of ẙ Byble, Allso to Instruct and Larne him ẙ S^d orphin Such Lawfull wayes or Wayes that he may be able after his Indentured time Expired to gitt his own Liveing and to Allow him ẙ S^d orphin Suffent Meat Drink washing *and Lodging and apparill untill ẙ Experation of ẙ S^d Indented time and after ẙ finishing of ẙ S^d time to pay him ẙ S^d Edward Carter all Shuch Allowances as ẙ Law Directs in Shuch Casses as allso to Keep ẙ afore S^d parish Dureing ẙ afore S^d Indented time from all manner of Charges or being any wayes Burdensom to The Said Parish. In Witneſs where of ẙ partyes above Named have Interchangably put their hands and Seales ẙ day and year above Written

Signed Sealed and Delivered
In P'sence of us

[146]

THIS INDENTUR mad ẙ Twenty Seventh day of Feby In ẙ year of oure Lord God on Thousand Seven hundred and

Eighteen and In y͏ͤ fifth yeare of y͏ͤ Reign of our Soveraine Lord George of Gratt Brittiane France and Ireland King Defender of y͏ͤ faith &c: WITNEſSETH that I John Carter Clarke of petso parish Vestry In Gloster County doe firmly In y͏ͤ Name and Behalf of y͏ͤ Parish above S͏ͩ Bind unto Jane Miner of y͏ͤ S͏ͩ Parish and County one orphin boy Named William Duglace of y͏ͤ age of Nine yeares old y͏ͤ Last day of Decemb͏ͬ: Next Inſueing untell Hee arive at y͏ͤ age as y͏ͤ Law Derects, To Serve her y͏ͤ S͏ͩ Jane Miner her heires &c: In all manner of Lawfull Serveis and Imployments that Shee Shall Sett him about and y͏ͤ S͏ͩ Jane Miner Doth Bind and oblidge herself her heires &c to give y͏ͤ S͏ͩ Orphin boy Three yeares Schooling and Carefully to Inſtruct him afterwards that he may Read well In any part of the Bible, allso to Inſtruct and Larne him y͏ͤ S͏ͩ orphin Shuch Law full Wayes or wayes that hee may be able after his Indentered time Expired to Gitt his one Liveing and to allow him Suffent meat Drinck waſhing Lodging and apparill untell y͏ͤ Expration of y͏ͤ S͏ͩ Indented Time and after y͏ͤ finiſhing of y͏ͤ S͏ͩ time, to pay him y͏ͤ S͏ͩ William Duglace all Shuch Allowances as y͏ͤ Law Derects In Shuch Caſes as allso to Keep y͏ͤ aforeſaide parish dureing the aforeſaide Indented time from all manner Charges or be[ ]g any wayes Burdenſom to y͏ͤ S͏ͩ Parish

In WITNEſS whereof wee have hereunto Interchangably Set our hands and Seales y͏ͤ day and yeare above Written

              Signum
Signed Sealed and Delivered   Jane   J   Miner
In P͏ͬsences of us
 Richard Hunley
  Signum
 Jn͏ᵒ   J   Grymes

[147]

THIS INDENTUR mad y͏ͤ tenth Day of June in y͏ͤ Yeare of our Lord god one thousand Seven hundred and Nineteen and in yᵉ fifth year of our Soverane Lord George of Gratt brittiane France and Ireland King Defender of yᵉ faith &c Witneſseth that I John Carter Clark of Petso Parish Vestry in Gloster County doe firmly in yᵉ Name and behalfe of yᵉ Parish above Said bind unto William Anderson of yᵉ Same Parish and County one orphin girll Named Mary Sarnderlens of yᵉ age of Nine Years old yᵉ Twenty day of November Next Insueing untell She arive at yᵉ age as the Law Dericts to Serve him yᵉ Sᵈ William anderson his heires &c, in all Manner of Lawfull Servises and Imployments that he Shall Sett her about and yᵉ Sᵈ William Anderson Doth bind and oblidge himself his heires &c: to give the Said orphin three years Schooling and Carefully to Instruct her afterwards that She may Read Well in any part of yᵉ bible allso to Instruct and Larne yᵉ Sᵈ orphin Such Lawfull waye. or wayes that She may be able after her Indentured time Expired to gitt her one Liveing and to alow her Sufficent mett Drinck Washing Lodging and apparil untell yᵉ Experation of yᵉ Sᵈ Indentured time and after the finishing of yᵉ Same time to pay yᵉ Sᵈ Mary Sarnderlens all Such allowances as the Law Dericts In Such Casses and allso to Keep yᵉ afore Sᵈ Parish Dureing yᵉ aforesaid Indentured time from all manner of Charges or being any wayes burdensom to yᵉ Said Parish In Witneſs whereof yᵉ Partyes above Named have put theire hands and Seales yᵉ day and yeare above Written

          Signum
Signed Sealed and Delivered Willᵐ S Anderson (Seal)
in Prˢence of
 John Carter
 Sarah Carter

[148] Note! This page is blank except for the words: "Francis Duval his Book" which are wrtten across the page near the top. C. G. C.

[149]

THIS INDENTUR mad the Sixth day of July in Yeare of our Lord God one thousand Seven hundred and Nineteen and in yᵉ fifth year of our Soveraine Lord George of gratt Brittian France and Ireland King Defender of the faith &c: WITNEſSETH that I Thomas Cook Church wardin of petso parish, in Gloster County, doe firmly, in the Name and behalfe of the Vestry of the Said Parish, bind unto John Carter of the Same Parish and County, one orphin Girll Named Elizabeth Rock, of the age of Eight Years old the tenth Day of the date of these Pʳsences, untell She arive at the age as the Law Dericts to Serve him the Sᵈ John Carter his heires &c: in all manner of Lawufull Servises and Imployments that he Shall Sett her about, and the Sᵈ John Carter doth bind and oblidge himself his heires &c: to give the Sᵈ orphin three years Schooling, and Carefully, to Instruct her, afterwards, that She may Read well in any part of Bible, allso to Instruct and Larne, her yᵉ Sᵈ orphin Such Lawfull waye or wayes, that She may be able after her Indentured time is Expired to gett her one Liveing, and to allow her suffent meat Drinck washing Lodging and apparill untell yᵉ Experation of the Said time, and after yᵉ finishing of the Sᵈ time, to pay her the Sᵈ Elizabeth Rock, all Such allowance as the Law Dericts in Such Cases, as allso to Keep the aforesaid Parish, Dureing yᵉ afor[ ]Said Indentured time, from all manner of Charges, or being any wayes Burdensom to the Sᵈ Parish, in Witneſs Whereof the partyes above Named have Interchangably put theire hands and Seales the day and yeare above Written
Signed Sealed and Delivered
in Pʳsences of
    Will: Miller   Jnᵒ Carter
    Thoˢ: Scott

[150] Note! This page is blank. C. G. C.

[151]

*Att a Vestry held

Att A Vestry held for Petso Parish Sepm^r ye 12th 1719 by Virtue of an ord^r: of Gloster Court dated ye 27th. day of August Last)

P^{r}sent M^r Em^{ll}: Jones minist^r
Capt Thos Buckner ⎫ Mr Auguston Smith
Mr John Royston ⎬ Mr John Read
Mr Phillip Smith ⎭
Mr Thos Cooke Church Warden

It is ordered by this P^{r}sent Vestry that the Clarke of the Vestry Record all ye Returns of Procefsionings which Shall be Returned by the Procefsioners and allso all the Return[] of Juryes which Shall be Returned by the County Court to the Church Wardens, In the Record Booke

(1) Septm^r ye 12th: 1719

In obedence to an ord^r. of Gloster Court dated ye 27th: day of Augst last This P^{r}sent Vestry has ordered that M^r. John Throckmorton and m^r John Pryor begin on the Twelveth day of octo^r next att Mr John Pratts too See the Lands within the first Precinct of this parish Procefsioned the Said Precinct Extending Crofs the parish as far as ye Branch between Mr Hanffords and the Said pryors and allso that thay make a Returne of theire Profeedings to the Clarke of Vestry of this Parish Some time between the above date and the Last of march next

(2) Sepm^r ye 12th: 1719

In obedence to an ord^r: of Gloster Court dated the 25th day of august Last This P^{r}sent Vestry has ordered that Mr Francis Thornton & Mr Seth Thornton begin on the nineteenth day of octo^r. next att M^r W^m. Thorntons too See the Lands within

---

*Note! These four words have been smudged out in the MS, but are still legible.—C. G. C.

yͨ Second Precinct of this Parish Proceſsioned the Sͩ precinct begining at the branch between John Pryors and Mʳ Hanſfords and up the parish to Mʳ thorntons mill Swamp and allso that thay make a Returne of theire proſeedings to the Clarke of the Vestry of this parish Some time between the above date and the Last of March Next

[152]   (3) Septmʳ yͨ 12ᵗʰ: 1719

In obedience to an ordʳ: of Gloster Court dated the 27ᵗʰ: of August Last This Pʳsent Vestry has ordered that Mʳ John Stubbs and Mʳ Thoˢ: Scott begin on the Twenty Sixth day of octoʳ: Next att Capᵗ Allexandʳ: Quarter In the Neck too See the Lands within the Third precinct of this Parish Procſsioned the Said Precinct Containing all the Lands between Mʳ Thornetons mill Swamp and popler Spring Swamp and allso that thay make a Returne of theire Proſeedings to the Clarke of the vestry of this Parish Some time between the above Date and the Last of March Next

(4) Septmʳ yͨ 12ᵗʰ: 1719

In obedience to an ordʳ: of Gloster Court dated the 27ᵗʰ day of August last This Pʳsent Vestry has ordered that Mʳ Wᵐ: Miller and Mʳ Henry Pursill begin on the third day of *octoʳ Novmʳ Next att Mʳ Wᵐ Millers too See the Lands within the fourth Precint of this Parish Proceſsioned the Said Precinct Containing all the Lands between Popler Spring Swamp and paytts mill Swamp and Bryerry branch as far as Stephen Jonsons and allso that thay make a Returne of theire Proſeedings to the Clarke of the Vestry of this parish Some time between the above date and the Last of March Next

(5) Sepmʳ yͨ 12ᵗʰ. 1719

In obedience to an ordʳ: of Gloster Court dated yͨ 27ᵗʰ day of August last This Pʳsent vestry has ordered that Mʳ Francis Lee

---

*Note! This word is scratched through in the MS., but is still legible.—C. G. C.

and Mr Robt Carter begin on the Twelveth day of of octo^r Next att Mr Richd Hubbards too See the Lands within the fifth Precinct of this parish Proceſsioned the S^d precinct Containing all the Lands from Mr Paytts mill Swamp to Docto^r Backers Swamp taking in Mr James Dudleys and Docto^r Crymes Land and allso that thay make a Returne of theire Proſeedings to the Clarke of the Vestry of this Parish Some time between the above date and the Last of March Next

[153]   (6) Septm^r ye 12th: 1719

In obedence to an ord^r of gloster Court dated the 27th day of august last This P^{r}sent Vestry has ordered that Mr Wm Brooking and Mr *George *Haynes Charles Royne begin on the Seventeenth day of Novem^r Next att Mr Wm Brooking too See the Lands within the Sixth Precinct of this parish Proceſsioned the ſ^d precinct Containing all the Lands on the left hand of the Road to the Dragon *Road Bridge and allso that thay make a Returne of theire Proſeedings to the Clarke of the Vestry of this Parish Some time between the above date and the last of March Next

(7) Septm^r ye 12th 1719

In obedence to an ord^r of Gloster Court dated the 27th day of August last This P^{r}sent Vestry has ordered that Mr Seth Thurston and Mr George Haynes begin on the Twenty fourth day of Novem^r Next att Mr Seth Thurstons too See the Lands within the Seventh Precinct of this Parish Proceſsioned the S^d Precinct Containing all the Lands from Docto^r Backers Swamp on the right hand of the Dragon Road to the bridge and So Croſs the parish to the Richland Swamp and allso that thay make a Returne of theire Proſeeding to the Clarke of the Vestry of this parish Some time between the above date and the Last of March Next

---

*Note! These words are scratched through in the MS., but are still legible.—C. G. C.

(8) Septm^r ye 12th 1719

In obedence to an ord^r of Gloster Court dated the 27th day of August Last this P^rsent Vestry has ordered that Mr Thos Read and Mr Will Corlawne begin on the Second day of Decem^r Next att Mr Auguston Smiths too See the Lands Within the Eight Precinct of this Parish Proceſsioned the S^d precinct Contaning all the Lands from ye S^d Smith to Stephen Jonsons and Croſs the Parish from the Richland Swamp to Coll^o John Lewies mill Swamp and allso that thay make a Returne of theire Proſeedings to the Clarke of the Veſtry of this Parish Some time between the above date and the Last of March Next

(9) Sepm^r ye 12: 1719

In obedence to an ord^r: of Gloster Court dated the 27th day of August last This P^rsent Vestry has ordered that Mr Richd Seaton and Mr Fra Wyat begin on the Twelveth day of octo^r Next att Mr Fra: Wyatt too See the Lands within the Ninth Precinct of this parish Proceſsioned the Said Precinct Containing all the Lands from Coll^o John Lewies mill to the out Sid of the Parish and allso that thay make a Returne of of theire Proſeedings to the Clarke of the Vestry of this Parish Some time between the above date and the Last of March Next

True Entry Teſt Jno Carter C^l p p V

[154]

Att A Vestry held for Petso Parish Octo^r ye 7th 1719
P^rsent M^r Em^ll. Jones Miniſt^r

Capt Thos Buckner	Mr Richd Seaton
Mr Wm Miller	Capt Henry Willis
Mr John Royſton	Mr Jno Reade
Mr Phillip Smith	Mr John Washington
Mr Augustan Smith	Mr Francis Wyatt Church Warden

Petso Parish is	Dr Tobo
To Mr Emll Jones minist'.	16000
To Joseph Ledford Clerke of ye Church	1000
To John Carter Clerke of Vestry	1000
To Ann Tryplowe as Sestonis	622¾
To Ellenr. Shillard as Sextons	374½
To Francis Thornton for Keeping George Stichall	800
To Capt Buckner for goods for Eliza. Gibson	213
To Capt David Alexandr for Keeping a basterd Child	800
To William Anderson for bureing Dorothy Rock	500
To John Willcocks Accot	15
To Collo: Beverlyes Accot	194
To Susanah Warters for Keeping Doro: Rockes Child	800
To Mr Thos Cookes Accot £4‖17s‖00d at 2d pr lb is	532
To Edwd Walford bord and Cure of Eliza Gibson	1600
To Edwd Walford bord and medensons for Mary Serrerd	1400
To John Day for Church Land	200
To Mary Hill for Relefe	300
To Mr James Dudley for Keeping and Cureing Ela Gibson	666¼
To Samll. Whitesed for Relefe	400
	27417½
To Caske of 11208½ at 8 pr Ct is	896
To Sallary of 27417½ at 5 pr Ct is	1370
	29683½
By Cr by the Church Wardens Last year	55¼
	29628¼
To 732 Tythables at 40½ pr pole is 29646	
	lb
Theire Remaines Due to the Parish	18

[155]

It tis ord' by this P'sent Vestry that the Church Wardens Receive of Every Tythable Person in this Parish fifteen pounds of Tob° or one Shilling and Six pence in Current money for the Repareing of the Glebe house which Comes to 10980^{lb} pounds of Tob° or £54∥18^s∥00^d in money and uppon Refusall of the Paym^t of the Same the Church Wardens are hereby Required to make Deſtreſs and that the Church Wardens are to be Allowed 5 p' C^t for Receiveing ye above Tob° or money

Itt tis ord' by the P'sent Vestry that Mr John Reade be Church Warden in Mr Fra: Wyatts Rume in the Uper Preceinct of this Parish and that Mr Fra Wyatt be Diſcharge from his Church Warden Ship

Memorandom Mr James Dudley is oblidged to Cure Eliz^a Gibſons Legg and allso to Keep it hole for one Whole yeare

True Entry Teſt Jn° Carter Cl: p: p: V

[156]

Att A Vestry held att the Church ye 13th of Decem^r 1719

P'sent

Mr Thos Cook & Mr John Reade Church wardens

Capt Thos Buckner   Mr Robt Pourtus
Mr Wm Miller
Mr John Royston

Itt tis ord': by this P'sent Vestry that Mr John Fleming Stand Proceſsioner in the Room of Mr John Stubb Deceaſed to See the Lands Within the Third Precinct Proceſsioned

True Entry Jn° Carter

Att A Vestry held for Petso parish June y˚ 30th 1720

P'sent Mr Em^ll: Jones Minijtr

Capt Thos Buckner ⎫ Mr Augt Smith
Mr Wm Miller   ⎬ Capt Henry Willis
Mr John Royston   ⎨ Mr Thos: Green
Mr Phillip Smith   ⎭

Mr Thos: Cook Church Warden

It tis Ordered by this Prejent Vejtry that Mr Thos: Green be Vejtry Man In the Lower Preceinct of this Parish in Mr Robt Pourtues Roome

True Entry Tejt Jn˚ Carter
C¹ p: p: V:

[157]

Att A Vestry held for Petso Parish Octor y˚ 7th: 1720

P'sent Mr Em^ll Jones Minijtr

Mr Wm Miller   ⎫ Capt Henry Willis
Mr John Royston   ⎬ Mr Thos Green
Mr Phillip Smith   ⎨ Mr John Reade Church W:
Mr Augstiane Smith ⎭

Petso Parish is	Dr	Tob˚
To Mr Em^ll Jones Minir		16000
To William Grumly Cl of y˚ Church		1000
To John Carter Clearke of Vestry		1000
To Ann Tryplow as Sextonis		1000
To Mr Fra: Thornton for Keeping Geo: Stichall		0800
To John Carter for Keeping Eliza Gibson		0600
To Mr John Reades Accot for Communian Wine £1: 15s: 0d @ 2d pr		0213
To Mr John Cleaytons Accot Cl of Gloster Court		0071
To John Willcocks Sherrife of Gloster Court		0015
To Sarah *Yeaman for Keeping Benja Carter Child of Sarah Carter		0466

*Note! This name was hard to make out. I may have read it wrong.—C. G. C.

To Mr Thos Cookes Acco{t} for Two barrells of Corne to Samll Whitſeead	0150
To Mrs Ann Allexander for Keeping a Baſterd Child	0800
To Fra: Eaſter for Mending ye Church Dore and three Horse blocks and Some pues	0060
To Doctr Richd Edwards for Cure of Eliza Warner	1000
To Mr Em{ll} Jones Acco{t} for £2: 10{s}: 2d @ 2d: ℔ lb is	0301
To Samll Whitsead for Releafe	0400
To Mary Hill for Releafe	0300
	24176
To Caſk for 8090{lb} Tob{o} @ 8 ℔ C{t} is	647
To Sall{ry} for 24176 @ 5 ℔{r} C{t} is	1208
	26031

    P{r}   Con{r}   C{r}

By Tob{o} Due to the parish from ye C: W	00018
	26013
By 742 Thythables @ 35 ℔ pole is 25970 Tob{o}	25970
and There Remaines Due to ye Church: W: on this Acco{t}	00043
	26013

          Carrid Over

[158]   Brought Over

It tis Ord{r} by this P{r}sent Vestry yt ye Church Wardens Receive of Every Tythable Person In this parish one hundred pound of Tob{o} or tenn Shill{s} in Current Money for ye building of a New Church Which Comes to 74200{lb} of Tob{o} or Three Hundred and Seventy won pounds in Current Money and uppon Refusall of ye payment of the Same ye Church Wardens are Hereby Required to Make Diſtreſs and that ye Church

Wardens are to be Allowed 5 ℔ C^t for Receiveing ye Above Tob^o or Money

It tis o^r by this P^{r}sent Vestry that Mr Thos Green be Church Warden In Y^e Lower Preceinct of this parish In Mr Thos Cooks Roome and that Mr Thos Cook be Descharged from his Church Warden Ship

Itt tis ord^r allso by this P^{r}sent Vestry that ye C^l of ye Vestry gitt a Copia of ye List of Tythables of this Parish Every Yeare for the futer

True Entry Test Jno Carter Cl P: p: V

[159]

Att A Vestry held for Petso Parish Jan^ry ye 18th: 1720/1

P^{r}sent M^r Em^{ll}: Jones Miniſt^r
Capt Thos Buckner   Mr Augt Smith
Mr Wm Miller   Mr John Read: C: W:
Mr John Royston   Mr Thos: Greene: C: W:

It tis ordered and Agreed by this P^{r}sent Vestry that Mr James Skilton bild the New Church at Popler Spring, and that he is to have Eleven Hundred and Ninty Pounds Current Money for the bilding of the above Said Church, and that he is to doe his Work well and Workman Like According to Agreement with the above Said Vestry and Church Wardens

It tis ordered by this P^{r}sent Vestry that ye Cleark of the Vestry Provide bonds with Conditions to bind Mr James Skilton to performe the Articles of Agreement with the Above Vestry and Church Wardens to bild the New Church at Popler Spring

True Entry Test Jno Carter C^l: p: p: V

[160]

Att a Vestry held for Petso parish ye 4th: Day of Feb^r 1720

P'sent Mr Em^{ll} Jones Minist
Capt Thos Buckner   Mr Richd Seaton
Mr William Miller   Capt Henry Willis
Mr John Royston   Mr John Washington
Mr Phillip Smith   Mr John Read Church Warden
Mr Augt Smith   Mr Thos: Green: C: W:

Att A Vestry held the 18th Day of Janu^{ry}: 1720 it was ordered and Agreead that Mr James Skelton Should build the New Church at popler Spring and that he was to have Eleven hundred and Ninty pounds Current Money of Virginia for the building the above Church but there Being Not A full Vestry it was Refurred tell the above Vestry mett; and it was alſo ordered and Consented to by this p'sent Vestry that Mr James Skelton Should build the New Church at Popler Spring and that he Should have the above Sum and that it Should be payd him as followeth Viz: he is to have Three Hundred and fifty pounds payd him the 23th day of Aprill Next Insueing and Three Hundred and fifty pounds payd him the 23th: day of April in the year of our Lord Christ: 1722 and Three Hundred and fifty Pounds payd him the 23th: day of Aprill in the year of our Lord Christ: 1723 and one Hundred and forty pounds the Remainder part of the above Sum one the 23 day of Aprill in the year of our Lord Christ. 1724

True Entry Test Jno Carter: C^l: P: P: V:

[161]

Att A Vestry held for Petso parish June 9th: 1721

P'sent M^r Em^{ll}: Jones Minist^r:
Capt Thos: Buckner   Mr Phillip Smith
Mr Wm Miller   Mr Aug^t: Smith
Mr John Royston   Mr Thos: Greene C: Warden

It tis ord^r by this p'sent Vestery that the Church Wardens of this parish bind out a Barsterd Child which is at Maddam Ann Allexanders belonging to Marther Thomas as Soone as possible they Can gitt any body to take it off them

True Ent^rr: Test Jn° Carter

[162]

THIS INDENTUR made y° Twenty Eight day of Augt in the year of Oure Lord God one thousand Seven hundred Twenty & one and in y° Eight yeare of Oure Soveraine Lord George of Gratt Brittiane France and Ireland King: Defender of the faith: &c: WITNEſSETH that I John Carter Clerk *of *petso *parish *Vestry of Petso parish Vestry in Gloster County doe firmly in the Name and behalf of the *Sd parish above S^d bind unto William Wats of y° S^d parish and County one Orphin boy Named James Watkins of the Age of Eight yeares old y° Six day of Feb^ry Next Insueing untell he Arive att the Age as the Law Derects To Serve him the S^d William Wats his heires &c In all Manner of Lawfull Servises and Imployments that he Shall Sett him about, and the S^d William Wats Doth bind and oblidge himself his heires &c: to give the S^d orphin boy Three Yeares Schooling and Carefully to Instruct him afterwards that he May Read Well In any part of the bible Allso to Instruct and Larne him the S^d orphin Such Lawfull Waye or Wayes that he may be able after his Indented time is Expired to gitt his one Liveing and to Allow him Suffeint meat Drinck Washing Lodging and Apparill untell y° Expiration of the S^d Indented time and after the Finishing of the S^d time to pay him the S^d James Watkins all Such allowances as the Law Derects In Such Cases as allso to Keep the aforesaid parish Dureing the aforesaid Indented time from all manner of Charges or being any Wayes Burdensom to the

---

*Note! These words have been scratched through in the MS, but are still fairly legible.—C. G. C.

S⁴ parish, In Witneſs Whereof Wee have hereunto Interchangeably put our hands and Seals the Day and yeare above Written

                                              Signum

Signd Seald and Delivered   William W Wats
In P'sence of
   Jnᵒ Carter
   Sarah Carter

[163]

Att A Vestry held for Petso parish yᵉ 4 day of Octoʳ: 1721

          P'sent Mʳ Emˡˡ Jones Ministʳ
    Capᵗ Thoˢ: Buckner   Mʳ Tho: Cooke
    Mʳ William Miller   Mʳ Fra Wyatt
    Mʳ John Royston   Mʳ John Reade C W
    Mʳ Augᵗ Smith   Mʳ Thoˢ: Greene C W

Petso Parish	is	Dʳ	Tobᵒ
To Mʳ Emˡˡ Jones Ministʳ:			16000
To Wᵐ Grumly Cl of yᵉ Church			01000
To Ann Tryplow as Sextonis			01000
To John Carter Cl Vestry			01000
To Mʳ Fra Thornton for Keeping Geo: Stichall			00800
To John Allexander for Keeping a barstard Child of Marther Thomas			00800
To Doctʳ Edwᵈ Walfard for Keeping a barstard Child of Jane Mackneles Six Mounths			00400
To Doctʳ Edwᵈ Walford When he has Cure'd Elizᵃ Warner			01000
To Doctʳ Edwᵈ Walford for bord and Meddensons to Elizᵃ. purſshur			01000
To Johanah Hubbard for bord of Mary Yates from yᵉ 9ᵗʰ of June to the first of Septemʳ			00180
To Doctʳ James Boyd for Visitts and Meddensons to Mary Yates			01000

To John Willcocks Sheriff Glo: Cour: Acco^t	00050
To Mr John Cleayton Cleark of Glo: Cour:	00163
To Mr Thos: Cooke part of his Acco^t Allow^d: for bord and Cure of Mary Taler	00318
To Mr John Read for Goods to Eliz^a: parssur £1: 00^s: 05^d @ 10^s ℔^{r} C^t:	00204
To John Carter for Keeping Eliz^a Gibſon one year	00800
To Sam^{ll} Whitsead for Releavff	00400
To Mary Hill for Releavef	00400
To Mr John Reades for Thos: Mareyes Leiveies not paid Last Year	00135
To m^r John Reade & Mr Thos Greene: C: W: Due from ye parish ye Last y^r	00043
To Mr John Reade & Mr Thos: Greene: C: W: for Takeing bond and Security of Mr James Skelton to build the New Church at popler Sp	00500
To George Haynes for bord of Eliz^a Warner	00050
To Thos: Grindley fr Releavfe	00300
To Mr Thos: Greene C: W: for bottles for ye Communian Wine	00035
	27578
To Sall^{ry} and Caske @ 13 ℔^{r}. C^t of 27578 is	03585
	31163

P^r C^r

By 761 Tythables @ 41 ℔^{r} pole is	31201
There Remaines Due to the parish one this Acco^t	00038

Carrid Over to the other Side

[164] Brought Over

Itt tis ord^r by this P^{r}sent Vestry that the Church Wardens Receive of Every Tythable person in this parish one hundred and Twenty five pounds of Tob^o or tenn Shill^s: In Current

Money Which Comes to 95125 pounds of Tob°: or £380: 10°: 00ᵈ: in Money for the building of A New Church and Uppon Refusall of the Payment of the Same the Church W: are hereby Required to Make Distreſs and that the C: W: are to be Allowed five ₱ʳ Cᵗ for Receiveing the above Tob°: or money

Itt tis allso ordʳ by this Pʳsent Vestry that Mʳ John Washington be Church Warden in yᵉ upper preceinct of this parish in Mʳ John Reades Roome and that Mʳ John Reade be Diſcharged from his Church Warden Ship

This Day Mʳ Tho°: Reade Junʳ Was Elected and Chosen Vestry Man in the Upper precinct of this parish In Mʳ Richᵈ: Seatons Roome: Deceᵈ:

This Day Mʳ Fra: Thornton Was Elected and Chosen Vestry Man In the Lower preceinct of this parish In Capt Henry Willis Roome be being Listed In Ware parish

This Day Mʳ John Reade produceing to this pʳsent Vestry by Accoᵗ that he has paid Mʳ James Skelton £175: 5ˢ: 6ᵈ: itt being his part of the parish Money Due to the Sᵈ Skelton one this yeares payment, Itt tis ordʳ: by this pʳsent Vestry that he be Diſcharged from yᵉ Sᵈ Sum

True Entry Test Jn° Carter Cˡ P P V:

[165]

THIS INDENTUR maid yᵉ third day of July in the Yeare of Our Lord God one thousand Seven hundred twenty and two and in the Eight yeare of Our sovereign Lord George of gratt Brittiane France and Ireland KING Defender of the faith &c WITNEſSETH that John Carter Cleark of petso parish Vestry in the County of Gloster Do firmly in the Name and behalf of the Vestry of the above Sᵈ Parish bind unto mʳ Francis Easter of the Same parish and County one orphen Boy
*old*the*forth
Named Danell More of the Age of Eleven yeares of Next

---

*Note! These words are interlined in the MS, as above.—C. G. C.

*Insuing
March untell he Arive at the age as the Law derects to serve him the S⁴ Francis Eaſter his heires &c: in al Maner of Lawfull Services and Imployment that he Shall set him About and the S⁴ Francis Easter doath bind and Oblidge himself his heires &c: to give the S⁴ orphan three yeares Schooling and to Carefully Instruct him after wards that he may Read well in any part of the bible allso to Instruct and Larn him the S⁴ orphin such Lawfull way or wayes that he may be Able after his Indented time Expire'd to gitt his Liveing and to allow him Seuffent meat Drinck Washing Lodging and apparill untell the Experation of the S⁴ time and after the finishing of the S⁴ time to pay the S⁴ Danell More all such allowances as the Law Derects in Such Cases as allso to Kep the afores⁴ parish dureing the aforeS⁴ Indented time from all ṁaner of Charges or being any Wayes burdensom to the S⁴ parish in Witneſs whereof the partyes above Named have Interchangably put theire hands and Seales the day and yeare above Writen

    The Words Interlined before Sealed
     (old) (the) (forth) (Insueing)
Sign'd Sel'd & Delivered
In P'sence of
   Signum
  James I Booker   Francis Easter (Seal)
  Jnᵒ Carter

[166]

  Att a Vestry held for petso parish Apʳˡˡ: yᵉ 3ᵗʰ: 1722
    P'sent Mʳ Emˡˡ: Jones Ministʳ
  Capᵗ Thoˢ: Buckner Mʳ John Read
  Mʳ William Miller Mʳ Thoˢ: Green: C: W:
  Mʳ Augᵗ Smith Mʳ John Wasington C: W

---

*Note! These words are interlined in the MS., as above.—C. G. C.

Att this p'sent Vestry M' John Throckmorton was Elected and Chosen Vestry man in y° Lower preceinct of this parish in M' Phillip Smiths Room he being Listed in Ware parish

True Ent'' Test Jn° Carter C: p: p

Att A Vestry held for petso Parish Aug': y° 1th: 1722

P'sent M' Em^{ll}: Jones minist':
Cap' Tho': Buckner ⎫ M' John Read
M' William Miller ⎬ M' Tho': Green C: W:
M' John Royston ⎥ M'. John Washington C: W:
M' Aug' Smith ⎭

It tis Ord': and Consented to by this p'sent Vestry that the Pulpit shall be on the North side of the Church in the same place Where it tis fixed

True Ent'' Test Jn° Carter C p: p: V

[167]

Att A Vestry held for petso parish y° 3th: of Octo' 1722

P'sent M' Em^{ll}. Jones Minist'
Capt Tho': Buckner ⎫ M' Tho': Green C: W
M' William Miller ⎬ M' John Washington C: W
M' John Royſton ⎥ M' Tho': Read Jun':
M' Aug' Smith ⎭ M' John Throckmorton

Petso Parish	D'	Tob°
To m' Em^{ll} Jones Minist'		16000
to William Grumly C' Church		1000
to Ann Tryplow as Sextonis		1000
to John Carter C' Vestry		1000
to Fra Thornton Keeping Geo: Stichall		0800
to M' John Clayton C' of Gloster Cou'.		0197
to John Willcocks Sheff of Gloster Cou':		0080
to Edwd Walford for Cure of Mary Shurrad		0800
to Doct' Edwd Walford Cure of Eliz' Shurred		1200

to Doctr Edwd Walford for Cure of an orphin girll at Geo Schools	0300
to Doctr Edwd Walford for Cure of Elizᵃ purshur	1100
to Thoˢ: Jackſon for Keepin Mary Yates Six weeks	0150
to John Crockford for Keepin Elizᵃ: Purshur foure mounths	0264
to Geo: Fary for Keeping Elizᵃ Warner five mounths & haff	0360
to George Haines for Keeping Elizᵃ Waner Seven mounths	0460
to mr Thomas Greens Accot £1: 3ˢ: 8ᵈ @ 10ˢ/ ℔ Cᵗ	0236
to Sarah Goram for Keeping Mary Yats five weeks	0100
to James Haines for Keepin Mary Yates one mounth	0080
to John Crockford Keepin Elizᵃ Gibson one year	0300
to Richᵈ Dance for Keeping Samˡ Whitseed one Year	0541
to Thoˢ Grindley for Releaf	0300
to mr John Washington for 13 bottles of Communion wine 2/6 and 1 ℔ Shoues to Elizᵃ Warner £1: 16ˢ: 6ᵈ @ 10 ℔ Cᵗ	0365
to Madm Ann Allexander for Keeping a barsterd Child	0800
to Richᵈ Hopkins one Leive over paid Last year	0041
to James Skelton one Leive over paid Last year	0041
to mary Hill for Releaf	0400
to Samˡ Whitseed for Releaf	0700
	28622

Pr	Conr	Cr
*By *Tobᵒ *due *to *the *parish *from *yᵉ *C: *W: *Last *years *Accoᵗ		*38
*By *Mr *Francis *Thorntons *bill		*170
		*208

*Note! These words and figures are scratched through in the MS., but are still fairly legible.—C. G. C.

	*32134
To Caske for 28622 @ 8 ℔ Cᵗ is	2289
To Salʳʸ for 28622 @ 5 ℔ Cᵗ is	1431
Carrid Over	3234[2]
[168] Brought Over from the other Side	32342

Pʳ   Conᵗʳ   Cʳ

By Tob°: Due to the parish from yᵉ C: W: one Last years Accᵗ   38
By Mʳ Fra Thorntons bill   170

   208

By 776 Tythables @ 41 ℔ pole is 31816 Tob°   32134
There Remands Due to the C: Wardens on this Accoᵗ †288¹ᵇ Tob°

It tis ordʳ by this P'sent Vestry that the Church Wardens Receive of Every Tythable person in this parish *one 125¹ᵇ of Tob°: or 10ˢ/ in Current Money. which Comes to 97000¹ᵇ of Tob° or £388: 00ˢ: 00ᵈ: Current Money for the building of A new Church and uppon Refusall of the payment of the Same the Church Wardens are hereby Required to make Distreſs and that the C: W: are to be allowed 5 ℔ Cᵗ for Receiveing the above Tob° or money

It tis allso Ordʳ by this P'sent Vestry that Mʳ Thoˢ Read Junʳ and Mʳ John Throckmorton be C: Wardens *this *P'sent *year for this Next year and that Mʳ John Washington and Mʳ Thoˢ: Green be Diſcharged from theire C. W. Ship

---

   *Note! These words and figures are scratched through in the MS., but are still fairly legible.—C. G. C.
   †Note! A remarkable piece of subtraction.—C. G. C.

It tis allso ord' by this P'sent Vestry that M' John Washington pay Rich'd Hopkins Tenn Shill' Current Money *out of the parish money which is in his hands and M' James Skelton Tenn Shill' more of the S'd money it being for two Leives they over paid Last year

Memorandon that M' John Allexander for the Consideration of Eight hundred pounds of Tob°: paid him this P'sent Year he has pomust to Keep a barsterd Child Called Marget Thomas from being any Charge to the Parish for the futer

morand'm M' Tho'. Read C: Warden has got Edw'd Wests bill for 500'lb of Tob°.

*and *M' *John *Throckmorton *has *got

[169]

Att A Vestry held for petso Parish March y° 9th: 1722/3

P'sent M' Em'll: Jones Minister
Cap' Tho' Buckner   M' John Reade
M' William Miller   M' John Washington
M' John Royston   M' Tho' Green
M' Aug' Smith   M' John Throckmorton C:W:
                      M' Tho' Reade Jun': C:W

Upon the Petion of John Shepard to this P'sent Vestry that he being very old and past his Labour the Gen'll:men of the Vestry thought fit to set him. Leivie free for the futer

Memorandom/ m' James Skelton has agreed with this P'sent Vestry to tar the new Church at popler Spring well, and that he is to have foure pounds Current money for the Same, and allso to Civer the pedements over the dors with Lead, and to bring in the Charge to the Gent'll: of the Vestry

---

*Note! These words scratched through in the MS, but are still legible.—C. G. C.

it tis alls ord': by this P'sent Vestry that the Church Wardens take Ceare of Sarah Yaman and allso to bind out her Children

Memorandon that John Mᶜ:Williams has agreead With this P'sent Vestry to Clear all the brick batch and looſe durt that is faceing the New Church and to Leavell all Round the New Church within one *Corse of the Are holds, and to pull down the old Church at popler Spring and to Carry it off of the Church Land, and to Cleane all the Church Yard of all Rubbidg and trash, and in Consideration of the Said Work the Gell: of the Vestry has Agreed to give the Said Jnº: MᶜWilliams two Thousand pounds of Tobº: at the Laying of the Next Leiveie

[170]

Att A Vestry held for Petso Parish Aprll: yᵉ 16: 1723

P'sent Mʳ Emll: Jones Ministʳ:
Capᵗ Thoˢ: Buckner ⎫ Mʳ John Reade
Mʳ William Miller   ⎪ Mʳ Thoˢ: Green
Mʳ John Royston   ⎬
Mʳ Augᵗ Smith   ⎭

Mʳ James Skelton petissioning to this P'sent Vestry that he haveing not time Enough to finish the New Church According to the first Agreement, this P'sent Vestry has thought fitt to give him tell yᵉ 24 day of June it being one Mounth, and that he has Agreed with the Gentle: men of the Vestry to finish the Church in the above time, and not to have any Longer time

---

*Note! There is no doubt that the words "Corse of the Are holds" are a correct rendering of the MS. I take these words, with the two preceding ones, to mean "within one course of brick from the bottom of the air holes"; i. e., within three or four inches of the bottom of the holes in the foundation left for the purpose of ventilation.—C. G. C.

Itt tis o^r: by this P'sent Vestry that George Fery Shall dessist in proceading to go on with the Work that Mr Thos Read C:W: Agreed with him to do at popler Spring Church and that the Cleark of the Vestry give him a Copia of the Said order

Itt tis ord^r by this P'sent Vestry that the Church Wardens pay Mr James Skelton the over plush of the parsh money which they have in thire hands and that they take Mr James Skeltons Recepts for the Same and and produce them to the Gent^{le}:men of the Vestry

True Entry Test Jn° Carter C^l: P: P:

[171]

Att a Vestry held for petso parish June ye 28th: 1723

P'sent M^r Em^{ll}: Jones Minist^r
Capt Thos: Buckner   Mr Augt Smith
Mr William Miller   Mr John Read
Mr John Royston   Mr Thos: Greene
                         Mr Thos. Reade Junr: C: W:

It tis ord^r: and agree'd by this P'sent Vestry with Mr James Skelton that he is to Lath and plaſter the walls of the house that he now Lives in: and to Seeal it over head with Laths and to plaster it with Lime and heare thereon and that he is to plaster the Chimbly with Lime and heare and to build a good Subſanceall brick back: and to Cover ye Said house with Sypraſs hart bords and to put two windows in the body of the S^d house and to make a good Subſanceall planck dore and to tare the Ruff of the S^d huse well; and in Conſiderratio[ ] of the S^d house and work this p'sent Vestry has agreed to give the S^d James Skelton Twelve pounds Current money of Virginia

Tru Entry Test Jn° Carter C^l ℔:℔ V

[172]

THIS INDENTUR made yᵉ 22 day of June 1724 the year of our Lord god one thousand Seven hundred twenty and four and in the ninth year of Our Sovereign Lord George of Gratt Brittian France and Ireland KING defender of the faith &c Witneſseth that I John Carter Clark of petso parish Vestry in Gloster County do firmly in the Name and behalf of the Vestry of the parish above Sᵈ bind unto Mʳ William Miller of the Sᵈ parish and County one orphin Girll Named Ellianer Butler untill She arive at the age as the Law Dericts to Serve him the Sᵈ William Miller his heires &c in all manner of Lawfull Services and Imployments that he Shall Sett her about, and the Sᵈ William Miller doth bind and oblidge him Self his heires &c to give the Sᵈ orphin Girll three years· Schooling and to Carefully to Inſtruct her after wards that She may Read well in any part of the bible allso to Inſtruct and Larne her Such Lawfull way or wayes that She may be able after her Indented time is Expiraed to gitt her one Liveing and to allow her Sufficient meat drnck *and waſhing and apparill untill the Expiration of the Sᵈ time and after the finishing of the Sᵈ time to pay the Sᵈ Ellianer Buttler all Such allowances as the Law dericts in Such cases as allso to Keep the afore Sᵈ parish dureing the afore Sᵈ Indented time from all manner of Charges or being any wayes Burdensom to the Sᵈ Parish in wittneſs Whreof wee have Interchangeably put our hands and Seals the day and year first above written

        (of yᵉ parrish) interlind before Sin'd)
Signd Sealed in
P'sence of   Will: Miller   (Seal)
   James Dudley
   Robert Carter

---

*Note! This word is scratched through in the MS but is still legible.—C. G. C.

[173]

THIS INDENTUR made y⁰ 24th day of July in the Yeare of Our Lord God one thousand Seven hundred twenty and three and in the Ninth year of our Sovereign Lord George of Grate Brittian France and Ireland KING defender of the faith &c: Wittneſseth that I John Carter Clarke of Petso Parish Vestry in Gloster County do firmly in the Name and *and behalf of the Vestry of the Parish above Sᵈ bind unto Benjᵃ: Baker of the Same parish and County on one Orphin Girll Named Franceſs Simco untell Shee arive at the age as the Law Dericts to Serve him the Sᵈ Benjᵃ: Baker his heires &c: in all manner of Lawfull Services and Imployments that he Shall Sett her about and the Sᵈ Benjᵃ: Baker doth bind and oblidge him Self his heires &c: to give the Sᵈ orphin Girll three yeares Schooling and to Carefully to Inſtruct her afterwards that She may Read well in any part of bible Allso to Inſtruct and Larn her Such Lawfull way or wayes that She may be able after her Indented time is Expiraed to gitt her own Liveing and to Allow her Sufficient meat drinck Washing Lodging and Apparill untell the Expiration of the Sᵈ time and after the finishing of the Sᵈ time to pay the Sᵈ Franceſs Simco all Such allowances as the Law dericts in Such Caſes as allso to Keep the afore Sᵈ parish dureing the afore Sᵈ Indentured time from all Manner of Charges or being any wayes burdenſom to the Sᵈ parish in Wittneſs whereof wee have Interchangeably put our hands and Seales the day and Yeare first above Written
Signd Seal'd in
P'sence of
    Jnº: Carter   Benjᵃ: Baker (Seal)
        her
    Sarah ſ Carter
        mark

*Note! This word is scratched through in the MS., but is still legible.—C. G. C.

[174]

Att a Vestry held for petso parish y⁰ 2ᵗʰ: day of Septʳ: 1723

P'sent Mʳ Emˡˡ Jones Miniſtʳ
Capᵗ Thoˢ: Buckner   Mʳ Fra Wyatt
Mʳ William Miller   Mʳ John Read
Mʳ John Royston   Mʳ John Washington
Mʳ Thoˢ Cooke   Mʳ Thoˢ: Green
Mʳ Augᵗ Smith   Mʳ Fra Thornton

Itt tis ordʳ by this p'sent Veſtry that y⁰ Clarke of the Vestry Record all Returns of p'oseſsioning and juryes which shall be Returned to y⁰ Vestry

Itt tis allso ordʳ by this p'sent Vestry that y⁰ first Precienct of this parish Come to the head of Bennits Creke

Att a Vestry held for Petso parish Septʳ y⁰ 2ᵗʰ 1723

In obedeince to an ordʳ: of Gloster Court dated y⁰ 22ᵗʰ: day of augᵗ last this P'sent Vestry has ordʳ: that John Clarke and John Smith Sawer Begin at Mʳ John Pratts on y⁰ Eleventh day of Octoʳ Next to See the Lands within y⁰ first Precinct of this Parish Profeſsioned y⁰ Sᵈ Precinct Extending Croſs the Parish as far as the head of Bennits Creek, and to take and Return to y⁰ Veſtry an Accoᵗ of Every p'ſons Land they Shall profeſsion and of the p'sons p'sent at the Same and of What Lands *they in their Precinct they Shall faile to Profeſsion and of the Particular Reaſons of Such failure by the Last of March Next Coming

Att a Vestry held for petso Parish Septʳ 2ᵗʰ: 1723

In obedence to an order of Gloſter Court dated y⁰ 22ᵗʰ: day of Augᵗ Last this p'sent Vestry has ordered that William Thornton Junʳ and Lewis Neal Begin at Mʳ William

Thorntons on the Sevententh day of Octo' Next to See the Lands within y° Second ℙrecinct of this parish procefsioned the S⁴ precinct begining at the head of Bennits Creek and up the Parish to m' Thornes mill Swamp and to take and Return to the Veftry an Account of Every p'son Land they shall ℙrocefsion and of the p'sons p'sent at the Same and of what Lands in their ℙrecinct they Shall fail to Procefsion and of the Particular Reafons of Such failure by the Last of March Next Coming

[175]

*Sept' Att a Vestry held for petso parish Sept' 2ᵗʰ: 1723

In obedence to an order of Glofter Court dated the 22ᵗʰ day of Aug' Last this P'sent Vestry has ordred that Tho': Scott and John Fleming begin at Cradd Allexanders Quarter in the Neck on the forth day of Octo' Next to See the Lands within y° third precinct of this parish Procefsioned the S⁴ ℙrecinct Containing all the Lands between M' Thornes Mill Swamp and popler Spring Swamp and to take and Return to the Veftry an account of Every ℙerfons Land they Shall Procefsion and of the P'sons p'sent at the Same and of what Lands in their precinct they Shall fail to Procefsion and of the Particular Reafons of Such failure by the Last of March Next Coming

Att a Vestry held for Petso parish Sept': y° 2ᵗʰ: 1723

In obedence to an ord': of Gloster Court dated y° 22ᵗʰ: day of Aug' last this P'sent Vestry has ord': that Edw⁴ Simmonds and Rich⁴ Crittenden begin at m' William Millers on the fourth day of Novem' Next to See the Lands within the forth ℙrecinct of this Parish Procefsioned the S⁴ ℙrecinct Containing all y° Lands Between poplar Spring

---

*Note! These words are scratched through in the MS., but are still legible.—C. G. C.

Swamp and patts mill Swamp and Bryer Branch as far as Stephen Johnſons and to take and Return to the Veſtry an Account of Every ₱'sons Land they Shall Proceſsion and of the ₱'sons ₱'sent att the Same and of what Lands in their ₱recinct they Shall fail to ₱roceſsion and of the ₱articular Reaſons of Such failur by the laſt of March Next Coming

At a vestry held for petso parish Sept' y' 2ᵗʰ: 1723

In obedence to an ordd of Gloſter Court dated y' 22ᵗʰ: day of Augᵗ laſt this ₱'sent Vestry has ordered that Robert Carter and Benjᵃ Baker begin att Henry Hubbard's on the tenth day of Octoʳ Next to See the Lands within the fifth ₱recinct of this ₱arish Proceſsioned the Sᵈ ₱recinct Containing all the Lands from pats Mill Swamp to Doctoʳ Walfords Swamp takeing Mʳ James Dudleyes and Doctoʳ Crymes Land, and to take and Return to the Veſtry an Accoᵗ of Every ₱'sons Land they Shall ₱roceſsion and of the ₱'son ₱'sent at the Same and of what Lands in their precinct they Shall fail to ₱roceſsion and of the ₱articular Reaſons of such failur *of by the Last of March Next Coming

[176]

Att A Vestry held for petso ₱arish Septem' 2ᵗʰ 1723

In Obedence to an ord' of Gloster Court dated the 22ᵗʰ day of Augᵗˢ Last this ₱'sent Veſtry has ordered that William Brooking and Allexander Rone begin on the 13ᵗʰ: day of Novem' att William Brookings to See the Lands within the Sixt ₱recinct of this parish ₱roceſsioned the Sᵈ ₱'ceinct all the Lands from Walfords Swamp on the Left hand of the Road to the Dragon Bridge and to take and Return to the veſtry an Account of Every ₱'sons Land

---

*Note! This word is scratched through in the MS, but is still legible.—C. G. C.

they Shall P'rocession and of the P'sons P'sent at the Same and of what Lands [ ]in their P'recinct they Shall faile to P'rocession and of the P'articular Reasons of Such failur by the Last of March Next Coming

Att A Vestry held for petso Parish Septr 2th: 1723

In Obedence to an ord^r of Gloster Court, dated ye 22th: day of Aug^{ts} Last this Present Vestry has ordered that m^r Seth Thurston and George Haines begin on the 20th day of Novem^r Next at Seth Thurstons to See the Lands within the Seventh P'recinct of this Parish processioned the S^d P'recinct Containing all the Lands from Docto^r Walfords Swamp on the Right hand of the Road to the Dragon bridge and So Cross the parish to the Rich land Swamp and to take and Return to the Vestry an Acco^t of Every P'sons Land they Shall P'rocession and of the P'sons P'sent at the same and of what Lands in their P'cinct they Shall fail to P'rocession and of the P'articular Reasons of Such failur by the Last of March Next Coming

Att A Vestry held for petso parish Septem^r the 2th: 1723

In Obedence to an ord^r: of Gloster Court dated the 22th day of Aug^{ts} Last this P'sent vestry has ordered that William Collawn and Conquest Wyatt begin the 2th day of Decem^r: at m^r Augt Smith to See the Lands within the Eaight P'recinct of this parish Processioned the S^d P'recinct Containing all the Lands from the S^d Smiths to Stephen Johnsons and Cross the parish *to *the Richland Swamp to Coll^o: John Lewis Mill and to take and Return to the vestry an Acco^t of Every P'sons Land they Shall procession and of the P'sons P'sent at the Same and of what Lands in their precinct they Shall fail to P'roces-

---

*Note! Above these two words appears in the MS the word "from" interlined.—C. G. C.

sion and of the Particular Reasons of Such failur by the Last of March Next Coming

[177]

Att A Vestry held for Petso parish Septem' the 2th: 1723
In Obedence to an ord' of Gloster Court dated y° 22th: day of Aug'' laſt this P'sent Vestry has ordered that John Wyatt and Rich⁴ West begin on the 14th day of Octo' Next at m' Franceſs Wyatts to See the Lands within the Ninth Precinct of of this Parish proceſsioned the s⁴ Precinct Containing all the Lands from Coll° John Lewis mill to the out Sid of the Parish and to take and Return to the veſtry an Acco' of Every p'ſons Land they Shall Proceſsion and of the P'sons P'sent at the Same and of what Lands in their Precinct they Shall fail to Proceſsion and of the particular Reaſons of Such failur by the Last of March Next Coming

      Copia Teſt Jn° Carter C': V:

[178]

Att a Vestry held for Petso parish Octo': 12th: 1723

    P'sent m' Em'' Jones Miniſter
Cap' Tho'': Buckner	M' Tho'': Green
M' William Miller	M' Fra Thornton
M' John Royston	M' John Throckmorton C: W
M' Aug' Smith	M' Tho'': Read Jun' C: W
M' John Read	M' John Washington

Petso Parish is Dr.	Tob°
To M' Em'' Jones miniſt'	16000
To William Grumly C' Curch	01000
To ann Tryplow Sextonis	01000
To John Carter C' Veſtry	01000
To M' Fra: Thornton for Keeping Geo Stichall	00800
To M' Tho'' Green for Keeping Sarah Yannan	00374

To Capt Thos: Buckner for Keeping Mary Shurred	00500
To John Wilcocks Sheriff Acct	00205
To Mr Augt Smith for Keeping John Barnett a baſter'd	00590
To John Timberlick one Leivei over paid laſt year	00041
To William Webb one Leivei over paid *last year 1721	00041
To Maj Henry Willis for Six buſhells Corne to Mary Shurred	00120
To John Grimes for Keeping Eliza ℔ursher Six Mounths	00400
To Jnº McWilliams for pulling down the old Church and Cleareing the Church yarde	02000
To doctor Edwd Walford takeing Care of Mary Shurreds legg	00400
To Doctor Walford Keeping Mary Shured foure Mounths	00264
To Geo Ferry Keeping Eliza Warner on year mr renolds	00800
To William Brooking one Leivie over paid in the year 1722	00041
To Thos: Grindee for Releaf	00400
To Saml Whitseed for Releaf	00500
To Mary Hill for Releaf	00400
To Mr John Throckmortons Acct	00041
To Mr Thos: Read Acct	00277
To Mr John Cleaytons Acct	00519
	27773
To Cask and Salry 27773lb Tobº is	3610
	31383

By 774 Tythables @ 41 ℔r pole is 31,734
There Remaines due to the parish   351

---

*Note! This word has been scratched through in the MS, and interlined above occur the words "in the."—C. G. C.

[179]

It tis ordʳ by this ℘ʳsent Vestry that the Church Wardens pay George fferry one hundred pound of tob⁰ out of the tob⁰ Due to the parish

It tis ordʳ by this ℘ʳsent Vestry that the Church Wardens Receive of Ever tythable person in this parish fifty pounds of Tob⁰ or *tenn five Shillˢ in Current money for the payment of the New Church and other Creditors which comes to 38700 pounds of Tob⁰ or £ 193 10ˢ Current money and uppon Refuſall of the payment of the Same the C.W. are hereby Required to mak distreſſ and that the Church Wardens are to be Allowed 5 ℘ʳ Cᵗ for Receiveing the above Tob⁰ or Money

It tis allso ordʳ by this ℘ʳsent Vestry that Mʳ John Royston be Church Warden in the upper ℘recinct of this parish and Mʳ Francis Thornton in the Lower ℘recinct of the parish and that Mʳ Thoˢ: Read and Mʳ John Throckmorton be discharged from theire Church Warden Ship

At this ℘ʳsent Thoˢ: Eaſter was Elected and Chosen Sextonis of the Church

True Entʳʸ Test Jn⁰ Carter Cˡ V:

[180]

This Indenture made the 22 day of June in the year of our Lord God one thousand Seven hundred twenty and foure and in yᵉ Ninth Year of our Sovereign Lord George of gratt Brittian France and Ireland King Defender of the faith &c Witneſseth that I John Carter Clarke of petso parish Veſtry in Gloceſter County do firmly in the Name and behalf of the veſtry of the parish above Sᵈ Bind unto William Brōking of the Same parish and County one orphin boy Named James Barnett of the age of thirteen

---

*Note! This word is scratched through in the MS, but is still legible.—C. G. C.

yeares old or there about untill he arive at age as the Law Derects to Serve him the S⁴ William Brooking his heires &c: in all manner of Lawfull Services and Imployments that he Shall sett him about and the S⁴ William Brooking doth bind and oblidge himſelf his heires &c: to give the s⁴ orphin boy three yeares shooling and Carefully to Inſtruct him afterwards that he may Read well in any part of the bible allso to Inſtruct and larne him Such Lawfull way or wayes that he may be able after his Indentured is Expire'd to gitt his one Liveing and to allow him sufficent meet drinck waſhing Lodging and apparrill untell the Expiration of the s⁴ time and after the finishing the S⁴ time to pay the s⁴ James Barnett all Such allowances as the Law derects in such Caſses as allso to Keep the aforeſ⁴ Parish dureing the aforeſ⁴ Indentured time from all manner of Charges or being any wayes Burdenſom to the s⁴ Parish in Wittneſs whereof wee have Interchangeably put our hands and Seales the day and year first above Written Signed Sealed in
P'sence of

 James Dudley   W Brooking
 Robert Carter
         Francis Duval

[181]

This Indenture made the 22⁴ day of June In the Year of our Lord God one thouſand Seven hundred & Twenty four And in the Ninth year of the Reigne of Our Sovreign Lord George of Great Brittaine France & Ireland King Defender of the faith &ᵉ Wittneſseth that I John Carter Clark of Petso Parriſh Vestery in Gloster County Do firmly in the Name & behalf of the Vestry of the pariſh Aforſ⁴. Bind Unto George Fary of the Same Pariſh and County one Orphen Boy Named Thomas Barnett being Eleven Years of Age or therabouts to Serve Untill he Arives to the Age as the Law Dyrects to Serve him the Said George Fary his heirs &ᶜᵃ, in all maner of Lawfull Servis & Imployment that he Shall Set him about And the Said George Fary Doth bind & Oblidge himſelf his heirs &cᵃ, to give the Said Orphen boy three years Schooling & Cearfully to Instruct him Afterwards that he may Read Well in Any part of the Bible Alſo to Instrut and Learn him Such *Such Lawful way or Ways that he may be Able After his Indentured time is Expired to get his own Living and to Alow him Sufficent meat Drink Waſhing Lodging & Apperil Untill the Expiration of the Said Time And After the Finishing the Said time to pay the Said Thomas Barnet All Such Allowances As the Law Dyrects in Such Caſes As Alſo to Keep the Parriſh harmleſs During the Said Indentered time from being Anyways Cargable or burdunſom to them In Witneſs Whearof We have hearunto Set our hands & Seals the day & Yea[ ] Above Written the Word (Sufficent) Interlined before Aſsignᵈ.

Signed And Sealed
In Preſents of
    W Brooking   Gerg ferry (Seal)
    Robert Carter

                                        †Gerg fary

[182]   Note! This page of the M.S. is blank.—C. G. C.

[183]

In Obedence to an Act of the Generall Aſsembly Entituled an Act for the better and more Effectuall improveing the Staple of Tobacco A Vestry whoſe Names are here

---

    *Note! This word is scratched through in the MS., but is still legible.—C. G. C.
    †Note! This signature is in a different hand from that of the signature above. It is evidently not an autograph signature.—C. G. C.

Mentioned was holden for Petso ℔arish the 22ᵗʰ: day of June 172[ ]

   Pʳsent

The Revernᵈ: Emˡˡ: Jones ⎫   Capt John Washington
 Capt Thoˢ Buckner | Mʳ Thoˢ: Greene
 Mʳ William Miller   ⎬   Mʳ Fran: Wyatt
 *Mʳ John Royston C:V | Mʳ John Reade
 Mʳ Augᵗ Smith   ⎭   Mʳ John Throckmorton
 Mʳ John Royston & Mʳ Fra: Thornton C: V:

It tis ordʳ by this ℔ʳsent Vestry that Mʳ Thomas Green & Mʳ John Smith Examine & Count or Number the Tobᵒ: plants in the first and Second ℔recinct of the Sᵈ ℔arish as the Law them Directs

It tis ordʳed by the Sᵈ Vestry that Capᵗ John Allexander and mʳ John Royston Examine Count or Number the Tobᵒ: plants in yᵉ third and fourth ℔recinct of yᵉ Sᵈ parish as the Law them Directs

Itt tis ordered by the Sᵈ Vestry that mʳ William Brooking and Robt Carter Examine Count or Numbʳ: the Tobᵒ: plants in yᵉ fifth and Sixth precinct of yᵉ Sᵈ parish as the Law them Directs

Itt tis ordered by the sᵈ Vestry that mʳ Seth Thurston & Benjᵃ Baker Examine Count or Numbʳ the Tobᵒ: plants in yᵉ Seventh ℔recinct of yᵉ Sᵈ ℔arish as the Law them Directs

Itt tis ordered by yᵉ Sᵈ Vestry that mʳ John Reade and mʳ Thomas Whiting Examine Count or Numbʳ the Tobᵒ: plants in the Eight and Ninth ℔recinct of the Sᵈ ℔arish as the Law then Directs

   True Entʳʳ   Teſt Jnᵒ Carter Cˡ ℔ ℔ V

---

*Note! This whole name has been scratched through in the MS., but is still legible.—C. G. C.

[184] Note! This page of the MS. is blank.—C. G. C.

[185]

Att A Vestry held for Petso Parish Octo^r ye 8th: 1724

P'sent the Revn^d Em^{ll} Johes Minist^r
Capt Thomas Buckner
Mr William Miller   ⎫   Mr Francis Wyatt
Mr Augt Smith   ⎪   Mr Thos Reade
Mr Thos. Green   ⎬   Mr John Royston & Mr Fra thorn-
Mr John Reade   ⎭   ton C:W:

Dep^r	Toba
To the Revend Em^{ll}: Jones Minist^r	16000
To William Grumly C^l Church	01000
To Thos Eastor Sextonis	01000
To D^o Eastor for his first labour in Cleaning the Church	00200
To John Carter C^l Vestry	01000
To Mr Fra Thornton for Keeping Geo: Stichall	00800
To John McWilliams Acco^t	00235
To Mr Augt Smith for Keeping John Barnett	00800
To John Willcocks Acco^t	00040
To Capt John Claytons Acco^t	00165
To Docto^r Walford for Keeping Mary Shurrud	00800
To Robt Pourtus Keeping John Marvill a Child Nine Months	00600
To Maj^r: Henry Willis 4 barrills of Corne D D ye wid^o Terry & Sam^{ll} Whitseed	00240
To John Grimes Keeping Eliz^a Pursur Six Weeks	00099
To William Miller one Leive over Charged the Last year	00041
To Mr John Royston for Keeping Thos Wooten 6 weeks and Buriall & Regt^r	00203
To Mr Thomas Green for Regt^r Sarah Yaman	3
To Mary Hill for Releffe	00300

To Thoˢ Grindly Senʳ for Releff	00300
To Jane May for Releff	00300
	24126
By Tobᵒ Due from yᵉ C:W:	169
	*23955
To Caske & Sallʳʸ: of 23955ˡᵇ Tobᵒ: @ 13 ℔ʳ Ct. is 3114	3114
	27069
Credʳ:	
by 832 Tithables @ 33ˡᵇ Tobᵒ ℔ʳ pole is	27456
By Tobᵒ: Due to the Parish the Next Year	387
	27456

[186]

Ordred by this P'sent Vestry that mʳ Francis Thornton Pay the Reverend Emˡˡ: Jones £3:00ˢ:10½ᵈ it being the money in his hands Due to the Parish & mʳ John Royston pay him 3ˢ:3½ᵈ

It tis allso ordʳ yᵗ mʳ John Royston pay the Revenᵈ Emˡˡ Jones £6:12ˢ:3ᵈ being all the Parish money in his hands   It tis Allso ordʳ that mʳ John Royston pay John Grimes £00:19ˢ:09ᵈ out of the Parish money in his hands and mʳ William Miller five Shillˢ: for one Tythable over Charged him the Last year

Ordred that Geo: Stichall have but 500ˡᵇ Tobᵒ: the Next Year and for to Choose his Maſtʳ

Ordred that John Barnett orphint Child be bound to mʳ Augᵗ Smith at two yeares old and mʳ Augᵗ Smith to have 500ˡᵇ of Tobᵒ: then for takeing the Sᵈ Child

---
*Note the mistake in subtraction.—C. G. C.

Ord^r: It tis allso ordrd by this ℙ^{r}ſent Vestry that all orphants Children bound out by the ℙarish hereafter that if they canot Read at thirteen years old that then they Shall be Sett free from theire then S^d Maſt^r or Miſt^{rs} or to taken from them

Children Read 13

It is Agreed by this ℙ^{r}sent Vestry that Doct^r Walford Keep Mary Shurrud Dureing her Life the parish finding her Cloathes & paying him 800^{lb} of Tob°: ℙ^r Annum So Long as he doath Keep her and that the C^l of the Vestry Take his bond to the Church Wardens of the parish *to *perform for his performance of the Agreement

Ordred that William Grumly C^l Church have but 800^{lb} pound of Tob°: and Cask the Next Year

Ordred that the C^l of the Vestry have but 500^{lb} Tob°: and Cask the Next Year

Ord^r that m^r Augt Smith be Church Warden in the upper ℙrecinct of this parish and Mr William Miller for the Lower ℙ^{r}ct

Ordred that m^r John Royston and m^r Fra Thornton be Diſcharged from their C:W: Ship

[187]

Ordred that the Church Wardens Recive of Every Tythable Person in this ℙarish 33^{lb} pound of Tob°: and uppon Refusal of the payment of the Same the Church Wardens are hereby Required to Make Diſtreſs for the Same

True Entry Test

---

*Note! These words are scratched through in the MS., but are still legible.—C. G. C.

184   VESTRY BOOK OF PETSWORTH PARISH

fine money from Eᵈ. West } Entry April yᵉ 8ᵗʰ 1725
That Mʳ Augustin Smith Chur Warden Recᵈ of Mʳ Francis Thornton £2:4ˢ To be Distributed to the pore of the Pariſh As after mentionᵈ: Alſo £1:17ˢ more pᵈ To Mʳ William Miler Chur. Warden for Uſe aforsᵈ. and Distributed a foloweth

Mʳ Smith to pay vizᵗ } To Widdow Bond 10ˢ. To Widdow Terry 10ˢ To Katherine Smith 10ˢ. To Jnᵒ. Galleman 10 and to the Widdow Siner 4 Shillings

Mʳ Miller to pay vizᵗ } To Daniel Danbee 10ˢ. To Jane May 10ˢ To Thomas Easter 10ˢ To Richᵈ Halcomb 7ˢ

True Entry Test   W Brooking Cl Vestry

[188]

At A Vestry held for Petso Pariſh the 28ᵗʰ day of June 1725

Preſent
The Reverᵈ. Emanul Jones
Capᵗ Thomas Buckner   Mʳ John Reade
Mʳ Thomas Cooke   Mʳ Thomas Green
Mʳ John Royston   Capᵗ John Waſhington
Mʳ Francis Wyatt   Mʳ. Thomas Reade
    Mʳ William Miler Church Wardin

In purſuant to An Act of Aſsembly Intituld An Act for the better and more Effectual Improving the Staple of Tobacco This preſent Vestry has Ordered the Tobᵒ. Counters in Each precinct of this pariſh As foloweth
Vizᵗ

Ordered that Mʳ. Thomas Green and Mʳ. John Smith Take the Number of Tobᵒ. plants growing in the first &

Second precint of This parifh according to the Dyrections of the Abovfaid Act of Afsembly

Ordered that Cap: John Alexander & Mr John Royston take the Number of Tob^o plants in the Third and fourth precint As afors^d.

Ordered that Mr Robert Carter & Wm Brooking Take the Number of plants in the fifth & Sixth precint as Aforsaid

Ordered that Mr Seth Thurston & Mr Benj^a Baker Take the Number of plants In the Seventh precint As aforsaid

Ordered that M^r. John Reade & Mr Thomas Whiting Take the Number of plants in the Eight & Ninth precint of the Said parifh as aforfaid

True Entry Test   W Brooking Cl V

[189]

THIS INDENTURE, mad the Thirtenth day of April In the Year of our Lord God one thoufand Seaven hundred & Twenty five and In the tenth year of the Reigne of Our Soverigne Lord King George of Great Brittaine, France & Ireland, Defendor of the faith &^{a}, WITNEfSETH that I Wm Brooking Clark of ye parifh of Petso In Gloster County Do firmly and In the name and behalf of the Vestry of the parifh afors^d bind Unto Augustin Smith Gent^n Church warding of the Parifh afors^d. One Orphen boy named John Burnett of the Age of Two years 14th las Jan^{ry} from thence to Serve Untill he Arives to the Age as the Law Dyrects to Serve him the Said Augus^{tn} Smith his heire Executors adm^{rs}. and Afsignes in all maner of Lawfull Servis and Imployment that he Shall Set him About And the Said Augustin Smith Doth bind & Oblidge himfelf his heirs & Afsignes &^{a}, to give the Said John Burnet three years Schooling and cearfully Instruct him Afterward that he may read well in Any part of the Bible and alſo to Instruct & Learn him Such Lawful way or ways that he may be Able After his Indentured time is Expired to get his own living and to allow him good Sufficent meat Drink waſhing lodging & apperil During his Indenterd Time and After the Said time is Expired to pay him all Such Allowances as the law Dyrects In Such caſes as alſo to Keep the pariſh harmleſs from his being any ways Chargable or burdenſom to them During his Indentured time IN WITNEſS whearof we have hearunto Set our hand & Seals this day & year firs Written

 Sealed and Signed
 In preſents of Uſs
   his   Aug^{tn}: Smith (Seal)
 Thoˢ T Roſs
   mark
 Susᵃ: Brooking

[190]

At a Vestry Held for Petso Pariſh the 6th day of October 1725

Preſent
The Revr^{d}. Emanuel Jones

Mr John Reade   Cap^{n} John Waſhington
Mr Thomas Green   Mr Thomas Reade
Mr William Miller & Mr Aug^{n}. Smith Ch Wardens

   Petso Pariſh Detter this Year In Tobacco

To the Rever^{d}. Emanuel Jones	16000^{lb}
To Thomas Easter Sextorn of the Church	01000
To Wm Brooking Clark of the Church & Vestry 10^{m} month	01167
To W^{m}: Grumley for 2 mo: Servis as Cl of Chur	00133
To Mr Augustin Smith for Keeping John Burnet	00700
To Mr John Cleyton for Clarks fees to parish	00178

To M'r Augustin Smith for perticuler Charges	00585
To Robert Portuse Esq'r for Keeping Two bars-terd Children viz't John & Watkinſon Marvil	01333½
To M'rs. Stubbs Upon Acc't of Geo Stichal Maintanince	00500
To M'r John Carter for Keeping Eliza Gibſon & Clothes	00800
To Capn. Steven Robbins for Eliza. Purſers pasage to Englanᵈ	00600
To M'r William Miller for Keeping Eliza Karr	00800
To M'r Francis Easter for Comunion Wine	00090
To John Mᶜwilliams Acc't	00035
To Thomas Grindee for Keeping Mary Sherard 10 month	00416½
To Mary Hill for Relief	00300
To Margret Bond for Keeping Thomas Griffing	00500
To Richᵈ. Halcomb for Relief	00200
To Jane May Widdow for Relief	00300
To the Church Wardins for the Uſe of Daniel Danbee	00300
	25938
To Cask & Salery on 25938 @ 13 ℔ Cent	3372
Totall	29310

Petso Parish Credit

By 819 Titheables at 36ˡ ℔ pole is	29484	25938
	29310	
		65
By Ballance due from the Church Warden	174	
By Ballance Due the Last Year	137	
Caryed up	311	

[191] Brought Upp

It is ordered by this preſent Vestry that Mʳ William Miller And Mʳ Augustin Smith Church Wardens Collect of Every Titheable perſon In this parish 36ˡ of Tobᵒ. to Discharge the parish debts As Aforsaid

Upon the Motion of Capᵗ Thomas Buckner deſiring to be Excuſed from Serving As A Vestryman any longer he is discharged of the Said office

This day Capⁿ John Alexander Was Elected And Choſen Vestryman in the Rome of Capⁿ Buckner & Took the Oaths of Vestrymen &cᵃ

Upon the petetion of John Wills Seting fourth that he is Antient & not able to labour for a livehood he is discharged from paying Any more pariſh leveys for the futer

True Entry Test WBrooking Cl Vestry

*Att thomas Kemps

Att A Vestry held for Petso Parrish the 7ᵗʰ Day of June 1726

Present
The Reverᵈ. Emanuel Jones
Mʳ. Augustin Smith Church Warding

Mʳ John Royston   } Mʳ Fra: Thornton
Mʳ Fra: Wyatt   }
Mʳ. John Reade   } Capⁿ Jnᵒ Washington

At this Vestry Majʳ. Henry Willis Was Ellected And Chosen Vestryman In the Rome of Mʳ Wᵐ Miller Decᵈ & Stands Church Warden In his Stead

---

*Note! The words "Att thomas Kemps" are in a different hand from that of the other entries on this page, and they appear to have been carelessly scrawled rather than to have been carefully written. It is the opinion of the editor that they are not a part of the original record.—C. G. C.

Upon the Motion of David Lewis Moving The Vestry that He is Very Indigent & Dropsical & Not able to Labour It is ordered that he bee to the Cear of Majʳ Willis and that he orde[ ] means to him for his helth at the Charge of the Parish

It is alſo Ordered that he pay No more pariſh levey

    Turn over
[192]   At this Vestry

In purſuant to an Act of Aſsembly Intituld An Act for the Better & more Effectual Improving the Staple of Tobacco this present Vestry as on the Other side mentioned have Ordered and appointed the Tobacco Counters In Each precint of this Parish As followeth Vizᵗ

Ordered that Mʳ William Barnard and Mʳ John Smith Take the Number of plants In the first and Second precint of this parish According to the Dyrections of the Said Act

Ordered that Majᵒʳ Henry Willis & Mʳ John Royston Take the Number of plants In the third & fourth precint a aforsaid

Ordered that Mʳ Robert Carter & William Brooking Take the Number of plants Groing the fifth & Sixh precint as aforesaid

Ordered that Mʳ Benjamin Baker and Mʳ Alexander Roane Take the Number of plants Groing In the Seventh precint as aforsaid

Ordered that Mʳ. Conquest Wyatt and Mʳ Wᵐ. Cemp Take the Number of plants Groing In Eight & Ninth precint as aforesaid

    True Entry Test
      W Brooking Cˡ V

[193]

At A Vestory held for Petsoe Parish Octobʳ: yᵉ 5ᵗʰ, 1726

Preſent Vizᵗ   The Reverᵈ Emanuell Jones
        Mʳ Augustin Smith Ch. Warden
  Mʳ John Royston   Mʳ Fra: Thornton
  Mʳ Fra: Wyatt   Mʳ Jnº Throckmorton
  Mʳ John Reade   Mʳ Thomas Reade
                      Cap: Jnº Alexander

Petso Parish mad Dʳ: In Tobacco this Year

To the Revᵈ Emanuel Jones	16000
To Thomas Easter Sexton	1000
To Wᵐ Brooking Cleark of the Church & Vestry	1600
To John Fleming for making a Coffin for David Lewis	200
To Henry Greenwood for making a Coffin for John More	200
To Cap: John Cleytons Accº. ℔ List of Titheabls	20
To Thomas Grindy for 2 Coffins & burials of Mary Sherd And A Child & for Keeping Mary Sherard 2 months	496
To John Grimes for Keeping Elizᵃ. Purser 6 weaks	92
To Doʳ. Edward Walford for Keeping Eliz. Gibſon one Year	800
To Mʳ. Thomas Reads Account for Goods for the pore	287½
To Thomas Driver for Keeping & Burying Geo Stichal	300
To Mʳ Augustin Smith for yᵉ paymᵗ: of 7ˡᵇ: 18ˢ: 2ᵈ to Ann Denis	1581
To Mʳˢ. Ann Miller Upon Account of Elizᵃ Karr	190
To Mʳˢ Fra Easter for 3 botls of Wine & Erecting a Dyal post	165
To Mʳ Law: Smith for Keeping John Marvil a baster Child	800

To the Rev⁴ Em¹. Jones for paying the q'rents of the Glieb land	705
To Mag': Bond for Keeping Thomas Griffing 6 months	300
To the Rev⁴ Em°. Jones for q'rents of the Glieb land this Year	54
To Maj': Henry Willis for paying of £6. 0ˢ 0ᵈ Cash	1200
To Mʳ Augⁿ Smiths Acc°. £4. 4. 8ᵈ & 45¹ᵇ Tob°.	888
To Mʳ Wᵐ. Thornton for 1 baril of Corn to Da. Lewis	80
To Mary Hill for Relief	600
To Jane May for Relief	600
To Richᵈ Halcomb for Relief	200
	28358½
Cask and Salery	3686
Parish Debt	32045
Parish Credit	
By 852 Titheables @ 39¹ᵇ ⅌ pole is	33228
Parish Debt is	32045
Remanes Due Upon Ballance	1183

Turn over

[194]   Brought Over

It is Ordered by this preſent Vestory that the ballance Due to the parish As on the Other Side is Given to the Reverᵈ Emanuel Jones for the Intent that A Tobacco house Should be built on on the Glieb At his Charge & the Ch: Wardens to pay the Same

At this preſent Vestory Mʳ Augustin Smith Was Dischargeᵈ from Being Church warden he having mad Up his Accoumpᵗˢ With the Vestory And Mʳ Francis Wyatt is Elected Church Warden for the Uper precincts of Petsoe Parish in his Stead

It is ordered by the present Vestory that Major Henry Willis and Mʳ Fra Wyat Collect of Each Titheable person Within their Respective Precint Within this Parish 39ᵇ Tobacco to Discharge the Parish Debts

It is Ordered that John Marvil A Basterd Child be bound to Mʳ Lawrance Smith And Upon Consideration of the Payment of 800ᵇ Tobacco to the Said Smith Capⁿ. Thomas Buckner Did promise the Vestry that the Said John Marvil Should be no more Burdensom to the Parish

True Entry Test WBrooking Cl Vestry

A A Vestry Held for Petso Parish December yᵉ 23ᵈ: 1726

Present The Revᵈ Emanuel Jones ⎫ Mʳ Fra: Thornton
    Mʳ Augⁿ. Smith ⎬ Mʳ Thomas Green
    Mʳ John Read ⎭ Capⁿ Jnᵒ Washington
    Mʳ Francis Wyat Church Warden

Upon the Motion of Mʳ Francis Wyatt moving the Vestory yᵗ he might be protected in the Execution of his Office it is Ordered that the Church wardens of the Parish of Petso be Allowed All Such Charges as they Shall be At In the due Execution of their offices At the Charg of the parish

Capⁿ. John Washington Desired that It might be Entred that he Doth not Consent to the Making the Abosᵈ. Order by Reason he Doth not Agre to the laying of the levey this present Year

At this Vestory Mʳ. John Reade Struck his Name Out of the Vestory Book And Would Stand No longer Vestory man

True Entry Test WBrooking Cl Vestry

[195]

THIS INDENTURE mad the Sixh day of Febuary in the Year of our Lord God one Thousand Seaven hundred

And Twenty Six And in the Eleventh year of the Reigne of
Our Sovereigne Lord King George of Great Brittaine
France & Ireland Defendor of the faith &ᶜ Wittneſseth that
I William Brooking Cleark of Petso Parish Vestory In
Gloster County Do firmly And in the name and Behalf of
the Vestory aforesᵈ. Bind Unto Mʳ Lawrance Smith one
Bastard Child Named John Marvil of the Age of Two years
or thearabouts from thence to Serve the Said Lawrance
Smith his heirs And Aſsignes Untill he arives to Lawfull
Age In all & all maner of Lawfull Imployment As he or
they Shall Set him About. And the Said Lawrance Smith
doth bind And Oblidge himself his heirs Executors Admʳˢ.
& Aſsignes to Give the Said John Marvil three years
Schooling & Cearfully Instruct *him Cause to be Instruct
Afterward that he may Read Well In Any part of the
bible And Alſo to Learne or Couse to be Lerned or In-
structed Such Lawfull Way or Ways that he may be Able
after his Indentured time is Expired to Get his Own Living
and Alſo During his Indentured time to †Expired Alow
him Good Sufficent meet Drink Washing Lodging And
Apperil And at the Expiration of the Said time to pay him
All Such Allowances As the Law in Such Cases do Allow
As Alſo to Keep the Parish harmleſs from his being Any
Ways Chargeable or Burdenſom to them During the Said
Term In Wittneſs Wherof We hereunto Sat our hands
& Seals this day & Year first Written

Signed And Seald In prestˢ. of
   Alexʳ Roane
                                   Lawʳ. Smith (Seal)
   Tho Tho Baytop

---

   *Note! Over—not above—the word "him," which is otherwise unerased in the MS., has been written by the same hand the word "Or." Both words are entirely legible.—C. G. C.

   †Note! The word "Expired" is scratched through in the MS., but is entirely legible.—C. G. C.

And Twenty Six And in the Eleventh year of the Reigne of Our Sovereigne Lord King George of Great Brittaine France & Ireland Defendor of the faith &ᶜ Wittneſseth that I William Brooking Cleark of Petso Parish Vestory In Gloster County Do firmly And in the name and Behalf of the Vestory aforesᵈ. Bind Unto Mʳ Lawrance Smith one Bastard Child Named John Marvil of the Age of Two years or thearabouts from thence to Serve the Said Lawrance Smith his heirs And Aſsignes Untill he arives to Lawfull Age In all & all maner of Lawfull Imployment As he or they Shall Set him About. And the Said Lawrance Smith doth bind And Oblidge himself his heirs Executors Admʳˢ. & Aſsignes to Give the Said John Marvil three years Schooling & Cearfully Instruct *him Cause to be Instruct Afterward that he may Read Well In Any part of the bible And Alſo to Learne or Couse to be Lerned or Instructed Such Lawfull Way or Ways that he may be Able after his Indentured time is Expired to Get his Own Living and Alſo During his Indentured time to †Expired Alow him Good Sufficent meet Drink Washing Lodging And Apperil And at the Expiration of the Said time to pay him All Such Allowances As the Law in Such Cases do Allow As Alſo to Keep the Parish harmleſs from his being Any Ways Chargeable or Burdenſom to them During the Said Term In Wittneſs Wherof We hereunto Sat our hands & Seals this day & Year first Written

Signed And Seald In prestˢ. of
   Alexʳ Roane

                              Lawʳ. Smith (Seal)
   Tho Tho Baytop

*Note! Over—not above—the word "him," which is otherwise unerased in the MS., has been written by the same hand the word "Or." Both words are entirely legible.—C. G. C.

†Note! The word "Expired" is scratched through in the MS., but is entirely legible.—C. G. C.

It is Order^d that Mr Francis Wyatt & Mr Seth Thornton Ch: Wardens Petetion the Court to move Thomas Griffing & Eliz^a Marcey to the Respective Parishes from Whence They came

It is Ordered that the Church Wardens Petetion the Court for to turn the Road back of the Vestry house by the Church

It is Ordered that Elizabeth Wethers An Orphen Girl be bound to Francus Arthur if She will Take her; if Not to be bound to Mr Conq^t Wyatt

      True Entry WBrooking Cl Vestory
[197]

THIS INDENTURE made the fourth day of Decemb^r In the Year of Our Lord God: one Thousand Seaven hundred & Twenty Seven WITNEſSETH that I William Brooking Cleark of Petso Parish Vestory in Gloster County Do firmly and in the Name and Behalf of the Vestory Aforsaid Bind Unto Mr Francis Wyatt One Orphen Girl Named Elizabeth Sanders about the Age of Twelve Years or therabouts from thence to Serve the Said Francis Wyatt his heirs And Aſsignes Untill She Arive to *the Age †of ‡Eighteen in all and all maner of Lawfull Employments As he his heirs or Aſsignes Shall Sat her About And the Said Francis Wyatt his heirs Executors am^rs. And Aſsignes Do oblidge themſelves to Give the Said Orphen Girl Thre years Schooling or In Struct or cause to be Instructed that She may Read perfectly in Any part of the bible And Also to Lern or Cause to be Learned & Instructed Such Lawfull Way or Waies that She may be Able After her Indentured time is Expired to get her own living And Also to allow the Said Elizabeth Sanders Good Sufficent

---

 *Note. The word "the" in the MS. has been scratched through and the word "Lawfull" written above it.—C. G. C.
 †Note! The word "of" in the MS. has been scratched through. —C. G. C.
 ‡Note! The word "Eighteen" in the MS. has been scratched through.—C. G. C.

meet Drink washing Lodging And Apperil During the Said Term And At the Expiration of the Said Term to pay her all Such Allowances as the Law in Such caſes alows As also to Keep the parish harmleſs and Indamnified by her being Any waies Chargable or burdenſom to Them During the Said Term In Wittneſs Whearof the parties have put their hand And Seals this day & Year first Written
Sealed And Delivered
In Presents of Uſs   (Lawfull) Enterlined
   Jnº Alexander
   Seth Thornton   Francis Wyatt   (Seal)

[198]

At A Vestry on Thursday the 31ᵗʰ day of August 1727

Present   The Revᵈ: Emanuel Jones
Mʳ Augustin Smith   ⎫   Cap Jnº Alexander
Mʳ John Royston   ⎬   Mʳ Conqᵗ. Wyatt
Mʳ: Fra: Thornton   ⎭   Mʳ Seth Thornton Ch Ward
Cap: Jnº Washington

It is Ordered by this preſent Vestory that Francis Brown An Orphen Boy of George Brown Decᵈ. be Bound to Richar Adams Bricklayer according to Order of Court to Learn his Trade

It is Ordered that Edward Carter Roſs Son of Christian Roſs Decᵈ. Be bound to Mʳ Augustin Smith to Serve till Lawfull Age

It is ordered that Sarah Sanders An Orphen Girl be Bound to William Robinſon Untill Lawful Age

It is Ordered that Mʳ John Clark & Mʳ John Smith Sawyer See the Lands preceſioned Within the first Precints of this Parish According to Law

It is Ordered Mʳ William Thornton Jnʳ & Mʳ Thomas Cook Junʳ See the Lands preceſioned Within the Second prects of this Parish According to Law

It is Ordered that Mʳ Thomas Scot & Mʳ Francis Easter See the Lands preceſioned Within the Third precint of this Parish According to Law

It is Ordered that Mʳ John Carter & Mʳ Richar Crittenden See the Lands preceſioned Within the *fifth precint of this Parish According to Law

It is Ordered that Mʳ Robert Carter and William Brooking See the Lands Within the fifth precint of this Parish Preceſioned According to Law

It is Ordered that Mʳ. Alexander Roane and Mʳ Thomas Amis See the Lands Within the Sixth precint Preſesioned According to Law

Caryed Up

[199]

It is Ordered that Mʳ Benjamin Baker and Mʳ John Garland See the Lands Within the Seventh Precint preceſioned According to Law

It is Ordered by this preſent Vestory that Mʳ John Reade & Mʳ Thomas Whiting See the Lands Within yᵉ Eight precint of this Parish poſseſioned According to Law

It is Ordered that Mʳ John Wyatt And Mʳ James Wyatt See the Lands Within the Ninth Precint of this Parish precſioned Acording to Law

True Entry Test

WBrooking Cl Vestry

---

*Note! So in the MS. Evidently a mistake for "fourth."— C. G. C.

At a Vestory held for Petsoe Parish December the 4th: 1727

Present the Rev^d. Emanul Jones

Mr Augustin Smith ⎫ Mr Fra: Wyat Ch wad^n.
Mr Thomas Green   ⎬ Cap John Aalexander
Mr Francis Thornton ⎭ Mr Seth Thornton Ch wd^n

It is ordered by this present Vestory that Grace Brown Orphen of George Brown Be bound to Frances Semonds Widow to Edward Semonds Dec^d. According to an order of Gloster County Court mad to the Said Edward Baring date the 26 day of January 1726

It is ordered by this Vestory that an orphen Girl named Jane Dowling Be bound to Edward Whitehorne According to An Order of Gloster County Court Baring Date the 24th day of August 1727

True Redgester Test

WBrooking Cl Vestry

[200]

THIS INDENTURE, Mad ye 14 day of Novemb^r. In the year of Our Lord God one Thousand Seaven hundred and Twenty ſeeaven and in the first year of the Reigne of our Sovereign Lord King George the Second of Great Brittaine France & Ireland Defend^r of the faith &c^a Wittneſseth that I Will. Brooking Cleark of the Parish of Petsoe in the County of Gloster Do in the name and Behalf of the Vestry of the Said Parish aforesaid (According to An Order of Gloster County Court Dyrected to them) Bind unto Richard Adams Bricklayer one orphen Boy named Francis Brown about the age of thirteen from thence to Serve the Said Richard Adams his heirs and Aſsignes after the maner of An Apprentis Untill he arives to the age as the Law Directs during Which time the Said Richard Adams doth promis for himself his heirs Exo^rs. Adm^rs & Aſsignes to give Unto the Said Francis Brown three years Schooling or Teach or cause to be taught that he may

Read perfectly in any part of the Bible and also to Teach or cause to be Taught to the S^d. Francis the art Trade or mistry of A Bricklayer and allſo to allow the S^d. Francis Good Sufficent meat Drink washing Lodging & Cloathing fit for Such an apprentis and at the Expiration of the Said Term to pay him all Such Allowances as are Uſuall & Allowed to apprentis'es in Such cases and alſo to Keep the Parish harmleſs from his being Any waies chargable or Burdenſom to them During the time as aforsaid IN WITTNEſS We have hearunto Interchangably Set our hands & Seals the day & year first Written
Signed & Seald
in the Presents of

   his
Thomas   T   Roſs
  mark   Richard Adams (Seal)
John Waller

[201]

THIS INDENTURE mad the Seventh day of Octob^r. In the year of our Lord God one Thousand Seaven hundred and Twenty Seven and in the first year of the Reigne of our Sovereigne Lord King George by the grace of God King of Great Brittaine France & Ireland Defendor the faith &^{ca} Wittneſseth that I William Brooking Clerk of Petso Parish Vestry in Gloster County Do firmly and in the name and Behalf of the Vestry aforsaid Bind Unto m^r Augustin Smith one Basterd Boy named Edward Carter Roſs of the age *of *the *age of Thirteen Next Febuary from thence to Serve the Said Augustin Smith his heirs and aſsignes in all and all maner of Lawfull Emplyments Untill he Shall arive to Lawfull Age, and the Said Augustin Smith his heirs &c^a Do Oblige Themſelves to give the Said Boy as aforsaid Three years Schooling

---

*Note! These words have been scratched through in the MS, but are still legible.—C. G. C.

or Instruct or cause to be Instructed that he may Read perfectly in any part of the Bible alſo to Learn or cause to be Lerned & Instructed Such Lawful way or waies that he may be able after his Indentured time is Expired to get his own Living and Alſo to Allow the Said Edward Carter Roſs Good & Sufficent meat drink Waſhing Lodging and apperil During the Said Time And At the Expiration of the Said Term as aforsaid to pay him all Such allowances as the Law in Such caſes Allowes as alſo to Kee the parish harmleſs and Indamny^d from his being any waies Chargable or Burdenſom to Them During the Said Term In Wittneſs wherof we have Interchangeably Set our hands & Seals this day & year first Written Signed And Seald
in the Presents of
 John Royton   Aug^{tn}: Smith (Seal)
 Conq^t: Wyatt

[202]

At A Vestory Held for Petso Parish on Saturday the 7th oct^r 1727

Present The Revd Emanul Jones
Mr Augustin Smith   Capⁿ John Alexander
Mr John Royston   M^r. Conq^t Wyatt
Mr Thomas Green   Mr Seth Thornton Ch ward

Petso Parish made Detter this Year (Viz)	Tob^o
To the Revd Emanuel Jones	16000
To Will Brooking Clerk Chur: & Vestry	1600
To Thomas Easter Sexton of the Church	1000
To Cap Jno Cleytons acc^o	0020
To Mr Francis Wyatts Acc^o	0350
To William Brookings Acc^o	0139
To Benjamin Bakers Acc^o	0100
To Mr Augustin Smiths Acc^o	0090
To Mr Seth Thorntons Acc^o	0120

To Doc' Hugh Nodens Acc° for Sarah Smiths Legg	1740
To the Rev⁴ Em⁸ Jones Acco	615
To John Flemings Acc°	350
To Francis Easters Acc° for Wine	280
To Geor Farys Acc° for Looking after Th°: Griffin	695
To Margret Bond Acc°	039
To the Rev⁴ Em⁸. Jones for q'rents the Glib Land	054
To Daniel Dickenſon for Keeping Sarah Smith	240
To Susanah West Wid°. for Relief	350
To Richard Holcomb for Relief	244
Parish Debt	24033
Cask & Salery @ 13 ℔ C	3124
Total Sum in Tob°	27157

Par is Credit

By 823 Tytheables @ 33ᵗᵇ Tob° ℔ pole	27159
Par Debt	27157
Remaind'	00002

Petso Parish alſo Detter To 1 Shiling In mony or 12ᵗᵇ Tobacco ℔ pole Which amounts to £41: 3ˢ or 9876¹ Tob. Which the Church Wardens are to Collect Towards the Building A Brick Wall Round the Church.

It is Order that Grace Brown be Bound to Edward Semonds till Lawfull age

WBrooking Cl Vestr

[203]

This Indenture mad the Ninth day of January In the year of our Lord God one Thousand Seven hundred & Twenty Seven And in the first Year of the Reigne of Our Sovereigne Lord King George the Second King of England Scotland France & Ireland Defender of the faith &ᶜ Wittneſseth that I

William Brooking Clerk of Petso Parish Vestory In Gloster County Do firmly & In the name and behalf of the Vestory of the Said Parish Bind Unto Mrs Frances Semonds one Orphen Girl Named Grace Brown about the Age of Eleven Years or therabouts from thence to Serve the Said Frances Semonds her heirs And Aſsignes in all & all maner of Lawfull Serves & Employments that Shee the Said Frances Semonds her heirs and aſsignes Shall Lawfully Set her the Said Grace Brown About Untill She Arive to Lawfull Age And the Said Frances Semonds for herſelf her heirs Aſsignes Doth promis covenant & agree to give Unto the Said Grace Brown Three Years Schooling or to Cearfully teach or Cause to be Taught that She may Read perfectly in Any part of the Bible and alſo to teach or Cause to be taught Unto the Said Grace Brown ſuch Lawfull way or wais that She may be able after her Indentured time is Expired to Get her own Living and Alſo to Alow her good Sufficent meet Drink Waſhing Lodging & Apperil During the Said Term and at the Expiration of the time Aforsaid to pay her all Such allowances as are Uſeial & as the Law Allowes in Such Caces and alſo to Keep her from being any waies Chargeable or Burdenſom to the parish Aforsaid During the S^d: Term In Wittneſs Wee have Set our hands & Seals the day & year first Written
Signed Seald And Testified
  In Preſents of Us

    Thos: Scott
       his
    Edward Ⱳ Whithorn   Francis Simands (Seal)
       mark

[204]

THIS INDENTURE mad the Ninth day of January in the year of our Lord Christ one Thousand Seven hundred and Twenty Seaven & in the first year of the Reigne of Our

Sovereigne *of *our *Sovereigne Lord King George the Second of Great Brittaine France & Ireland King Defender of the faith &ᶜᵃ WITNEſSETH that I William Brooking Clark *of of Petso Parish Vestory in Gloster County Do firmly and In yᵉ Name and Behalf of Mʳ Francis Wyatt and Mʳ Seth Thornton Gentmⁿ Church Wardens of the Parish of Petso In Gloster County According to An Order of Gloster County Court Dyrected to them Bind Unto Edward Whitehorn one orphen Girl named Jane Dowling About yᵉ Age of Ten Years or Therabouts ——— from thence to Serve the Said Edward Whitehorn his heirs & Aſsignes in all & all maner of Lawfull Serveces & Employments that he the Said Edward Whitehorne his heirs & Aſsignes Shall Set her About Untill She arives to Lawfull Age & the Said Edward Whitehorn for himself his heirs and Aſsignes Doth promis Covenant & Agree to Give the Said Jane Dowling Three years Schooling or to Cearfully Teach or Cauſe to be taught that She may Read perfectly in any part of the Bible and Alſo To Teach or Cause to be Taught Unto The Said Jane Dowling Such Lawfull way or Waies that She may be able after her Indentured Time is Expired to get her own Living and Alſo to Allow her Good Sufficent meat Drink waſhing Lodging And Apperrill During the Said Time and At the Expiration of the Time As Aforsaid to pay her all Such Allowances as Are Uſeiall and As the Law allows in Such Caces And Alſo to Keep her from being Any Waies Chargable or Burdenſom to the Parish As aforsᵈ. During the Said Term In Wittneſs Wee have Set our hands and Seals Interchangably to Each other the Day & year first Written

Signed Seald & Declard
  In Preſents of Us
    Thoˢ: Scott
    Thoˢ. Greene

                          his
                    Edward ᴍ Whitehorn (Seal)
                         mark

*Note! These words have been scratched through in the MS., but are still legible.—C. G. C.

[205]

*I At a Vestory held for Petsoe

THIS INDENTURE mad the Twenty fourth day of may In the Year of our Lord God one Thousand Seven hundred & Twenty Eight & In the first Year of the Regne of our Sovereigne Lord King George the Second of Great Britaine France & Ireland Defedor of the faith &ª WITTNEſSETH that I William Brooking Cleark of Petsoe Parish Vestory in Gloster County Do firmly & in the Name & Behalf to the Genⁿ Church Wardens & Vestory of the Parish Aforsaid *bind According to An Order of Vestry dated Thursday the 29 of June 1727 Bind Unto Frances Arther one Orphen Girl named Elizabᵗʰ Wethers of the Age of Twelve yeas old Las January —— from thence to Serve the Said Frances Arther her heirs or Aſsignes in all & all maner of Lawfull Serveses & Employments as She Shall Set her About Untill She Arives to Lawfull Age and the Said France[] Arther Doth promis Covenant & Agree to Give the Said Orpen Girl Three Years Schooling (Together with what She has had) and Cearfully Teach & Instruct her afterwards that She may Read perfectly in any part of the Bible and Alſo to Teach or Cause to be Taught Unto the Said Elizabeth Wethers Such Lawfull way or Waies that She may be Able After her Indentured time is Expired to Get her own Living and Alſo to Allow her Good Sufficent meat Drink Waſhing Loging And April During the Said time And at the Expiracon of the time as aforsᵈ. to pay her all Such Allowances As Are Uſeial and as the Law in Such Cases alowes as alſo to Keep the Parish harmleſs & Indamnified from her Being Any waies Chargable or Burdenſom to them During the Time as aforsaid IN WITTNEſS We

---

*Note! This whole line has been scratched through in the MS., but is still legible.—C. G. C.

have Enterchangably Set to our hands & Seals the day & year first Written

her	her
Susana + Barnes	Frances F Arther (Seal)
mark	mark
Susanna Brooking	

[206]

At A Vestory held for Petso Parish on Tusday the 21th day of may 1728

Present

The Revd Emaluel Jones

Mr John Royston
Mr Aug^n Smith
Mr Thomas Green
Mr Fra: Thornton

Mr John Throckmorton
Mr Conq^t Wyat
Mr Seth Thornton Ch Warden

It is ordered that the fine of Easter Terry being 500^{lb} Tobacco & Cask at 2^d ℔ ^{lb} amo^t. to £4: 6: 4^d in the hands of the Rever^d Emanuel Jones be Distributed to the folowing Perſons viz to Margret Bond Wid° 20 S to the Wid° West 20 S to Eliz^a Brown Wi^{do} 20 S to Jeffry Bourk 20 S to Marcus Bendixon 6^s: 4^d *the *Reverend to be paid in Goods by Mr Jones

It is ordered that Mr Seth Thornton Church warden agree With A Joynor to mend the Church dore that is Broke

It is ordered that the Church Bible be Sent to England to be New Bound & a New Comon Prayer Book be Sent for for the Uſe of the Church & alſo four Duz: panes of London Duble Crownd Glaſs of about 11 & 13: Size to be Sent for by the Rever^d Emanuel Jones At the Charge of the Parish

True Redgester Test
WBrooking Cl Vestry

---

*Note! These words have been scratched through in the MS., but are still legible.—C. G. C.

[207]

At A Vestory Hedl for Petsoe Parish on Saturday ye 5th day of June 1728

Present

The Revd Emanuel Jones

Mr Aug^n Smith	}	Mr Francis Thornton
Mr Thomas Cook		Cap: Jno: Washington
Mr John Royston	}	Cap^n Jno Alexander
Mr John Throckmorton		Mr Conq^t Wyatt
Mr Thos: Green		Mr Seth Thornton C-Wa

According to the Dyrections of An Act of Aſsembly for the Beter & mor Effectual Improving the Staple of Tobacco This present Vestory has Ordered And Appoin^d the Tob^o Tellers in Each precint of this Parish Accordingly (viz)

It is ordered that Mr Thomas Green & Mr John Throckmorton · take the Number of plants Groing in the first & Seccond precint of this Parish According to the Dyrections of the Said Act

It is ordered that Cap^n John Alexander & Mr John Royston Take the Number of plants Growing in the Third & furth precints of this praish According to the Dyrections of the Said Act

It is ordered that Robert Carter & William Brooking Take the Number of plants in the fifth Sixh & Sevent[] precints of this parish According to the Dyrections of the Said Act

It is ordered that Mr Conq^t & Mr James Wyatt Take the Number of plants in the Eight & Ninth precin[] precints of this parish According to the Dyrections of the Said Act

True Redgister Test

WBrooking Cl Vestry

[208]

At a Vestory held for Petsoe Parish the 2ᵈ day of Octʳ 1728

Present   The Revᵈ Emanuel Jones
- Mʳ Augustin Smith
- Mʳ John Royston
- Mʳ Francis Wyat C W
- Mʳ John Throckmorton
- Mʳ Thomas Green
- Mʳ Fra Thornton
- Cap Jnᵒ Alexander
- Mʳ Seth Thornton
- Mʳ Conq Wyatt

	Petsoe Parish mad Detter in Tobᵒ this Year	Tobᵒ
To	the Revᵈ Emanuel Jones	16000
To	Wᵐ Brooking Cl Church & Vestry	1600
To	Thomas Easter Sextorn	1000
To	Capⁿ John Claytons Accᵒ	106
To	Mʳ John Smith Sher: Accᵒ	015
To	Thomas Driver for Keeping Ann Haines & Burying	217
To	Mʳ Francis Wyatts Acco: for Delinqᵗˢ	152
To	Mr Seth Thorntons Accᵒ	834
To	Eliz Hanford for Keeping & Buring Ruth Roboton	300
To	Eliz: Ennis for Keeping Ruth Robotons Child 9 Mᵒ	600
To	the Revᵈ Emˡ Jonses Accᵒ for Qutrents the Glieb	054
To	the Revᵈ Emᵒ Jones Accᵒ — Dᵒ	17
To	Mʳ John Read for Keeping Eliz Mercy 8 mᵒ	533
To	Richᵈ Halcomb for Relief	300
		21728
To	Cask & Sallery @ 18ˡᵇ ℔ C	3911
		25639

Parish Creditt

By 811 Tithables @ 32 ℔ pole	25952
Parish Debt is	25639
Due to the Parish	313

By Delinquents put Into M′ Conq Wyatts hand to Collect
  By John Blakes Levey   33 & *1*S*mony
  By Thomas Swepſons   D° 33
  By Frank Loes   D° 33 & 1 Shil
                                        ———
                                         99
  By Geo Grimes Wife   32 & 1: 6
  By Thomas Drivers Wife 32 & 1: 6

[209]   Brought forward

It is Ordered And Agreed that A Brick Wall be built Round the Church at Popler Spring And that M′ John Moore Undertake the Work Giving Bond & Security to the Churchwardens of Petsoe Parish for the performance of the Said Wall According to Agreement And that he Is to be paid one hundred & forty pounds Corant mony for the Same

It ordered that An Aſseſs of 1/6 ℔ pole or 18ˡᵇ Tobacco be Leveyed on the Titheable perſons of this Parish this present year & to be Gathered to Gether by M′ Conqust Wyat Church Warden Collector of the Said Parish towards the building & paying for the Said Wall

It is Ordered that Capᵗ John Alexander & M′ Conquest Wyat Be Church Wardens In the Roome of †M′ †Augustin †Smith M′ Francis Wyatt & M′ Seth Thornton they having mad Up their Accompts & Discharged

It is ordered that M′ Conquest Wyatt be Collector of the parish of Petsoe this present year & that he Well & truly performe his Several Duties therin Giving Bond & Security for the true performance of the Same According to Law

True Entry Test
WBrooking Cl Vestory

---

*Note! The words "1 S mony" have been scratched through in the MS., but are still legible.—C. G. C.

†Note! These words have been scratched through in the MS., but are still legible.—C. G. C.

[210]

THIS INDENTURE mad the Sixh day of November in the year of our Lord Christ one Thousand Seven hundred & Twenty Eight and In the Second year of the Reigne of Our Sovereigne Lord King George the Second of Great Brittaine France & Ireland Defender of the faith &c[a]:) Wittneſeth that I William Brooking Cleark of Petso parish Vestory in Gloster County Do in the name And Behalf of Cap[t] John Alexander and M[r] Conquest Wyatt Gent[n] Churchwardens for the Parish of Petso In the County A forsaid According to An order of the Said Vestory Dated on Thursday the Thirty first day of August 1727 Bind Unto William Robinſon one Orphen Girl named Sarah Sanders of the Age of Eleven Years the fifteenth day ot December Next Enſuing from thence to Serve the Said William Robinſon his heirs & aſignes In all & all maner of Lawfull Imployments Untill She shall Arive to Lawfull Age And the Said William Robinſon his heirs And Aſsignes Do Oblidge themſelves to Give the Said Sarah Sanders Three years Schooling or Instruct or Cauſe to be Taught & Instructed that She may Read perfectly Well in Any part of the Bible & alſo to Lern or Cauſe to be Lerned & Instructed Such Lawfull way or Waies that She may be Able after her Indentured time Is Expired to Get her own Living And Alſo to allow the Said Sarah Sanders Good Sufficent Meat Drink Waſhing Lodging & Apperil During her Indentured Time And At the Expiration of the Said Time to pay her all Such Allowances As Are Uſeial & As the Law In Such Caſes Allows As Alſo to Keep the parish harmles from her being Anywais Chargable or Burdenſom to them During the Said time In Wittneſs Whearof we have [*] Interchangably Set our hand & Seals the Day & Year first Written

Signed Seald & Delivered   W[m] Robinson (Seal)
In the presents of Us
    Mary X Lambarth
    Susanne Brooking

*Note! A word here has been scratched through and rendered il-

[211]

THIS INDENTURE mad the fourtenth day of November In the Year of our Lord Christ one Thousand Seven hundred & Twenty Eight WITTNEſSETH that I William Brooking Clerk of Petso Parish Vestory in Gloster County Do In the Name & Behalf of Capt John Alexd^r & Mr Conq^t Wyat Gen^n Church Wardens for the Parish Aforsaid According to the Dyrections of An order of Gloster County Court Dated on the Twenty Second day of Aug^t: Last past to bind out the Children of Mary Netles Do According Bind Unto Mr Edward Wyatt one of her Children Named Wm Netles About the Age of Ten years from thence to Serve the Said Edward Wyatt In all & all maner of Lawfull Servis & Imployments that him the Said Wyatt his heirs Eo^{rs}. &^{ca}. Shall Set him About & the Said Edwd Wyatt his heirs Exo^{rs}. &^{ca}. Do Oblidge themſelves to Give the Said Wm Three Years Schooling or Instruct or Cause to be Taught or Instructed the Said William that he may Read perfectly Well In Any part of the Bible During the Said Time And Alſo to Lern or Instruct or Cause to be Lerned & Instr^d Unto the Said Wm Such Lawfull way or Trade that he may Be Able After his Indentured time Is Expred to Git his own Living And Also During the Said Time to Allow the Said William Good Sufficent meat Drink Waſhing Lodging & Aperil And at the Expiration of the time Afores^d. to Allow him All Such Allowances As Are Uſeial & as the Law in Such Caſes Alws As Alſo to Keep the parish harmleſs from his being Any Waies Chargable & Truble ſome to them During the Said Time In Wittneſs Whearof We have Interchangeable Set our hands & Seals this Day & year first Written

 Test   Edwd Wyatt (Seal)
Jno: Reade
Benj^a Baker

[212]

THIS INDENTURE mad the Twentififth day of Novr. In the year of our Lord Christ one Thousand Seven hundred and Twenty Eight Wittneſseth that I William Brooking Clerk of Petsoe Parish Vestory in Gloster County Do In the Name and Behalf of Capt John Alexander & Mr Conquest Wyatt Gent^n Churchwardens for the Parish Aforsaid. According to An Order of Gloster County Court Dated on the Twenty Second day of August Last to Bind out the Children of Mary Nettles Do Accordingly Bind Unto Mr John Reade one of her Children Named Sollomon Nettles About the Age of Seven Years from thence to Serve the Said John Read his heirs Exo^{rs} & Aſsigns In all & all maner of Lawfull Servis & Employments Untill he Shall Arive to Lawfull Age And the Said John Read his heirs Executors & Aſsignes Do promis Covenant & Agre to Give the Said Sollomon Nettles three years Schooling During the Said time or Cearfully teach or Cause to be Taught That he may Read perfectly in Any part of the Bible & And Alſo to Lern or Instruct or Cause to be Learned & Instructed Unto the Said Sollomon Nettles Such Lawfull Way Trade or Buisneſs that he may be Able after his Indentured time is Expired to Get his ow Living & Alſo During the Said time to Allow him good Sufficent meat Drink Waſhing Lodging & Apperil and At the Expiration of the time As aforsaid to pay & allow him all Such Allowances as are Uſeial & as the Law in Such Cases Allowes As Alſo to Keep the Parish harmleſs from his being Any Waies Chargable or Burdenſom to them During the Said time In Wittneſs Whearof we have Interchangably Set our hands & Seals the Day & Year first above Written
Signed & Seald in
Preſents of Uſs   John Reade (Seal)

[   ] : Lan[ ]ford   Copia Test   WBrooking Cl Ves
[   ]ris Loe

[213]

THIS INDENTURE made the Twentieth day of November in the Year of our Lord Christ one Thousand Seven hundred & Twenty Eight Wittneſseth that I William Brooking Clerk of Petsoe parish Vestory In Gloster County Do in the name & Behalf of Capt. John Alexander Church Wad^n of the Parish aforsaid According to An Order of Gloster County Court Dated on the Twenty Second day of August Last to Bind Out the Children of Mary Nettles Do Accordingly Bind Unto Mr Conquest Wyatt one of her Children Named Mary Nettles About the Age of Eleven years from thence to Serve the Said Conquest Wyatt his heirs Executors & Aſsignes in all & all maner of Lawfu[] Serveses & Emplyments Untill She Shall arive to Lawfull Age And the Said Conquest Wyatt his heirs Eo^rs. and Aſsignes In Conſideration As aforsaid Do Oblidge themſelves to give the Said Mary Nettles Three years Schooling or Cearfully Teach or Cauſe to be taught that She may Read perfectly in Any part of the Bible During the Said time and Alſo to Lern & Instruct or Cause to be Lerned and Instructed Unto the Said Mary Nettles *that *She Such Lawfull way or waies that She may be able after her Indentured time is Expired to get her own Living and Alſo during the Said time to Allow her good Sufficent meat Drink Waſhing Lodging And Apperil And At the Expiration of the time As Aforsaid to pay her all Such Allowances As Are Uſial and As the Law in Such Cases allows As Alſo to Keep the Parish harmleſs from her being Any Wais Chargable or Burdensom to them During the Said time I Wittneſs Wherof Wee have Interchangably Set our hands & Seals the day & year Above Written

    Signed Sealed & Delivered
      In Preſents of Uſs   Conqueſt Wyatt (Seal)
        Edward Wyatt
            his
        Thomas T Roſs
           mark

[214]

THIS INDENTURE mad the third day of Febuary in the second year of the Reigne of our Sovereigne Lord King George the Second of great Brittaine France & Ireland Defendor of the faith &c[a]. and in the year of Our Lord Christ one thousand Seven hundred and Twenty Eight Wittneſeth that I William Brooking Cleark of Petsoe Parish Vestory in Gloster County Do firmly in the Name and Behalf of Cap: John Alexander & M[r] Conquest Wyatt Gent[n] Church wardens for the Parish aforsaid According to An Order of Gloster County Court Dated on the Twentysecond day of August 1728 Durected to the s[d] Church wardes to Bind Out the Children of Mary Nettles Do According to Order bind Unto M[r] Sam[ll] Coleman one of her Children Named George Nettles about the Age of fourteen years or therabouts from thence to Serve the S[d]. Samuel Colman his heirs Execut[rs]. adm[rs]. And Aſsignes in all & all maner of Lawfull Serveſes and Employments Untill he Shall Arive to Lawfull Age and the Said Samuell Colman his heirs Exec[rs] adm[rs]. &c[a]. in Conſideration of the Servis as afors[d]. Do Oblidge theſelves to give the Said George Nettles three years Schooling or to Cearfully teach or Cauſe to be taught that he may Read perfectly in the Bible And Alſo During the Said time to allow him good Sufficent meet Drink Washing Lodging & Apperil And Alſo to Teach or Cause to be taught Unto the Said George Nettles Such Lawfull way trade or Buisneſs that he may be Able after his Indentured time Is Expir[d] to Get his own Leving and at the Expiration of the time As Afors[d] to pay and allow him all Such Allowances As Are Uſeiall And As the Law in Such Cases Allowes as allso During the Said time to Keep the Said Parish harmleſs from his Being Any wais Burdenſom to them In Wittneſs Wherof we have hearunto Set our hands & Seals the day & year first Written

   Signed Sealed & Declared
   In Preſents of Us

                              Sam[l] Coleman (Seal)

     Jn[o] Smith
     John Crittenden

[215]

At A Vestory held for Petsoe Parish ye 16th day of June 1729 In order to appoint the Tobacco Tellers in Each Precint of the Said Parish According to the Dyrections of An Act of Aſsembly Intituled An Act for the more Effectual Improving the Staple of Tobacco

Members Present

   The R^d. Emanuel Jones

Mr John Royston	Mr Francis Thornton
Cap John Washington	Mr Seth Thornton C W
Mr John Throckmorton	
Mr Thomas Green	Mr Conq^t Wyat Ch Wd^n

It is ordered by this preſent Vestory that Mr Thomas Green and Mr John Throckmorton Take the Number of Tobo Plants groing In the first & Second Precints of this Parish according to the Dyrections of the Act of Aſsembly for the More Effectual Improving the Staple of Tobacco

It is ordered by this present Vestory that m^r Thomas Scott & m^r John Carter Take the Number of Tobacco plants Growing in the Third & fourth precints of this Parish According to the dyrections of An Act of Aſsembly for the more Effectual Improving the Staple of Tobacco

It is ordered that Robert Carter & Willm. Brooking Take the Number of Tobacco plants Growing in the fifth Sixth & Seventh precints of this Parish According to the Dyrections of An Act of Aſsembly for the more Effectual Improving the Staple of Tobacco

It is ordered by this present Vestory that m^r James Wyatt & m^r Edward Wyat Take the Number of Tobacco plants Growing In the Eight & Ninth precints of this Parish According to the Dyrections of An Act of Aſsembly for the More Effectuall Improving the Staple of Tobacco

It is ordered that m`r` Francis Thornton be paid Twelve Shiling by the Parish for A Dyal to be Set Up at the Church

       Entry Test W Brooking Cl Ves

[216]

This Indenture mad the 17`th` day of July one Thousand Seven hundred & Twenty Nine and in the *Second *year *of *the *Reigne *of *our *Sovereigne *Lord *King *George *the *Second Third year of the Reigne of our Sovereigne Lord King George the Second of Great Brittane France & Ireland &`cr`. Wittneſseth that I William Brooking Clerk of Petsoe Parish Vestory In Gloster County Do According to Order & Dyrections of the Gent`n`. Churchwardens of the Parish aforsaid Bind Unto John Stublefield one Parish Boy Named Alexander Young Rowbottom about the Age of three Years from thence to Serve the Said John Stublefield his heirs And Aſsignes in all & all maner of Lawfull Serves & Employm`t` Untill he Shall Arive to Lawfull Age and the Said John Stublefield his heirs Exo`rs`. & aſsignes Do oblidge themſelves to give the Said boy as aforsaid three years Schooling & Cearfully Teach or Cause to be taught that he may Read perfectly in any part of the Bible within the Said time and also to Learn & Instruct or Cause to be Learned & Instructed Unto the Said Boy as aforsaid Such Lawfull way traid or buisneſs that he may be able after his Indentured time is Expired to Get his own Living and also During the Said time to Allow him Good Sufficent meat drink washing Lodging & Apperil and at the Expiracon of the Term of the Time As Aforsaid to pay him all Such Allowances As Are Uſeiall as the Law in Such Cases Allowes As Also to Keep the Parish harmleſs and Indamnified from his being

---

*Note! These words are scratched through in the MS., but are still legible.—C. G. C.

Any more Chargable *or *burdenſom to them During his Indentured time In Wittneſs we have Interchangably Set our hand & Seals the day & year first Written

Signed Sealed & Deliverd
In Presents of Us

Jnº. Reade   John Stubblefield (Seal)
Thomas T Roſs

[217]

This Indenture mad the first day of October in the year of Our Lord God one thousand Seven hundred & Twenty Nine And In the Third year of the Reigne of Our Soverigne Lord King George the Second of Great Brittaine France & Ireland Defender of the faith &cᵃ, Wittneſseth that I William Brooking Clerk of Petsoe Parish Vestory in Gloster County Do According to Order & Dyrection of mʳ Conquest Wyat Church warden of the Parish Aforsaid Bind Unto Mʳ William Thornton Juʳ one Orphen Boy Named   Haines about the Age of   years from thence to Serve the Said William Thornton Juʳ. his heirs Exoʳˢ. & Aſsigns in all & all maner of Lawfull Serves'es & Employments yᵗ they Shall Set him about Untill he Arrives to Lawfull Age & the Said Wᵐ. Thornton his heirs and Aſsignes do Oblidge themſelves to give the Said   Haines three years Schooling or Cearfully teach or Cause to be taught that he may Read perfectly in Any part of the bible within the Said time and Also to lern & Instruct or Cause to be Lerned & Instructe[] Unto the Said Haines as Aforsᵈ Such Lawfull way trade or Buisneſs that he may be able after his Indentured time is Expired to Get his own Living and Also during the Said time to Allow him good Sufficent meet Drink Washing Lodging & Apperil & at the Expiracon of the time as aforsᵈ. to pay him all Such Allowances As Are Uſeiall & As the Law in Such Cases Allowes as Also to Keep the Parish as aforsᵈ harmleſs from his being Any Waise Cargable or Burdensom to them During the time As Aforsᵈ. I

---

*Note! These words are scratched through in the MS., but are still legible.—C. G. C.

Wittnefs Whearof We have Interchangably Set our hands &
Seals the Day & year first Spercified
 Signed And Seald
 In Prefents of Ufs

                                                                   (Seal)

[218]

At A Vestory held for Petsworth Parish Octr. y^e. 1th. day 1729

              present the R^d. Em^{ll} Jones

Mr Augustin Smith	Mr Thomas Green
Mr John Royston	Mr Fran^s. Thornton
Mr Thomas Read	Mr Conq^t Wyat C W
	Cap Jno Alexander C W

    Petsoe Parish mad D^r. this present Year In Tobacco

To the Rev^d. Emanuel Jones Minister	16000
To Alexander Roane Clerk Church 9 month	750
To Wm Brooking Cl Vestry & Cl Church 3 mo	850
To Thomas Easter Dec^d. Sexton	1000
To Thomas Easter D^o for 2 days labour	25
To Cap: John Alexander for 8 botles of Wine to the Church	240
To Mr Augustin Smith for 3 botles D^o.	75
To Elizabeth Ennis for Keeping Robotoms Child 9 mo	600
To John Stublefield for Taking An Indenture for S^d Child	1200
To m^r John Read for Keeping Eliz. Marcy 3 mo & 6 days	319
To Mr James Dudley Juner for 2 hors blocks & 2 benches	250
To Mr Francis Thornton for A dyal	120
To Mr William Camp for one Levey overcharged Last year	47
To the Revd Em^{ll} Jones Acc^o. for Books & Glas for the Church	1005
To D^o for quitrents for the Glieb Land as Useial	54
	22535

To 18 ⅌ Cent Upon the Whole for Cask & Salery	4056
Total Debt Amount to	26591
Par is Credit By 867 Tithables @ 31 ⅌ pole	26877
Parish Debt	26591
Ballance Due	286

Petsworth Parish Also mde D^r. In Mony or Tobacco *To *Mony *aſseſsed Toward the building the Wall £65: 0^s: 6^d or 13005^{lb} Tobacco

Petsworth Parish Credit
By 867 Titheabls @ 1/6^d ⅌ pole £65: 0^s: 6^d or at 15^{lb} Tobacco p^r. pole is 13005^{lb} Tobacco

[219]   Brought forward

It is ordered And appointed that m^r Conquest Wyat Church Warden Be Collector for the Parish of Petsworth this present Collection Giving Bond & Security to proforme his Several Duties therin According to Law

It is ordered that Mr Conquest Wyat Collect of Every Titheable perſon Within this parish this year 31^{lb} of Tobacco & 1/6^d or 15^{lb}. of Tobacco ⅌ pole to pay of And Satisfie the Several Parish Creditors or Upon Refussal to make Distreſs as the Law dyrects

Upon Cap^n. John Allexanders Going out of the Parish Mr Francis Buckner is this day Ellected and Chosen Vestry man & Church warden for the Lower precint of this Parish in his Rome

True Entry Test
WBrooking Cl V

Memorandum that James Booker Is Chosen Sexton of the Chur by M Jones for the time Insuing

---

*Note! These words are scratched through in the MS., but are still legible.—C. G. C.

[220]

At A Vestory held for Petsoe Parish April the 13—1730

Present The R⁴ Em¹, Jones

M' Augustin Smith   M' Tho⁸ Green
M' John Royston   M' Seth Thornton
M' Thomas Read   M' Conq' Wyatt
M' John Throckmorton   M' Sam¹ Buckner C. W.

At this Vestory M' Sam¹¹. Buckner Was Elected & Chosen Vestory man And Church warden in the Rome of M' Francis Buckner Dec⁴. and took the Oaths of Allegiance Supremesey Vestory man &ᶜᵃ

It is ordered that the fine of Rich⁴. Crittenden & Charles Roane being Ten Shilings in the hands of M' Conquest Wyatt be paid to Richard Halcomb In Consideration of his Indigencey And that the Said Wyat take Recept for the Same

True Entry Test
WBrooking Cl Ves

[221]

At A Vestory held for Petsoe Parish the 6ᵗʰ day of July 1730

Present the Rev⁴ Emanuel Jones

M' Augⁿ. Smith
M' Jnᵒ. Royston
M' Tho: Read   } M' Fra: Thornton
M' Jnᵒ. Throckmorton   M' Seth Thornton
                          M' Tho⁸ Green
         M' Conq' Wiat Ch Warden
         M' Sam¹¹ Buckner Ch Warden

Upon the Negligence of M' John Moore in his Nonperformance In building the Brick Wall at Popler Spring Church According to his Artickls of Agreement With the Church Wardens of this parish It is ordered by this present Vestory that the present Church Wardens for the parish A forsaid bring Action In behalfe of the parish Against the Said Moore As the Law In that Behalf Requirs &ᶜᵃ.

At this Vestory Mʳ Jones Informᵈ. the Vestory that the Mancion house & Other building on the Glieb are in So Ruinouse a Condition that rather then Undertake to put & Keep them In Such Repair as the law Requirs he must quit his Incumbancy the Vestory being Very Sencable that if Mʳ Jones Should Refigne the Living No Minister Would Receive the Buildings in the Codition they are in at present And Very Ardently defireing his Continuance Do Agre And Accordingly Order that the present buildings on the Gleib be Repaird at the Charge of the parish untill New ones Are Erected

It is therefore Accordingly Ordered that the Churchwardens Do With All Convenient Speed hire Worke men to make all Such Repairs as is Nessefsary on the Gleib And Tarr the houfes At the Charge of the parish

True Entry Test

WBrooking Cl Ves

[222]

At A Veftory held for Petsoe Parish the 7ᵗʰ day of Octʳ 1730

Present
- The Rᵈ. Em̃ˡˡ Jones
- Mʳ Augⁿ. Smith
- Mʳ John Royston
- Capⁿ Jnᵒ. Washington
- Mʳ Jnᵒ. Throckmorton
- Mʳ Thoˢ. Green
- Mʳ Fra: Thornton
- Mʳ Conqᵗ Wyat C W
- Mʳ Samˡ Buckner C W

Petsoe Parish made Dettoʳ this year In Tobacco (viz)

To the Rᵈ Emanuel Jones for his Sallery	16000
To Allexʳ Roane Clerk Church	1000
To Wᵐ Brooking Cl. Vestory	600
To James Booker Sextorn	1000

To Capⁿ John Cleytons Acc°	165
To Capⁿ Cleyton D° for Last year	118
To Mr Augustin Smith for four Botles of Wine	100
To Mr Conq^t. Wyats Acc° for four bottles D°.	160
To Mr Francis Easter for Three Bottles D°.	67½
To Capⁿ Sam^{ll} Buckner for Three Bottles D°.	90
To Jn° Wilcocks Sheriff Acc°	80
To Jn° McWilliams Acc° for making 3 hors blocks	300
To Thomas Booker for a Levey over charged Last year	31
To Thomas Davis for bording the Widd° Steers 3 mo: & 10 d^s	334
To George Haines for buring Eliz^a. Warner	300
To Jn° Routon for fixing the Led on the Pedemend	050
To the R^d Emanuel Jones for q^trents of the Glieb	54
To Conq^t Wyat for Two Delinq^{ts} Graves & Knight & C mony	92
To Richd Halcomb for Relief	400
To Capⁿ Sam^{ll} Buckner for finding 16 bottles of Wine & bread for the Ufe of the Comunion this Next year Enfuing	400
	21341
To Cask & Sallery at 18 ℔ C^t	3841
Parish Debt in all amounts to	25182
Parish Creddit By 881 Tithables @ 29 ℔ pole	24969
By Tob°. Remaining In Mr Wyats hands Last year	286
	25255
	25182
By Tob° Due to the Parish from Mr Wyat	00073

[223] Brought forward

At this Vestory Mr Conquest Wyat is Continued Church warden In the Rome of Cap{n} John Washington he agreeing to Stand Church warden in his Rome And it is agree by the Vestry that Cap{n}. Washington Shall be Discharged it being his Turn to Serve

At this Vestory Mr Conq{t}. Wyat is appointed Collector fo the Uper Precint of this Parish & Cap. Samll. Buckner for the Lower They Giving Bond & Security As the Law Dyrect for ther Due Performance of their Several Offies as the Law Dyrect

It is Ordered that Mr Conq{t}. Wyat & Cap{n}. Samuel Buckner Collect of Every Titheable Person in this Parish in their Several Precints 29^{lb} of Tobacco or Upon Refusial to make Distreſs as the Law Dyrects to pay of the Several Parish Creditts

    True Entry Test
      WBrooking Cl Vestry

[224]

At A Vestory Hed for Petsoe Parish on Tusday Ap{l}. ye 20 1731

Present

The Revd. Em{l} Jones	Mr Fra: Thornton
Mr John Royston	Mr Thos. Green
Cap{n}. Thomas Reade	Mr Seth Thornton
Mr Conqest Wyat C W	Mr Thomas Booth

At This Vestory Mr Thomas Booth Was Ellected & Chosen Vestry man in the Rome of Mr Frances Wyat Dec{d} and has Taken the Oaths Supremacy & Vestry man &{ca}

It is Ordered that Cap{n}. Samuel Buckner pay to the Poore of this Parish As hereafter Allotted £3:3:6 It being for 500^{lb} Tob{o} & Cask paid by Geo Gardner for the fine of

Eliz Ennis Viz to Richd Halcomb 10/ to Sam^{11}. Whittew's Wife & Children 20/ To Thomas Jackſons Wife & Children 15/ to Widdow Carter 20/6 the Above Said Money's to be paid In Goods In Mr Montagues Store

It's Alſo Ordered that the fine money in the Hands of Mr Conqest Wyat being £5-5^s-0 be Distributed to the following perſons Viz to Vicares Nettles 20/ to John Eastwood 15/ to Jeffry Bourk 15/ to James Lewis 15/ to Widd^o Steers 30/ to Widd^o. Bond 10/ the Above S^d Mony to be paid in Goods by Mr Wyat at Reaſonable Rates As Can be bought Else Where for Redy mony

      True Entry Test
        WBrooking Cl Ves

[225]

      Proceſsioning Orders

At A Vestory Held for Petsworth Parish the 10th day of Augt 1731

    Present the R^d. Em^l. Jones

Mr Aug^n Smith	Mr John Throckmorton
Mr John Royston	Mr Seth Thornton
Mr Thomas Green	Mr Conq^t Wyat C.W.
Mr Fra Thornton	Mr Thomas Booth

In Pursuant to An Order of Gloster County Court Dated on Thursday the 22^d Day of July 1731 to Lay Out this Parish into Several precints And Appoint proceſsioners in every precint to See the Lands Within the Same procesioned According to Law. This Vestory has Therefore Ordered And Appointed the Several procesioners as followeth viz

1. It is ordered that Mr William Thornton Ju^r & Mr John Stublefild See the Land proceſioned Within the first precinct of this Parish And to begin at Jno. Smith Sawyers on the first Tusday In Sep^r.

2. It is Ordered that Mr William Thornton Senr. & Mr John Thornton See the Lands Within the Second precint poſesioned & to begin on the Second Tusday in Sepr at m^r Thomas Cooks

3^d It is ordered that Mr Thomas Booth & Mr Thomas Scott See the Lands Within the Third precint Poſesioned And to begin the Third Tusday in Sepr at Mrs Stubb's

4th. It is ordered that Mr John Carter and Mr Richard Crittenden See the Lands Within the fourth precint poſesioned And that They Begin the fourth Tusday in Sepr. at Henry Purſels

5th It is ordered that Mr Robt. Carter & W^m. Brooking See the Lands Within the fifth precint proceſioned and that they Begin on the first Wednesday in Sepr at Henry Hubbards

6th It is Ordered that Mr Edward Wyat And Mr Alex^{dr} Roane Se the lands Within the Sixth Precint proceſioned and that they begin on the Second Wednesday In Sepr at Jo^s: Bardins

7th It is order'd that Mr Benj^a Baker and Mr John Garland See the Lands Within the Seventh precint Proceſioned and to begin on the Third Wedneſday in Sepr at Jno Smith[ ]

8th It is ordered that Mr John Reade & m^r George Fary See the Land Within the Eight precinct of this Parish Proceſioned and that they begin the fourth Wedneſday In Sepr at Mr Aug^n Smiths

           Turn Over

[226]   Brought Over

9th It is Ordered that Mr James Wyat and Mr Rich^d. West See the Lands Within the Ninth precint proceſioned And that they Begin on the Second Thursday in Sepr At James Wyats

Forasmuch As An Order of Vestory has been heartofore made that the Church wardens of this Parish Should With all Convenient Speed Hire workmen to make all Such Repairs on the Glieb House that they Should find Neſseſary to be done, They being *altogether Negligent in proforming the Same, It is Therefore Ordered that Mr Jones may hire Any Workman As he Shall Think fit to doe the Same As Alſo to buy Tar & Tar the House's at ye Charge of the Parish

      True Entry Test
        WBrooking Cl Ves

[227]

At A Vestory held for Petsoe Parish the 6th day of Octo^r 1731

    Present the Revd Em^l Jones

Mr Augustin Smith	Mr Seth Thornton
Mr John Royston	Mr Conq^t Wiat C W
Mr Fra. Thornton	Cap Saml Buckner C W
Mr Jno Throckmorton	Mr Thomas Booth

Petso Parish	Dr
	Tobacco
To the Revd Em^l Jones Sallery	16000
To Mr Alexd^r Roane Clerk of the Church	1000
To Wm Brooking Clerk of ye Vestory	0600
To James Booker Sexton	1000
To Cap Jno Cleytons Acc^o Cl Fees	0053
To Thos. Stubb's Sheriffs Acc^o	0070
To James Booker's Wife for Waſhing the Scurplis 5 Times	0200
To Widd^o Arther for one Levey overcharged Last year	0031
To Cap. Saml. Buckner Acc^o.	0058
To Henry Griffin for one hors Block	0050

 *Note! This word has been scratched through in the MS, but is still legible.—C. G. C.

To Thomas Laughlin for one Levey Last year	0029
To Lewis Neele for one Levey D°	0029
To Francis Easter for Keeping the Orphens of Thoˢ Easter Decᵗ	1000
To Fra: Easter D°. for Taking One of the Orphens of the Parish	1000
To Peter Bell for Taking An Indentur for James Easter of the Parish	1000
To Mʳ Conqest Wiat for Ballance Accᵒᵗ	0062
To Mʳ John Smith Sheriff's Accᵒ.	0060
To Thomas Pool of Keepinging Elizᵃ Whitrence A Child Untill the Next Octobʳ Enſuing on Codition of an Indentʳ for yᵉ same	1250
To Mary Paine for Cure Susᵃ Steers	0400
To Mʳ Jones for Qtrent of the Glied Land	0054
To Cap Buckner for Comunion Wine the yʳ Enſuing	0400
To mʳ Jones for Repair the Glied & finding Nailes	2500
To Widᵒ. Steers for Relief	0500
To Richᵈ Halcomb for Relief	0400
To Doʳ Semers Accᵒ for Susᵃ. Steers	1800
	29546
Caske & Sallery @ 18 ℔ Ct	5318
Paris Debᵗ	34864
By Parish Credit	
By 851 Titheables @ 41ᴵᵇ ℔ pole	34891
Due to the Pariſh	27

        Turn Over

[228]   Brought Over

At this Vestory Mr Thomas Booth was Chosen Church Warden In the Rome of mʳ Conqest Wiat for the Lower precint Precint of this Parish & Capⁿ. Buckner for the Upper

It is Appointed that Cap. Samuel. Buckner Church Warden be Collector of the Parish and that he Collect of Every Titheable Perſon forty one pounds of Tobacco by Way of Inspectors Notes As the Law Dyrects to pay of & discharg the Severl Parish Debts he Giving Bond for the Due performance of his Office therein According to Law

It is Ordered that Eliz: Whitrence A bastard Child be Bound to Thomas Pool tell Lawfull Age

It is Ordered that James Easter Orphen of Thomas Easter Be bound to Peter Bell As An Apprentis till he Comes to Lawfull Age

True Entry Test

WBrooking Cl Vestry

[229]

At A Vestry held for Petsworth Parish the 18th of January 1731

Present the Rd Eml Jones

Mr John Royston	Mr Seth Thornton
Mr Thoˢ. Green	Capn Saml Buckner C W
Mr Fra Thornton	
Mr Conqt Wyat	Mr Tho Booth C W

Whereas at A Vestory held for Petsworth Parish the 10th day of Auguſt 1731 Mr John Carter and Mr Richd Crittenden Was Appointed to See the Lands Within the fourth Precint of this Parish Proceſioned the Said John Carter Deceasing Without fulfiling the Said proceſioning It Is Therefore Ordered by this Preſent Westory that Mr David Alexander be Appointed in his Rome With Mr Crittenden to Make And Return the Said proceſioning According to Law

And Whearas at A Vestory held Auguſt the 10th Mr John Reade Was appointed With George Fary to See the Lands Within the Eight Precint of this Parish Proceſioned the

Said John Read being Long Sick And Not able to proſome the Same It is Therfore Ordered that Mʳ Augustin Smith be proceſionʳ In his Rome to See the Lands Within the Said precint Proceſioned According to Law

True Entry Test
W Brooking

At this Vestory Upon the Motion of Wᵐ Brooking Seting fourth that he Ought to be paid for all Indentures he Provides for Orphens Bound by the Church wards dyrections to him As Cleark It is Thought fit to Order that he Shall be paid five Shilings Coranᵗ for Every Pair of Indentures he Shall provide hearafter by the Partyes to whom the Said Children Be bound

Tes WBrooking Cl V

Nota from this place all Indentures are Moved to the Later part of this Book

[230]

At a Vestry held for Petsoe Parish the 9ᵗʰ day of Octobʳ 1732

Present The Revᵈ. Emˡ. Jones
Mʳ Augⁿ Smith   Cap. Thomas Reade
Mʳ John Royston   Mʳ Seth Thornton
Mʳ Fra. Thornton   Mʳ Thomas Booth Ch W
Mʳ Thomas Green   Cap Samˡ Buckner C W
                       Mʳ David Alexander

Petsoe Parish Dʳ this Year in Tobacco viz)

To the Revᵈ. Emˡ Jones his Sallery	16000
To Alexander Roane Clerk of the Church	01000
To James Booker Sextom	01000
To William Brooking Cleark of Vestry	00600
To Cap John Cleytons Clerks Accᵒ	00059

To James Booker for his Wifes Washing the Surplis Twice	00080
To Mr Seth Thornton for one baril of Corn to Wid^o Knoles	00060
To Mr Georg Gardner for Dyal post	00150
To Cap Barnard for 2 Leveys Overcharged	00058
To Joseph Meacham for Taking Eliz Knoles by Indenture	01200
To Mr John Moors Acc^o Not Leveyed Last year	00300
To Thomas Goulder for Taking Wm Knoles by Indenture	00200
To Wid^o Edwards for Taking Robt Knoles by Indenture	01000
To Wid^o Steers for Relief	00400
To Wm Brooking for finding Wid^o Steers a house	00100
To Simon halcomb for Keeping his father 8 Months	00350
To John Gilbert Moore for D^o Keeping 4 Months	00250
To Mr Thomas Booth to be laid Out in Clothes for D^o	00200
To Revd Em^l Jones for Quitrent of the Glieb Land	00054
To Mr Thomas Booth for finding Comunion Wine ye year Enſuing	00400
	23461
To 8 ℗ Cent Leveyed	1876
Total Parish Deb^t	25337
Petso Parish Credit	
By 848 Titheables @ 31 ℗ pole is	26288
Due to ballance to the Parish	951
By Tob^o from Cap Buckner Last year	27
By Tob^o from Richd Crittenden	39
Due in all	1017

[231]

At This Vestory M⁰ David Alexander is Chosen Vestry man in the Rome of Mʳ Thomas Cooke (Who Relinquisht his place by reſon of Age & Infirmity) and Is appointed Church Warden in the Roome of Capⁿ Buckner for the Upper precint of Petsoe Parish

It is Ordered That Mʳ Thomas Booth Churchwarden be Collector for the Parish the Enſuing year and that he Receive of Every Titheable person the Sum of 31ˡᵇ of Tobacco (Without the Allowance of 10 ℔ Cᵗ as the Law perscribes it not being Laid On) to pay of the Several Parish Creditts Giving Bond and Security as the Law Dyrects

It is Ordered that Mʳ Thomas Booth Receive of Richᵈ Crittenden 39ˡᵇ of Tobᵒ Due by Clearks note Against the Said Richard Upon the Informacon of A Grand Jury at Gloster Court

     True Entry Test
       WBrooking Cl V

[232]

At A Vestory held for Petsworth Parish the 18ᵗʰ day Of Octʳ 1733

   Present the Rd: Emˡ. Jones

Mʳ Augⁿ. Smith	Mʳ Fra Thornton
Mʳ John Royston	Mʳ Seth Thornton
Majʳ John Washington	Capⁿ. Samˡ Buckner
Cap Thoˢ Reade	Mʳ Tho: Booth Chur Warden
	Mʳ David Alexand Ch Warden

  Petsworth Parish Dettʳ this Year in Tobacco

To the Revᵈ. Emuel Jones his Sallery	16000
To Dᵒ. for Quitrents of the Glieb Land	54
To Mʳ Alexander Roane Clerk of the Church his Sallery	1000
To James Booker Sextorn his Sallery	1000

To Dº: for his Wifes Washing the Surplis Twice	80
To Wm Brooking Clerk of the Vestory his Sallery	600
To Dtº. for Bording Thomas Walles Six Month	300
To Dº for Rent An house to Widdº Stears	100
To Thomas Pool for Keeping Eliz. Whitrence A Child Without Any more Charge to the Parish	1250
To Cap John Cleytons Accº	90
To Mr Thomas Stubbs Sherifs Accº	40
To Docr. Semors Accº £4 @ 2d ℔ lb	480
To George Farys Accº £1: 4: 1d @ 2d p lb	144½
To Saml Whittus for Keeping & Burying Symon White	400
To John Nettles for a Levey Overcharged in the yr. 1731	37½
To Eleanar Edwards for Buring Widº Grindey	200
To John Ward for Making the Coffin & Diging the Grave	50
To Cap Saml Buckner for A Coffin for Wm Smith Decd	50
To Dittº for 3 delinquents in the year 1731	112
To Jnº Gilt More for Keeping Rd. Halcomd Last year & find Neſeſary'	800
To Mary Cox for Nursing A basterd Child 8 Mo @ 8lb ℔ Annum	533
To Mr David Alexander for Taking An Indenture for Thomas Grindy Without any more Charg to the Parish	1600
To Mrs Arthur for Taking An Indenture for Christyan Grindy as afosd	700
To Mr Thomas Booth for 2 delinqts Last year	62
To Mr Davd Alexander for Comunion Wine the year Enſuing	400
To Widdº Stears for Relief	300
	26383

To Sallery At 8 ⅌ Cᵗ	2111
	28494
By Tobᵒ. Due in Mʳ Booths hands	955
Total Parish Debᵗ Due	27539
By Credit for 842 Tithaᵇ @ 33 ⅌ pole	27786
By Tobaccᵒ Due Remaining	247

[233]　　　Brought forward

four Year Old
Feb 1736

It is Ordered that Thomas Grindy An Orphen Boy be bound to Mʳ David Allexander Till Lawfull Age he discharging the Parish of his being any more Chargable to them

It is Ordered that Christyan Grndy be Bound to Richᵈ Arſhur And his Wife Till Lawfull Age They discharging the Parish of her being any more Chargable to them

It is Ordered that Mʳ Thomas Green be Church Warden in the Lower precint in the Rome of mʳ Thomas Booth

It is Ordered that Mʳ David Allexander be Collector of the Parish this Enſuing and that he Collect of Every Titheable Person the Sum of 33ᵗᵇ Tobᵒ to pay of the Several Parish Creddits

　　　　　　　True Entry Test
　　　　　　　WBrooking Cl Vestory

[234]

At A Vestory held for Petsorth Parish the 16ᵗʰ apʳ 1734

Present The Revᵈ Emanuel Jones

Mʳ Thomas Green C W ⎫ Cap Samˡ Buckner
Mʳ Francis Thornton　 ⎬ Mʳ Thomas Booth
Mʳ Seth Thornton　　　⎭ Mʳ David Allexander C W

At This Vestory it is Ordered that the fine money in m^r David Alexandrs hands being Two pounds Ten Shilings be distributed to The following poore people of this Parish vizt

  To John Sprat Twenty Shilings
  To Wid° Sinar Ten Shilings
  To Wid° Smith Ten Shilings
  To James Lewis five Shilings
  To Thomas Jackson five Shilings

The above Said money to be paid in Goods in Mr James Hubbard's Store by Order of the Said Alexand^r The Several Above mentioned pore

It is Ordered that Mr David Alexander Repair ye Vestry houſe at Popler Spring With all Convenient Speed & bring in his Charge to the Parish At the Next Laying the Levey

    True Entry Test
     WBrooking Cl Vestry

[235]

At A Vestory held for Petsworth Parish the 2^d day of Octr 1734

Present the Revd Em^l Jones Mr Thomas Green C W
  Mr John Royston Cap Saml. Buckner
  Mr Augustin Smith
  Cap Thomas Read Mr Thomas Booth
  Mr Francis Thornton Mr David Alexander C W

Petsworth Parish Dett^r	Tobacco
To the Rev^d. Emanuel Jones his Sallery	16000
To Ditt°. for Quitrents for the Glieb Land	00054
To Alexander Roane Cleark of the Church	01000
To Wm Brooking Cleark of the Vestory	00600
To D°. for finding a Coffin & Buring Joseph Mansfild	00120
To James Booker Sextorn	01000
To Cap^a Cleytons Acc°	00100
To Thomas Stubbs Sheriffs Acc°	00070

To Cap Samuel Buckner for Taking An Indenture fo Daniel M°clare Without any more Charge	01000
To Mary Ellis for a Levey Overcharged Last year	00033
To M' Augustin Smith for Three Seats for the Church Yard	00300
To John Routon for Leding the Windoes	00150
To M' David Alexander Repair the Vestory houſe and Three barils of Corne to Widd° Smith	00626
To M' Alexander for John Siners Levey	00033
To M' Thomas Booth for Siners Levey In 1732	00031
To Francis Easter for one hors Block & mending one	00075
To Thomas Boaden of King & Queen County upon provisoe he Take an Indenture for Wid° Smith Child	01600
To Mary Cox for Keeping A basterd Child One Year	00500
To Jn° Gil More for Keeping Rich⁴ Halcomb 129 days	00282
To Susanah Steers for Relief	00300
To Doc'. Semer for Cutting Off Tho Fleming Arme & Bord	900
To the Rev⁴ Em¹ Jones for Law Book for the Parish	00152
To M' Thomas Green for Cumunion Bred & Wine	00400
To Jm' Lewis for Relief	00500
	25820
To 8 ℔ Cᵗ	2066
	27886
℔ Co Credit	27895

By 864 Tithables @ 32 ℔ pole	27648	Due	00009
By Tob° Due from M' Alexander	00247		

                        27895   Cᵈ 50¹ Tob° More

        Turn Over

[236]

At This Vestory *that Mʳ Thomas Green is Appointed Collectʳ of this Parish and that he Collect of Every Titheable person the Sum of Thuurty Two pounds of Tobacco to pay off the Several parish Creditts Without the abatment of 10 ℔ Cent the Same Not being laid On As Alſo to Receive of Mʳ Da Alexander Two hundred forty Seven pounds of Tob Due in his hands And to pay of All the Several parish Creditors As the Law Dyrects

It is Ordered that Mʳ John Royston be Church warden of the Upper precint of this Parish In the Rome of Mʳ David Alexander it being his Turn

It is Ordered that John Mᶜclaran be Bound to Zach Leigh Till Lawfull Age

It is Ordered that Daniel Mᶜclaran be Bound to Cap Samuel Buckner Till Lawfull Age

It is Ordered that Jane Smith Decᵈ Child be bound to Thomas Boaden of King & Queen County if he will Take him if not to Any Other that Will for the Tobacco Leveyed this Vestory

     True Entry Test WBrooking C V

[237]

At A Vestory held for Petsworth Parrish April yᵉ 8ᵗʰ 1735

 Present

The Revᵈ Em¹ Jones	Mʳ Thomas Green C W
Mʳ Augustin Smith	Mʳ Seth Thornton
Mʳ John Royston C W	Mʳ Thomas Booth
Majʳ Jnᵒ Washington	Cap Sam¹ Buckner
Mʳ Fra Thornton	Mʳ David Alexander

At this Vestory Capⁿ John Smith Is Ellected and Choſen Vestoryman In the Rome of Mʳ John Throckmorton Decᵈ

---

*Note! This word has been scratched through in the MS., but is still legible.—C. G. C.

At this Vestry the fine Mony of Phillis Cilligrue And Mary Adamſon In the hands of Mr Augustin Smith and Mr David Alexander being five pound be deſtributed to the folowing pore People of This Parish Mr Smith to pay Vizt James Lewis 10/ Vicares Nettles 10/ Margret Bond 10/ Jeremia Darling 10/ Thomas Wollis 10/ Mr Alexander to pay vizt Wido Jackson 10/ Wido Bowen 10/ Wido Neal 10/ Richd Hope 10/ Simon Halcomb 10/

True Entry Test
WBrooking Cl V

Memorandom At this Vestory There was Great Subscriptions mad by ye Present Vestory for an Organ to be Purchasd. for the Uſe of the Church of Petsworth

[238]

At A Vestory held for Petsworth Parrish the 13th day of June 1735

Present the Revd Em͡l. Jones
    Mr Augustin Smith   Mr Seth Thornton
    Mr John Royston C W
    Mr Fra Thornton   Cap Sam Buckner
    Mr. Tho. Green C W   Mr Tho. Booth

It Is Ordered And Agreed that Mr Augustin Smith Receive the Money Given for the purchaſe of An Organ for the Uſe of Petsworth Church of the Several perſons yt Subscribed And Chang the Same Into Sterl And With What Convenient Speed he Can Send for As Good An Organ As the Said Money shall purchaſe In Great Brittaine And to have the Same Enſured the Danger of the Seas In and beſtow the Same to the Uſe Aforsd when Returned

It is Ordered that Margret Hartwel be bound to Daniel Hunter Till Lawfull Age

It is Ordered that Mʳ Guyn Reade be Chosen Vestry man in the Rome of Cap Smith Decᵈ (for the Uper precinct)

     True Entry Test
      WBrooking C V

[239]

At A Vestory held for Petsworth Parish the 3ᵈ day of Sepʳ. 1735

Present the Revᵈ Em̄¹ Jones   Cap Thoˢ Reade
  Mʳ Augⁿ Smith   Cap Sam¹ Buckner
  Mʳ Jnº Royston C W   Mʳ Thoˢ Booth
  Mʳ Tho Green C W   Mʳ David Alexander
  Mʳ Fra Thornton

In purſuant to An Order of Gloucester County Court dated on Thursday the 28 day of August 1735 to appoint proceſioners in Each precint of this parish to See the Lands proceſioned and to make Return to their proceedings by the Last day of March According to Law Wee Do therfore Order and appoint them as followeth vix

1 It is ordered that mʳ William Thornton and mʳ Thomas Cook See the Lands in the first precint proceſioned According to Law and bin at Claybank the first wedneſsday in Octʳ.

2 It Is Ordered that Mʳ John Thornton and mʳ Benj Cooke See the Lands in the Second precint proceſsioned According to Law and begin on the Second friday in Octʳ at Mʳ Thomas Cooks

3 It is Ordered that Mʳ Francis Easter and Mʳ Thomas Bolton See the Lands in the Third precinct proceſsioned According to Law and begin the Secconday in Octʳ at Mʳˢ Stubb's

4 It is Ordered that Mʳ James Dudley & Mʳ Geo Dudley See thee Lands in the fourth precint Proceſioned According to Law and Begin on the Seccond friday in Octoʳ at Mʳ Crittendens

It is Ordered that Mʳ Francis Lee and Wᵐ Brooking
5 See the Lands in the fifth precint proceſsioned According to Law and begin On the Third Wedneſday in Octoʳ. at Mʳ Rob Carters

It is Ordered that Mʳ Alexander Roane and mʳ James
6 Amis See the Lands in the Sixth precint proceſioned According to Law & Begin On the third friday in Octoʳ. at Mʳ Jnᵒ Garlands

Turn Over

[240] Brought Over

It is Ordered that Mʳ Benjᵃ Baker and Mʳ Tho Dudley
7 See the Lands in the Seventh precint proceſsioned According to Law and begin on the fourth Tuesday in Octʳ at Mʳ Jnᵒ Moors

It is Ordered that Mʳ Gwin Read and Mʳ John Col-
8 lawne See the Lands in the Eight precint proceſioned According to Law And begin on the fourth Monday in Octoʳ At Mʳ Augⁿ Smiths

It is Ordered that Mʳ Peter Kemp and Mʳ Bayley Sea-
9 ton See the Lands in the Ninth precint proceſsioned According to Law and begin On the Seccond Tuesday in Octoʳ at Mʳ Seatons

True Entry Test

WBrooking Cl V

[241]

At A Vestory held for Petsworth Parish the 8ᵗʰ day of Octʳ. 1735

Present the Revᵈ Emˡ Jones
    Mʳ Augⁿ Smith
    Mʳ John Royston C W
    Mʳ Thomas Green C W
    Mʳ Francis Thornton

Mʳ Seth Thornton
Cap Samˡ Buckner
Mʳ Thoˢ Booth
Mʳ Davᵈ Alexander
Mʳ Gwyn Reade

	Tobacco
Petsworth Parish Dʳ	
To the Revᵈ. Emanuel Jones his Sallery	16000

To Quitrents of the Glieb Land Dt°.	00054
To M' Alexander Roane Sallery	01000
To Wm Brooking Clear Vestory	00600
To James Booker Sextorne	01000
To Henry Griffin for a Coffin for Ellis Whitseeds	00050
To Cap^n Claytons Acc°.	00071
To Daniel Hunter for Taking Margret Hartwell by Indent^rs	01200
To D° for keeping McClareys Child 25 days	00058
To George Gardners Acc° for Work	00039
To W^m. Browns Acc° for Work	00021
To Mr Thomas Greens Account To Thos Fleming	00056
To John Ryley for a Levey Overcharged Last year	00032
To Cap Saml Buckner for painting the Gates	00150
To Mr John Royston for Communion Wine the y^r Insuing	00400
To Thomas Wallis for Releif	00200
To Tobacco Leveyed for the Gallery	2208
Parish Debt	23139
Cask & Saller @ 8 ℔ C^t	1851
Total Debt	24990
Parish Creddit By 833 Tithables @ 30 ℔ pole is	24990
Ther Remains	00000

Turn Over

[242] Brought Over

It is Ordered that Mr John Royston Church Warden Collect of Every Tithable perſon the Sum of 30^lb Tobacco to pay off The Severall parish Debts this year Without the Allowance of 10 p C the Same Not being Laid On

It is Ordered that Mʳ Francis Thornton be Church warden In the Lower precint in the Rome of Mʳ Thomas Green

      True Entry Test
         WBrooking C V

[243]

At A Vestory held for Petsworth Parish on Wedneſday Octʳ. yᵉ 6 1736

Present The Revᵈ. Eṁanuel Jones
- Mʳ Augⁿ. Smith
- Mʳ Jnᵒ Royston C W
- Mʳ Thoˢ Green
- Mʳ Fraˢ Thornton C. W
- Cap Thoˢ Reade
- Mʳ Conq Wiat
- Mʳ Seth Thornton
- Capⁿ Samˡ Buckner
- Mʳ Davᵈ Alexander
- Mʳ Gwyn Reade

   Petsworth Parish Debttʳ. in Tobacco

To the Revᵈ Eṁanuel Jones his Sallery	16000
To Dᵒ. for Quitrents of the Glieb Land	054
To Mʳ Alexandʳ Roane Cleark of the Church	1000
To James Booker Sextorn	1000
To Wᵐ Brooking Cleark of the Vestory	600
To Wᵐ Harington for Keeping & Bording Mary Mount one year till the 11ᵗʰ of Novʳ. next	600
To Capⁿ: Clayton Accᵒ for List of Tithables	20
To Henry Griffin for Two horſe Blocks	100
To Thomas Jones for 2 Leveys overcharged Last year	060
To Daniel Hunter for finding Coffin & bur: Mary Mᶜclaron	120
To Jer: Darnal for Keeping Dorothy Gorgy 5 Monts	333
To Dʳ. John Edward Accᵒ @ 2ᵈ ℔ lb in Tobacco	285
To Dʳ Symmers A Dᵒ	600

To Mr Francis Thornton for Bred & Wine ye ye^r Enſuing	400
To Tob^o Leveyed for the Gallery	1098
	22270
To Cask & Sallery @ 8 ℔^{r} C^t	1781
Total Deb^t Amount to	24051

Petsworth Parish Credit in Tobacco	
By 859 Tithables @ 28 ℔^{r} pole is	24052
Parish Deb^t	24051
There Remaines Due	·00001
Turn Over	
[244] Brought forward	

It is Ordered the Three pounds five Shilings fine money In the hands of Mr Augustin Smith be Distributed to the folowing poore people Viz^t To James Lewis 25 Shiling To Jeremiah Darnel 20 Shilings & to the Widd^o Sinar 20 Shiling to be paid in Goods by the Said Smith at Redy mony Rates

It is Ordered that Mr Augustin Smith be Chosen Churchwarden for the Uper precint of this Parish in the Rome of Mr Jno Royton

Ordered that Mr Francis Thornton be Collector of the Parish for the Enſuing year and Receive of Every Tithable perſon the Sum of 28^{lb} Tobacco to pay of the Severall parish Debt

           Tru Entry Test   WBrooking C V

[245]

At A Vestory held for Petsworth Parish the 16th day of Febru 1736

Present

The Reverd Em^l Jones	M^r. Francis Thornton C W
Mr Aug^a Smith C W	M^r. Conq Wiat
Mr John Royston	Mr Seth Thornton
Maj^r John Washington	Cap^n. Saml Buckner
Cap^n Thomas Reade	Mr Thomas Booth
Mr Thomas Green	Mr David Alexander

It is Agreed at this vestory that Mr William Ran Undertake & Build A Good & Substantial Gallery at the west End of the Church at Popler Spring for the Uſe of placing an Organ Winscoted painted hanſom and Substantialy Well Built Workman like for the Uſe afors^d withall Convenient Speed & Upon the Due performance of the Said building it is agred by the Said Vestory that the Said Ran have forty pounds Corrant that is 20^£ to be paid in hand and the Remainder to be paid by the Last day of March in the year 1738

At this Vestory Mr Bayley Seaton is Choſen Veſtoryman in the Rome of Mr Gwyn Reade

It is Agreed At this Vestory with Mr Em^l Jones that forasmuch that 2500^lb of Tobacco by a former Order hath been Leveyed and paid to the Said Mr Em^l Jones for the Repairs on the Glieb & *finding the Said Repairs not being Done It is Agreed that if they are not Done by the Laying the Next Parish Levey that then the Said Jones Refund the Said Tobacco or money at the Rate of Ten ℔ Centum

True Entry Test   WBrooking C V

---

*Note! This word has been scratched through in the MS., but is still legible.—C. G. C.

To Mr Francis Thornton for Bred & Wine yͤ yeʳ Enſuing	400
To Tobᵒ Leveyed for the Gallery	1098
	22270
To Cask & Sallery @ 8 ℔ʳ Cᵗ	1781
Total Debᵗ Amount to	24051

Petsworth Parish Credit in Tobacco
By 859 Tithables @ 28 ℔ʳ pole is   24052
Parish Debᵗ   24051

There Remaines Due   ·00001
Turn Over

[244]   Brought forward

It is Ordered the Three pounds five Shilings fine money In the hands of Mr Augustin Smith be Distributed to the folowing poore people Vizᵗ To James Lewis 25 Shiling To Jeremiah Darnel 20 Shilings & to the Widdᵒ Sinar 20 Shiling to be paid in Goods by the Said Smith at Redy mony Rates

It is Ordered that Mr Augustin Smith be Chosen Churchwarden for the Uper precint of this Parish in the Rome of Mr Jnᵒ Royton

Ordered that Mr Francis Thornton be Collector of the Parish for the Enſuing year and Receive of Every Tithable perſon the Sum of 28ˡᵇ Tobacco to pay of the Severall parish Debt

            Tru Entry Test   WBrooking C V

[245]

At A Vestory held for Petsworth Parish the 16th day of Febru 1736

Present

The Reverd Em¹ Jones	Mʳ. Francis Thornton C W
Mʳ Augᵃ Smith C W	Mʳ. Conq Wiat
Mʳ John Royston	Mʳ Seth Thornton
Majʳ John Washington	Capⁿ. Samˡ Buckner
Capⁿ Thomas Reade	Mʳ Thomas Booth
Mʳ Thomas Green	Mʳ David Alexander

It is Agreed at this vestory that Mʳ William Ran Undertake & Build A Good & Substantial Gallery at the west End of the Church at Popler Spring for the Uſe of placing an Organ Winscoted painted hanſom and Substantialy Well Built Workman like for the Uſe aforsᵈ withall Convenient Speed & Upon the Due performance of the Said building it is agred by the Said Vestory that the Said Ran have forty pounds Corrant that is 20ˢ to be paid in hand and the Remainder to be paid by the Last day of March in the year 1738

At this Vestory Mʳ Bayley Seaton is Choſen Veſtoryman in the Rome of Mʳ Gwyn Reade

It is Agreed At this Vestory with Mʳ Em¹ Jones that forasmuch that 2500ˡᵇ of Tobacco by a former Order hath been Leveyed and paid to the Said Mʳ Em¹ Jones for the Repairs on the Glieb & *finding the Said Repairs not being Done It is Agreed that if they are not Done by the Laying the Next Parish Levey that then the Said Jones Refund the Said Tobacco or money at the Rate of Ten ℔ Centum

True Entry Test WBrooking C V

---

*Note! This word has been scratched through in the MS., but is still legible.—C. G. C.

[246]

At A Vestory held for Petsworth parish the 7th day of Ap^l 1737

Present

Mr John Royston	Cap Saml Buckner
Mr Aug^n Smith C W	Mr Tho Booth
Mr Fra Thornton C W	
Mr Seth Thornton	Mr David Alexander

At this Vestory Mr Augustin Smith Suing that he having Rec^d of the Several Subscribers the mony Given for the purchaſe of An Organ the Said Subscriptions amounting to more mony then the Said Organ Cost. this preſent Vestory is of Oppinion that the Overplush of the Mony in the hands of Mr Aug^n. Smith Ought to be Apropriated towards the Suport and Maintanance of the Said Organ, and it is further Orderd And Agreed by the Gent^n. of the Vestory hear present that if Any of the Overplush of the mony is demanded Back by Any of the Subscribers or any Sute of Law Commenced Against the Said Smith for the Same that the Said Aug^n. Smith Shall Stand A Sute of Law for the Same and Emply An Attorney and that he be paid his Costs & Charges Out of the mony that Shall Remaine in his hands

True Entry Test
WBrooking C Ves

Memorandom

That the Gentl^n. that Subscrib^d. for the Organ hear preſent Unanimousely Agreed And Subscribed to An Instrument of Writing that the mony Given Towards the Organ that is Over & Above the purchase of the Said Organ Shall & Ought to Goe Towards the Support and bennifit of the Same As the Vestory Shall Think fitt to Order it

[247]

At A Vestory held for Petsworth Parish the 29th day of June 1737

<blockquote>
Present The Revd Em^l Jones   Cap Thomas Reade
Mr John Royston   Mr Conq^t Wiat
Mr Augustine Smith   Mr Seth Thornton
Maj^r Jno Washington   Mr Thomas Booth
Mr Thomas Green   Mr David Alexander
Mr Francis Thornton   Mr Baley Seaton
</blockquote>

It is Ordered that Mr Anthony Collins be Entertained An Organist for the Parish Church of Petsworth from the Eight day of April last and that he be paid as Shall be appointed at the laying the next parish Levey

It is Orderered that the Order of Vestory dated the Seventh day of April for M^r. Augustin Smith to Stand a Trial at Law for the mony that Should be Demand^d. back Given for the purchase of the Organ Be Reversed & of No Effect

At this Vestory Mr Bayley Seaton was Sworn Vestory man for this Parish in the Rome of Mr Gwyn Reade

Memorandom that Mr Augustin Smith Ch Warden Acquaint^d the Vestory that he Agreed with Mr James Dudley for the Keeping & Cure of Margret Thomas her Legg at the Uiseal Rate ℔ Annum from this date

<blockquote>
True Entry Test
WBrooking
</blockquote>

[248]

At A Vestory held for Petsworth Parish the 12th day of Ocr. 1737

Present the Revd Emanuel Jones
- Mr Augustin Smith C W
- Mr John Royston
- Major Jno Washington
- Mr Francis Thornton C W
- Mr Conqt Wiat
- Mr Thos Green
- Mr Seth Thornton
- Capn Saml Buckner
- Mr Thomas Booth
- Mr David Alexander

Petsworth Parish Dettr in Tobacco

To the Revd Emanuel Jones his Sallery	16000
To Ditto. for Extrodinary Charge in Repairing the Glieb houſe	319
To Ditto. for Quitrents of the Glieb Land As Uſeial	054
To Mr Alexander Roane Cleark of the Church	1000
To James Booker Sextorn of Church	1000
To Wm Brooking Clark of the Vestory	600
To Cap John Claytons Acco for List of Tithables	020
To Mr Frances Thornton for 2 ℔ Ct not Charged Last year	445
To Do for 2 Leveys Ward & Allard Not to be found	056
To Jeremiah Darnel for Keeping Dorothy Goargy one year	800
To Wm Harington for Keeping Mary Mount one year	300
To James Dudley for Keeping Margret Thomas 3 mos & 14 days	233
To Mr Augustin Smiths Acco in Mony @ 18 ℔ Ct is	196
To Capn Buckner & Mr. Booth for *bringunt Up the Organs	500
To Mr Francis Easters Accu	055

*Note! A hard word to decipher. I may have read it incorrectly.—C. G. C.

To Mʳ Augustin Smith for Comunion Wine the Year
Enſuing   400
To Tobacco Levied for the Uſe of the Parish to be
Sold for Cash   1395

                                                                    23373
    To Cask & Sallery @ 10 ℔ Ct Amᵗ to   2337

            Paris Debt   25710
    By Credit ℔ 857 Tithabes @ 30 ℔ pole   25710

            Ballance Due is   00000
            Carryed forward
[249]   Brought forward

At This Vestory Mʳ Augustin Smith Church warden is Appointed Collector for the parish this year and that he Collect of Every Titheable Person 30ᵇ of Tobacco to Discharg the Several Parish Credits

At This Vestory Mʳ Seth Thornton is apointed Churchwarden in the Lower precint in the Rome of Mʳ Francis Thornton he being Discharge from the Said office

It is Ordered that Mʳ Anthony Collins be paid Ten pound Corrt mony by Mʳ Augustin Smith Out of the Mony Remaining in his hands it being for Six Months Servis as an Organist And Continue at the Same Rate ℔ Annum he duly Officiating in the Said office & Oblidging himsel To Teach Som Other fit perſon in the Mistory of the Said Musick with all Convenient Speed he Can

It is Ordered And Agreed that Mʳ Augustin Smith have 7½ ℔ Cᵗ for Collecting the Mony Due for the purchasing the Organ And after the Making Up of the Said Account he has Made A present of the said ℔ Ct to be Laid Out by the Ustory of this Parish Towards the Support and bennefit of the Said Organ or Organist

True Entry Test
WBrooking Cl Vestory

[250]

At A vestory held for Petsworth Parish y⁰ 29ᵗʰ of June 1738

Present the Revᵈ Emˡ. Jones
Mʳ Augustine Smith C W   Mʳ Seth Thornton C W
Mʳ John Royston   Capⁿ Samˡ. Buckner
Majʳ Jnᵒ. Washington   Mʳ Thomas Booth
Mʳ Thoˢ Green   Mⁿ David Alexander

At this preſent vestory it is Ordered And Agreed with Mʳ Samuel Peacock that he Do with what Convenient Speed he Can hanſomly paint the Aulter peace of Popler Spring Church in ye parsh afosᵈ as alſo the paint Coving Within the Church that has bent Spoilt by mens of the Leacage of the Roofe of the Church Angles As alſo to paint all the Cornish Doors Windors and Sashes and All Otherwork that Requirs painting And to find all the Oyles & Coulers Except the Leaf Gould that is to be made Uſe of for the Carving Work and Other work that is to be Done on the Said Aulterpeace And for the Due performance of the Said Work Well & workmanlike to be Done and performed it is Agreed that the Said Samˡ Peacok or his Order is to have & Receive fifteen pounds Corᵗ Mony by Vertue of this Order from the parish Aforsᵈ.

At this Vestory Mʳ William Thornton Jnʳ. is Choſen Vestory man in the Rome of Mʳ Fra Thornton Deᵈ. for the Lower precints of this Parish

It is by this Vestory Agreed With Mʳ. Augustine Smith Gentⁿ Church warden that he Doe with all Convenient Speed he Can Send for 700 Leaves of Leafe Gould for yᵉ

Uſe of the Aulter peace and that he be paid for it by The parish @ y° Rate of 5 ℔ Cent from the prime Cost in Corant Mony

Cary[d] forward

[251]

It is Agreed With Cap[a]. Samuel Buckner that he provide Six Barrels of Tarr and Cause the Same to be made Uſe of In Tarring the Roofe of Popler Spring Church as allso to find Shingles and put in And mend All the places Where Any of the Old Ones is Decay[d] or Gon and further it is Agreed that if ther is more Tar then Six barils to be made Uſe of in Well Tarring the Said Church to provid it & that y° Said Buckner is to be allowed his Charge for the Same And in the Due performance of the Said Work he is to be Allowed And paid Seven pounds Corant Mony

True Redgister Test
WBrooking C. Ves.

[252]

At A Vestory held for Petsworth Parish the 18th day of Oct[r]. 1738

Present

M[r] Augustin Smith	Cap Sam[l] Buckner
M[r] John Royston	M[r] Thomas Booth
Maj[r] John Washington	M[r] David Alexander
M[r] Thomas Green	M[r] Bayley Seaton
M[r] Seth Thornton C W	M[r] W[m] Thornton

Petsworth Parish Dett[r] in Tobacco this Year Vizt

To the Rev[d] Em[l] Jones his Sallery	16000
To Ditt° for Quitrents of the Glieb Land	54
To M[r] Alexander Roane Cleark of the Church his Sallery	1000
To James Booker Sextorn of the Church his Sallery	1000
To W[m] Brooking Cleark of the Vestory his Sallery	0600

To Mr Seth Thornton for Communion Wine the year Enſuing	0400
To Richard Lovel for Saudering the Organ pips	0028
To Benj^a Baker for Keeping Margret Thomas one year	0600
To Mr Augustin Smith Acc° for Goods for the pore	0060
To Jeremiah Darlin for Keeping Dorothy Gorgy one year	0800
To Wm Thorntons Acc°. for Elizabeth Malton	0112
To Wm Devals Acc° for Making Steps for the Organ	0066
To Saml Whitus for Keeping 2 Children of Mary Hilton	0350
To Henry Griffin finding A Coffin & Sheat for James Lewis	0100
To Wm Harington for Burying Mary Mount	0070
To Mr Francis Easter for 2 horſe Blocks	0100
To Capⁿ Saml Buckner for Taring the Church	0777
To Mrs Anne Thorntons Acc°.	0027
To Tobacco Leveyed for the Uſe of the Church	4240
	26384
To Cask and Sallery @ 10 ℔ Ct	2638
Total parish Deb^t	29022
Parish Creditt By	
By 900 Tithables @ 32 ℔ pole is	28800
Ther Remains Due to the Collector	00222

Caryed forward
[253]   Brought forward

It is Ordered that Mr Augustin Smith pay Mr Anthony Collins Twenty pounds Corrant Ouut of the Mony Remaining in his hands Raised for the purchaſe of the Organs

At this Vestry M[r] William Thornton Toock the Oaths of Vestry Man for the Parish Afors[d].

At this Vestry M[r] Bayley Seaton is Chofen Church warden in the Rome of M[r] Augustin Smith for the Uper precints of this Parish

It is Ordered And Appointed that M[r] Seth Thornton Church warden be Collector for this parish the year Enfuing and that he Collect of Every Tithable perfon the Sum of 32[lb] of Tobacco to pay of the Several parish Creditts

True Redgester Test
WBrooking C V.

At A Vestory held for Petsworth Paris y[e] 6th. day of Nov[r] 1738

Present the Rev[d] Em[l]. Jones

M[r] John Royston
M[r] Thomas Green
Cap[n] Thomas Reade
M[r] Seth Thornton

Cap[n] Sam[l] Buckner
M[r] Thomas Booth
M David Alexander

At this Vestory it Ordered And it is Defired that Cap[n] Sam[l] Buckner Soliciate the Afembly With A petetion for An Act *of *Afsembly for the parish of Petsworth to pay their Organist by a pole Tax And that he be paid his Charge for the Same by the parish

True Entry Test
WBrooking C V

---

*Note! These words are scratched through in the MS., but are still plainly legible.—C. G. C.

[254]

A A Vestory Held for Petsworth Parish the 9th day of Febr. 1738

Present the Revd Eml Jones

Mr John Royston	Mr Thomas Booth
Mr Augustine Smith	Mr David Alexander
Majr John Washington	
Capn Saml Buckner	Mr Baley Seaton C W

At this Vestory it is Ordered that Whearas at A Vestory held for This Parish Dated the 18th day of October last at the Laying of the Parish Levey it was Ordered that Mr Seth Thornton Churchwarden Should Receive of Every Tithable perſon the Sum of 32lb of Tobacco which with the Allowance of 10 ℔ Ct was Two ℔ Ct more then what the Law Allows for Collecting of Parish Tobo it is Thought fit by this Vestory that the Said 2 ℔ Ct be Remitted. But that he Receive the Said 32lb. of Tobo. ℔ pole and Account for the Said Two ℔ Ct to the Uſe of the Parish Which Amounts to 305lb of Tobo more then What the Parish Debt was

It is Ordered that Mr Seth Thornton Receive of Mr Augustin Smith 467lb. of Tobo. it being for 2 ℔ Ct that was levyed more yn was Due by Law for the year 1737. And Alſo it is Ordered that he Receive of Mrs Anne Thornton 445lb Tobo it being for the 2 ℔ Ct Leveyed for Mr Francis Thornton more then the Law Allowed in his Collection for the year 1736 And that he Accot for the Said Tobo. for the Uſe of the Parish

True Entry Test

WBrooking Cl V.

[255]

At A Vestory held for Petsworth Parish June y⁰ 20ᵗʰ 1739

Preſent the Revᵈ. Emˡ. Jones
  Mʳ Augustin Smith
  Majʳ John Washington
  Mʳ Thomas Green
  Mʳ Seth Thornton C W
  Mʳ Conquest Wiat
  Mʳ Thomas Booth
  M Capⁿ Buckner
  Mʳ David Alexander
  Mʳ Bayley Seaton C W

At this Vestory it is Ordered And Agreed that Seven pounds One Shiling In the hands of Mʳ Bayley Seaton Church Warden being mony Due to the pore of this parish for the fine Of Ann Hopwood being Sold Be distributed to the Several perſons as followeth viz To Thomas Poole £2 ‖ 10ˢ and to Vicares Nettles Michael Willis Wiᵈᵒ Elizᵃ Lewis Wᵈ. Jane Haines Wiᵈᵒ & Mary Sprat Wiᵈᵒ Each 18/2ᵈ Which Amounts to the Said Sum

At This Vestory Mʳ James Hubard is Choſen Vestory man in the Rome of Cap Thomas Reade Decᵈ for the Uper precints of this Parish

It is Also *Ordered Deſired by this present Vestory that Mʳ Bayley Seaton Write to Mʳ Charles Carter for his painter to Undertake the painting Work of the Aulter peace of the Church

                True Entry Test
                    WBrooking Cl V

---

*Note! The word "Ordered" has been scratched through in the MS., and the word "Deſired" written above it.—C. G. C.

[256]

At A Vestry held for Petsworth Parish the 28 of July 1739

Present the Revd Eml Jones

Mr John Royston
Maj^r John Washington
Mr Thomas Green
Cap Saml Buckner

Mr David Alexander
Mr Bayley Seaton C W
Mr William Thornton

At This Vestory it is ordered And Agreed With Richard Cooke and him In behalf of his Master Mr Charles Carter That he Doe With all Convenent Speed provide Oyle & paint; to Do and proforme the work hear next Mentioned that is to Say the Aulter peace to be Neatly Painted: the Ground work of the Pannels to be Jappand; the Creed Lords Prayor & Ten Comandments to be Done In A Leagable hand In fair Gold letters and All the Carvingwork to be Guilded And to paint all the Coving in the Angles Whear it has bene Spilt or Defased And to hanſomly paint Six Pues In the Church Within & Without of A Windscote Couler And to New Paint the pulpit And Cañopy And to New paint and Prime all the Doors of the Church window frames Sashes Cornish Churchyard Gates And posts And to find And provide all the Oyle & Coullers Except the leaf Gould that is to be made Uſe of in the Work. And for the Due Proformance of the Said Work that then the Said Vestory Do Oblidge themſelves to pay Twenty pounds Corant Mony of Virg^a. At the finishing of the Work And Twenty pounds more being the full payment At this date Twelve month. Scafoling Only Exceped Which the Gent^{en}: of the Vestory Oblidge them Selves to find

True Entry Test
WBrooking

agred to in the behalf of
Charles Carter

Richard Cooke

[257]

At A Vestory held for Petsworth Parish the 12ᵗʰ day of Octobʳ 1739

Present The Revᵈ Emˡ: Jones
- Mʳ John Royston
- Mʳ Augustin Smith
- Majʳ John Washington
- Capᵃ Samˡ Buckner
- Mʳ Tho: Booth
- Mʳ Bayley Seaton CW
- Mʳ Wᵐ Thornton

Petsworth Parish Dʳ. In Tobacco this year

To the Reverᵈ Emˡ Jones his Sallery as ℔ʳ Annum	16000
To Dittº for the Quitrents of the Glieb Land	0054
To Mʳ Alexander Roane Cleark of the Church Sallery	1000
To James Booker Sextorn his Sallery	1000
To Wᵐ Brooking Cleark of the Vestory his Sallery	0600
To Mʳ Augustin Smiths Accº for Goods to Dorothy Gorgy	0193
To Mʳ Bayley Seatons Accº for Goods to Margret Thomas	0200
To John Guilbert More for Keeping Thomas Hilton a Child	0600
To Wᵐ Duvals Accº for work done to the Church	0160
To Mʳ Seth Thornton for Charges to Robert Lodge	0127
To Jeremiah Darnel for Keeping Dorothy Gorgy	0800
To Capᵃ Samˡ Buckners Accº & for Scaffels for the painter	0374
To Docʳ Simmer for Bording Margret Thomas	0600
To Mʳ Seth Thornton for a Levey Overcharged last year	0032
To Elizabeth Hilton for Keeping her Child Two Month	0100

To Mr Bayley Seaton for Comunion wine the year Enſuing		0400
To Tobacco Raised for the Uſe of the Parish		2700
		24940
To the 8 ℔ Ct on the wole		1995
Total Parish Debt Amt to		26935
Parish Credit viz		
By 906 Tithables @ 30 ℔r pole is	27180	
	26935	
Remander Due	00245	

Turn Over

[258] Brought forward Octor. ye. 12. 1739

It is Ordered that Mr Augustin Smith pay Mr Anthony Collins Organist Twenty Pounds Corrant out of the mony Remaining in his hands Raised for the purchase of the Organs

It is Ordered that Mr William Thornton be Churchwarden in the Rome of his Brother Mr Seth Thornton for the Lower precint of this Parish

It is Ordered that Mr Bayley Seaton be Collector for the Parish the Enſuing Year And that he Collect of Every Tithable perſon the Sum of Thirty pounds of Tobo. to pay of the Severall Parish Credits

At this Vestory it was alſo Ordered And Appointed the Severall proceſsions to See the Lands in the Severall precints of this Parish Proceſioned According to Law And to begin On the Times And places As followeth viz

1. Mr Thomas Minor & Mr Wm Oliver begin On the Second Monday In November At Mr William Thorn-

tons in the first precnt of this Parish And to Make their Return by the Last day of March According to Law

2 Mʳ *Seth John Thornton & Mʳ William Thornton the Yunger begin on the Seccond Thursday in November at the Said Wᵐ Thorntons And to Make their Return As aforsᵈ.

3 Mʳ Francis Eastor & Mʳ Wᵐ Fleming to begin on the *Seccond Third Tuesday in Novʳ. At the Said Flemings And to Make their Return As Aforsaid

4 Mʳ Richard Crittenden & Mʳ Henry Purcil begin on the Third Friday in Novʳ At the Said Crittendens And to Make their Return According to Law

Goe forward

[259]   Brought forward Octʳ. yᵉ. 12ᵗʰ. 1739

5ᵗʰ Mʳ Francis Lee & William Brooking Begin on the Third Tuesday In November At Mʳ James Hubards & to make their Return According to Law

6 Mʳ Alexander Roane and Mʳ James Amies Begin on the Second Wedneſday in Novʳ. at Mʳ John Garlands and to make their Return According to Law

7 Mʳ James Dudley & mʳ George Dudley Begin on the fourth Monday in Novʳ. at mʳ John Moors And to Make their Return According to Law

8 Mʳ David Alexander and Mʳ John Collawn Begin On the Second Thursday in Novʳ. At Mʳ Augustin Smiths And to Make their Return According to Law

9 Mʳ James Wiat and Mʳ Francis Wiat Begin On the Third Thursday in Novʳ. at Mʳ Martin Connor's and to Make their Return According to Law

True Entry Test
WBrooking Cl Ves

---

*Note! These words are scratched through in the MS., but are still legible.—C. G. C.

[260]

Petsworth Parish

On November the 5ᵗʰ. 1739 The Gentⁿ. of the Vestory being Preſent viz Mʳ John Royston Capⁿ Samuel Buckner Capⁿ David Alexander Mʳ James Hubard

It is Thought fitt to Order that Whearas Charles Roane being Unleagally Sent into this Parish being Sick & lame And not in A Condition to be Removed to the Parish of his Last Reſidency the Gentlemen of the Vestory As aforsᵈ. has thought fitt to Order that the Church wardens Provide for him Untill Such Time as he Shall be Capable of being Removed According to Law

It is Alſo Ordered that Mʳ Richard Aſhur be proceſsioner in the Rome of Capⁿ David Alexander for the 8ᵗʰ precint of this Parish

     True Redgester Test
       WBrooking Cl Ves

[261]

At A Vestory held for Petsworth Parish the 8ᵗʰ day of June 1739

Present

Mʳ John Royston	Capⁿ Samˡ Buckner
Mʳ Augustin Smith	Mʳ Thomas Booth
Majʳ John Waſhington	Capⁿ David Alexander
Mʳ Thomas Green	Mʳ William Thornton C W
Mʳ Conqᵗ Wiat	Mʳ James Hubard

At This Vestory it is Ordered that Whearas by the Deceaſe of the Late Reverᵈ. Mr Emañuel Jones this Parish of Petsworth is become Vacant of A Minister This Vestory do therefore Unanimouſely Consent And Agree to Chuſe the Reverᵈ. Mʳ Robert Yeats for their Minister And that As Soon As It Shall Please God that he Shall Safe

Arive from Great Brittaine To Take the Cure of the Parish And to be Allowed All Such Salleryes And perquisits As Are Uſeial and As the Law dyrects And Untill Which Time the Revᵈ. Mʳ John Reade & the Revᵈ. Mʳ Yeats of Middleſex has Agreed to Officiate As Minister Or procure Some Other Minister in their Stead to Preach at pople Spring On Sundays Or On Wedneſdays weakly As they Shall Appoint And to Allow the Sallery to the Widdᵒ. And famely of the Said late Deceasᵈ Emˡ Jones Untill the first wedneſday In Octʳ Next

At this Vestory Mʳ Edward Wiat is Choſen Vestory Man in the Rome of Mʳ Seth Thornton Decᵈ

True Entry Test WBrooking Cl V

[262]

At A Vestory held for Petsworth Parish yᵉ 8ᵗʰ day of April 1740

Present

Mʳ John Royston	Mʳ David Alexander
Mʳ Thomas Green	Mʳ Bayley Seaton C W
Mjʳ John Washington	Mʳ Wᵐ Thornton C W
Cap Samˡ Buckner	Mʳ James Hubard
Mʳ Thomas Booth	Mʳ Edward Wiat

At this Vestory it was put to the Voate Whether the Repairs On the Glieb Oaught not to be put in Repair At the Coast of the Reverᵈ. Emanuel Jones Decesᵗ Estate or At the Charge of the Parish And it was Carryᵈ. by the Voate that the Building On the Glieb Ought to be put in Such Like Repairs As they were in At the Pasing the Act of Aſemby made in the year 1727 for the Better Suport of the Clergy of this Dominion &ᶜ At the Cost And Charg of the Said Deceaseᵈ. Estate: (The Gentlemen that Opposᵈ it Deſir'd that they might be Enterd of the Contrary

Opinion Viz M\ː John Royston Cap\ᵃ Sam\ˡˡ Buckner M\ʳ James Hubard)

At this Vestory it is Ordered And Agreed with Cap\ᵃ Sam\ˡˡ Buckner that he Undertake to make All Such Repairs on the Mantion houſe On the Glieb As Shall be found Neſsesary And to build one 16 & 12 foot dary one Meat houſe 12 foot Square One Stable 24 & 16 foot one Neſseſsary houſe 8 & 6 foot And to do and performe the Said Work with all Convenient Speed And to bring in his Charge to the Next Vestory to be held after the Due performance of the Said Work And to be paid his Charge *At *the As the then Preſent Vestory Shall Appoint

True Entry Test
WBrooking C V

[263]

At A Vestory held for Petsworth Parish 15\ᵗʰ of Oct\ʳ 1740

Present Mʳ John Royston   Mʳ Da Alexander
         Mʳ Thomas Green   Mʳ Wᵐ Thornton
         Majʳ John Washington   Mʳ James Hubard
         Mʳ Conqᵗ Wiat
         Cap Saml Buckner

To the Revᵈ Emˡ Jones Decᵈ Estate	4000
To Mʳ Alexander Roane his Sallery	1000
To James Booker Sextorn	1000
To Wᵐ Brooking Clear of the Vestory	0600
To Mʳˢ Ann Jones for 8 Mo Sallery for Mʳ John Reads & Mʳ Yeates Offisiating As Minister	12000
To Mʳ James Hubard for Goods to Charles Roane	00277
To Mʳˢ Mary Thorntons Accᵒ	00135
To Thomas Boulton for his Cart	00050
To John Trivilion for bording hiltons Child	00600

*Note! These words are scratched through in the MS., but are still legible.—C. G. C.

To Dʳ Symers Accᵒ for A Woman	01000
To Dᵒ for Charles Roans bord	00250
Do Docʳ Stretchey for Charles Roane	00800
To Tobacco Leveyd for the Uſe of the Parish to be disposᵈ *for [By] the †Uſe [Vestry] of the parish	06400
To Mʳˢ Cook for Dorothy Gorgis bord	00800
To Mʳ Wᵐ Thornton for Comūnion Wine Next year	00300
	29212
Credit by Mʳ Edward Wiat	250
Total Sum	28962
To 8 ℔ Ct Upon the Whole	2317
	31279
Parish Credit by 878 Tithables @ 36 ℔ pole	31608
Due to the Parish & to be paid to Mʳ Amis Upon Accᵒ of Charles Roane	329

It is Order by this preſent Vestory that Mʳ James Hubard be Church warden in the Rome of Mʳ Baley Seaton

Tur Over

[264]

It is Ordered that Mʳ James Hubard And Mʳ Wᵐ Thornton Agree with Som Minister to Officiat in the Cure of this Parish Untill Mʳ Yeats Shall be Recᵈ. in this Parish or Som Other Minister

It is Orderd that Mʳ Augustin Smith pay Mʳ Anthony Collins Twenty pound Corand & Eight Shilings for for his Servis and Mending the Organ

---

*Note! Over the word "for" has been written the word "by," but the word "for" is still legible.—C. G. C.

†Note! Above the word "Use," which is not scratched through in the MS. has been written the word "Vestry."—C. G. C.

It is Ordered that Mr Daniel New be Cleark of the Church And Upon his Due performance to have 1000 pds of Tob° ℔ Annum

It is Orderd that Mr Anthony Collins Officiate as Organis Untill Such Time As the mony in the hands of Mr Augin Smith be Expended At the Rate of 20 pound per annum

It is Ordered And Agreed As A Standing Rule to be Observ^d in the Vestory that all Orders made by the Vestory Shall be ſigned by Two of the Eldist Vestory men then preſent And that All Orders Not So Signed Shall be Invaled And of No Effect

       John Royston
       Thos Green

21 of Ot^r

John Hardcaſtle Confest And Are Chargeable to pay his 3 Leveys @ 36 ℔^r pole Which is to be Accounted for by the Collector

      ℔ WBrooking C V

[265]

At A Vestory held for Petso Parish the 14th of Octr. 1741

Present

Mr John Royston	Maj^r Buckner
Mr Augⁿ Smith	Mr Wm Thornton C W
Mr Tho Green	Cap Alexander
Maj Jn° Washington	Mr Ja^s Hubard C W

To the Revd Mr Ford for year Sallery   16000
†T Dan New Clerk Church   1000

 *Note! This whole order (enclosed between asterisks) has been scratched through in the MS., but is still entirely legible. The rule laid down in the order appears to have been observed for about six years.
 †Note! This line was evidently inserted after what are now the first and third lines were written; the third line therefore refers to the Rev. Mr. Ford and not to Dan. New.—C. G. C.

To his Ferrages	1000
To Wm Brooking Cl of the Vestry	600
To Jas Booker Sextorn	1000
To Ann Trivillion for Hiltons Childs Bord	0600
To Anne Crittenden for Keeping Dolly Gorgit	0800
To the Collector for the Communion	0400
To John Blasingame for Benches & hors blocks	0720
To Wm Thornton for Burying Eliz Hilton	0200
To Mary Sprat for Bording Jos Stears	175
To Do^r Mackinza	822
To Mr Seaton 2 Levies	072
To Sollom Hall's Levey	36
To Do^r Symer for Cha Roans Bord	600
To Cap Claytons Acc°	20
To Mr Hubard for Bal Due to Col° Carter	300
	24417
	1953
	26370
	26550
Due	180

Thes Proceedig Taken by Jam^s Carter And Entered by me

                        W Brooking Cl Vestory

                A Coppy

It is Ord^d that James Hubard be Colleter the Enſuing year and that he Receive 29½ Tobo of Every Tithable perſon

Maj^r Saml Buckner is Choſen Church warden in the Rome of m^r William Thornton

[266]

At A Vestory held for Petso Parish the 9th of Novr. 1742

Presesent

Mr Rob Yeats Minister
   Mr John Royster   Mr Wm Thornton
   Mr Thomas Green   Cap Da: Alexander
   Mr Conq^t Wyat   Mr James Hubard
   Maj^r Buckner C W

Petsworth Parish D^r.

To the Revd Mr Yeats his Sallery and for Quitrents of the Glieb Land	16054
To Daniel New Cl Church	1000
To Jas Booker Sextorn	1000
To Wm Brooking Cl Vestry	0600
To Maj^r Buckner for Comunion	400
To Anne Crittenden for bording Dor Gorgit	700
To Tho: Stubs for buring D^o	175
To Anne Trivillon for bording Hiltons Child	600
To Jno Moore for bording Steers	250
To Cap Clayton for Cop list Tithabls	020
To Mr James Hubard for Goods to Jo Sters	355
To Do^r Mackenseys Acc^o for Steers & Gorgit	800

To Doc^r Symer's Acc^o for Cha
  Roane viz   £ 21. 4. 3^{d}½

To his Ac^o Whilst at Amis	2. 02. 0	in Tob^o. & for bord 7 Months	3385
To his Charge for Medicin & Dreſing whilst with him	15 10		
To D^o. for Cloathing	3. 12. 3 ½		
	21. 4. 3 ½		

To Francis Brows Acc°	185
To John Blasingam's Acc°	60
To Tobacco Levey for the Uſe of the Parish	1200
Par Deb	26784
Cask & Sallery	2678
Total Acc°	29462

Cap Sam¹ Buckner is App⁴ Collector And that he Receive 32ˡ Tob° ℔ʳ pole to pay of the Several Parish Debtˢ

Mʳ Edward Wiat is Appointed Churchwarden in the Rome of Mʳ James Hubard

It is Orderᵈ that the Churchwardens Agree With Some Workmen to Make all Such Repairs at the Glieb as is Wanting

It is Orderᵈ that the Churchwardin Advise With Some Lawyere to bring Sute for the Recovery of Certain Charges Relating to Charles Roane Against the parish from Whome it may be Recoverable

John Royston
Thoˢ Greene

[267]

At A Vestory held At the Glieb yᵉ 16ᵗʰ of Decʳ. 1742

Present
the Revᵈ Mʳ Rob Yeats } Cap Alexander
Mʳ Augⁿ Smith } Mʳ J. Hubard
Mʳ Tho Green } M Ed Wiat
Capⁿ Sam¹ Buckmer }

It is Ordᵈ that Mʳ James Carter have for pailing a Garden at the Glieb and other Serveses 857ˡᵇ Tob to be paid by the Collector Out of the Tob° Levey⁴ for the Uſe of the Parish for Such Servises

Augustine Smith
Thoˢ. Greene

True Entry Test WBrooking

[268]

At A Vestory held for Petso Parish yᵉ 5ᵗʰ of Octʳ 1743

the Revᵈ Mʳ Robᵗ Yeats
Mʳ John Royston
Mʳ Augⁿ Smith
Mʳ Tho Green
Majʳ Washington
Mʳ Conqt Wiat

Cap Buckner
Mʳ. Jaˢ Hubard
Capⁿ Edᵈ Wiat

To the Revᵈ Mʳ Robᵗ Yeats & Qᵗ rents	16054
To Mʳ Danˡ. New	1000
To James Booker	1000
To Wᵐ Brooking Cl Vestory	600
To Mʳ James Hubard Acc° £1. 1. 4ᵈ. @ 15/℔ C	143
To Ann Trivilion for Keeping Hiltons Child	600
To John Gilb More for Going to Mʳ Powers	067
To Doʳ. Mackenzey for Reb° Harington & a Child	313
To Majʳ Buckner for find Comunion Bred & Wine	450
To Tobacco for the Uſe of the Parish	2000
To 4 pʳ. Cᵗ. for Cask on 23116ˡᵇ Tob°	889
To 6 pʳ. Cᵗ. for Collecting	1386
	24502
By 950 Tithables @ 26 ℔ pole	24700
Due to yᵉ parish	198

the Overplush Orderᵈ to Anne Jones

Mʳ Thomas Green is appointed Churchwarden in the lower precint

Ord Mʳ John Shermer Vestory Man

Mʳ Edward Wiat is Chosen Collector the Year Inſuing

The Several proceſsioners is Chosen As followeth

It is Orderᵈ that Mʳ Wᵐ Thornton & Thoˢ Minor be proceſsioner in the first precint & begin on the Second Monday in Novembʳ. Next

It is Ordered that Mʳ John Thornton & Thomas Thornton be proceſsioners in the Second precinct & begin on the Second Thrsday in November Next

[269]
It is ordered that Robᵗ Proyor & Wᵐ Fleming be proceſioners in the third precinct & begin on the third Monday in Novʳ. Next

It is Orderᵈ that Thomas Stubs & John Ware be proceſsioners in the fourth precint and begin on yᵉ Third [   ] day in Novʳ. Next

It is Orderᵈ that Mʳ Francis Lee & Wᵐ Brooking be proceſsioners in the fifth precint & begin the fourth Monday in Novʳ. Next

It is Ord that Mʳ James Amis & Wᵐ Keningham b proceſiʳˢ in the Sixt precinct & begin on the Second Tuesday in Novʳ Next

It is Orderᵈ that John Thurston & Thᵒ Dudley be proceſions in the Seventh precint & begin on the Second thursday in Novʳ.

It is Orderᵈ that Mʳ Jnᵒ Shermer and John Collawn be proceſʳˢ in the 8 precint and begin on the Third Monday in Novʳ Next

It is Orderd that Mʳ Peter Kemp & Mʳ Martin Connor be proeſ [   ] in the 9ᵗʰ precinct And begin on the third thursday in Noʳ Next it is Ordered that the Several fines due to the pore of this Parish be distributed to the Several pore people in this parish as folow^t

 to Elizbth Jonſon ten Shil in Mr Hubards hands
 to Mary Sprat 30/ in Maj^r Buckners hands
 to Wid° Luis 17/6 in Mr Buckners hands & 10/ in Mr Stubbs hands
 20/ in Maj^r Washings hands & 4/6 in Mr Wiats hands to D°. Harington
 15/ in James Carters hands to W^d Jackson

Ordered that the Churchwardens agree with Some person to Stop the leak in the Church and to put a New Collum under the Gallerry

          John Royston

[270]

At a Vestrey held for Petsworth Parish the 3 day of October
        1744

Present ye Revd Mr Yeats
 Mr John Royston
 M^r. Aug^n. Smith
 Mr Thos: Green   Capt. Alexander
 Mr Conq^t Wiatt   M^r: Ja^s: Hubard
 Mr Will^a: Thornton   M^r: John Shermer

To y^e. Rev^d: Mr Yeates	16000
To D°. Quitrents for the Glieb	00054
To M^r: Daniel New	01000
To Mr *James Sexton	01000
To W^m: Brooking Cl Vestrey	00600
To Capt Claytons acc^t	0091
To M^r: James Hubard for Doc^r. Simers Charge for a Sute in Case of Charles Roane	0720

 *Note! By mistake the Clerk omitted the Sexton's last name; i. e. "Booker."—C. G. C.

To Chr° Macdonald for taking hiltons Child	1500
To Fra⁸. Stears for burying Moors Daughter	0175
To Mʳ. Thoˢ Greens Accᵗ	0100
To Tob° for the Use of the parish	4400
To Ann Jones for keeping moors Child 5 months	250
To Elizabeth Jackson for Relief	0500
To Mary Spratt for Relief	0500
To Ann Jones wido for Relief	0500
	27390
To Caske & Collection	2739
	30129
by Parish Credit	
by 916 Tithables @ 33	30228
Due to the Parish	99

[271]

It is Ordred that Mʳ Thomas Green be Collector for the year Insuing

It is Ordered that Mʳ John Shermer be Churchwarden in the Upper precinct of this Parish

It is Orderᵈ that the Churchwardens bind Out Such of the Children of Thomas Jones Decᵈ as is Chargable to the Parish

It is Ordered that the Present Churchwardens *and *the Bring Action for Certaine Charges Relating to Charles Roane Against the Parish where it may be Recovered in the County of Orang

John Royston
Augustine Smith

[272]

At A Vestry held for Petsworth Parriſh the 6th Day of November 1744

Preſent The Revd Mr Yeates
Maj^r. Waſhington
Maj^r. Buckner
Mr Thos. Green
Mr James Hubard
Captn. David Alexander
M^r. W^m. Thornton

Ordered that Daniel New is Clark of this Vestry in the Room of M^r. W^m. Brooking

Thos. Greene
John Washington

Teſt Da^l. New C. V.

[273] Note! This page of the MS. is blank.—C. G. C.

[274]

At a Vestory held for Petsworth Pariſh the 16th Day of Aprill 1745

Present the Revd Robt Yeates   Maj^r. Sam^{ll}. Buckner
M^r Ag^n: Smith   Captn David Alexander
Maj^r. Jno Waſhington   M^r. Jno Shermer
Mr Conq^t Wiat   Captn Bayley Seaton

Tis order'd that the three Pounds, for fines in M^r. Francis Lee's hand, be Diſtributed to the several Poor of the Pariſh as foloweth

To Rebecca Jenkins one Pound, To Mary spratt twelve shi^{ll} & 6 To Eliz^a. Lewis twelve Do & 6 To Willm. Harington seven Shill and Six pence   To Edwd Balston seven and six pence

Mʳ Alexander Mackinsie is Chosen Vestory Man in the Room of Captⁿ Edwᵈ. Wiat Deceas'd

>Augustine Smith
>John Washington
>
>>Test Daˡ: New C V

[275]

At a Veſtry Held for Petsworth Pariſh the 1ˢᵗ. day of Augˢᵗ. 1745

Preſant The Revᵈ Robᵗ Yates

  Majʳ Jnᵒ Waſhington ⎫ Captⁿ David Alexander
  Mʳ. Thoˢ. Green   ⎬ Mʳ. John Shermer
  Majʳ Samˡˡ. Buckner ⎭ Captⁿ Bayley Seaton
  Mʳ. James Hubard

It is Order'd By this Preſant Vestry that Mʳ. John Shermer Provide Maſters for the two younger Sons of Thoˢ Jones Deceᵈ. and to agree with the said Maſters to take them at as Cheap a rate as he can

Order'd that the Colector of the Pariſh Levy, Pay unto Doctʳ Symer one Thousand and fifty Pounds, of the Tobᵒ Levied for the use of th[ ] Parish in the year 1744

Order'd that Mʳ John Shermer Churchwarden receive of the Exe[ ] Mʳ of Eduard Wiat Deceas'd Two Thousand Pounds of Tobacco and Casque, which was Levied for the use of the Pariſh in the year 1743 which the sᵈ. Wiat Never Accounted for

Mʳ Thoˢ. Stubbs is Elected By this Vestry, (Vestryman) in the Room of Mʳ William Thornton Deceas'd

>Thoˢ Green
>John Washington
>
>>Test Daˡ New Clk P P V

[276]

At a Veſtry Held for Petsworth Pariſh the 9th. October 1745

Preſent   The Revd Mr Robt Yates
- Mr. John Royston
- Mr. Augun. Smith
- Mr Thos. Green
- Majr. Saml¹. Buckner
- Mr James Hubard
- Mr. John Shermer
- Mr. Thos Stubbs

Petsworth Pariſh in Tobacco	Dr
To the Reverd. Mr Robt Yates	16000
To Do for Quitren of the Glebe Lane	54
To James Booker Sexton	1000
To Dal. New Clark of the Church & Vesr	1600
To Comunion Bread and Wine	450
To Captn. Claytons Charge	60
To Mrs Hunter for Boarding the Widdow Joneses Child	400
To William Lamb for taking the Widow Joneses Child and diſcharging the Pariſh of the same	800
To Jacob Rice for taking another Do	1000
To Doctor Mackinsie for Looking after the Widow Willis Edwd Batston & Wm Shanks	2149
To Mildred Kiningham for Takeing one of Greenwoods Children and Diſcharging the Pa	1000
To Willm. Harington for Relief	400
To the Widow Jackson for Do	400
To Edwd. Batston for Do	400
To Mrs Hunter for taking care of the widow Joneses Child, and Diſcharging the Pariſh of the same	1200
To Mr. James Hubard for Wm. Shanks	200
To Mr. Thos. Stubb's for two Levy's not rec'd	66
To Majr Buckner for his acct. agt. Batston	100
the amount of the Debts	27279

10 ℔ C^t on Which is	2727
	30006
[277] Brought up	30006
℔ Contra	C^r
By 944 Tithables @ 32^{lb} ℔ Pole is	30208
Ball due to the Parifh	202

Tis ordered By this Veftry that M^r. Thos Stubbs be Church Warden in the Room of M^r. Thos Green

Mr John Shermer is appointed Colector & that he Collect of Every Tithable, 32 Pounds of Tobacco to Difcharge the several Parifh Debts

John Royston

Augustine Smith

[278]

At A Veftry Held for Petsworth Parifh the 1st Aprill 1746

Prefant   The Rev^d. M^r. Robt. Yates

M^r. Aug^n. Smith	Captn David Alexander
Mr Thos Green	M^r. John Shermer
Capt Conq^t Wiat	M^r. Thos Stubbs
Maj^r Sam^{ll}. Buckner	

Order'd that the Church Wardens Give Notice to Workmen to meet at the Gebe at some Convenient time, and under take to make such repairs as the Vestry shall think Nesefsary, and that Mr Green Maj^r Buckner Captn Alexander M^r. Shermer Mr Stubbs Meet at the Glebe and agree with Workmen accordingly

N. B. that any three of the above Mentioned Veftrymen is sufficient to agree with the Workmen

[279]

At a Veſtry Held for Petsworth Pariſh the 28 day of May 1746

Preſent　　The Revᵈ. Mʳ. Robᵗ Yates
　Mʳ. Augⁿ. Smith　　　　Capⁿ. Bayley Seaton
　Mʳ Thoˢ Green　　　　 Mʳ John Shermer
　Majʳ Samˡˡ. Buckner
　Mʳ. John Royston
　Mʳ. Conqᵗ. Wiat

*Ordered this Preſent Veſtry, have thought it Better to Build a New Glebe house rather then to Repair the old one, therefore tis ordered by the sᵈ. Veſtry that there be a New Dwelling house Fifty two feet Long and twenty feet wide from out to out Built on the said glebe, and that the Veſtry meet on the first Wednesday in August Next to agree with Workmen accordingly

　　　　　　　　　　John Royston
　　　　　　　　　　Augustine Smith

At a Veſtry Held for Petsworth Pariſh the 6ᵗʰ Day of Augᵗ 1746

Present　　The Revᵈ. Mʳ. Robᵗ. Yates
　Mʳ. Augⁿ. Smith　　　　Majʳ. Samˡˡ. Buckner
　Mʳ. Jnᵒ Royston　　　　Captⁿ David Alexander
　Majʳ. Jnᵒ Waſhington　Mʳ. Jnᵒ Shermer
　Mʳ. Thoˢ Green　　　　Captⁿ. Bayley Seaton
　　　　　　　　　　　　 Mʳ. Thoˢ. Stubbs

Mʳ. John Thornton is Chosen Veſtry man, by this Veſtry, in the Room of Mʳ Alexander Mackensie who Refuses to act as a Veſtryman

---

*Note! This word is scratched through in the MS., but is still plainly legible.—C. G. C.

Order'd that the Church Wardens Enter into Bond with Mr. Samuel Duvall to Build a Glebe House, Persuant to the Laſt order of Veſtry

      John Royston
      Augustine Smith

[280]

At a Veſtry Held for Petsworth Pariſh the 1ſt. day of Octobr. 1746

Preſant Mr. Augn. Smith   Capn Conqust Wiat
  Mr. John Royston   Mr. John Shermer
  Mr. Thos Green   Mr. Thos: Stubbs
  Coll. Saml1. Buckner

Petsworth Pariſh in Tobo:	Dr
To the Revd. Mr. Robt Yates	16000
To Quitrents for the Glebe Land	00054
To James Booker Sexton	01000
To Daniel New Clark of the Church and Vestry	01600
To Comunion Bread and Wine	00450
To Captn Clayton for a Coppy of the List	00060
To Doctr Mackenzie's Accot	00800
To Mr. James Hubard's Accot	00237
To Mr. Blasingame for Glazing the Church windows	00260
To Mr John Shermer's Accot	00270
To Mr. Duval for a Coffin for Mary Titbery	00036
To James Booker for Diging her Grave	00018
To Mary Spratt for keeping Mary Titbery	00250
To Jane Haines for Relief	00300
To the Widow Jackson for Relief	00400
To Edwd. Batston for Relief	00400
To Mary Spratt for Do	00400
The amount of the Debts	22535
10 ℔ Ct on which is	2253
which Added makes the Total	24788

℔ʳ Contra	Cʳ
By 963 Tithables @ 26ᶫᵇ of Tobº ℔ tithe is	25038
Due to the Pariſh	250

Order'd that Mʳ. Thoˢ. Stubbs be Colecter the Insueing year, and that he receive 26. of Tobº. ℔ Pole to Diſcharge the several Parish Debts and 30ᶫᵇ of Tobº. or three Shillings in Cash. ℔ Pole, toward Building a Glebe House

            Caried Forward

[281]

By the above Vestry Mʳ. Warner Waſhington is Chosen Vestry man in the room of his Father Deceas'd

Mʳ John Thornton is appointed Church Warden in the Room of Mʳ John Shermer

            Teſt
            Daˡ New C: P: P: V

At a Veſtry held for Petsworth Pariſh the 7ᵗʰ. day of Octoʳ 1747

Preſant   The Revᵈ Mʳ. Robᵗ. Yates

    Mʳ. Augⁿ. Smith   Capᵗ. Conqᵗ. Wiatt
    Mʳ. Jnº. Royston   Mʳ. Thoˢ. Stubbs
    Coˡˡ. Samˡˡ. Buckner   Mʳ. Jnº. Thornton
    Capᵗ. Davᵈ. Alexander

Petsworth Parriſh in Tobacco	Dʳ
To the Reverᵈ. Mʳ. Robᵗ. Yates	16000
To Quitrents for the Glebe Land	54
To Communion Bread and Wine for the Ensueing year	450
To James Booker, ſexton	1000
To David New. Clk Church and Vestry	1600
To Mʳ. William Fleming, for taking Care of and Burying John Salmon	250

To Mʳ James Hubard's Accoᵗ	308
To Mʳ John Thornton for Burying Elizᵃ. Jackson	390
To Doctʳ Alexander Mackenzie, for Medecines and Board for Joseph Mears	2213
To Capᵗ. Clayton for Coppy of the List of Tithables	20
To Mʳ. Yates, for a Surpliſs	942
To Mʳ. Thoˢ. Stubbs for four Levies not receivᵈ.	104
To Willᵐ. Harington for relief	300
To Rebeckah Jenkins for relief	400
To Mary Spratt for Dᵒ	400
the amᵗ. of the Debts Caried Forward	24431

[282] Brought over

The Amount of the Debts	24431
To 10 ℔ Cᵗ. for Casque and Colection	2443
Total Debt	26874
By 974 Tithables at 28ᵗᵇ of Tobᵒ. ℔ Tithe is	27272
Due to the Pariſh in the hand of Colectʳ	398

Order'd *by *this *Vestry that the Colecter receive of every Tithable 28 Pounds of Tobacco to Discharge the several debts of the Pariſh

Mʳ. John Thornton is appointed Collecter of the Pariſh dues for the Ensueing year

Mʳ Warner Waſhington is appointed Church Warden in the uper Precinct in the room of Mʳ. Thoˢ. Stubbs.

Order'd that Vicaris Nettles, be paid two Pounds four Shillings, which is due to the Pariſh, in the hand of Mʳ. Thoˢ. Stubbs

*Note! These words are partly erased in the MS.—C. G. C.

Order'd, that the Collecter receive for every Ttihable two shillings, in Cash, or twenty Pounds of Tobacco, for the use of the Parriſh

[283]

At a Veſtry held for Petsworth Pariſh the 18ᵗʰ day of July 1748

Preſant   The Revᵈ. Mʳ. Robᵗ Yates
     Mʳ. Jnᵒ Royston ⎫ Mʳ. Thoˢ: Stubbs
     Coˡˡ. Samˡˡ. Buckner ⎮ Mʳ Warner Waſhington
     Mʳ. James Hubard ⎰ Mʳ. John Thornton
     Capᵗ: Bayley Seaton ⎭

By this preaſant Vestry. Captⁿ. John Stubbs, Captⁿ. William Thornton, and Mʳ. James Carter, are Elected Veſtrymen in the Room of Mʳ. Thoˢ: Green, & Captⁿ Conquest Wiat Deceased, and Mʳ. John Shermer, who is gone out of the Pariſh.

                       Teſt Daˡ New Cl:k : V

At a Veſtry Held for Petsworth Pariſh the 23ᵈ Day of septʳ 1748

Presant Coˡˡ. Smˡˡ. Buckner ⎫ Mʳ John Thornton
     Capᵗ. David Alexander ⎮ Mʳ Warner Waſhington
     Capᵗ. John Stubbs ⎰ Capᵗ. Wᵐ T[ ]rnton
     Mʳ. Thoˢ. Stubbs ⎭ Mʳ. James Carter

	Petsworth Parish in Tobᵒ	Dr
To the Revᵈ. Mʳ. Robᵗ Yates		16000
To Quitrents for the Glebe Land		54
To Coˡˡ Buckner For Comunion Bread and Wine		500
To James Booker, Sexton		1000
To Daˡ New Clk of the Church and Veſtry		1600
To Vicars Nettles for Relief		300
	Caried Forward	

[284]

To Edw⁴. Badston For Dº	300
To William Harington for Dº	300
To John White for Dº	300
To Capᵗ Clayton, fo a Coppy of the Liſt	18
To Mʳˢ Dudley for Takeing Care of Stears	450
To Levied for the use of the Pariſh	1000
	21822
To 10 ℔ Cᵗ for Casque and Colection	2182
Total Debt	24004

℔ Contra   C'

By Tobacco in Mʳ. John Thornton's hand	398
By 945 Tithables @ 25ˡᵇ of Tobº ℔ Tithe is	23625
	24023
Due to the Parish	19

By the above Veſtry Capᵗ. William Thornton is Chosen Churchwarden in the room of Mʳ. John Thornton

Mʳ. Thoˢ. stubbs is *Chosen appointed Collecter for the ensueing year, and that he Receive for Every Tithable 25 pounds of Tobº to Diſcharge the several debts

it is Order'd that the Church Wardens agree with Workmen to do such work to the out houses of the Glebe, as they shall think proper.

Order'd that the Ballance Left in Mʳ. Thoˢ. stubb's hands, be paid to Mʳ Samˡˡ. Duval, as also the two shillings a Head, Levied in year 1747

Order'd that the Church Wardens lay out the Tobº. Levied for the Poor, as they shall think proper

Teſt

Daˡ New Clk P. P. V

---

*Note! This word has been partly erased in the MS.—C. G. C.

[285]

At a Vestry Held for Petsworth Parish the 16ᵗʰ day of Octobʳ 1749

Preſant   The Revᵈ. Mʳ. Robᵗ. Yates
  Mʳ Augⁿ. Smith   ⎫ Capᵗ. John Stubbs
  Coˡˡ. Samˡˡ. Buckner   ⎪ Capᵗ. Bayley Seaton
  Mʳ. James Hubard   ⎬ Capᵗ. William Thornton
  Mʳ. John Thornton   ⎪ Mʳ. James Carter
  Mʳ. Warner Waſhington   ⎭

	Petsworth Pariſh in Tobᵒ.	Dʳ
To the Revᵈ. Mʳ. Robert Yates Miniſter his Salery		16000
To Quitrent for the Glebe Land		54
To Coˡˡ. Buckner for Comunion Bread and Wine		500
To James Booker Sexton		1000
To Daniel New Clerk of the Church and Veſtry		1600
To Capᵗ Clayton for copy of the Liſt of Tithables		1[ ]
To Mʳˢ Fleming, for Taking Ann Spratt a Baſtard, by Indenture off of the Pariſh		1500
To Thoˢ Wright, for one Levy Overpaid in the Year 1747		42
To Vicars Nettles for Relief		300
To Rebeckah Jenkins for Dᵒ		200
To Mʳˢ. Sarah Dudley, for Takeing Care of Stears &c		150
To William Arington for Relief		300
To Thoˢ. Sadler for Dᵒ.		300
To Edwᵈ Badston for Dᵒ.		300
To John White for Dᵒ.		300
To James Booker jʳ. for takeing John Spratt, a Baſtard Child of Chriſtian Spratts off of the Pariſh by Indenture		900
To James Howard for Boarding the sᵈ. John Spratt		200
To Mʳ James Hubards Accoᵗ against the Pariſh		572
To Coˡˡ Buckner, Doctʳ Makenzies Accoᵗ for Takeing care of Spratt		511

To Tho[s] Booker for Makeing Clothes for Jos: Stears	50
To Doct[r] Leith's Acco[t]. for takeing care of Several Poor Indigent Sick persons to this time	1900
Caried forward	26697
[286] Brought Over	26697
To Will[m] Grumley for Relief	200
To M[r]. Warner Waſhingtons Acco[t]	740
To Mary Hunter for keeping Jos Steers till Next May	300
To Co[ll]. Buckner for Expences at Williamsburg in a Law Sute with Straton Major Parriſh	210
To Capt[n]. William Thornton for Boarding Chriſtian Spratt	200
To Joſeph Eastwood for Takeing two Orphans, Named James Sins and William Sins off the Pariſh	1040
To four ℔ C[t]. on M[r]. Yateses Salery	640
To four ℔ C[t]. on Dan[l]. New's Salery	64
The Debts am[t].	30091
Six ℔ C[t]	1805
	31896
℔ Contra C[r]	
By 950 Tithables @ 34[lb]. of Tob[o] ℔ Tithe is	32300
Due to the Pariſh	*504

it is Order'd that Tho[s] Sadler be Diſcharg'd from paying Pariſh Levy for the future

M[r] Peter Kemp is Chosen Vestryman, in the room of M[r]. Royston Deceas'd, and is appointed Church Warden in the room of M[r]. Warner Waſhington

---

*Note! First written "404," and then changed to "504."— C. G. C.

Order'd that Capt William Thornton be Colector of the Parifh dues the Infueing year, and that he receive for Evry Tithable 34ˡᵇ of Tob° to Difcharge the Parifh Debts

Order'd that Capt William Thornton agree with a Workman to Build a Tobacco house on the Glebe, and Make a Sufficient Chimney to the Old Glebe house for a Kitchen

     Tefte Daˡ New C.l.k PPV

[287]

At a Veftry Held for Petsworth Parifh the 9ᵗʰ day of Novʳ. 1750

    The Revᵈ. Mʳ Robert Yates

Prefent
- Coˡˡ Samˡˡ Buckner
- Mʳ James Hubard
- Mʳ. Jn° Thornton
- Capt. Bayley Seaton
- Capt. John Stubbs
- Mʳ Warner Wafhington
- Mʳ Thoˢ Stubbs
- Mʳ James Carter

Petsworth Parifh in Tob°	Dr
To the Revᵈ. Mʳ. Robt. Yates his salary	16000
To Quitrents for the Glebe Land	54
To James Booker Sexton	1000
To Coˡˡ. Samuel Buckner for Comunion Bread & Wine	500
To Capt Clayton for Copy of Lift of Tithables	18
To Danel New Clk of Church & Veftry	1600
To Mʳ. James Hubards Accot	85
To John Blafingame for work done at the Glebe	30
Order'd that Coˡˡ. Samˡˡ. Buckner have for Laying a Thrafhing Floor, in a Tob° house at the Glebe, 20 feet by 12	420
To Mʳ. Richad Jones'es Accot for Cloathing &c for Jof: Stears the year 1747	47
To Capt. Bayley Seaton, for tending the Parifh Cause against Stratonmajor Parish, at Williamsburg	300

To Capt. Bayley Seaton for a Secretaries Note	88
To Co^{ll}. Buckner for Building a Tob^o. House on the Glebe	2175
To Vicris Nettles for relief	300
To Thos. Sadler for D^o	200
To William Harington for D^o.	200
To Doct^r Charles Leith, in full of his acco^t against the Par^{sh}	504
To 4 ₩ C^t. on Mr Yates & Daniel News Salery	704
To Eight hundred Levied for Mr Yates to make his Tob^o Neet	800
	25023
To six ₩ C^t for *Casque *and Colection	1502
	26525

Caried Forw^d

[288]   Brought Forward   lb Tob^o

The Whole amount of the Parish Debts   26525

₩ Contra   C^r

By 950 Tithables a^t 28^{lb} of Tob^o ₩ Tithe is   26600

Due to the Parish in the Colectors hand   75

Order'd that 404^{lb} of Tob^o. in Capt Thorntons hand, due to the Parish be Paid to Mary Hunter for Boarding, Cloathing & Takeing Care of Joseph Stears, the Ensueing year

M^r. Richard Jones is Chosen Vestry man, in the Room of Capt. David Alexander Dec^d. and is apointed Church Warden in the room of Capt. William Thornton

M^r. Peter Kemp is apointed Colector the Ensueing year and that he Receive for Every Tithable 28^{lb} of Tob^o. to discharge the Parish Debts

*Note! An unsuccessful attempt was made to erase these words by scratching them through with a pen.—C. G. C.

Order'd that the Church Wardens of This Parifh, Bind James Camel Baftard son of Margret Camel, to Richard Guthrie of King and Queen County, upon his giving Security to the Church Wardens of the s⁴ Parifh, to keep the Said Child from being Chargable to the Parifh according to Law

Tefte Da¹ New Cl:k P.P. V.

[289]

At a Vestry held for Petsworth Parifh Sept'. 4ᵗʰ. 1751

The Revᵈ Mʳ. Robᵗ. Yates

Presant
- Mʳ Augⁿ. Smith
- Colⁿ. Samⁿ. Buckner
- Mʳ. James Hubard
- Mʳ. John Thornton
- Mʳ. Richᵈ Jones
- Mʳ Thoˢ Stubbs
- Mʳ. James Carter
- Mʳ. Peter Kemp
- Capᵗ. John Stubbs
- Capᵗ. William Thornton

Persuant to an Order of the Court of Gloucester County bearing Date the 25ᵗʰ day of July, to Appoint Pofsefsioners *to in Each Precinct of this Parifh, to see the Land Pofsefsion[ ] and to make return of their proceedings by the laft day of March, according to Law, wee do therefore order an[ ] appoint them as followeth ———

Order'd that Mʳ. Thoˢ. Minor, and Mʳ. Mordecai Cooke see the Land pofsefsion'd in the first Precinct, and to begin the first thursday in October, on the Land of Mʳ. Thoˢ Minor

Order'd that Mʳ William Thornton, & Mʳ. Francis Stubbs, see the Land pofsefsion'd, in the Second Precinct, and to begin on the Land of Robᵗ Porteus Esqʳ. on the secound Thursday in October

---

*Note! An unsuccessful attempt was made to render this word illegible by scratching it through with a pen.—C. G. C.

Order'd that M`r`. John Scott & M`r`. Rich`d`. Jones, see the Land poſseſsiond, in the third Precinct, to begin on the Land of M`rs` Ann Brown, on the third Thursday in October

Order'd that M`r` Lewis Booker and M`r` Conquest Royston see the Land Poſseſsiond, in the Fourth Precinct, to begin on the Land of M`r`. Rich`d`. Critenden Deceas'd, on the fourth Munday in October

Order'd that M`r`. Humphry Mackentree & M`r` W`m` Brooking see the Land Poſseſsion'd, in the Fifth Precinct, to begin on the Land of the Said Mackentree, on the first Thursday in November

Caried Forward

[290]

Order'd that M`r`. John Stubbs Jun`r`. and M`r`. John Amis, See the Land Poſseſsion'd in the Sixth Precinct, to begin on the Land of the S`d`. Amis on the first thursday in November

Order'd that M`r` Benjamin Baker, and M`r`. John Keningham See the Land Poſseſsion'd in the Seventh Precinct, to begin on the Land Co`ll`, Samuel Buckner (Near the Dragon Swamp) on the Secound Thursday in November

Order'd that M`r` John Reade & M`r`. Thomas Kemp See the Land Poſseſsion'd in the Eighth Precinct, to begin at M`r` Augustine Smiths, on the Third Thursday in November

Order'd that M`r` Conq`t` Wiatt and M`r` John Wiatt See the Land Poſseſsion'd in the Ninth Precinct, to begin on the Land of Cap`t`. Bayley Seaton Dec`d`: on the Fourth Monday in November

At this Veſtry M`r`. John Scott is Elected Veſtryman in the room of Capt`n`. Bayley seaton Dec`d`.

This Veſtry has impower'd M`r` Augustine Smith to Send to England for a Pulpit, and Table Cloth, and Cuſhon, for the use of Petsworth Parish Church, on the Receipt of which, the S⁴, Vestry do agree to Pay, the S⁴ M'. Augustine Smith, Fifty ℔ C'. on the first Cost of the same. the Cloth to be of Crimson Velvet, with a Gold Frienge & Lace, to come in a Very Strong Oak Chest, for the use of the Parish

     Teste Dan¹ New C,lk P, P, V

[291]

At a Vestry Held for Petsworth Parish th 16ᵗʰ Oct': 1751

    *The Rev⁴ M'. Rob' Yates

Presan M'. Augustine Smith ⎫ Cap William Thornton
   M'. John Thornton | M' Peter Kemp
   Cap'. John Stubbs ⎬ Col¹¹ Samuel Buckner
   M'. Thoˢ Stubbs | M'. Richᵈ. Jones
   M'. James Carter ⎭

Petsworth Parish in Tob°	D'
To the Rev⁴. M'. Robert Yates, his Salary	16640
To Quitrent for the Glebe Land	54
To Amy Booker for being Sexton	1000
To Cap'. Clayton for List of Tithables	81
To Da¹ New, C,l,k of Church & Vestry	1600
To M' Thoˢ: Boswell, serving a Writ on Elizᵃ Mills	27
To Humpʸ: Mackentree, for Removing Thoˢ: Burk	100
To Captain Thornton for Levies not rec⁴.	306
To M'. James Hubard, for Fees Paid	81
To M'. Peter Kemp, for Levyes not rec⁴	280
To M' Peter Kemp, for Sundrys for the Poor	108
To M'. John Clark, sundrys for Edw⁴, Badston	53
To M'. Rich⁴. Jones, for Sundries found for the use of the Parish	1105
To William Grumley for Benches	150

*Note! An attempt has been made to erase this entire line from the MS., the erasing being done with a pen knife.—C. G. C.

To Charles Tompson for work done to the Church & Glebe	200
To Doct' Symmer for Dance £2‖13‖9: in Tob°	327½
To Doct' Symmer for John White £1‖0‖8. in Tob°.	124
To John White for Relief	400
To Vecarius Nettles, D°	300
To Tho° Sadler D°	400

Caried *up forward

[229]   Brought forward

To William Harington for Relief	200
To Elizth. Lewis D°	200
To Rebeckah Jenkins D°	300
To Mary Hunter for Stears	500
To W^m. Roundtree for Care of Bluefords Baſtard one year	1000
To Margaret Nettles for Care of another of Bluefords Baſtards	500
To John Shepard for Takeing Care of Lucy Clarks Child	800
To John Burk for relief	200
To Mary Dance for Rich^d. Dance	800
To Comunion Bread and Wine	500
To 4 ℔ C^t. on Mr Yates, & News Tob°.	704
	29040½
To Six ℔ C^t for Collection	1742
Total	30782½
P C C^r	
By 933 Tithables at 33^{lb} of Tob° ℔ Tithe	30789
	7½

*Note! This word has been scratched through with a pen in the MS.—C. G. C.

Order'd that the Collector Receive for every Tithabe 33ᴸᵇ of Tobacco to Diſcharge the Pariſh Debts, and Eighteen Pence in Cash or fifteen Pounds of Tobᵒ. to pay for Ornaments for the Church

Mʳ. Richard Jones is Chosen Collector, in the room of Mʳ Peter Kemp

Mʳ. James Carter is Chosen Church Warden with Mʳ. Richᵈ. Jones

[293]

At a Veſtry held for Petsworth Pariſh the 14ᵗʰ Novʳ. 1752

Preſent
- Mʳ Augⁿ Smith
- Coˡˡ, Samˡˡ Buckner
- Mʳ. James Hubard
- Capᵗ John Stubbs
- Mʳ Waner Washington
- Mʳ Thoˢ Stubbs
- Mʳ John Thornton
- Mʳ Peter Kemp
- Mʳ James Carter
- Capᵗ Richᵈ Jones

Petsworth Parish in Tobᵒ	Dʳ
To the Revᵈ Mʳ Robert Yates his Salary	16640
To Quitrents for the Glebe Land	54
To Amy Booker for being Sexton	1000
To Daniel New C.l.k of the Church & Veſtry	1600
To Capᵗ Clayton for Liſt of Tithables	20
To Mary Lamb for Bluefoots Child	500
To Wᵐ Wright for Masons two Children	800
To Free Robin for Covering Haringtons House	200
To Mʳ James Carter for Nails for the same	27
To Mʳ James Hubard for Fees &.c.	1153
To Mary Dance for Care of her Father one year	700
To Humphry Mackentree for Horse blocks	100
To Capᵗ Richᵈ. Jones for Expences to & From WᵐˢBurg	575
To Meſsʳˢ Jones & Scott, for Clothing for the Poor	286

To Jnº Blaſingame for mending the Church & Glebe Wind:	286
To Doctʳ Leith for his care of Sarah Barden	953
To Mʳ Thoˢ: Stubbs for Summoning two Witneſses	54
To Doctʳ Symmer his Accoᵗ for Wᵐ Harington	105
To Mʳ James Carter for Communion Bread & Wine	500
To 4 ℔ Cᵗ on Mʳ. Yates & Daˡ News Tobº.	729
Aded	26548
[294] Brought up	26548
To Coˡˡ. Throcmorton for Moving the Poor	200
To John White for Relief	400
To Vicares Nettles Dº	300
To Elizª Lewis for Dº	200
To Mary Hunter for her Care of Stears	500
To William Harrington for Relief	200
To Vicars Nettles for one of Bluefoots Children	400
To Thomas Burk for Relief	400
To John Shepard for Care of Clarks Child the Ensuing year	500
Debt	29648
To 6 ℔ Ct on the above Tobº, for Collection is	1778
Total	31426
Contra Cʳ	
By 948 Tithables at 34ˡᵇ, of Tobº ℔ Tithe is	32232
Repoſited in the Collectors Hands	806

Order'd that the Colectʳ. Receive 34ˡᵇ of Tobacco ℔ Tithe to diſcharge the Debts of the Pariſh

Order'd that the Collecter Receive (for every Tithe) one Shilling in Caſh or twelve pounds of Tobacco, over and above the Charges as abov

Capt John Stubbs is Chosen Church Warden in the room of Capt Jones

Mr James Carter is appointed Collect^r for the Ensueing year

John Blasingame is Chosen Sexton, in the room of Amy Booker

       Teſte Danl New Clk P.P. V

[295]

At a Vestry held for Petsworth Parish, the 13th July 1753

Preſent
- Colo^{ll} Sam^{ll} Buckner
- Mr Aug^n. Smith
- Mr James Hubard
- Mr James Carter
- Mr Thos: Stubbs
- M^r. Richd Jones
- Mr Peter Kemp

At this Vestry Mr Augustine Smith brought the Ornaments for the Church, which he had sent for by Order of Vestry bearing Date the 4th of September 1751, which Cost £103||4||4¾ Which the S^d Vestry hath Receiv'd, and agree'd to pay him £154||16^S||6^D cur^t Money for the Same, of which sum the S^d. M^r. Augustine Smith hath receivd £61||9^S||3^D. being the Ballance remaining in the hands of Capt. Richard Jones, of the Money Collected by him in in the Year 1752

Order'd that Mr James Carter pay unto Mr Augustine Smith the Money in his Hands, ariseing from the Money Levied (for the use as above) in the Year 1752

     Teste: Da^l New Cl.k P: P: V:

[296] This page of the MS. is blank.—C. G. C.

[297]

At a Vestry held for Petsworth Parish the 9th of Nov'. 1753

M'. Augustine Smith
Co'': Sam'' Buckner
M' James Hubard
Pre∫ant Cap' John Stubbs
M' Peter Kemp
M' Tho⁵ Stubbs
M' James Carter
Cap' W'" Thornton
M' Warner Washington

Petsworth Parish in Tob°	D'
To the Rev⁴ M' Rob'. Yates his Salary	16640
To Quitrents for the Glebe Land	54
To John Blasingame, Sexton	1000
To Dan' New Clk: &c	1600
To Cap' Clayton for List of Tithables	20
To Communion Bread and Wine	500
To John Blaingames Acco': for Work done	200
To Mary Lamb, for Bluefords Child	500
To Tho⁵ Hall for Moving Henry Carter into Kingston	60
To Co'': Buckner for Smiths work and Dial	241
To Cap': Thornton for Levys overpaid Last year	65
To M' Peter Kemp for Levys not receiv'd the year 1751	196
To Cap' W'" Thornton for Charges in a Suit in Law with Howard Conserning Spratts bastard Child	624
To M' Francis Stubbs for a Levy overpaid	34½
To M'⁵ Fleming for takeing care of Mary Dance 6 Months	300
To Doct' Leith for what he has done, and is to do for D°.	300
To John White for Relief	300
To Vicars Nettles for D°.	300

To William Harington for D°	400
To Eliz⁸. Lewis for D°.	300
Caried over	23634½
[298] Brought up	23634½
To Mary Hunter for Stears the ensueing Year	500
To Vicars Nettles for Bluefords Child untill Next Aprill	500
To Thoˢ Burk for Relief the next Year	800
To John Shepard for Clarks Child, to discharge the Parish of The same	800
To Dorothy Bond for relief, to be Laid out with Mʳ Hubard	300
To Richᵈ: Dance for relief	300
To 4 ℔ Cᵗ. on Mʳ Yateses, and Daˡ News Salary	729½
Debts	27564
To 6 ℔ Cᵗ for Collection is	1654
Total Debt	29218
℔ Contra	Cʳ
By Tob°. in Mʳ James Carters Hand	296
By 950 Tithables at 31ˡᵇ. Tob° ℔ Tithe is	29450
The whole Credit	29746
Due to the Parish	528

Order'd that the Collector Pay unto Mʳ Augustine Smith £49||19ˢ||1ᴰ, in full for the Church Ornaments

Order'd that the Collector Receive for every Tithable 31ˡᵇ of Tob°. to Discharge the Parish Debts, Likewise 1ˢ||3ᵈ, or thirteen Pounds of Tob°. ℔ Tithe, to discharg the above £49||19ˢ||1ᴰ to Mʳ Smith

Note at the above Vestry M[r] Augustine Smith declin'd serving any longer as Vestry man, and M[r] Ludwell Grymes was Elected in his room, and M[r] Fran[s]: Stubbs, in the room of M[r] John Scott who is remov'd out of the County

M[r] Ludwell Grymes is appointed Church Warden with Capt[n] John Stubbs, in the room of M[r] James Carter

Cap[t]: John Stubbs is appointed Collector for the ensueing year

[299]

At a Vestry held for Petsworth Parish the 30th day of Octob[r] 1754

Co[ll] Samuel Buckner
M[r] James Hubard
Cap[t] John Stubbs
M[r]. Tho[s]: Stubbs
Cap[t] W[m] Thornton
M[r] Peter Kemp
Cap[t] Rich[d] Jones
M[r] James Carter
M[r] Fran[s]: Stubbs
M[r] Ludwell Grymes

Petsworth Parish in Tob[o]:	D[r]
To the Rev[d] M[r] Robert Yates his Salary	16640
To Qutrents for the Glebe Land	54
To John Blasingame for being Sexton	1000
To Daniel New Clk of the Church & Vestry	1600
To Capt Clayton for List of Tithables	20
To Communion Bread and Wine	500
To Mary Horsley for 2 of her Children	400
To Eliz[a]: Sadler for Relief and a Levy	250
To M[rs] Fleming for Relief	150
To Mary Lamb for keeping Blufords Child and to secure the Parish from the same	900
To William Harington for Relief	500
To Eliz[a] Lewis for D[o]	250
To Co[ll] Buckner for a Cow and Calf for the S[d] Eliz[a] Lewis	250

To Vicars Nettles for Relief	300
To Vicars Nettles for taking Nany Blueford and discharging the Parish of the same	600
To Elianna Edwards for Relief	300
To Thos: Burk for Ditto	800
To William Wright for D°.	300
To John White D°.	300
	*25414
[300] Brought over	†25114
To Mary Hunter for Stears	300
To Rich^d. Dance for Relief	300
To Mr Striplehill Camp for one Levy overpaid the Last year	31
To further alowance to Mrs Hunter for Stears	200
To 4 ℔ C^t on Mr Yateses Tob°	640
To 4 ℔ C^t on Daniel News Tob°	64
To 6 ℔ C^t for Collection	1599
Total	28248

℔ Contra   C^r
By Tob°. in Capt John Stubses hand   241 ⎫
By 957 Tithables at 29½^{lb} of Tob°   ⎬ 28232 ⎬ 28473
      ℔ Tithe   ⎭
                                        28473 ⎭
                        Due to the Parish   225

---

*Note! This addition is incorrect.—C. G. C.
†Note! The amount brought over does not agree with the amount to be forwarded.—C. G. C.

Petsworth Parish in Cash		Dʳ
To paid Doctor Leith 10/		£0‖10
To Paid Mʳ Dunlavy for his care of, and burying of Michel Moreing		1‖10
To be paid to the Collector for the use of the Parish		2‖17‖1
		£4‖17‖1
℔ Contra	Cʳ	
By Cash in Capⁿ: John Stubbses hand		£4‖17‖1

Mʳ Ludwell Grymes is Chosen Collector, and that he receive 29½ᴸᵇ of Tobᵒ ℔ Tithe, to discharge the Debts of the Parish

Mʳ. Franˢ. Stubbs is appointed Church Warden, in the room of Capᵗ. John Stubbs

Richᵈ: Coal is Chosen Sexton in the room of John Blasingame

Teſte Danˡ New Clk V

[301]

At a Veſtry held for Petsworth Paſiſh the 26ᵗʰ day of Augᵗ. 1755

Preſant
Coˡˡ. Samuel Buckner
The Reveᵈ. Mʳ Robᵗ Yates
Capᵗ John Stubbs
Mʳ Warner Washington
Capᵗ Richard Jones
Mʳ. James Carter
Mʳ Francis Stubbs
Mʳ. Thomas Stubbs

Persuant to an Order of Gloucester County Court bearing Date the 24ᵗʰ day of July 1755, to appoint Poſſeſsioners in each Precinct of this Parish and to make returns of their proceedings by the last day of March, according to Law, we do therefore Order, and appoint them as followeth

Order'd that M^r. John Throckmorton, and Mr Mordecai Cooke See the Land Poſseſsion'd in the first Precinct, to begin on the Land of M^r. Thomas Minor, on the first Thursday in October

1st

Order'd that M^r. William Thornton, and M^r. William Fleming See the Land Poſseſsion'd in the Second Precinct, to begin on the Land of Robt. Porteus Esqr. on the Second Thursday in October

2^d

Order'd that Captain Rich^d. Jones & M^r. George Booth see the Land Poſseſs in the Third Precinct, to begin on the Land of Captain John Stubbs on the third thursday in October

3^d

Order'd that M^r. Lewis Booker, & M^r. Conquest Royston see the Land Poſseſsion'd in the fourth Precinct, to begin on the Land of M^r. Peter Stubbs on the fourth Monday in October

4th

Order'd that Mr George Dillard & Mr William Grumley See the Land Poſseſsion'd in the fifth Precinct, to begin on the Land of Humphry Mackendree on the first Thursday in November

5th

Caried forward

[302]

Order'd that M^r. John Stubbs Junr and M^r. John Amis see the Land Poſseſsion'd in the sixth Precinct, to begin on the Land of the Said Amis, on the Second thursday in November

6th

Order'd that M^r. Benjamin Baker and M^r. John Keningham see the Land Poſseſsioned in the seventh Precinct, to begin on the Land of Co^{ll} Samuel Buckner, near the Dragon Swamp, on the third thursday in November

7th

Order'd that Mr Thomas Kemp & Mr. Richard Roys-
8th ton see the Land Poſseſsion'd in the Eighth Precinct,
to begin on the Land of Mr. Augustine Smith, on the
fourth Monday in November

Order'd that Mr: Conquest Wiat & Mr. John Wiat
9th see the Land Poſseſsion'd in the Ninth Precinct, to begin on the Land of Capt Bayley Seaton Dec{d}. on the
first Munday in December

Mr. John Scott is Elected Vestry Man, in the room of
Mr John Thornton who is remov'd out of the Parrish

Capt. John Wiatt is Elected Vestry Man in the room of
Mr William Thornton, who is remov'd out of the Parrish

True Entry Da{l} New Clk

[303]

At a Veſtry held for Petsworth Parish the 28th of October 1755

the Revd: Mr. Robt. Yates	Mr. Peter Kemp
Mr James Hubard	Mr. Warner Waſhington
Co{ll}. Samuel Buckner	Mr. Ludwell Grymes
Preſant Capt John Stubbs	Mr. John Scott
Mr Thomas Stubbs	Mr. John Wiatt

Petsworth Parish in Tob°.	Dr	lb
To the Revd. Mr. Robt Yates his Salary		16640
To Quitrents for the Glebe Land		54
To Richard Cole Sexton		1000
To Daniel New Clk Church & Veſtry		1600
To Captn Clayton for List of Tithables		20
To Communion Bread and Wine		500
To Doctr. Leath for loking after Stears & Wright		2000
To Thos Burk for Relief		800
To Mrs Hunter for Stears		600
To Willm Wright, and Elianna Edwards each, 350{lb}		700

To John White for Relief	400
To Richard Dance for Ditto	250
To Mary Horsley for two of her Children	400
To Co^{ll} Buckner for his Acco^t	106
To Vicarius Nettles for Relief	300
To Eliz^a Sadler for her Son	200
To William Harington for Relief	500
To Eliz^a. Lewis f Ditto	250
To Ann West for D°	250
To Rich^d. Cole for keeping James Power's Child	400
To Mildred Power for her Children	400
Caried forward	27370
[304] Brought over	27370
To 4 ⅌ C^t. on M^r. Yateses Salary	640
To 4 ⅌ C^t. on Daniel New's Tob°:	64
To Mr Ludwell Grymes for Levy's not rec^d.	113
To M^r. James Carter for Nails	50
To 6 ⅌ C^t. for Collection	1694
Total Debt	29931
⅌ Contra C^r	
By 969 Tithables at 31^{lb} of Tob°. ⅌ Tithe, is	30039
Due to the Parish	108

Ordered that Daniel New, have the above 108^{lb} of Tob°.

Mr Francis Stubbs is Chosen Collector the Ensuing year and that he receive, for every Tithable 31^{lb} of Tob°; to discharge the Several Debts of the Parish

Captain John Wiat is Chosen Church Warden with M^r. Francis Stubbs, in the room of Mr Ludwel Grymes

True Entry. D. N. C V

[305]

At a Vestry Held for Petsworth Parish, the 12 of May 1756

Preſant
- The Revᵈ. Robᵗ Yates
- Coloⁿ Samⁿ Buckner
- Mʳ. Warner Washington
- Mʳ. Thomas Stubbs
- Mʳ. James Carter
- Capᵗ John Wiat
- Capᵗ John Stubbs
- Mʳ. Francis Stubbs
- Capᵗ. Richᵈ Jones
- Mʳ. Peter Kemp
- Mʳ. John Scott

At this Vestry it is Order'd that the Clerk of the Vestry Advertise the Building of Several Houses on the Glebe Vizᵉ: a Stable & Hen House &c. and some Repairs about the Church,

Danˡ New Clk

[306]

At a Veſtry held for Petsworth Parish Octobʳ. 20ᵗʰ. 1756

Presant
- The Revᵈ Mʳ Robᵗ. Yates
- Capᵗ. Ludwel Grymes
- Mʳ. Warner Washington
- Mʳ. Thoˢ. Stubbs
- Mʳ. Peter Kemp
- Captⁿ. John Wiat
- Mʳ. Francis Stubbs
- Mʳ. James Hubard
- Capᵗ. John Stubbs
- Mʳ. James Carter
- Mʳ. John Scott

Petsworth Parish In Tobᵒ.	Dʳ
To the Revᵈ. Mʳ. Robᵗ Yates his Salary	16640
To Quitrents for the Glebe Land	54
To Richᵈ Cole Sexton	1000
To Daniel New Clk of Church & Vestry	1600
To Captⁿ. Clayton for Liſt of Tithables	20
To Communion Bread & Wine	500
To Capᵗ. John Wiat for Buildings on the Glebe,	2700
To Majʳ. Tompkies for Insolvents, Last year	155
To Doctʳ Read for Medicines for the Poor	1350

To Mr. James Hubards Acco^t. of Sundrys for the poor	200
To Mr. Yates for Land Tax paid the Year 1755	18
To Mary Darnold for care of Hopkins	700
To Richard Marcey	70
To Thomas Burk for Relief	800
To Mrs Hunter, for Stears	400
To Elianna Edwards, for her Self & Son Wm Wright	1000
To John White for relief	400
To Mary Horsley for two Children	400
To Vicars Nettles Ditto	300
	28307
[307] Brought up	28307
To Eliz^a. Sadler for her Son	300
To Rebecca Arington for some person to take care of her Husband	400
To Ditto for Relief	600
To Eliz^a. Lewis for Relief	250
To Mildred Power for her Children	400
To Jane Hains for Relief	300
To Mary Thomas for D°	300
To 4 ℔ C^t. on Mr. Yateses Tob°.	640
To D° on New's Tob°.	64
	lb
To Collection on	31561
of Tob° is	1893
Total Debt	33454
℔ Contra:	C^r
By 960 Tithables at 35^{lb}. of Tob° ℔ Tithe,	33600
Due to the Parish	146

GLOUCESTER COUNTY, VIRGINIA, 1677-1793   299

Order'd that Sarah Ellis Bastard Daughter of Ann Ellis be Bound to Richard Davis and his Wife ———

Order'd that Elizabeth Bluefoot be Bound to Mary Lamb.

Mr. John Scott is Chosen Church Warden, in the room of Mr. Francis Stubbs

Captn John Wiatt is appointed Collector for the ensuing and that he receive for every Tithable 35^{lb}. of Tob°. to discharge the Debts of the Parish

D. New Clk P. P. V

[308]

At a Vestry held for Petsworth Pariſh the 5th. of Octobr. 1757

Preſant
the Revd. Robt Yates
Coll. Saml. Buckner
Mr. Thoˢ. Stubbs
Mr. Peter Kemp
Mr. Ludwel Grymes
Mr. Franˢ Stubbs
Mr. John Wiatt
Mr. James Carter

Petsworth Parish in Tob°.	Dr
To the Revd. Mr. Robt Yates his Salary	16640
To Quitrents for the Glebe Land, and Tax	81
To Richd. Cole Sexton	1000
To Daniel New Clerk of Church & Vestry	1600
To Capt. Clayton for Coppy of the List,	20
To Communion Bread & Wine	500
To Mr Peter Kemp for work done for Nettles	93
To Thoˢ Burk for relief	800
To Joſeph Stears D°.	200
To Elianna Edwards, & Wm Wright D°.	800
To John White Do	350
To Mary Horſley for two Children D°.	350
To Vicars Nettles D°.	250
To Elizˢ. Lewis D°.	250

To Mildred Power for her Children	350
To Jane Hains for Relief	250
To Mary Thomas D°.	200
To Co¹¹. Buckner for Necessaries for the Poor	95
To Mʳ. Alexander Dalgleish for his Accᵗ. against the Pariſh	727
Caried up	24556
[309] Brought up	24556
To Mʳ. Francis Stubbs for work done on the Glebe	700
To 4 ℔ Cᵗ. on Mʳ Yateses Tob°.	640
To D°. on Daniel News Tob°.	64
the debts	25960
To 6 ℔ Cᵗ. for Collection	1557
Total Debt	27517
℔ Contra	Cʳ
By John Blaſingame	500
By 998 Tithables at 27½ᵇ of Tob°. ℔ Tithe	27445
Total Credit	27945
Due to the Parish	428

Order'd that the Acting Church Warden Settle the Accompt with Majʳ. Tomkies, and receive the Money in his hands due to the Parish ——

Order'd that the Church Warden Pay Richᵈ. Cole seven Shillings, Mʳ. Francis Stubbs Eight Shillings, & Bob Seven Shillings of the above Money ——

Order'd that Co¹¹ Buckner repair the Church Windows and apply the Depoſitum 428ᵇ of Tob°, as above to that purpoſe ——

Co¹¹ Samuel Buckner is chosen Church Warden, in the room of Capt. John Wiatt. ——

*collector

Mr. John Scott is Appointed the Ensueing year, and that he receive 27½ˡᵇ of Tobacco for every Tithable

True Entry. Danˡ New Clk V

[310 Blank]

[311]

At A Veſtry held for Petsworth Pariſh 11ᵗʰ. of Ocᵇʳ: 1758

The Revrᵈ Robt.. Yates	Capt.. John Stubbs
Cor¹¹.. Samuel Buckner	Mr.. Thoˢ.. Stubbs
Preaſant Mr.. James Hubard	Mr.. Jaˢ.. Carter
Mr. Warner Waſhington	Mr.. Peter Kemp
Capt Ludwell Grimes	Mr.. John Scott

Petsworth Parriſh in Tob°, at 2ᵈ. ℔ pound	Dʳ
To the Revrᵈ.. Mr.. Robt.. Yates his sallary	16640
To Quitrents for the Glebe Land	87
To Daniel New Clˣ.. of the Church & veſtry	1600
To Richard Cole sexton	100[ ]
To Communion Bread & wine	50[ ]
To Thomas Burk for Relief	600
To Joſeph Stears for D°.	150
To Elender Edwards & Wm.. Right D°	800
To Mildred Power for D°	250
To Mary Horsley for her Child	150
To Vicars Nettles for D°	250
To Elizabeth Lewis D°	200
To Jane Hains D°	200
To Mary Thomas D°	150
To John Shepard D°	150

*Note! The word "collector," which is written above the line in the MS., as here, is in a different hand from that of the rest of this entry; and the ink too is different.—C. G. C.

To Ann Hall D°	150
To Elizabeth Sadler	100
To John Howlit for Benches & Hors Blocks	660
To Capt.. John Wiatt for a ballance paid Ric^h Macy	33
To Richard Wi^{tt}.. Royston for Burying Arrinton	100
Carrid over	23770
[312] Brought over	23770
M^r.. John Scott for taking Fitsummunses Child	1000
To M^r.. Yates to make his Tob°.. Neat 4 ℔ C^t..	640
To M^r.. New for Do	64
The Debts am^d	25474
To 6 ℔ C^t.. for Collection	1528
Total Debt is	27002
℔ Contra C^r	
By 972 Tithables at 28^{lb} of Tob°.. ℔ Tith is,	27216
Due to the Parish	214

Cor^{ll}.. Samuell Buckner is appointed Collecter for the Ensuing Year & that he receave 28^{lb} of Tob°.. ℔ Tith to discharge the Sevurrall Debts of the parrish ———

Mr James Hubard is Chosen Church Warden in the Room of M^r.. John Scott ———

Ja^s.. Baker is Chosen Cl^k.. of the Church & Vestry by The above Vestry in the Room of M^r.. Dan^{ll}.. New Who declind it ———

Orderd that that the Church Wardens apply to Major Tomkies & M^r.. Francis Stubbs for the money in there hands belonging to the poar of the parish Which if they Refuse payment to bring sute for the same

True Entry Ja^s.. Baker Cl^k. V

[313]

At A Veſtry held for Petſworth Pariſh the 7 day of Augt. 1759

Preſant,
The Revrd. Robart Yates
Corn.. Samuell Buckner
Mr James Hubard
Mr. Thos.. Stubbs
Mr. Warner Waſhington
Capt. John Stubbs

Mr.. Peter Kemp
Capt. Richard Jones
Capt.. Ludwell Grymes
Mr. Francis Stubbs
Mr. John Scott
Capt. John Wiatt

Purſuant to an order of Glouceſter County Court Bearing Date the 28 day of June 1759 To appoint Poſseſsioners in Each Precinct of this Pariſh & to make returns of there procedings By the Laſt Day of March According to Law, we do therefore Order & appoint them aſs followeth

1th Orderd that Mr.. Mordica Cook & Mr.. William Thornton Juner see the Land Poſseſsiond in the furſt precint to begin on the Land of Mr.. Thomas Minor on the first Thurſday in October

2th Orderd that Mr.. John Stubbs juner & Mr.. Francis Stubbs see the Land Poſseſsiond, in the second Precint to begin on the Land of Robart Porteer, Eſqr.. on the second Thurſday in October

3th Orderd that Capt.. Richard Jones & Mr.. John Scott see the the Land Poſseſsiond in the thurd Precint to begin on the Land of Capt. John Stubbs on the Third Thurſday in October

4th Orderd that Capt. Ludwell Grymes & Mr.. Lewis Booker see the Land Poſseſsiond in the fourth Precinct to begin on the Land of Mr.. Peter Stubbs on the foarth munday in October

Orderd that Mʳ.. Richard Wiatt Royston & Mʳ. William Pollard see the Land Poſseſsiond in the fifth Precint to begin on the Land of Mʳ.. Humphry Macingtree on the firſt thurſday in Novb

5ᵗʰ

Carrid forward

[314]

Orderd that Mʳ. Peter Kemp & Mʳ.. Robart Garlant see the Land Poſseſsiond in the sixth Precint to begin on the Land of Mʳ.. Robart Daniel on the second thurſday in Novʳ.———

6ᵗʰ

Orderd that Mʳ.. Benjamun Baker & Mʳ. John Killingham see the Land Poſseſsiond in the Seventh Precinct to begin on the Land of Corⁿ.. Samuel Buckner near the Draggon on the third Thusday in Novᵇʳ..

7ᵗʰ

Orderd that Mʳ Warner Waſhington & Mʳ.. Thomas Kemp see the Land Poſseſsiond in the Eighth Precint to begin on the Land of Mʳ.. John Smith on the foarth Munday in Novᵇʳ

8ᵗʰ

Orderd that Capt.. John Wiatt & Mʳ.. John Wiatt see the Land Poſseſsiond in the Ninth Precint to begin on the Land of Capt.. Baley Seaton Deceaſt on the furſt munday in December

9ᵗʰ

Mʳ George Booth is Elected Veſtryman in the Room of Mʳ.. James Carter Deceaſt by the above Veſtry ———

Orderd that Corⁿ.. Buckner & Capᵗ. Ludwell Gryes Agree with workmen for what Repairs are wanting to be Dun on the Glebe ———

True Entry James Baker Clk V

[315]

At A Veſtry held for Petſworth Pariſh 19ᵗʰ of Novᵇʳ.. 1759

The Revrᵈ, Mʳ Robᵗ.. Yates
    Mʳ James Hubard
Preaſant Mʳ Thoˢ, Stubbs
    Mʳ Warner Waſhington
    Capt. John Stubbs

Mʳ Peter Kemp
Capt. Richard Jones
Capt. Ludwel Grimes
Mʳ.. Francis Stubbs
Mʳ. George Booth

Petſworth Parrish in Tobº,	Dʳ
To the Revʳᵈ.. Mʳ. Robᵗ.. Yates his Salry	16640
To 4 ℔ Cᵗ. to make Mʳ Yates Tobº. Neat	640
To Quitrents for the Glebe Land	87
To Communion Bread & wine	500
To Richard Cole sexton	1000
To James Baker Clᵏ.. of the Church & Veſtry	1664
To Capᵗ.. John Clayton for the Liſt of Tiths	18
To Capt. Clayton for part of his Account	275
To Thoˢ. Burk for Relief	800
To Joſeph Stears for Dº	200
To Elendʳ.. Edwards & Wᵐ.. Right for Dº	1000
To Mildrid Power for Dº	250
To John White for Dº	400
To Mary Horſley for Dº	150
To Vicars Nettles for Dº	500
To Elizabeth Lewiſs for Dº	300
To Jane Hains for Dº	300
To Mary Tomaſs for Dº	200
Carreyᵈ, Over	24924
[316] Brought Over	24924
To John Shepard for Relief	200
To Elizabeth Sadler for Dº	100
To John Bain for Dº	300
To James Bentley for Keeping Fitzsummers Child	1000

To Coll°.. Samuell Buckner for sevurrall infolvments	336
To Capt.. Ludwel Grymes for work dun on the Glebe	5220
To M^r.. Francis Stubbs for To^{bo}.. Not Recv^d. of John Blafingim	500
To M^r.. Francis Stubbs for five Leveys not Recev^d,	138½
To Mr Francis Stubbs for Brufh Broom &^{c},	48
The Debts amount	32766½
To 6 ℔ C^t.. for Collection is	1965
	34731½
By Coll°.. Samuell Buckner	214
Total Deb^t.	34517½
℔ Contray	C^r
By 985 Tiths at 35½^{lb} of Tob°.. ℔ Tith is	34867½
Due to the Parifh	350

M^r Ja^s.. Hubard is appointed Collecter for the Enfuing year And that he Receve 35½^{lb} of Tob°. ℔ Tith to Discharg the Severall Deb^{ts}.. of the parifh

Mr George Booth is Chofen Church Warden in the Room of Coll°. Buckner

Orderd that M^r.. Hubard Receve the fines Due to the parifh afs allso to Receve of Coll°. Buckner the 214^{lb} of Tob°. the Depofitom of the Laft year

True Entry Ja^s.. Baker Clk V

[317]

At A veſtry held for Pets^th.. Pariſh the 6 day of March 1760

The Revr^d. M^r.. Robt. Yates ⎫ M^r. Peter Kemp
Co^ll.. Samuel Buckner   ⎪ Mr Francis Stubbs
M^r Ja^s. Hubard   ⎬ Capt. Ludwel Grimes
M^r. Thos. Stubbs   ⎪ Capt. John Wiatt
Capt Rich^d. Jones   ⎭ M^r. John Scott

M^r. John Buckner is Choſen Veſtryman in the Room of Capt. John Stubbs Deceaſt by the above Veſtry

      Teſt Ja^s.. Baker Clk: V

     James Baker
    Teste
     James Baker

[318]

At A Veſtry Held for Petſworth Parſ^h. 18th Nov^br.. 1760

    The Rev^rd.. M^r. Robt. Yates Capt. Lud^ll.. Grymes
    M^r. James Hubard   M^r. John. Scoot
Preſent Mr Thomas Stubbs   Capt. John Wiatt
    M^r. Peter Kemp   M^r. George Booth
    Capt. Richard Jones   Mr John Bucker

	D^r	lb
Petsworth Parriſh in Tob^o,		
To the R^vd, M^r. Robt. Yates His Salry		16640
To 4 ⅌ C^t, to make Mr Yates's Tob^o, Neat		640
To Quitrents for the Glebe Land		87
To Communion Bread & Wine		500
To Richard Cole Sexton		1000
To James Baker Cl^k.. of the Church & Veſtry		1600
To 4 ⅌ C^t, to make His Tob^o, Neat		64
To Capt, John Clayton for the Coppy of the Liſt		18
To Capt Clayton for the Hier of Doc^t, Claytons Negro		200

To Thomas Burk for Releif	800
To Joseph Stears for Dº.	200
To Elender Edwards for Dº.	500
To William Wright for Dº.	500
To Mary Horsley for Dº.	150
To Vicars Nettels for Dº.	600
Carried up	23499
[319] Brought up	23499[1b]
To Elizabeth Lewis for Releif	400
To Jean Haynes For Dº.	400
To Mary Tommas For Dº.	300
To John Lawson For takeing Care of Mary Tommas	300
To John Sheppard For Releif	300
To John Bain For Dº.	400
To Briget Cotes For Dº.	400
To Jerimiah Darnold For Dº.	400
To Mʳ James Hubard For his Account	93
To Mʳ George Booth For Dº	240
To Docᵗ Dalglish For Dº	631
	27363
To 6 ℔ Cᵗ, for Collection	1641
The Amount of the Debts	29004
℔ Contra Crdᵗ, by 981 Tiths at 30ᵇ of Tobº, ℔ Tith is	29430
Depositom Due to the Parrish	426

Orderd that Conqᵗ, Wiatt pay Mildred Power 3ˢ 10ˢ of the fines that he has Receiv,d

M^r. George Booth is Appointed Collector for the Enſuing Year & that he Receive 30^{lb} pounds of Tob^o, to Diſcharge the Severall Debts of the Parriſh

M^r, John Buckner is Appointed Church warden in the Room of M^r, James Hubard

Orderd that the Churchwardens Receive of Maj^r, Tomkeys the Fines in His hands Belonging to the Poor of the Parriſh Which if he Refuſeth to pay to Bring Sute for the same ———

True Entry   James Baker Clk, of the Veſtry

[320]

At A Veſtry Held for Petſworth Parrth.. 2th of March 1761

	Co^{ll}. Samuel Buckner		M^r. Warner Waſhington
	M^r. James Hubard		M^r. Francis Stubbs
Preaſan^t.	Mr Thomas Stubbs		Capt, Rich^d. Jones
	M^r. Peter Kemp		Capt. John Wiatt
	Mr John Scott		Mr George Booth

Mr Charels Mynn's Thruſton & M^r. John Rootes is Electe'd Veſtry men in the Room of Mr Ludwell Grymes and M^r. John Buckner, Who has Remov,d out of the Parriſh

Mr Charles Mynn's Thruſton is appointed Church Warden in the Room of M^r, John Buckner

Order'd that the Church Wardens take the money out of M^r. Williſes & Mr Rows hands for not paying the Intreſt in due time ———

Orderd that the Church Wardens of this parriſh write to the Church wardens of Chriſt Church Parriſh to indemnyfie the Parriſh if they will Let Joſeph Stears Live there ———

Enterd by James Baker C.lk V

[321]

At A Veſtry Held for Petſworth Parriſh Oc^{tbr}.. 14th day 1761

Preſent
- Co^{ll}, Samuel Buckner
- M^r. James Hubard
- M^r. Thomas Stubbs
- M^r. Warner Waſhington
- M^r. Peter Kemp
- Capt. Richard Jones
- Capt. John Wiatt
- M^r. George Booth
- M^r. Charls Mn^s, Thruſton
- M^r. John Roots

Petſworth Parriſh in Tob^o.	D^r. lb
To the Rev^d, M^r. Robt. Yates His Salry	16640
To 4 ℔ C^t. to M^r. Yateses Tob^o. Neat	640
To quitrents for the Glebe Land	87
To Communion Bread & Wine	500
To Richard Coal Sexton	1000
To James Baker Cl^k.. of the Church & Veſtry	1600
To 4 ℔ C^t. to make Bakers Tob^o. Neat	64
To Capt. John Clayton for A Coppy of the Liſt	18
To M^r. James Hubards Ac^t.	18
To Doc^t. Alx^d.. Dalgliſh Ac^t.	2500
To Capt. John Claytons Ac^t.	140
To M^r. George Booths Ac^t.	188
To Co^{ll}. Samuel Buckners Ac^t.	600
To Thos. Burk for Relief	800
To Elendor Edwards for D^o	500
To W^m.. Wright for D^o.	500
To Capt. Thruſton Ac^t. for goods to M^{rs}.. Nettles	94
To Vicars Nettles For Releif	600
To Elizabeth Lewis for D^o	400
Carried Over	26889
[322] Brought Over	26889
To Jean Haynes for Releife	400

To Vicars Nittles for takeing Care of Beaufords Child	200
To Mary Tommas for Releif	300
To John Lawson for Boarding of Mary Tommas	300
To John Bane for Relief	400
To Brigᵗ, Coats for Dº.	400
To Jeremy Darlin for Dº.	200
To Cathrine Waſher for Dº.	200
To Ann Weſt for Dº.	200
To Mildred Power for Dº.	200
To Elizabeth Proſser for Dº.	200
To Mary Driver for Nurſing A Baſtard Child	500
	30389
To Collection at 6 ₩ Cᵗ. is	1823
	32212
Depoſᵗ. of the Laſt year is	426
total Debᵗ. is	31786
₩ Contra Cʳᵈᵗ	
By 945 Tithables at 34ˡᵇ of Tobº. ₩ Tith is	32130
Depoſᵗ. in the Hands of the Collector	344

Orderd that Capᵗ Charles Mnº.. Thruſton Be Collecttor for the Enſuing year & that He Receive 34ˡᵇ of Tobº. ₩ Tith to Diſcharge the several Debts of the Parriſh

Orderd that Capᵗ. John Roots Be Church Warden in the Room of Mʳ. George Booth

Orderd that Capᵗ. Thruſton Pay David Dickison 150ˡᵇ of Tobº for Keeping of Mary Horſly One Month Out of the Depoſᵗ. in his Hands

Order'd that the Clark of this Veſtry Employ Mʳ. David Kar to Bring Suit Againſt Mjʳ Tomkies for the fines in his Hands Belonging to the Poor of this Parriſh

Entred By James Baker Clᵏ V

[323]

At A Veſtry Held for Petſworth Parriſh 13ᵗʰ of November 1761

Preſent
- Coˡˡ, Samuel Buckner
- Mʳ. James Hubard
- Mʳ. Thomas Stubbs
- Mʳ. War Waſhington
- Mʳ, Peter Kemp
- Capᵗ, Richard Jones
- Mʳ. Francis Stubbs
- Capᵗ, John Wiatt
- Mʳ. John Scott
- Mʳ. George Booth
- Mʳ. Charles Mnˢ, Thruſton
- Capᵗ, John Roots

It is Reſolv'd by this preſent Veſtry, upon the Motion of the Revᵈ, Mʳ William Yates, that the Salry of this preſent year be Proprated, for the Uſe of the Widow & Orphins of the Late Revᵈ. Mʳ. Robart Yates, Upon Mʳ.. William Yates Seeing the Parriſh Supplid By him self or some Other Minniſter; ——

True Entry James Baker Clᵏ.. Vsʳʸ..

[324]

At A Veſtry Held for Petſworth Parriſh 30ᵗʰ of Decᵇʳ 1761

Preſent
- Coˡˡᵒ.. Samuel Buckner
- Mʳ Peter Kemp
- Mʳ. Francis Stubbs
- Capᵗ, John Wiatt
- Mʳ.. John Scott
- Capᵗ, Charls Mnˢ, Thruſton
- Mʳ.. John Roots

The Revᵈ, Mʳ.. Richard Hueit is by this Veſtry Unamouſly choſen Miniſter of this Parriſh, in the Room of the Revᵈ, Mʳ.. Robᵗ, yates deceaſ'd, & is to enter into this

Parriſh at the Laying of the Next Parriſh Levy or on the 10 day of Oct⁰, Next to take upon him the cure of the sᵈ, parriſh, & to be Endue'd with all the benefits & spirituallities due to A miniſter of the Church of England, by the Laws of Virginia

     Teſt James Baker Clᵏ, of yᵉ Veſtry

[325]

At A Veſtry Held for Petſworth Parriſh the 13 of Sepᵗ, 1762

  Coˡˡ. Samuell Buckner Capᵗ, Richard Jones
Preſent Mʳ. James Hubard Mʳ. John Scott
  Mʳ. War. Waſhington Capᵗ, Charls Mnˢ, Thruſton
  Mʳ. Peter Kemp

Orderd by this preſent Veſtry that Coˡˡ, Samuel Buckner Capᵗ, Richard Jones Mʳ.. John Scott Mʳ.. George Booth Capᵗ. Charˢ, Mnˢ, Thruſton or any three of them meet at the Gleebe to see What repairs Are Wanting and to Agree With Workmen for doing the same

     Teſt James Baker Clk. of yᵉ Veſtry

[326]

At A Veſtry Held for Petſworth Parriſh the 11ᵗʰ of Octᵇʳ.. 1762

Preaſent
 Coˡˡᵒ.. Samˡˡ.. Buckner Capᵗ, John Wiatt
 Mʳ.. James Hubard   Mʳ John Scott
 Mʳ.. War Waſhington Mʳ George Booth
 Mʳ.. Peter Kemp   Capᵗ, Charˢ, Mnˢ, Thruſton
 Capᵗ, Richard Jones   Capᵗ, John Roots
 Mʳ.. Francis Stubbs

Petſworth Parriſh in Toᵇᵒ..	Dʳ	lb
To the Revᵈ. Mʳ.. Wᵐ.. Yates for the Use of the Widow Yates & Chlⁿ		16640

To 4 ℔ Cᵗ, to make Mʳ Yatesʳˢ Tobᵒ.. Neat	640
To Quitrents for the Glebe Land	87
To Communion Bread & Wine	500
To Richard Cole Sexton	1000
To James Baker Clᵏ.. of Church & Veſtry	1600
To 4 ℔ cᵗ.. to make Baker's Tobᵒ.. Neat	64
To Capᵗ, John Clayton for Coppy of the Liſt & Acᵗ..	54
To Capᵗ, John Wiatt his Acᵗ,	394
To Capᵗ, Charˢ, Mnˢ, Thruſton his Acᵗ,	656
To Mʳ.. George Booth's Acᵗ,	27
To David Dickinson's for Boarding Mary Horſley his Acᵗ,	750
To Mʳ Henry Purſell for two Levies Over paid Laſt year	68
To Mʳ.. Livingſton for Seven inſolvents	238
To Thomas Burk for Releif	700
To Elnʳ.. Edwards for Dᵒ.	450
To William Wright for Dᵒ.	350
To Vicars Nettles for Dᵒ.	500
To Jean Haynes for Dᵒ.	400
Carryed up	25118
[327] Brought up	25118
To Mary Tommas for Relief	250
To John Lawson for Boarding Mary Tommas	250
To John Bane for Relief	500
To Bridget Cotes for Dᵒ	400
To Bridget Cotes for Keeping of Mildred Powers Child two months	100
To Cathrine Waſher for Relief	200
To Ann Weſt for Dᵒ.	200
To Mary Darnold for takeing care of Ann Weſt & Child	200
To Elizabeth Proſcer for Relief	200
To Mary Driver for Keeping of Lucy Clarkes Baſtard	600

To W^m.. Brooking for takeing Care of & Buriing Mary Horſley	350
To John Soles for Keeping a baſtard Child till the firſt of Deb^r	1000
To Frances King for D° to keep till the firſt of Novb^r	1000
To Rhode Horſley for Relief	500
To Edward Sanders for D°	400
To Thomas Booker for Keeping of Boolses Child	600
To W^m.. Morris for Keeping one of D°.	350
To John Brown for Boarding Mary Horſley 10 Days	50
Tob°.. Levi'd to Wards Repairing the Glebe	4000
	36268
To Collec^{tn}.. at 6 ℔ C^t, is	2176
	38454
By A ballance of the Laſt years Depoſitom	194
Total Debt is	38260
℔ Contra Crd^t, by 977 Tiths at 40^{lb} ℔ pole is	39080
Depoſ^t, in the Hands of the Collect^r, is	820

It is Orderd that John Blaſingame have 320 of the s^d, Depoſ^t, And that the Remaining 500 be put to the use of the Glebe

Orderd that Capt, John Roots be Collecter for the Enſuing year and that he Receive 40^{lb} of Tob°.. ℔ pole to Diſcharge the severall Debts of the Parriſh

Carried Over

[328]   Brought forward

As the Rev^d, M^r.. Rich^d, Hewit has failed to come to this Parriſh at the time as he Waſs to become Miniſter, this vestry Do Unamousely chuse the Rev'd, Robert Reade to be Minister of this Parish & to take upon himself the Cure of the s'd. Parish & to be enduid with all the Benifits & Speritualities due to A minister of the Church of England by the Laws of Virginia, provided the Rev'd. M'. Reade will come to this Parish Between this & the first Day of December ———

M'r Alexander Dalgleish is Chosen Vestryman in the room of M'r. Thomas Stubbs Deceast, & is appointed Church Warden In the Room of Cap't, Charls Mn'., Thruston ———

Test James Baker Cl'k. of Vtry

[329]

At A Vestry Held for Petsworth Parish Deb'r.. 8th, 1762

Present
Col°. Samuel Buckner
M'r.. Peter Kemp
Cap't, Richard Jones
M'r Francis Stubbs
M'r. John Scott

Cap't, John Wiatt
M'r. George Booth
Cap't, Charls Mn'., Thruston
M'r.. Al'r, Delgleish

As the Rev'd, M'r.. Rob't, Reade who Was Chosen Minister of this Parish the 11 Day of Oc't, Last did not come to the Parish by the appointed time this Parish is become vacant, this Vestry therefore hath thought propper to Recommend M'r James Fountain to his Lordship the Bishop of London to be Ordained A Minister of the Church of England, he promising to go to England as soon as he conveniently can, & at his return to Virginia after Ordination, this present Vestry do Agree to receive Him as Minister of this Parish, & it is resolved by this present Vestry to receive Him as Minister, Provided He comes to the Parish Within two months after his arival in Virginia & take upon him the Curateship of the Parish, & that he shal Be endowed With all the Spiritualities & Temparilities due to

A Minifter of the Church of England by the Laws of Virginia

It is further Order'd that this Veftry addrefs the Governor And that Col°. Buckner & Cap', Wiatt wait on the Governor With the said Addrefs, it is Likewife Order'd that Col°.. Buckner & Cap', Wiatt Agree With some Minifter to officiate in this Parrifh untill M' Fountain Goes to & returns from England

      Teft James Baker Cl*. of y° Veftry

[330]

At A Veftry Held for Petfworth Parrifh the 16 of Sep', 1763

Prefen',
- Col°. Sam¹, Buckner
- M'. James Hubard
- M'. Peter Kemp
- Cap'. Rich⁴. Jones
- M'. Francis Stubbs
- Cap', John Wiatt
- M'. John Scott
- M'. George Booth
- Cap', Char° Mn°, Thrufton
- M'. Al*. Dalgleifh

Purfuant to An Order of Gloucefter County Court Bearing date the 28 Day of July 1763 to Appoint Procefsiners in Each procinct of this Parrifh & to make returns of there proceedings by the Laft day of March According to Law, We do therefore Order & appoint them as followeth ———

1

Orderd that M'. John Throckmorton & M'. Tho°, Miner see the Land Procefsion'd in the firft procinct to begin on the Land of M', Tho° Minor on the firft Thurfday in October

2

Order'd that M'. William Thornton & M' Mordaca Cook see the Land procefsion'd in the second procinct to begin on the Land of Rob', Poortees Efq'. on the second Thurfday in October

3

Order'd that Capt, Richd, Jones & Mr George Booth see the Land procession'd in the third procinct to begin on the Land of Mr. Richd, Talleforo on the third thurſday in October

4

Order'd that Capt, Chars, Mnˢ, Thruſton & Mr. Lewis Booker see the Land procession'd in the fourth procinct to begin on the Land of Mr. Henry Purſell on the fourth monday in October.

5

Order'd that Mr. John Wood & Mr. William Pollard see the Land Proceſsion'd in the fifth procinct to begin on the Land of Mr Humphry Macingdree Decoaſt on the firſt thurſday in November

Carried forward

[331]
6

Order'd that Mr.. Robt, Garland & Mr Warner Rone see the Land procession'd in the sixth procinct to begin on the Land of of Mr. Robt, Daniel on the second Thurſday in Novbr..

7

Order'd that Mr. Benjamon Baker & Mr.. John Kilingham see the Land procession'd in the seventh procinct to begin on the Land of Colo. Smll. Buckner near the Dragon on 3th Thurſday in Novbr

8

Order'd that Mr. Thos.. Kemp & Mr Henry Whitting see the Land procession'd in the Eighth procinct to begin on the Land of Mr.. Auguſtin Smith on the fourth munday in Novb

9

Order'd that Mr. Peter Wiatt & Mr. Francis Rofs see the Land procefsion'd in the Ninth procinct to begin on the Land of Capt, Baley Seaton Decr. on the firft monday in Debr

True Entry James Baker Clk

[332]

At A Veftry Held for Petfworth Parrifh Octbr.. 16th 1763

Colo Saml. Buckner   Capt, John Wiatt
Mr. James Hubard   Mr. John Scott
Mr. Peter Kemp   Mr.. George Booth
Capt.. Richard Jones   Doctor Alx Dalgleifh

Petfworth Parrifh in Tobo.. Dr..	lb
To the Rvd, Mr.. James Horrox	12000
To 8 ℔ ct, To make his Tobo.. Neet	960
To quitrents for the Glebe Land	87
To Communion Bread & Wine	500
To Richd, Cole sexton	1000
To James Baker Clk.. of Church & Veftry	1600
To 4 ℔ Ct to make Bakers Tobo.. Neet	64
To James Baker Clk.. for further servicies	1000
To Capt, John Clayton for A Coppy of the Lift	18
To the Rvd, Mr.. Fox for 17 Tiths Over charg'd Laft year at 40	680
To Mr. Cornls.. Livingfton for One Infolvment	40
To Thos. Burk for Relief	800
To Elender Edwards for Do.	500
To Wm.. Wright for Do.	400
To Jane Hayns for Do.	400
To Jane Hayns for Keeping of Sarah Buredges Child	400
To Mary Tommas for Relief	300
To John Lawson for Boarding of Mary Tommas	300

To John Bane for Relief	800
To Bridget Coats for D°.	400
To D°. for Keeping of Mildred Butchers Child 6 months & buriing it	400
To Catherrine Waſher for Releif	200
Carried up	22849
[333] Brought up	22849ᵇ
To Mary Darnold for Boarding of Ann Weſt &c.	600
To Mary Driver for Keeping of Lucy Clarks Child &c.	850
To John Soles for Keeping A baſtard Child of Mgᵗ, Addams	600
To Frances King for Keeping Another of D°.	600
To Rhode Horſley for Relief	800
To Edward Sanders for D°.	500
To Edwᵈ, Sanders for Keeping two of Bools'es Children 5 months	500
To Thoˢ. Booker for Keeping of D°. 5 months	500
To Mʳ. James Pullar jnʳ for Keeping of one of Elizᵗʰ Procers Children 6 months	300
To Thoˢ Lewis for Keeping two of Kilᵐⁿ.. Killihams Chlᵈ, 1 month	100
To paying him towards Keeping them Another year	400
To George Norton for Keeping of Killihams Child 4 months	200
To D°. for Keeping the same Child off of the parriſh	1000
To Sarah Adderson for Relief	300
To Joſeph Steers for D°	400
	30499

Orderd that the Church Wardens reciev of Mr Batop for rent of the Glebe — 500

                       29999
To collection at 6 ℔ c^t, is   1799

       The total Debt is   31798
℔ Contra Crd^t, by 955 Tiths at 34 ℔ tithe is   32470

       Depoſ^t, in the hands of the Collector is   672

Orderd that Capt, Charls Mn^s Thruſton pay George Hayns 3$^£$ for his Ac^t, Againſt the Parriſh out of the money in his Hands belonging to the Parriſh

Orderd that Capt, Char^s. Mn^s. Thruſton pay M^r. George Booth 1$^£$||17^s||6^d for his Ac^t, Againſt the parriſh Out of the money in his hands belonging to the Parriſh

Carried Over

[334] Brought Over

Orderd that Capt, Char^s. Mn^s. Thruſton pay M^r. W^m.. Finnie 1$^£$ 10^s for his Ac^t, Againſt the Parriſh out of the money in his hands belonging to the Parriſh ———

Orderd that M^r. War. Waſhington be Church Warden in the Room of M^r. John Roots ———

Orderd that Doc^{tr}.. Al^x.. Dalglieſh be Collector for the Enſuing year & that he receive 34^{lb} of Tob^o.. ℔ pole to Diſcharge the several Debts of the parriſh ———

Orderd that Doc^{tr}.. Al^x.. Dalgliesh Apply to Mj^r.. Francis Tomkies for the money Due to the Parriſh in his Hands, Which he promiſ'd to pay, Which if he refuſes To commence A sute for the same ———

True Entry James Baker Cl^k, of Vestry

[335]

At A Veſtry Held for Petſworth Parriſh the 7 of March 1764

Preſent Mʳ..
Capᵗ, Richard Jones
Francis Stubbs
Capᵗ John Wiatt
Mʳ John Scott
Capᵗ, Charˢ, Mnˢ. Thruſton
Capᵗ, John Roots
Doctʳ Alˣ.. Dalgleiſh

Mʳ Auguſtin Smith is Elected Veſtry Man by the Above Veſtry in the Room of Colº. Samuel Buckner Deceaſt

Teſᵗ. James Baker Clk of V

At A Vestry held for Petſworth Parriſh the 12 day of sepᵗ, 1764

Preſent
Mʳ. War Waſhington
Mʳ. Peter Kemp
Capᵗ. Richᵈ. Jones
Mʳ. John Scott
{ Capᵗ. John Wiatt
M'. George Booth
Capᵗ. Charˢ. Mnˢ. Thruſton }

It is order'd by this Veſtry that Mʳ. John Scott bring suit Againſt Mʳ. Francis Willis for his bond due to this parriſh; And that he Apply to Mʳ. John Stubbs for security for the Money in his hands belonging to the parriſh, Which if he refuse'es to give then to Commence Suit for the same ———

Teſt James Baker Clk

[336]

At A Veſtry held for Petſworth Parriſh the 18 day of Sepᵗ 1764

Preſent,
Mʳ. War Waſhington
Mʳ. Peter Kemp
Capt Richard Jones
Mʳ. Francis Stubbs
Mʳ. John Scott
Capᵗ. John Wiatt
Mʳ. George Booth
Doctʳ. Alˣ. Dalgleiſh

As the Revᵈ, Mʳ. James Murra Fountain Who was Miniſter of this Parriſh has left it to go to Wear, this Parriſh is become vacant of a Miniſter this Veſtry therefore hath thought proper to recommend Mʳ Charˢ. Mnˢ. Thruſton to his Lordſhip the Biſhop of London to be Ordaind A Miniſter of the Church of England he promiſing to go to England as soon as he conveniantly can, & at his return to Virginia After ordination, this preſent Veſtry do Agree to receive him as Miniſter of this parriſh, & it is reſolv'd by this preſent Veſtry to receiv him as Miniſter, provided he comes to the parriſh Within two months After his Arrival in Virginia & take upon him the Curateſhip of the parriſh, & that he shall be Endow'd with all the spirituallities & temporalities due to A Miniſter of the Church of England by the Laws of Virginia, ———

It is further order'd that this Veſtry Addreſs the Governor & that Capᵗ. Rhᵈ. Jones & Capᵗ. John Wiatt wait on the Governer with the said Addreſs, ———

Teſt. James Baker Clᵏ

Note) at the above Veſtry Capᵗ. Charˢ. Mnˢ. Thruston declin'd serving Any longer as Veſtry Man, & Mʳ. James Hubard Jnʳ was Choſen in his room,

Teſt James Baker Clᵏ

[337]

At A Veſtry held for Petſworth Pariſh the 13 day of Novbʳ. 1764

Preſent
- Mʳ. James Hubard
- Mʳ. War Waſhington
- Mʳ. Peter Kemp
- Capᵗ. Rhᵈ. Jones
- Mʳ. John Scott
- Mʳ. George Booth
- Capᵗ. John Rootes
- Mʳ. Alʳ. Dalglieſh
- Mʳ. James Hubard Jnʳ

Petſworth Pariſh in Tobº.	Dʳ.	lb
To the Revᵈ. Mʳ. James Murra Fountain his salary		8000
To 8 ℔ ᶜᵗ. to make his Tobº. Neat		640

To Quitrents for the Glebe Land	87
To Communion Bread & Wine	500
To Richᵈ. Cole sexton	1000
To James Baker Clᵏ. of Church & Veſtry	1600
To 4 ℔ cᵗ. to make Bakers Tobᵒ. neat	64
To James Baker for further services	1000
To Capᵗ. John Clayton for Copy of the Liſt	18
To Capᵗ. John Clayton for Clarks notes	172
To William Baker Jnʳ. for one levy Over paid	34
To Thomas Burk for relief	800
To Mary Tommas for Dᵒ.	300
To John Lawson for Boarding of her	300
To John Bane for relief	800
To Briget Coats for Dᵒ.	400
To Catherine Waſher for Dᵒ.	200
To Rhode Horſley for Dᵒ.	800
To Joſeph Stears for Dᵒ.	600
To Elizabeth Draper for Dᵒ.	200
Carry'd over	17515
	lb
[338] Brought Over	17515
To Solomon Hall for relief	500
To William Hubard for Dᵒ.	600
To Mary Stubblefield for Dᵒ.	200
To Mary Buzbee for Dᵒ.	600
To Mary Darnold for Keeping of Dianah Weſt	600
To Mary Driver for Keeping of Jhⁿ. Procer & Purcilla Clark	1200
To John Soles for Keeping of Ann Shepard Adams	600
To John Soles for takeing care of Ann Wright	200
To Marget Darnold for takeing care of Dᵒ.	400
To Thomas Booker for Keeping of Peter & Stubblefield Bools	1200
To James Pullar snʳ. for Keeping of Sarah Procer	600

To Thoˢ. Lewis for Keeping of Kilmon Kallahams two Children	800
To James Haynes for his & his mothers Keeping of Sarah Burges Child	450
To Sarah Waſher tor Cloths for her Child	150
To Mʳ. James Hubard his Acᵗ.	475
To Tobᵒ. Levid for the use of the Parish	4000
	30090
To Collection at 6 ℔ cᵗ. is	1805
Total Debᵗ	31895
℔ Contra Crdᵗ. by 931 Tiths at 35ˡᵇ ℔ tith is	32585
Depoſit	690

The Said Depoſit to be Applid to the uſe of the parish

Orderd that Mʳ. Jaˢ. Hubard Jnʳ. be Church Warden in the room of Mʳ. Alˣ. Dalglieſh

Orderd that the Church Wardens Agree with some Miniſter to Officiate till Mʳ. Thruston returns from England

Carried up

[339]

Orderd that Mʳ. Washington, Mʳ. Rootes, Mʳ. Booth, Mʳ. Scott Mʳ. Hubard Jnʳ. & Capᵗ. Jones meet at some convenient time And Agree to the Leting & building of A Workhouse & that Any three of the above Veſtry men may let the same

Orderd that James Baker be Collector for this present year & that he receive 35ˡᵇ of Tobᵒ. ℔ Tith to Discharge the parriſh Debts And Mʳ. William Duval Agrees to be his security for the said Collection ———

Teſt James Baker Clk

[340]

At A Vestry Held for Petsworth Parrish the 2 day of March 1765

Preſent
M^r. James Hubard
M^r. War Washington
M^r. Peter Kemp
Capt. John Wiatt

M^r. John Scott
M^r. George Booth
M^r. John Roots
M^r. Al^x. Dalgliesh

Order'd that M^r.. Char^s. Mn^s. Thruston & M^r. Cornelious Livingston pay to Capt. Richard Jones the money they owe to the parrish with Intrest

Orderd that the Collector of the Parrish Levy pay the Tob^o. Levy'd for the use of the Parrish to Capt. Rh^d. Jones & that Capt. Jones pay M^{rs}. Pollard 10/ is being her Ac^t. Against the parrish for mending the surplis

Teſt   James Baker Cl^k.. of P. P.V

[341]

At A Vestry Held for Petsworth Parrish the 4 day of Novb^r. 1765

M^r. James Hubard sn^r.
M^r. Warner Washington
M^r. Peter Kemp
Capt. Rh^d. Jones
M^r. Francis Stubbs
M^r. John Scott

Capt. John Wiatt
M^r. George Booth
Capt. John Roots
M^r. Augustin Smith
Capt. James Hubard Jn^r.

Receiv^d. by the Above Vestry of Capt. Richard Jones, the House for the poor, done According to Agreement

Orderd that M^r. Henry Whiting be Vestry man in the room of Doct^r. Al^x. Dalgliesh who has remoov^d. out of the Parrish

M^{rs}.. Johannah Macingdree is Chosen M^{rs}.. of the poors house And she to be paid ten pounds ℔ year for the s^d. service

Teſt   James Baker Clk of P.P. Veſtry

[342]

At A Veſtry held for Petsworth Parrish the 13 of Novb^r. 1765

Present
M^r. James Hubard sn^r.
M^r. Warner Washington
M^r. Peter Kemp
Capt. Rh^d. Jones
M^r. Francis Stubbs
M^r. John Scott

Capt. John Wiatt
M^r. George Booth
Capt. John Roots
M^r. Augustin Smith

Petsworth Parrish in Tob°.	Dr.	lb.
To Quitrents for the Glebe Land		87
To Communion Bread & Wine		500
To Rh^d. Cole sexton		1000
To James Baker Clk of the Church & Vestry		1664
To Capt. John Clayton his Ac^t		246
To John Lawson for Buriing of Mary Tommas		100
To James Blasingam for A Coffin for Mary Tommas		80
To Mary Darnal for Keeping of Dianah West & Rich^d. Aderson		1200
To Mary Driver for Keeping of John Procer & Purcila Clark		1200
To M^{rs}.. Soles for Keeping of Ann Shepard Addams		600
To M^{rs}.. Duva^l. for Keeping of Peter & Stubblefield Bowls		1200
To M^{rs}.. Ann Puller for keeping of Sarah Procer		600
To M^{rs}.. Ann Puller for Keeping the s^d. child off of the Parrish On her giving good security		1000
To Thomas Lewis for keeping of Rhode Kallaham		600

To Sarah Washer for Keeping of her Daughter Nancy	600
To George Fary for Keeping of Flurinah Kallaham	600
Caryed up	11277

[343]

	lb
Brought up	11277
To M^{rs}.. Mary Soles for keeping of Ann Shepard Addams off of the Parrish Capt. John Wiatt being her security	1000
To Sarah Washer for Keeping her own Child the year 1766	300
To James Baker for Insolvents	830
To James Baker for mooving of M^{rs}.. Macingdree	50
To M^r. James Hubard for his Ac^t. for Beding &c. for the poor	860
To M^r. Augustin Smith for A beef & salt	350
To M^r. Peter Kemp for one Levy Over paid	34
Levied for provision & necefsary's for the Poor's house	3000
To Capt. Rh^d. Jones for Ballance of the Work House	1477
To Capt. Rh^d. Jones for Building a 12 foot square house	1500
	20678
To Collection at 6 ℔ c^t. is	1240
Total Debt is	21918
℔ Contra Crd^t. by 918 Tiths at 24^{lb} of Tob^o. ℔ tithe is	22032
Depoſ^t.	114

Orderd that Capt. Rh^d. Jones receive £10|| of Doct^r. Al^x. Dalgliesh it being for rent of the Glebe

Orderd that Mr. Augustin Smith be Church Warden in the room of Mr. Warner Washington

Orderd that Capt. James Hubard be Collector the insuing year & that he receiv 24^{lb} of Tobo. ℔ tithe to discharge the several debts of the Parrish, Likewise that he endeavour to receiv 900^{lb} of Tobo. the insolvents return'd to this Vestry

Order'd that the Church Wardens be impower'd to A Gree with any one Willing to take any of the poor Children off of the Parrish for 1000^{lb} of Tobo. Each, on there giving Bond & good security to Endamnifie the Parrish from Any further charge for the sd. Child or Children

Orderd that they who has the 172^{lb} Levi'd for Capt. Clayton in the year 1764 pay it to the Collector

    Teſt James Baker Clk of P. P. V

[344]

At A Vestry held for Petsworth Parish January 14th. 1767

Preaſent The Revd Mr. Chars. Mns. Thruston
 Mr. James Hubard { Mr. John Scott
 Mr. Warner Washington { Mr. George Booth
 Mr. Peter Kemp   { Capt. James Hubard Jnr.
 Capt. Rhd. Jones   {

Petsworth Parrish in Tobo.	Dr.	lb
To the Revd Mr. Charles Mins Thruston his sallery		16000
To 8 ℔ Ct. to make Mr. Thruston's Tobo. Neat		1280
To Quitrents for the Glebe Land		87
To Richard Cole sexton		1000
To James Baker Clark of Church & Vestry		1600

To 4 ℔ Cᵗ. to make Bakers Tobº. Neat	64
To Communion Bread & Wine	500
To Capᵗ. John Clayton of the List	20
To Capᵗ. James Hubard for insolvevents	360
To Mary Darnold for taking Ann West Child of the parrish John Wood her security	1000
To Mjʳ. Robᵗ. Danel for takeing Mary Hudson's Child of the parish	1000
To Mʳ. James Hubard his Acᵗ. £18‖18 at 2ᵈ ℔ lb is	2268
To Samuel Brooking for Thoˢ. Burks Coffin 90ˡᵇ at 2ᵈ ℔ lb	90
To Frances Grumbley for a sheat to bury Thoˢ. Burk 84 at 2ᵈ	84
To Sarah Blasingame for Bringing two women to bed	120
To Capᵗ. John Wiatt for Hire of a negro Woman for the workhouse £4 — — reduct 10/ for Mʳˢ.. Blasingame £3‖10	420
To Johanna Mᶜ.Kindree for minding the work house £10	1200
To Susanah Burk to pay her rent 210ˡᵇ Tobº at 2ᵈ ℔ lb	210
To Johanna Mᶜ.kindree for finding the Negro Woman Cloths at the work house & making them 17/6	105
To Wᵐ Stubb for his Acᵗ	68
To Lewis Booker for 5 Bushells of Corn Dº. of Wheat 17/6	225
Carried forward	27701

		lb
[345]	Tobº. Brought forward	27701
	To Capt. Rhd. Jones Act £18||11||0 at 2d ℔ lb is	2226
	To Tobº. Levyd. to buy Cloths & Provision for the Work house Youse for the year 1767	6000
		35927
	To Marget Hubbard for William Hubbard	300
		36227
	To 6 ℔ Ct. for Collection	2173
		38400
	Crdt. by 900 Tithes at 43lb of Tobº ℔ Tithe is	38700
	Depoſit	300

Orderd that Thoˢ. Scott be Collector this year & that he receive 43lb of Tobº. ℔ tithe to discharge the several Debtˢ. of the Parrish

Orderd that the Collector pay Mr. Washington, Mr Hubard & the Revd Mr. Thruston for the provision they find for the work house & that he shall Buey on the best terms Green or Blue plains Or half thick & Canvis to Cloth the poor Children, & Cottin for the Negro Woman at the Work house

Orderd that the Collector pay for Chairs & A Table out of the Depositum for the youse of the Vestry house

Mr. John Fox is Chosen A Vestry man in the Room of Mr. Francis Stubbs decd.. & is appointed Church Warden in the Room of Capt. James Hubard

M^{md}. M^r. Hubard is to find 10 Barrils of Corn at 13/6 ⅌ Bar^l M^r. Washington 20 D^o. at 13/6 D^o. to be paid for out of the 6000^{lb} Levy^d. for the work house at 2^d. ⅌ lb

The Rev^d. M^r. Thruston to be paid 18/ Groce ⅌ hundred [ ] his Pork & 30/ ⅌ hundred for Beef, out of the Tob^o. Levy'd for the youse of the Work House at 2^d ⅌ lb

True Entry ⅌ Ja^s. Baker Cl^k V

[346]

At A Vestry Held for Petsworth Parrish 1th of Decb^r. 1767

Present   The Rev^d. M^r. Chr^s. Mn^s. Thruston
            M^r. James Hubard   ⎡ M^r. George Booth
            M^r. Peter Kemp   ⎨ Capt. James Hubard
            Capt. Rich^d. Jones   ⎩ M^r. Henry Whiting
            M^r. John Scott

Pursuent to Order of Gloucester Court bearing date 6th. of Augst 1767 to Appoint porſesioners in this Parrish & to make return of there proseedings by the Last day of March according to Law we therefore Appoint them as followeth—Viz

Orderd that Thomas Miner & W^m.. Thornton see the Lands Prosesioned in the first Procinct to begin on the Land of Thos. Miner on the first friday in January ———

Ordered that John Blasingame & Thos. Stubbs see the Lands prosesioned in the second procint to begin on the Land of W^m.. Fleming Eſtate on the second Thursday in January ———

Orderd that Rh^d. Talifero & W^m.. Fliming see the Lands prosesioned in the third procinct to begin on the Land of Rh^d Talifero on the third Thursday in January ———

Orderd that Lewis Booker & John Wood see the Lands prosesioned in the fourth presinct to begin on the Land of James Baker on the fourth *fourth Thursday in January —

Orderd that W^m.. Pollard & Thos. Wright see the Lands prosesioned in the fifth procinct to begin on the Land of Humphrey Macindree Decs^d. on the first Friday in February ———

            Carried up

[347]   Brought up   †precinct

Orderd that Robt. Garland & Samuel Brooking see the Lands prosesioned in the sixth procinct to begin on the Land of Robt. Daniel on the second Thursday in Febuary

Orderd that Benjamin Baker & John Kiningham see the lands prosesioned in the seventh procinct to begin on the Lands of Robt. Kemp on the third Thursday in Febuary —

Orderd that Rh^d. Wiatt Royston & W^m.. Sears see the Lands prosesioned in the Eighth Procinct to begin on the Land of Augustin Smith on the fourth Thursday in Febuary ———

Orderd that John Wiatt sn^r. & Peter Wiatt see the Lands prosesiond in the ninth procinct to begin on the Land of Bailey Ceaton Decs^d. on the first Friday in March ————

          A True Entry ⅌ James Baker Clk P. P. V

---

*Note! This word has been scratched through with a pen in the MS., but is still plainly legible.—C. G. C.

†Note! This word is so written at the bottom of page 346 of the MS. and to the right of the words "Carried up."—C. G. C.

[348]

At A Vestry held for Petsworth Parrish 1ᵗʰ. of December 1767

Present the Revᵈ. Mʳ. Charles Mnˢ. Thruston

Mʳ. James Hubard
Mʳ. Peter Kemp
Capᵗ. Richᵈ. Jones
Mʳ. John Scott

Mʳ. George Booth
Capᵗ. James Hubard
Mʳ. Henry Whiting

Petsworth Parrish in Tobº.	Dʳ	lb
To the Revᵈ. Mʳ. Chrˢ. Mnˢ. Thruston his sallery		16000
To 8 ℔ cᵗ to make his Tobº. neat		1280
To Quitrents for the Glebe Land		87
To James Baker for Clk of the Church & Vestry		1600
To 4 ℔ Cᵗ. to make his Tobº. Neat		64
To Rhᵈ. Cole sexton to be paid to Lewis Booker ℔ Coles order		1000
To Communion Bread & Wine		500
To Capᵗ. John Clayton for the List of Tithables		20
To Johannah Macingdree for minding the Work house £10‖		1000
To Wᵐ.. Morris for Nursing Jaˢ. Brooks Child one year		600
To Capᵗ. John Wiatt for the Hire of a Negro Wench for the Work House belonging to Miſˢ. With at £4		400
To James Puller Jnʳ. for making the Church Gates £6‖5 Not to be paid till the gates are finished		625
To James Hubard for his Acᵗ. £1‖14‖9		174
To John Scott for his Acᵗ. £3‖9‖8		348
To Wilson Cary for his Acᵗ. £2‖11‖4		257
To Rhᵈ. Jones for his acᵗ. £4‖11‖3		457
To Rhᵈ. Cole for Diging Floʳ. Hutsing's grave		12

To Mary Hunter for finding A Coffin &c. for Mary Adams	75
To Ja⁵. Puller Jn͏ʳ. for makeing A Coffin for Floʳ Hutson 5/	25
Carryed up	24444

[349]

	lb
Brought up	24444
To Johannah McKindree for her Aᶜᵗ. 16/9	82
To Wᵐ.. Pollard for taking Ann Burage of the parrish	1000
To Wᵐ.. Baker Jnʳ. for takeing Danˡ. Powers of the Parrish	1000
To Susannah Burk to pay her rent &ᶜ.	250
To Britchet Coates 150ˡᵇ to be laid out by the Church Wardins for Cloathing for Her	150
To Joseph Stears for Cloathing & provision	250
To Tobᵒ. to pay for Provision's & Cloathing &ᶜ. for the poor at the work House	3000
	30176
To 6 ₱ᶜ. for Collection	1810
total debt is	31986
Crdᵗ. by 848 Tythes at 38 ₱ pole	32224
Deposit due to the Parrish	238

Order'd that the Collector Receive 38ˡᵇ of Tobᵒ. ₱ tithe to Discharge parrish Debts

Orderd that the Collector pay Rhᵈ. Jones for 20 Barˢ. of Corn at 10/ & to pay for 1000ˡᵇ of Pork & to buey Cloaths & salt for the poor at the Work house out of the 3000ˡᵇ of Tobᵒ. Levyᵈ. for that purpose

At this Vestry M‍ʳ. Rhᵈ. Talliferro is Chose Vestry man in the Room of Mʳ. Augsᵗ. Smith who has remoovᵈ. out of the Parrish, & Mʳ. Lewis Booker is Chose Vestry man in the room of John Fox who refuseth to serve As A Vestry man

Mʳ. Henry Whiting & Mʳ. Rhᵈ. Taliaferro is Appointed Church Wardins for this Parrish

Ordered that the Church Wardens Agree with workmen to build A Tobᵒ. House at the Glebe 40 foot Long & 20 foot wide

Coˡ. Francis Tomkies is appointed Collector for this presend Year, on his giving Bond & security

Teſt Jaˢ. Baker Clk P. P. V

[350]

At A Vestry Held for Petsworth Parrish 14ᵗʰ. day of March 1768

The Revᵈ. Mʳ. Charˢ. Mnˢ. Thruston   Capᵗ. Rhᵈ. Jones
    Mʳ. James Hubard Gen ᵗ   Mʳ. John Scott
    Mʳ. Warner Washington   Mʳ. George Booth
    Mʳ. Peter Kemp   Mʳ. Henry Whiting

Orderd that Mʳ. George Booth bring suit Against Mʳ. Benjamin Rows Executers, & Mʳ. John Stubbs snʳ. for the money in there hands belonging to the Parrish

At this Vestry Mʳ. William Thornton is Chose Vestry Man in the Room of Capᵗ. John Roots who has resigned — & Mʳ. John Wiatt is Chosen Vestry man in the Room of Capᵗ. John Wiatt who has remooved out of the Parrish

Teſt James Baker Clk V.

[351]

At A Vestry held for Petsworth Parish 4th. of Octobr. 1768

The Revd. Chars. Mns. Thruston
Capt. Rhd. Jones   Mr. Rhd. Taliafero
Mr. Jno. Scott   Mr. Lewis Booker
Capt. Jas. Hubard   Mr. Wm.. Thornton
Mr. Henry Whiting   Mr. Jno. Wiatt

Ordered that the Church Wardins speak to the Clark of the Court to dismiſs the suit Commenct Against John Stubbs & William Thornton for the money in there hands belonging to the parrish Left by the Late Mr. Augustin Smith

Teſt Jas. Baker Clk V

[352]

At A Vestry Held for Petsworth Parish 12th day of Decbr. 1768

Preasent
Mr. James Hubard   { Capt. Jas. Hubard
Mr. Peter Kemp   { Mr. Lewis Booker
Capt. Rhd. Jones   { Mr. John Wiatt
Mr. George Booth   {

Petsworth Parish in Tobo.	Dr.	lb
To the Revd. Mr. Chars. Mns. Thruston his sallery		16000
To 8 ℔ ct. to make his Tobo. neat		1280
To Quitrents for the Glebe Land		87
To Communion Bread & Wine		500
To James Baker Clk of Church & Vestry		1600
To 4 ℔ ct to make his Tobo. Neat		64
To Rhd. Cole sexton to be paid to James Hubard Gent.		1000
To Capt. Jno. Clayton for Copy of the List		18
To Mr. Jno Howlit for Building a Barn at the Glebe £24‖14‖6 in Tobo. at 20/ ℔ C is		2475

To W^m.. Pollard for takeing care of & buring Joseph Stears	300
To Ja^s. Hubard Gen^t. his Ac^t £2‖15‖6 in Tob°. at 20/ ⅌ C	278
To Johannah M^{c}ingdree £10—2 in Tob°. at 20/ ⅌ C	1020
To Jn°. Kiningham for Buring David Murray	150
To Rh^d. Cole for his Ac^t. 11/6 in Tob°. at 20/ ⅌ C	58
To Capt Rh^d. Jones for his Ac^t. £3—17 in Tob°. at 20/ ⅌ C	385
To the Ex^s. of Baytops Es^t. for Hire of A Negro woman	305
To Susanah Burk for releaf	300
To Briget Cotes for D°.	300
To Ann Brooking for D°.	200
To Ann Hall for D°.	200
Levy'd for the Use of the Work House	2100
Carryed up	28620
[353] Brought up	28620
To Ja^s. Baker for fetching the List 10/ in Tob°. at 20/ ⅌ C	50
Levyed for the use of the parish towards repairing the Glebe	3000
To the Rev^d. M^r. Thruston for two months sallery	2666
To 8 ⅌ c^t. to make the s^d. Tob°. Neat	208
	34544
To Com^s. at 6 ⅌ c^t. is	2072
total debt	36616
Crd^t. by 877 Tiths at 40^{lb} of Tob°. ⅌ tithe is	35080
	1536
Crd^t. by Col°. Fr^s. Tomkies for	1830
the Deposit is	294

Orderd that M^r. Rh^d. Taliafero Be Collector the ensuing year on giving bond with security for his performance & that he receav 40^{lb} of Tob^o. ₱ tith to Discharge the parish Debt

Orderd that M^r. Jno. Wiatt be Church Wardin in the room of M^r. Henry Whiting

At this Vestry the Rev^d. M^r. Ch^{rs}.. Mn^a. Thruston Agreed to resign this parish as Minister on the Last day of this month & the Rev^d. M^r. Auther Hamilton is Chose Minister in his room

M^r. William Duval is Chosen Vestry man in the room of M^r. Warner Washington who has resigned it

Ordered that the Collector pay to Capt. Rh^d. Jones & M^r. Lewis Booker out of the Tob^o. Leavyed for the use of the Work House According to there Act^s.

     Test James Baker Clk of the Vestry

[354 Blank]

[355]

At A Vestry Held for Petsworth Parish 13th. of Novb^r. 1769

    The Rev^d. Mr Auther Hamilton

James Hubard Gen^t. Capt. James Hubard
M^r. Peter Kemp   M^r. Lewis Booker
Capt. Rh^d. Jones   M^r. John Wiatt
M^r. John Scott   M^r. William Duval
M^r. George Booth

Petsworth Parrish in Tob^o.	D^r.
To the Rev^d. M^r. Auther Hamilton his salary	14000
To 8 ₱ c^t. to make his Tob^o. Neat	1120
To Quitrents for the Glebe Land	87
To Capt. Ja^s. Hubard for Communion Bread & Wine	500
To Ja^s. Baker Cl^k. of the Church & Vestry	1600
To 4 ₱ C^t. to make his Tob^o. Neat	64

To Rh^d. Cole sexton, to be paid to James Hubard Gen^t.	1000
To Capt. Jno. Clayton for Coppy of the List of tithes	18
To M^r Jno. Howlit his Ac^t. in Tob^o.	8000
To Capt. Jno. Hubard for Insolvents	288
To M^r. Robt. Garland for one Barrill of Corn for Burk 10/	50
To M^r. Jno. Wiatt his Ac^t. for 253^{lb} of Beef at 2^d ℔ lb £2∥2∥2	210
To M^{rs}.. Johannah M^c.ingdree for M^{rs}. of the Work house	500
To Ocly Philpots for takeing of Ja^s. Brooks'es Child Rebeckah	400
Levy'd for the youse of the Work House	2300
To buey 1000^{lb} of pork 12 Bar^s. of Corn ½ A Baril of Salt & Clothing	
To be paid M^r. Peter Kemp Susanah Burks rent	300
To Thos. Polard for mending the Church Kee 1/3 in Tob^o	7
To Susanah Burk 250^{lb} of Tob^o. to buey 5 Barrils of Corn of Capt. Ja^s. Hubard the Tob^o. to be paid to Capt. Hubard	250
Deb^t. is	30694
Com^s. at 6 ℔ c^t. is	1841
Carry'd Over	32535 lb

[356]

The Total Deb^t. Brought Over	32535
By Col^o. Fr^s. Tomkies	117
	32652
℔ Contra Crd^t. by 823 Tithes at 40^{lb} of Tob^o. ℔ Tithe is	32920
Deposit	268

Order'd that the sᵈ. Deposit be Apply towards giting Books for the Church

Order'd that Mʳ John Wiatt be Collector the Ensuing year & that he Receive 40ˡᵇ of Tobᵒ. ℔ tith to discharge the Parish Debt

Order'd that Mʳ. William Duval be Church Warden in the Room of Mʳ. Richard Taliafero

Order'd that the Church Wardins provide A Mistreſs for the Work House

Orderd that Church Wardins Imploy some Workman To repair the Church Windows

      Teſt James Baker Clk of V.

[357]

At A Vestry held for Petsworth Parish November 15ᵗʰ. 1770

    The Revᵈ. Mʳ. Arther Hamilton

Preasent { James Hubard Genᵗ.; Capᵗ. Richᵈ. Jones; Mʳ. George Booth; Mʳ. Richᵈ. Taliafero } { Mʳ. Lewis Booker; Mʳ. William Thornton; Mʳ. John Wiatt; Mʳ. William Duval }

Petsworth Parish in Tobᵒ. Dʳ	lb
To the Revᵈ. Mʳ. Arther Hamilton his Sallery	16000
To 8 ℔ cᵗ. to make his Tobᵒ. Neet	1280
To Quitrents for the Glebe Land	87
To Capᵗ. Jaˢ. Hubard for Communion Bread & Wine	500
To Jaˢ. Baker Clk of the Church & Vestry	1600
To 4 ℔ cᵗ. to make the said Tobᵒ. Neet	64
To Richᵈ. Cole sexton to be paid to William Hall	1000
To Capᵗ. John Clayton his Acᵗ.	90
To Mʳ. John Roots his Acᵗ. 17/6 in Tobᵒ. at 2ᵈ. is	105
To Benjamin Philpots for Coffin & sheet for Jean Potter 20/	120

To the Rev⁴. Mʳ. Hamilton for the Ballance of Books &c for the Church his Acᵗ. is 17/8 in Tobᵒ. at 2ᵈ	106
To Mʳ. Lewis Booker for one Bushell of wheat 5/	30
To Capᵗ. Richᵈ Jones for Cuting of wood & ½ A bushell of Salt for the work House £1‖11‖2	187
To Mʳ: Wᵐ.. Duvaˡ. his Acᵗ. for Horsblocks &c 1ˢ—9ˢ—2ᵈ	175
To Mʳ. Rhᵈ. Taliafero his Acᵗ. for A bucket for the Church 2/6	15
To Thoˢ. Pollards Acᵗ. for 3 pare of Hinges for Church gates 7/6	45
To Mary Lamb Mistreſs of the Work House £5..0	600
To Dᵒ. for finding some provision £1—5	150
To Rhᵈ. Cole his Acᵗ. 5/6 in Tobᵒ. to be to Mʳ. Lewis Booker	33
To Arnold Burk for takeing of Jaˢ. & John Stripling-Powers off of the Parish on his giving sufficient security to the Church Wardens	1000
Cary'd Over	23187
[358] Brought Over	23187
To Susanah Burk for relief	600
Levy'd for the Use of the Work House	2100
Levy'ᵈ. for & to be laid out by the Church Wardin for the use of the Church	1000
	26887
To Comˢ. at 6 ℔ Cᵗ.	1613
Total Debᵗ.	28500
℔ Contra Crdᵗ. by 849 Tithes at 34ˡᵇ of Tobᵒ. ℔ Tithe is	28866
Deposit	366

Orderd that Mr. John Fox be Vestry man in the Room of Mr Henry Whiting who has moved out of the Parish

Orderd that Mj{r}. Jonathan Watson be Vestry man in the Room of Mr. John Scott who has resign'd

Orderd that Mr. Lewis Booker be Church Wardin in the Room of Mr. John Wiatt

Orderd that Mr. John Wiatt be Collector the Ensuing year & 34^{lb} of Tob°. ℔ Tithe to Discharge the Parish Deb{t}

Orderd that the Church Warden Employ A Workman to Build A garden at the Worke House 80 feet square to be Compleated by the last day of March next, the Deposit to be Apploid to the sd. Use

[359]

At A Vestry held for Petsworth Parish Novb{r}. 15th 1771

The Revd. Mr. Arther Hamilton

Preasent
- Mr. James Hubard
- Mr. Peter Kemp
- Capt. Richard Jones
- Mr. George Booth
- Capt. James Hubard
- Mr. Rh{d}. Taliafero
- Mr. Lewis Booker
- Mr John Wiatt
- Mr. William Duva{l}.

Petsworth Parish in Tob°.	Dr.	lb
To the Revd. Mr. Hamilton his sallery		16000
To 8 ℔ c{t}. to make his Tob°. Neet		1280
To Quitrents for the Glebe Land		87
To James Baker Clk of Church & Vestry		1600
To 4 ℔ C{t}. to make Baker's Tob°. Neet		64
To Capt. Jn°. Clayton his Ac{t}. Neet		224
To Jn°. Kiningham for one levy Overcharg'd last year		34
To Mr. Wm.. Duval his Ac{t}. £3‖15‖8 in Tob°. at 20/ ℔ C is		378

GLOUCESTER COUNTY, VIRGINIA, 1677-1793 345

To Capt. Rh^d. Jones his ac^t. £2‖18‖9 in Tob°. at 20/ ℔ C is	294
To Rh^d. Cole his Ac^t. 5/ in Tob°. at 20/ ℔ C	25
To Rh^d. Cole sexton 1000^{lb} to be paid to M^r. W^m.. Hall a	1000
To Mary Lamb for M^{rs}.. of the work House £5— in Tob°. at 20/ ℔ C	500
To M^r. David Dickerson for takeing of Thos. M^c-Williams youngest Child of the parish on his giving Bond for the same	1500
To M^r. Henry Burton for one Levy Over charg'd last year	34
To M^r. John Howlet his Act for work dun at the Glebe & to be dun	200
To M^r. W^m.. Hall for Clothing of an Olphin Boy	150
To M^r. Joseph Pullar for rent of M^{rs}.. Burk	50
To M^r. Lewis Booker on Ac^t. of M^{rs}. Lamb	30
To Arnold Shumake Burk on giving Bond & security to the Churchwardins as A further indulgance for keeping two of Powers'es Children off of this Parish	1000
Carry^d. Over lb	24450
[360] lb	
Brought Over	24450
To Communion Bread & Wine	500
To M^{rs}.. Ann Pullar for one levy Over paid	40
To Levy'd for the Use of the Work House	2000
	26990
Crd^t. by M^r. John Wiatt for	125
	26865
To Com^s. at 6 ℔ c^t. is	1611
Total Deb^t.	28476
Crd^t. by 826 Tithes at 35^{lb} of Tob°. ℔ Tithe is	28910
Depoſt.	434

Orderd that the Collector pay Mary Austin 200^{lb} of the s^d. Depost And the remainder to be paid to Susanah Burk

Orderd that the Churchwarden Imploy A Workman to Lay A Threaching flour in the Barn at the Glebe 12 feet square, & to provide A Cushen for the alter & a spade & Hoe for the sexton

M^r. William Thornton is Appointed Church Warden in the Room of M^r. William Duva^l.

Test James Baker Clk of the V

[361]

At A Vestry held & continued for Petsworth Parish January 6th. 1772

James Hubard Gn^t	M^r. Lewis Booker
Capt. Rh^d. Jones	M^r. William Thornton
M^r. George Booth	M^r. Jno. Wiatt
Capt. James Hubard	M^r. Jno. Fox
M^r. Rh^d. Taliafero	

Capt. Rh^d. Jones & M^r. George Booth Agreed this day in vestry to be security for Arnold Shumake Burk Keeping of two of Powers'es Children off of this Parish

M^r. Chas. Tomkies Jn^r. is Appointed Collector for the Ensuing year & that he receive 35^{lb} of Tob^o. ℔ Tithe to discharge the Parish Deb^t. & M^r. Jno. Fox Agrees to be his security for the Performance of the same

Orderd that the Collector pay the 200^{lb} of Tob^o. Leavied for Mary Auston to M^r. George Booth

Teſt James Baker Cl^k. of the V

[362]

At A Vestry held for Petsworth Parish July 27th. 1772

Present Capt. Rh^d. Jones   M^r. Jno. Wiatt
M^r. George Booth   M^r. W^m. Duval
Capt. Ja^s. Hubard   M^r. Jno. Fox
M^r. Lewis Booker

M^r. Jno. Fox is Appointed Church Warden in the room of M^r. Wm Thornton Dec^d.

Test Ja^s. Baker Clk of ye Vestry

[363]

At A Vestry held for Petsworth Parish Novb^r. 18th. 1772

Present James Hubard Gn^t.   M^r. Rh^d. Taliafero
M^r. Peter Kemp   M^r. Lewis Booker
Capt. Rh^d. Jones   M^r. W^m.. Duval
M^r. George Booth   M^r. Jno. Fox
Capt. Ja^s. Hubard

Petsworth Parish in Tob^o.	D^r.	lb
To the Rev^d. M^r. Hamilton's sallery		16000
To 8 ⅌ c^t. to make his Tob^o. Neat		1280
To Quitrents for the Glebe Land		87
To Ja^s. Baker Cl^k. of Church & Vestry	to be paid to Ja^s Hubard Gn^t	1600
To 4 ⅌ c^t. to make Baker's Tob^o. Neat		64
To Capt. Ja^s. Hubard for Communion Bread & wine		500
To Rh^d. Cole sexton to be paid to W^m.. Hall		1000
To Capt. Jno. Clayton his Ac^t.		101
To Ja^s. Pullar his Ac^t. £4—18 in Tob^o. at 2^d		588
To M^r. Lewis Booker his Ac^t. £5—19—8¾ in Tob^o. at 2^d		718
To Col^o. Wilson Cary his Ac^t. £4— —4 in Tob^o. at 2^d		482

To Mr. Chars. Tomkies for insolvents & sffs note	370
To Mrs. Burk to be paid to Capt. Jones £3—2—6 in Tobo.	375
To Capt. Jones his Act. £1—5 in Tobo. at 2d ℔ lb	150
To Mr. Wm. Hall for Mrs. Burks rent	180
To Mary Hunter for three Bars. of Corn for Keeping of two Children of Jno. Washers to be paid to Mr Fox	225
To Mrs. Mary Lamb for Mrs. of the Work House	700
To the Collector for provision for the Work house £22 in Tobo. at 2d ℔ pound	2640
To 6 ℔ ct. for Coms.	1623
Total Debt.	28683
Crdt by 783 Tithes at 37lb of Tobo. ℔ tithe is	28971
Depost. is	288

Order'd that the Collector pay Wm. Austin out of the Depost 150lb of Tobo. & Jno. Shepard 138lb of Tobo. the Rmd. of Do

Mr Chars. Tomkies is Appointed Collector for this year & that he receive 37lb of Tobo. ℔ tithe to discharge the parish Debt and Mr. Jno. Fox his security for the performance of the same

Carry'd Over

[364]

Majr Jonathan Watson is Appointed Church Wardin for this year

Capt. Jno. Hubard is Chosen Vestry man in the room of Mr. Wm. Thornton Decd.

Test Jas. Baker Clk of the Vestry

To Capt. Rh^d. Jones his ac^t. £2∥18∥9 in Tob^o. at 20/ ℔ C is	294
To Rh^d. Cole his Ac^t. 5/ in Tob^o. at 20/ ℔ C	25
To Rh^d. Cole sexton 1000^{lb} to be paid to M^r. W^m.. Hall a	1000
To Mary Lamb for M^{rs}.. of the work House £5— in Tob^o. at 20/ ℔ C	500
To M^r. David Dickerson for takeing of Thos. M^c-Williams youngest Child of the parish on his giving Bond for the same	1500
To M^r. Henry Burton for one Levy Over charg'd last year	34
To M^r. John Howlet his Act for work dun at the Glebe & to be dun	200
To M^r. W^m.. Hall for Clothing of an Olphin Boy	150
To M^r. Joseph Pullar for rent of M^{rs}.. Burk	50
To M^r. Lewis Booker on Ac^t. of M^{rs}. Lamb	30
To Arnold Shumake Burk on giving Bond & security to the Churchwardins as A further indulgance for keeping two of Powers'es Children off of this Parish	1000
Carry^d. Over lb	24450
[360] lb	
Brought Over	24450
To Communion Bread & Wine	500
To M^{rs}.. Ann Pullar for one levy Over paid	40
To Levy'd for the Use of the Work House	2000
	26990
Crd^t. by M^r. John Wiatt for	125
	26865
To Com^s. at 6 ℔ c^t. is	1611
Total Deb^t.	28476
Crd^t. by 826 Tithes at 35^{lb} of Tob^o. ℔ Tithe is	28910
Depoſt.	434

Orderd that the Collector pay Mary Austin 200^{lb} of the s^d. Depost And the remainder to be paid to Susanah Burk

Orderd that the Churchwarden Imploy A Workman to Lay A Threaching flour in the Barn at the Glebe 12 feet square, & to provide A Cushen for the alter & a spade & Hoe for the sexton

M^r. William Thornton is Appointed Church Warden in the Room of M^r. William Duva^l.

Test James Baker Clk of the V

[361]

At A Vestry held & continued for Petsworth Parish January 6th. 1772

James Hubard Gn^t	M^r. Lewis Booker
Capt. Rh^d. Jones	M^r. William Thornton
M^r. George Booth	M^r. Jno. Wiatt
Capt. James Hubard	M^r. Jno. Fox
M^r. Rh^d. Taliafero	

Capt. Rh^d. Jones & M^r. George Booth Agreed this day in vestry to be security for Arnold Shumake Burk Keeping of two of Powers'es Children off of this Parish

M^r. Chas. Tomkies Jn^r. is Appointed Collector for the Ensuing year & that he receive 35^{lb} of Tob^o. ℔ Tithe to discharge the Parish Deb^t. & M^r. Jno. Fox Agrees to be his security for the Performance of the same

Orderd that the Collector pay the 200^{lb} of Tob^o. Leavied for Mary Auston to M^r. George Booth

Teſt James Baker Cl^k. of the V

[362]

At A Vestry held for Petsworth Parish July 27th. 1772

Present Capt. Rh^d. Jones
   M^r. George Booth
   Capt. Ja^s. Hubard
   M^r. Lewis Booker

M^r. Jno. Wiatt
M^r. W^m. Duval
M^r. Jno. Fox

M^r. Jno. Fox is Appointed Church Warden in the room of M^r. Wm Thornton Dec^d.

     Test Ja^s. Baker Clk of ye Vestry

[363]

At A Vestry held for Petsworth Parish Novb^r. 18th. 1772

Present James Hubard Gn^t.
   M^r. Peter Kemp
   Capt. Rh^d. Jones
   M^r. George Booth
   Capt. Ja^s. Hubard

M^r. Rh^d. Taliafero
M^r. Lewis Booker
M^r. W^m.. Duval
M^r. Jno. Fox

	D^r.	lb
Petsworth Parish in Tob^o.		
To the Rev^d. M^r. Hamilton's sallery		16000
To 8 ℔ c^t. to make his Tob^o. Neat		1280
To Quitrents for the Glebe Land		87
To Ja^s. Baker Cl^k. of Church & Vestry	to be paid to Ja^s Hubard Gn^t	1600
To 4 ℔ c^t. to make Baker's Tob^o. Neat		64
To Capt. Ja^s. Hubard for Communion Bread & wine		500
To Rh^d. Cole sexton to be paid to W^m.. Hall		1000
To Capt. Jno. Clayton his Ac^t.		101
To Ja^s. Pullar his Ac^t. £4—18 in Tob^o. at 2^d		588
To M^r. Lewis Booker his Ac^t. £5—19—8¾ in Tob^o. at 2^d		718
To Col^o. Wilson Cary his Ac^t. £4— —4 in Tob^o. at 2^d		482

To M*. Char*. Tomkies for insolvents & sff* note	370
To M**.. Burk to be paid to Cap*. Jones £3—2—6 in Tob°.	375
To Cap*. Jones his Ac*. £1—5 in Tob°. at 2ᵈ ℔ lb	150
To M*. Wᵐ.. Hall for M**.. Burks rent	180
To Mary Hunter for three Barˢ. of Corn for Keeping of two Children of Jn°. Washers to be paid to Mʳ Fox	225
To M**.. Mary Lamb for Mrˢ. of the Work House	700
To the Collector for provision for the Work house £22 in Tob°. at 2ᵈ ℔ pound	2640
To 6 ℔ cᵗ. for Comˢ.	1623
Total Debᵗ.	28683
Crdᵗ by 783 Tithes at 37ˡᵇ of Tob°. ℔ tithe is	28971
Depos*. is	288

Order'd that the Collector pay Wᵐ.. Austin out of the Depost 150ˡᵇ of Tob°. & Jn°. Shepard 138ˡᵇ of Tob°. the Rmᵈ. of D°

Mʳ Charˢ. Tomkies is Appointed Collector for this year & that he receive 37ˡᵇ of Tob°. ℔ tithe to discharge the parish Debt and Mʳ. Jn°. Fox his security for the performance of the same

Carry'd Over

[364]

Majʳ Jonathan Watson is Appointed Church Wardin for this year

Capᵗ. Jn°. Hubard is Chosen Vestry man in the room of Mʳ. Wᵐ.. Thornton Decᵈ.

Test Jaˢ. Baker Clk of the Vestry

[365]

At A Vestry Held for Petsworth Parish Novb^r. 13th. 1773

    M^r. Peter Kemp   M^r. W^m.. Duva^l.
    Capt. Rh^d. Jones   Mj^r Jonathan Watson
    Capt. Ja^s. Hubard   M^r. Jno. Fox
    M^r. Jno. Wiatt   Capt. Jno. Hubard

Petsworth Parish in Tob^o. D^r	lb
To the Rev^d. M^r. A Hamilton his sallery	16000
To 8 ℔ c^t. to make his Tob^o. Neet	1280
To Quitrents for the Glebe Land	87
To Capt. Ja^s. Hubard for Communion Bread & wine	500
To Ja^s. Baker Cl^k. of Church & Vestry	1600
To 4 ℔ c^t. to make his Tob^o. Neet to be paid to Ja^s. Hubard gn^t	64
To Rh^d. Cole Sexton to be paid to Matt Anderson	1000
To M^r. Char^s. Tomkies his Ac^t. £4—17—6 in Tob^o. at 12/6 ℔ C	776
To Ja^s. Batop's Estate for the Hire of A Negro £4 — —	660
To M^r. Jno. Fox his Ac^t. £10 — — in Tob^o. as Above	1600
To Rh^d. Cole his Ac^t. 13/	104
To Mj^r. Jonathan Watson His Ac^t. £5—9—	872
To Doct^r. W^m.. Carter his Ac^t. Allowd 12^s/6^d	100
To M^rs.. Mary Lamb Her Ac^t. 8/6	68
To D^o. for M^rs.. of the work House	800
To Jeremiah Darnold for A Coffin for Elizabeth Burk	100
To Line Shackelford for mooving Fr^s. Blan his wife &c	320
To M^r. Jno. Wiatt for insolvents the years 1770 & 71	171
To Capt. Rh^d. Jones for finding 16 Bar^s. of Corn for the Use of the Work House at 10/6 ℔ Bar^l. £8—8—	1344
To Tob^o. Lev^d. for meat & necessaries for the use of the work House	2800

To Jnº. Royston for A Coffin for Rhᵈ. Washer 15/	120
To Lewis Walden for Dº for Mary Austin 15/	120
To Elizabeth Pullar for Corn for her Children	400
To Catharine Crabbin for Dº.	400
Carᵈ. Over	31286
[366] Brought Over	31286
To Susanah Burk to pay her rent, to be paid to Wᵐ.. Hall	240
To Dº. to buey Corn	160
To Sarah Washer to pay her rent to be paid to Jnº. Wright	200
	31886
To Comˢ. at 6 ℔ Cᵗ. is	1913
Total Debt	33799
℔ Contra Crdᵗ. By 755 Tithes at 45ˡᵇ ℔ tithe is	33975
Depost	176

Capᵗ. Jnº. Hubard is Appointed Church Wardin in the room of Mʳ. Jnº. Fox

Mʳ. Charˢ. Tomkies is Appointed Collector & that he receive 45ˡᵇ of Tobº. ℔ Tithe to Discharge the Parish Debt Mʳ. Jnº. Fox his security for the performance of the same

This Parish Agrees to Endamnifie Struttin Mjʳ. Parish for any Charges that Mrˢ. Blan or family may be of to them

Test Jaˢ. Baker Clk of the Veſtry

[367]
At A Vestry held for Petsworth Parish Decb`r`. 30`th`. 1773

The Rev`d`. M`r`. A. Hamilton
Cap`t`. Rh`d`. Jones
Preasent M`r`. George Booth
M`r`. Lewis Booker
M`r`. Jn`o`. Wiatt

M`r`. W`m`.. Duval
Mj`r`. Jonathan Watson
Cap`t`. Jn`o`. Hubard

Where as at A Vestry Held for this parish Novb`r`. 13`th` last past the rates ℔ tithe were mention'd to be at 45`lb` of Tob`o`. & intended so to be & were vallued at 12/6 ℔ C weight but the sum in money was Omitted to be inserted According to the direction *of *the of the Act of Aſsembley of the 10 year of his present Majesty King George the 3`d` it is Order'd by this preasent Vestry, that the s`d`. order be Amended by inserting the Words or at 5`s`/7½`d` after the words 45`lb` of Tob`o`. ℔ Tithe

At the Request of the Rev`d`. M`r`. Hamilton it is Order'd that the Church Wardins serch the proper offices for the †terrier of the Glebe & Deeds thereunto belonging

True Entry ℔ Ja`s`. Baker Clk

[368]
At A Vestry held for Petsworth Parish Novb`r`. 15`th`. 1774

Preasent
The Rev`d`. M`r`. A. Hamilton
M`r`. Peter Kemp
Cap`t`. Ja`s`. Hubard
M`r`. Lewis Booker

M`r`. Jn`o`. Wiatt
M`r`. William Duval
Mjr Jonathan Watson
Cap`t`. Jn`o`. Hubard

Petsworth Parish in Tob`o`.   D`r`.
To the Rev`d`. M`r`. A. Hamilton his Salery   16000
To 8 ℔ C`t` to make his Tob`o`. Neet   1280

*Note! These two words have been scratched through with a pen in the MS.—C. G. C.
†Note! *The Century Dictionary* gives: "Terrier, (b) In modern usage, a book or roll in which the lands of private persons or corporations are described by their site, boundaries, number of acres, etc."—C. G. C.

To Quitrents for the Glebe Land	87
To Cap*. Ja*. Hubard for Communion Bread & Wine	500
To Ja*. Baker Cl* of Church And Vestry to be paid to	1600
To 4 ℔ c* to make Baker's Ja* Hubar* Tob°. Neet	64
To Rh*. Cole sexton To be paid to Matt Anderson	1000
To M*. Tho*. Nelson for Coppy of the list	20
To M*. Lewis Booker his Ac*. £1—19—10 in Tob°. at 20/ ℔ C	200
T Col°. Wilson Cary his Ac*. Omited in 72 £0—13 in Tob°.	66
To M*. Ja*. Bentley his Ac*. £5—8—6 D°.	542
To M*. Dan*. New jn* his Ac*. £2— D°.	200
To Cap*. Ja*. Hubard his Ac*. £1—1 D°	105
To Mj*. Jonathan Watson £2—18—2 D°	291
To Cap*. Rh*. Jones his Ac*. £3—17—6 D°.	387
To Mary Lamb for Mr*. of the Work House £5— D°	500
To M*. Jn°. Howlit his Ac*. £29—5 D°	2925
To M*. Phillip Taliafero by Levingstons order for hire £1—17—4 D°	187
For the Use of the Work House to be paid to Cap*. Ja*. Hubard	2500
To Sarah Washer to be paid to Henry Burton	100
To Susan Burk for relief £1—10 D°.	150
To Elizabeth Pullar for D°. £2—10 D°.	250
To Elizabeth Shaw for D°.	250
	29204
To 6 ℔ c*. for Collection is	1752
Total Debt is	30956
Crd*. by 771 Tithes at 41** of Tob°. ℔ tithe is	31611
Depost	655

Carry'd up

[369] Brought up

Orderd that Capt Jno. Hubard be Collector the insuing year & that he receive 41^{lb} of Tob^o. ℔ tithe to discharge the Parish debt

M^r. Peter Kemp is Appointed Church Wardin in the room of M^{jr} Jonathan Watson

Orderd that the Collector Apply to Col^o. Fra^s. Tomkies for the money he has in his hands belonging to the Parish

At A Vestry continued & held for Petsworth Parish Novb^r. 29th. 1774

The Rev^d. M^r. A. Hamilton

M^r. Peter Kemp	M^r. Jno. Wiatt
Capt. Rh^d. Jones	M^r. William Duval
M^r. George Booth	Maj^r. Jonathan Watson
M^r. Lewis Booker	Capt. Jno. Hubard

To M^r. Char^s. Tomkies his Ac^t. for Insolvents 371^{lb} of Tob^o. to be paid out of the Deposit

The Ballance of the Deposit to be Apply'd to wards Cloaths for Jno. Shepard & Hurt Washer

Orderd that the Collector receive 41^{lb} of Tob^o. or 8/2½ ℔ tithe at the Oction of the payer

Teſt James Baker Clk of ye Vestry

[370]

At A Vestry Held for Petsworth Parish August 24th. 1775

The Rev^d. M^r. A Hamilton

	Capt. Rh^d Jones	M^r. John Wiatt
Preſent	M^r. George Booth	M^r. William Duval
	Capt. James Hubard	M^r. John Fox
	M^r. Rh^d. Taliafero	Capt. John Hubard

Pursuent to order of Gloucester Court bearing date 3th day of August 1775 To Appoint proceſsioners in this parish

& to make return of there proceedings By the last day of March According to Law we the Vestry Therefore Appoint them as followeth ViZ

1. Orderd that Thos. Miner & Eleazar Willkins see the Lands procefsion'd in the first precinct to begin on the Land of Thos. Miner on the first Friday in January next

2 Orderd that John Blasingame & John Hunt see the Lands procefsiond in the second precinct to begin on the Land of Matthew Anderson on the second Thursday in January next

3 Orderd that Starling Thornton & Zac^h. Gardner see the Lands procefsiond in the third precinct to begin on the Land of Rh^d. Taliafero on the Third Thursday in January next

4 Orderd that Lewis Booker & Rh^d. W. Royston see the Lands procefsiond in the fourth precinct to begin on the Land of James Baker on the Fourth Thursday in January

5 Orderd that W^m.. Pollard sn^r. & Rh^d. Wright see the Lands procefsion'd in the fifth precinct to begin on the Land of Capt. John Hubard on Poropotanck Creek on the first monday in Febuary

6 Orderd that John Robinson & Saml. Brooking see the Lands procefsion'd in the sixth precinct to begin on the Land of Robt. Daniels Eftate the second Thursday in Febuary next

Carry'd up
[371]

7 Orderd that John Kiningham & Christopher Garland see the Lands procefsion'd in the seventh Precinct to begin on the Land of Doct^r Robt Sprat on the Third Thursday in Febuary next

8 Orderd that W^m.. Sears & W^m.. Collawn see the Lands proceſsiond in the Eighth precinct to begin on the Land of the Rev^d. Mr Thos. Price on the fourth Thursday in Febuary

9 Orderd that Peter Wiatt & George Green see the Lands proceſsion'd in the ninth precinct to begin on the Land of Baley Seaton Decs'd on the first monday in March next

The said Vestry do proceed to Chuse Vestry men as followeth ViZ

M^r. Sterling Thornton is Elected Vestry man in the room of Ja^s. Hubard Gen^t. Decs^d.

Mr Peter Wiatt is Elected Vestry man in the room of Mr Peter Kemp Decs^d.

M^r. W^m. Sears is Elected Vestry man in the room of Maj Jonathan Watson Who has moov'd out of the Coliny And Appointed Church Warden in the room of Mr Peter Kemp Decs'^d

M^{rs}.. Elizabeth Shaw is Appointed M^{rs}.. of the Work House in the room of M^{rs}.. Mary Lamb Decs'd

True Entry ⅌ Ja^s. Baker Clk V.

[372]

At A Vestry Held for Petsworth Parish Janr^y. 13th 1776

The Rev^d. M^r. A. Hamilton

Capt. Rh^d. Jones
M^r. Lewis Booker
M^r. Jno. Wiatt
M^r. W^m.. Duva^l.

Capt. Jno. Hubard
M^r. Peter Wiatt
M^r. W^m.. Sears

M^r. Peter Wiatt is Appointed Church Wardin in the Room of Capt. Jno. Hubard

Order'd that Capt. Jno. Hubard deliver the Church Plate to M^r. Peter Wiatt

Order'd that Mr. Wm.. Duval Over look the work House this present year,— & that the Gent. of the vestry take it Annully as they may be appointed by the vestry

Order'd that this vestry be Ajurn'd till Thursday senight

Test Jas. Baker Clk Vestry

At A Vestry continued & held for Petsworth Parish Janry. 25th. 1776

Capt. Rhd Jones
Capt. Jas. Hubard
Mr. Lewis Booker
Mr. Wm.. Duval.

Capt. Jno. Hubard
Mr. Peter Wiatt
Mr. Wm.. Sears

The Vestry is Ajurn'd till monday fortnight;—& that the Clk publish the same & give further notice to those that have not giving in there Lists of tithes for the last year to give them before that day or there will be notice taken of such that neglect

Test Jas. Baker Clk Vestry

[373]

At A Vestry Held for Petsworth Parish Febuary 12th 1776

Present Capt. Rhd. Jones
Mr. George Booth
Mr. Lewis Booker
Mr. Wm.. Duval
Mr. Jno. Fox

Capt. Jno. Hubard
*Mr. Peter Wiatt
Mr. Sterling Thornton
Mr. Peter Wiatt
Mr. Wm.. Sears

Petsworth Parish in Tobo	Dr.	lb
To the Revd. Mr. A. Hamilton his salary		16000
To 8 ℔ Ct. to make his Tobo. Neet		1280
To Quitrents of the Glebe Land		87

*Note! This name has been scratched through with a pen in the MS.—C. G. C.

To the Revᵈ. Mʳ. Hamilton for priseing sixteen Thousand pounds of Tobᵒ. at 2/6 ℔ Thousand is £2— in Tobᵒ. at 10/ ℔ C is	400
To 5/ ℔ Thousand for Carting the same to a publick Landing is £4— in Tobᵒ.	800
To Jaˢ. Baker Clk of Church & Vestry To 4 ℔ Cᵗ. to make Baker's Tobᵒ neet to be paid to Capᵗ Jnᵒ Hubᵈ	64
To Rhᵈ. Cole sexton	1000
To Mʳ. Peter Wiatt for Communion Bread & Wine	1000
To Mʳˢ.. Elizabeth Shaw for Mʳˢ.. of Work House	1000
To Mʳˢ.. Shaw her Acᵗ. £5—7 in Tobᵒ.	1070
To Mʳ. Wᵐ.. Duvaˡ. his Acᵗ. 9/ in Tobᵒ	90
To Capᵗ. Jnᵒ. Hubard his Acᵗ. £1—13—9 in Tobᵒ.	389
To Mʳ. Smˡ. Davis his Acᵗ. £2—1—6 in Tobᵒ.	415
To Mʳ. Danˡ. New jnʳ his Acᵗ. for insolvents £3—12 in Tobᵒ	720
To Mʳ. Jaˢ. Bentley his Acᵗ. £2—14—3 in Tobᵒ.	542
To Mʳ. Phill Taliaferro his Acᵗ. 18/8 in Tobᵒ	186
To Elisabeth Pullar for Corn;—to be paid to Capᵗ. Jones	300
To Rachel Wood her Acᵗ £2—0— in Tobᵒ.	400
Carried over	27343
[374] Brought Over	27343
For the Use of the Hospitol £12—10 to buey provision &ᶜ. in Tobᵒ	2500
	29843
To Commision at 13 ℔ Cᵗ. is	3879
Total Debᵗ.	33722
Crdᵗ. by 808 Tithes at 43ˡᵇ of Tobᵒ. ℔ Tithe is	34744
Deposᵗ.	1022

N. B. Those persons that do not pay there Levy in Tob° to pay 15/ ℔ C

M'. Jn° New is appointed Collector for the present year, & that he receve 43^{lb} of Tob° ℔ Tithe to discharge the Parish debt, According to the Ordinance;—on his giving Bond & security for the performance of the same

At A Vestry Held for Petsworth Parish April 17th. 1776

Present
The Rev^d M^r. A. Hamilton
Capt. Rh^d. Jones
M^r. George Booth
Capt. Ja^s. Hubard

M^r. Lewis Booker
M^r. W^m.. Duva^l.
Capt. Jn°. Hubard
M^r. W^m.. Sears

Where as M^r. Jn°. New refuseing to act as Collector M^r. Henry Pursell is appointed Collector in his room, & that he receive 43^{lb} of Tob°. ℔ Tithe to discharge the Parish Debt according to the Ordinance, on his giving Bond & security for the performance of the same

Teſt James Baker Cl^k. ye Vestry

[375]

At A Vestry Held for Petsworth Parish Decb^r. 31th. 1776

Preasent Capt. Rh^d Jones
M^r. George Booth
Capt. Ja^s. Hubard
Mr Lewis Booker
M^r. Jn°. Wiatt

M^r. W^m.. Duva^l.
Capt. Jn°. Hubard
M^r. Peter Wiatt
M^r. W^m.. Sears

Petsworth Parish in Tob°.   D^r

To the Rev^d. M^r. A. Hamilton his salery from the 14 day of Novb^r. 1775 to the first of Jany. 1777 according to Act of Aſsembly	18060
To 4 ℔ C^t. for shrinkage	722
To 4 ℔ C^t. for cask	722
To quitrents for the Glebe Land	87

To Jaˢ. Baker Clk of Church & Vestry from 15 of Novbʳ. 75 to the first of Janrʸ. 1777 with 4 ⅌ Cᵗ is To be paid to Capᵗ. Jnº. Hubard	1873
To Rhᵈ. Cole sexton from 15ᵗʰ. of Novbʳ. 75 to the first of Janrʸ 1777	1128
To Elisabeth Shaw for Mʳˢ.. of the Work hous from 15ᵗʰ. of Novbʳ. 75 till the first of Janrʸ 1777 £5—12—6 in Tobº. aᵗ. 15/ ⅌ C is	750
To Mʳ. Peter Wiatt for Bread & Wine	700
To Samˡ. Davis for takeing Wᵐ.. McWilliams	300
To Wᵐ.. Duvaˡ. jnʳ. for takeing Wᵐ.. Liall Gibson	300
To Susanah Burk for reliefe	1000
	25642
To 6 ⅌ Cᵗ. for Collection	1538
Total Debt	27180
Crdᵗ. by 801 Tithes at 35ˡᵇ of Tobº. ⅌ tithe is	28035
Deposit	855

Carried Over

[376]

Mʳ Sterling Thornton is appointed Church Wardin in the room of Mʳ. Wᵐ.. Sears

Mʳ. Danˡ. New is appointed Collector the Ensuing year & that he receive 35ˡᵇ of Tobº. ⅌ Tithe to discharge the Parish Debt on his giveing Bond & security for his performance

Teſt Jaˢ. Baker Clᵏ. Vestry

At A Vestry Held for Petsworth Parish January 26th 1778

Preasant Cap.t Rich.d Jones M.r W.m.. Duva.l
    M.r George Booth Cap.t Jn.o Hubard
    M.r Lewis Booker M.r Peter Wiatt
    M.r Jn.o Wiatt M.r W.m.. Sears

M.rs Judith Blasingame is Chosen sexton in the room of Rich.d Cole decs.d

Cap.t Rich.d Jones is appointed Church Wardin in the room of M.r Peter Wiatt

               Test Ja.s Baker Cl.k Vestry

[377]

At A Vestry Held for Petsworth Parish 2th. day of March 1778

Preasent Cap.t Rh.d Jones M.r Jn.o Wiatt
    M.r George Booth M.r W.m.. Duva.l
    Cap.t Ja.s Hubard M.r Peter Wiatt
    M.r Lewis Booker M.r W.m.. Sears

Petsworth Parish in Tob.o	D.r	ViZ
To Coppy for the List of Tithes		20
To tax for the Glebe Land		87
To James Baker Cl.k of the Vestry		600
To Hurt Washer for Releife		400
To Jn.o Sheapard for	D.o	400
To Elisabeth Pullar for	D.o	300
To Ann Brooking for	D.o	100
		1907
To 6 ₽ C.t for Com.s		114
		2021
Crd.t by 783 Tithes at 3.lb of Tob.o ₽ Tithe is		2349
Depost		328

Ordered that the Collecter receive 3^{lb} of Tob^o. or 1/6 ₱ Tithe to discharge the Parish Debt

Orderd that M^r. Peter Wiatt's Ac^t. of £1—1—4¾ be paid out of the Depos^t.

Orderd that Capt. Jno. Hubards Ac^t. of 9/7½ be paid out of the Depost

Orderd that the Parish Collecter of Petsworth for the last year pay Mrs Rachal Wood 500^{lb} of The Tob^o. out of the 1000^{lb} Levid for Susan Burk;—for her trouble with the s^d. Burk the Ballance to be paid to the Church Wardin

Mr Peter Kemp is Appointed Collecter this preasent year & that he receive 3^{lb} of Tob^o. or 1/6 ₱ Tithe to discharge the Parish debt, on his giving Bond & security for his purformance of the same

Test Ja^s. Baker Clk   Rich Jones

[378]

At a Vestry held for Petsworth Parish at the Church the 19th. day of Oc^r. 1778

Present Cap^n. Rich^d. Jones   { M^r. John Wiatt
          M^r. Geo^o. Booth   M^r. W^m.. Duval
          Cap^n. Ja^s. Hubard   Cap^n. John Hubard
          M^r. Lewis Booker

This day Richd W. Royston was Chosen Clerk of the Church and Vestry

M^r. Geo^o. Booth & Cap^n. John Hubard is Appointed Church wardens for the Insueing year

Ordered that the Clerk of the Vestry give in a List of those Persons that have not given in their List of Tithables to the Grand Jury

                                          Geo^o Booth

True Entry   Rich^d W Royston C.V.

[379]

At a Vestry held for Petsworth Parish Jan⁷. 12ᵗʰ 1779

Present

Capⁿ. Richᵈ Jones   Mʳ. John Wiatt
Mʳ. Geoˢ. Booth   Mʳ. William Duval
Capⁿ. Jaˢ. Hubard   Capⁿ. John Hubard
Mʳ. Lewis Booker   Mʳ. William Sears

Petsworth Parish				Dʳ	
To Jaˢ. Baker for 7 Months as Clerk of the Vestry		350	Tob°	or £	17‖10‖0
To Richᵈ W Royston 5 Months for D°		250ᶫᵇ	To°	or	12‖10‖0
To Jn° Shepard to Buy Corn		300ᶫᵇ	Tob°	or	15‖ 0 ‖0
To Hurt Washer for	D°	300	D°	or	15‖ 0 ‖0
To Johanah Purſel for	D°	400	D°	or	20‖ 0 ‖0
To Sarah Busby for	D°	600	D°	or	30‖ 0 ‖0
To Elizᵗʰ. Puller for	D°	600	D°	or	30‖ 0 ‖0
To Mary Spann for	D°	400	D°	or	20‖ 0 ‖0
To Ann Brooking for	D°	300	D°	or	15‖ 0 ‖0
To Elizᵗʰ. Shaw for	D°	400	D°	or	20‖ 0 ‖0
To Elizᵗʰ. Baker for	D°	300	D°	or	15‖ 0 ‖0
To Geo. Coats for	D°	400	D°	or	20‖ 0 ‖0
To 6 ℔ʳ. Cent for Collecting		276	D°	or	13‖16‖0
		4876		or	243‖16‖0
Crᵗ.					
By 808 Tithes @ 6ᶫᵇ Tob° or 6ˢ/ is		4848		or	242‖ 8 ‖0
		28			1‖ 8

Richᵈ *Wiatt Royston is Appointed Collector and to Receive 6ᶫᵇ. Tob° or 6 Six shillings ℔ʳ Tithable to be to

---

*Note! This name was first written "Richᵈ W Royston"; later, and evidently with a different pen, were added in very minute characters the letters "iatt" after the initial "W."—C. G. C.

be Paid in Tob° or money at the option of the Payer to discharge the Parish Debt

Order⁴ that the Collector Receive of Mʳ. Wᵐ. Duval Juʳ £4— and Carry it to the Parish Crᵗ.

Geo Booth

True Entry   Richᵈ W Royston C Vestry

[380]

At A Vestry held for Petsworth Parish on the 10ᵗʰ day of Febʳ. 1780

Present   Mʳ. Geoᵉ. Booth, Capⁿ. Jaˢ. Hubard, Mʳ. Richᵈ. Taliafero, Mʳ Lewis Booker, Mʳ. Jnᵒ Wiatt, Mʳ. Wᵐ. Duval, Mʳ. Sterling Thornton & Mʳ. Wᵐ. Seares

Capⁿ. Jaˢ. Hubard is Appointed Churchwarden in the room of Capⁿ. John Hubard Decᵈ

Mʳ Robert Yates is Chosen Vestryman in the room of Capⁿ. Jnᵒ Hubard Decᵈ

Then the Genⁿ. of the Vestry Persuant to an Order of Gloucester Court bareing date Sepʳ. yᵉ 2ᵈ 1779 did proceed to appoint Proceſsenors as follows

1ˢᵗ Order'd that Thoˢ. Mynor & Wᵐ. Harwood se the Lands proceſsion'd in the 1ˢᵗ precᵗ begining the Monday the 21ˢᵗ day of Febʸ 1780 on the Land of Thoˢ. Mynor & that they make Return of their proceedings by the Last of March Accᵍ. to Law ———

2ᵈ Order'd that Capⁿ. John Fox & Mʳ. Mattʷ. Anderson Juʳ. se the Lands proceſsion'd in 2ᵈ precᵗ, begining on the Lands Mʳ. Wᵐ. Finny *the on Monday yᵉ 21ˢᵗ. of Febʸ. 1780

*Note! This word has been scratched through with a pen in the MS.—C. G. C.

& make return of their proceedings by the Last of March Acc^s. to Law ———

3^d Order'd that M^r. Henry Purſel & M^r. Peter Stubbs se the Lands Proceſsion'd in the 3^d. prec^t. begining on the Land of Mr Rich^d. Talifaro on Monday ye 21st of Feby. 1780 & make return of their Proceedings by the Last of March Accord^g to Law ———

4 Order'd that M^r. W^m. DuVal Ju^r. & M^r. Lewis Wood se the Lands Proceſsion'd in the 4th. prec^t. begining on the Land of Ja^s. Baker Dec^d, on Monday ye 21st of Feby. 1780 & make return of their proceedings by the Last of March Accord'^{g} to Law ———

5th Order'd that M^r. W^m. Thrift & M^r. Richd Wright se the Lands Proceſsion'd in the 5th prec^t. begining on the Land of M^r W^m. Pollard on Monday ye 21st. of Feby. 1780 & make return of their Proceedings by the Last of March Accord'^{g} to Law ———

6th Order'd that M^r. Saml. Brooking & M^r. Swan Grumley se the Land proceſsiond in the 6th. prec^t. begining on the Land of M^r. Beverly Daniel on Monday ye 21st. of Feby. 1780 & make return of their proceedings by the Last of March Accord^g to Law

7th Order'd that M^r. Chri^n Garland & Benjn Robinson se the Lands Proceſsion'd in the 7th. prec^t. begining on the Land of Doc^r. Spratt on Monday ye 21st. of Feby. 1780 & make return of their proceedings by the Last of March Acc^g. to Law

8th Order'd that M^r. Chas Tomkies Jur & M^r. Ja^s Laughlin se the Lands Proceſsion'd in the 8th prec^t. begining on the Land of M^r. Chas. Tomkies on Monday ye 21st. of Feby. 1780 & make return of their proceedings by the Last of March Accord^g. to Law ———

[381]

9th Order'd that Mr. Wm. Hall Jur. & Mr. Antho. Davis se the Lands Procefsion'd in the 9th. prect. begining on the Land of Mrs Bushrod on Monday ye 21st of Febr 1780 & make return of their Proceedings by the Last of March Accord's to Law

Petsworth Parish	Dr
To *the *C Richd. W. Royston C Vestry	£ 60‖0‖0
To Mrs. Ann Brooking	£ 90‖0‖0
To Geo°. Coats	£ 30‖0‖0
To Mrs. Sarah Busby	£ 90‖0‖0
To Mrs. Mary Spann	£ 45‖0‖0
To Mrs. Elizth Pullar	£ 60‖0‖0
To John Shepard	£100‖0‖0
To Mrs. Ann Figg for keeping Thos. Figgs Child	£100‖0‖0
To Mrs. Sarah Edwards	£ 30‖0‖0
To 6 per cent for Collecting	£ 36‖6‖0
	£641‖6‖0
Ct	
By 828 Tithes @ 16s/ is	£662‖8‖0
Deposm.	21‖2‖0

Richd W Royston is Appointed Collector for the Insuing year

Geo.°. Booth

Tru Entry Richd W Royston C Vestry

---

*Note! These words have been smudged out in the MS.—C. G. C.

[382]

At a Vestry held for Petsworth Parish Jany 22^d. 1781

Present

Cap^n Richd Jones
M^r. Geo^e. Booth
M^r. Lewis Booker
M^r. W^m. Duval

M^r. Richd Talafaro
M^r. John Wiatt
M^r. Robt. Yates

Petsworth Parish			D^r
To Rich^d W Royston as Clerk Vestry	600^{lb} Tob^o.	or	£240—
To Ann Brooking	500 Tob^o.	or	200—
To W^m. Blake for Jno Sheperds Coffin	100 Tob^o.	or	40—
To John Hains for Hurt Washers Coffin	100 Tob^o.	or	40—
To Thos. Nelson for Coppy List Tithes	20 Tob^o.	or	*6—
To Thos. Hall as Clerk of the Church	1000 Tob^o.	or	400—
To Judth. Blasingham Sexton	1000 Tob^o.	or	400—
	3220		1326—
6 ₱^{r}. C^t. Commision Colec^t	199	or	79‖12
	3519		1405‖12
By 780 Tithes at 5^{lb} Tob^o. ₱ Tithe is	3900	or	1560
Depos^m.	381 Tob^o.	or	†152‖ 8

Order'd that Peter Kemp be appinted Collector for this year and that he Receive 5^{lb}. Tob^o. ₱^{r} Tithe or Eight Shillings ₱^{r}. Pound in Money & that he Apply for 10^{lb} Tob^o. ₱^{r} Tithe for the Rev^d M^r. Price for his services for the year 1780

M^r. Ja^s. Baytop is Chosen Vestryman in the Room of M^r. Peter Wiatt Dec^d.

M^r. Robt. Yates is appointed Churchwarden in the Room of M^r. Geo^e. Booth

Geo. Booth
True Entry Rich^d W Royston C^k. V

---

*Note! This figure is out of proportion.—C. G. C.
†Note! Rather remarkable subtraction.—C. G. C.

[383]

At a Veſtry held for Petsworth Parish Apˡ. 8ᵗʰ 1782

Present

Capⁿ. Richᵈ Jones
Mʳ. Geoᵉ. Booth
Capⁿ. Jaˢ. Hubard
Mʳ. Lewis Booker

Mʳ. Wᵐ. DuVal
Mʳ. Richᵈ Taliafero
Mʳ John Wiatt
Mʳ. Robᵗ. Yates

Petsworth Parish	Dʳ
To Thoˢ. Hall for his services as Clerk of yᵉ Church	1000ˡᵇ Tobᵒ
To Richᵈ W Royston as Clerk of the Vestry	600
To Judʰ Blaſinham Sexton	1000
To the Clerk of the Court for a Coppy of List Tiths	20
To Elizᵗʰ Puller	100
To Dᵒ the Rent of the Workhouse in 1781	
To Sarah Busby	200
To Mʳ. Jnᵒ Houlett for mending the Church windows	35
To 6 ℔ʳ. cent for Collecting	*177
	3138
By 743 Tithes @ 5ˡᵇ is	3715
Deposᵐ.	†583

Coll Jaˢ. Baytop is Chosen Churchwarden in the Room of Capⁿ. Jaˢ. Hubard

Order'd that the Churchwardens find Bread and Wine for the use of the Church & to be paid out of the Depoᵐ.

Mʳ. Peter Kemp is appointed Collector for this year and that he recieve 5ˡᵇ of Tobᵒ. of every Tithable in the Parish to

---

*Note! The number 183 was first written here; later a 77 was written over the 83 in heavy black figures.—C. G. C.

†Note! The number 577 was first written here; later an 83 was written over the 77 in heavy black figures.—C. G. C.

discharge the Parish Debt also that he recieve it of all those that have not given in their List & Acc^t. with the Vestry for the same

Robt Yates

Test Rich^d W Royston C V

[384]

At A Vestry held for Petsworth parish June the 11th. 1782

Present

Cap^n. Richd Jones	M^r. Richd Taliafarro
Mr Geo^e Booth	M^r. John Fox
Cap^n. Ja^s. Hubard	M^r. W^m. Sears
M^r. Lewis Booker	M^r. Robt. Yates
M^r. W^m. Duval	

The present Vestry has Unanimusly imploy'd and Continued the *M^r. Rev^d. M^r. Thos. Price as minister of this Parish and to be paid by the Subscription of the Inhabetents of the s^d. Parish ———

Order'd the Collector receive of the Subscribers to the Rev^d. M^r. Price 5^{lb} of Tob^o p^r. Tithe for his Services for the Last half year

M^r. Peter Kemp is Chosen Vestryman in the room of Co^l. Ja^s. Baytop who has refused to qualify and is appointed Churchwarden

R Yates

True Entry Rich^d W Royston Cl^k Vestry

[385]

At A Vestry held for Petsworth Parish March 17ᵗʰ 1783

Present

Capⁿ. Richᵈ. Jones
Capⁿ. Jaˢ. Hubard
Mʳ. Lewis Booker
Mʳ. Wᵐ.. Duval
Capⁿ. John Fox
Mʳ. John Wiatt
Mʳ. Robert Yates
Mʳ. Peter Kemp

Petsworth Parish	Dʳ
To Thoˢ. Hall Clerk of the Church	1000ˡᵇ Tobᵒ
To Judⁿ. Blasingame Sexton	1000
To Richᵈ W Royston Clerk of yᵉ Vestry	600
To Sarah Busby	225
To Elizᵗʰ. Puller	225
To *Chrisⁿ Pryer for a List Tithables	20
To Tobᵒ. for the poore	1500
To 6 ℔ʳ. Cent for Collecting	274
	4844

Crᵗ
By 779 Tithes @ 6½ˡᵇ Tobᵒ. is   5063

Deposᵐ.   219

Order'd that the Collector receive 950ˡᵇ Tobᵒ. or £9‖10 of Mʳ Peter Purcel for the Last years rent of the Workhouse & pay the Same to the Churchwarden

Order'd that the Collector receive of Capⁿ. Thoˢ. Baytop £5‖5 for the rent of the Glebe and pay the same to Churchwarden

Mʳ. Richᵈ. Taliafaro is apointed Church Warden in the room of Mʳ. Robᵗ. Yates

---

*Note! This name may be Chrisʳ (Christopher) and not Chrisⁿ (Christian) as here given; it is practically impossible to say whether the small ("superior") letter is an "n" or an "r."—C. G. C.

Rich⁴ W Royston is Apointed Collector and he giving Bond &c for the same

Order'd that the Collector Apply to Mʳ. Geoᵉ. Booth Mʳ. John S Stubbs Majʳ John Robinson & Alexʳ. Brown for the Intrust Due on the Bond Due to the Parish and if they refuse to pay it to Commence Sutes *for against them for the whole Bond

Orderd that the Churchwarden aply to Colˡ. Chaˢ. M Thruston for the Legascey Left this Parish By Hugh Spotswood Decᵈ. and if he refuses to bring Sute for the same

           Peter Kemp

True entry Richᵈ. W Royston C V

[386]

At A Vestry held for Petsworth Parish the 3ᵈ day of May 1784

Present

Mʳ George Booth	Mʳ. William Sears
Mʳ. Lewis Booker	Capⁿ John Fox
Mʳ. John Wiatt	Mʳ. Robᵗ. Yates
Mʳ. Richᵈ. Talleferro	Mʳ. Sterling Thornton
	Mʳ. Peter Kemp

In persuance to an Order of Gloucester Court bearing date the 5ᵗʰ. day of Febuary 1784 the Gentlemen of the Vestry did procede to Appoint Procesioners as follows Vzᵗ ——

1ˢᵗ Order'd that Thomas Minor & Richᵈ Leigh se the Lands Procesion'd in the First precinct to begin the second Thursday in June

2ᵈ Order'd that John S Stubbs & James Bentley se the Lands Procesion'd in the Second precinct to begin the Fourth Thursday in June

---

*Note! This word has been scratched through with a pen in the MS.—C. G. C.

3ᵈ Order'd that Preſley Thornton & Peter Stubbs se the Lands Proceſsiond in the Third precinct to begin the Second Thursday in July

4 Order'd that Lewis Wood & Thomas Thrift se the Lands Proceſsion'd in the fourth precinct to begin the Third Monday in July

5ᵗʰ. Order'd that William Thrift & Swan Grumly se the Lands Proceſsion'd in the fifth precinct to begin the Third Wednesday in July

6ᵗʰ. Order'd that John Keiningham & William Keiningham se the Lands Proceſsion'd in the sixth precinct to begin the Third Friday in July

7ᵗʰ. Order'd that Christopher Garland & Benjⁿ Robinson se the Lands Proceſsiond in the Seventh precinct to begin the First Wednesday in August

8ᵗʰ. Order'd that James Laughlin & James Dutton Se the Lands Proceſsioned in the Eighth precinct to begin the Second Wednesday in August

9ᵗʰ. Order'd that James Wiatt & William Wiatt se the Lands Proceſsiond in the Ninth precinct to begin the Second Friday in August

Mʳ. John Wiatt is Appointed Church Warden in the Room of Mʳ. Peter Kemp

Capⁿ. Charles Tomkies is Chosen Veſtryman in the Room of Mʳ. William Duval who Declines

Richᵈ. Taliaferro

True Entry
Richᵈ W. Royston C Vʸ

[387]

At a Vestry held for Petsworth Parish the 14th. day of May 1784

Present

M^r. George Booth
M^r. Rich^d. Taliaferro
M^r. John Wiatt
M^r. Sterling Thornton
M^r. Robt. Yates
M^r. Peter Kemp
Cap^n. Charles Tomkies

Pets Paris	D^r
To Rich^d W Royston as Clerk of ye Vestry	600^{lb} Tob^o.
To Thos. Hall Clerk of ye Church	1000
To Jud^h Blasingham Sexton	1000
To M^r. Pryer for List of Tithes	20
To Sarah Busby for relief	125
To Elizth. Puller for D^o	125
To Robt. Nettles for D^o	400
To Elizth. Haynes for her Children	200
To Thos. Minor for a Child of Hobdays	200
To Rich^d. Coleman for D^o. of D^o	200
for Bread & Wine for Use of the Church	500
To 6 p^r. Cent for Collection	270
	*4840
C^{rt}.	
By 769 Tithes @ 6½^{lb} Tob^o.	4998
Depos^m.	158

Order'd that Susana Luvel have the Depos^m. of 158^{lb} Tob^o

Rich^d. W Royston is Appointed Collector for this year and that he receive 6½^{lb} Tob^o of every Tithe to discharge the above Creditors

*Note! There is an error of 200 in the addition here.—C. G. C.

M^r. Meux Thornton is Chosen Vestryman in the room of Doc^r. Rich^d. Jones who resigns

Rich^d. Taliaferro

True Entry
Rich^d W Royston C V

[388]
At a Vestry held for Petsworth Nove^r. 24th. 1784

Present

M^r. Richd Taliaferro	M^r. Robt. Yates
Mr Lewis Booker	M^r. Wm Sears
M^r. John Wiatt	M^r. Peter Kemp
M^r. Sterling Thornton	

Order'd that the Rent Due from M^r. Peter Purſell for the work House be Collected and given to M^r. Peter Kemp for furnishing the Church with Bread & Wine for time Past

Rich^d W Royston is by this present Vestry Chosen Clerk of the Church & Sexton for which the s^d Vestry have agrea'd to Allow him 3000^{lb} Tob^o. Including the Salry for Clerk of the Vestry

Richd Taliaferro

True Entry
Rich^d W Royston C V

[389]
At a Vestry held for Petsworth Parish ye 31st of Jany. 1785

Present

M^r. George Booth	M^r. John Wiatt
Cap^n. Ja^s. Hubard	M^r. Sterling Thornton
M^r. Rich^d. Taliaferro	M^r. W^m. Sears
M^r. Lewis Booker	M^r. Peter Kemp

Petsworth Parish	D^r	Tob^o
To Rich^d W Royston as Clerk of Vestry		600
To Thos. Hall as Clerk of ye Church		1000

To Judah Blasingame as Sexton	1000
To M^{rs}. West for keeping Elizth. Haynes Child	500
To D° to D° for keeping D° the Last half year	150
To John Haynes for keeping a Child of Elizth Haynes	150
To Sarah Busby for Releif	125
To Elizth. Puller for D°	125
To Chris^n. Pryer for List of Tithes	20
To W^m. Haynes for Releif	150
To Robt. Nettles for D°	150
To the Churchwardens for Fra^s. Dunstons Child	500
To Elizth. Dickinson Fra^s. Dunstons Child time Past	200
To Lawrance White for keeping Elizth. Dudley	100
To 6 ℔. Cent for Collecting	274
	5044
By 814 Tithes @ 6½^{lb} Tob°. is	5291
	247

Order'd that the Collector Receive of Each Tithe 6½^{lb} Tob° to discharge the Parish Debt

Rich^d W Royston is Appointed Collector for this year

Rich^d. Taliaferro

True Entry
   Rich^d W Royston C V

[390]
   1785 March 28th. We the Subscribers being this day duly Elected Vestrymen for the Parish of Petsworth in Gloucester County do profeſs ourselves to be Members of the Protestant Episcopal Church

*Geo. Booth
Lewis Booker
Robert Yates

---

   *Note! The following thirteen names appear to be autograph signatures.—C. G. C.

M: Anderson
Peter Kemp
Wm Sears
Richd Taliaferro
Sterling Thornton
Ja^s. Baytop
Chas. Tomkies
W^m Du'Val
Thos Booth
Ben Dabney

[391]

At a vestry held for Petsworth Parish Ap^l. 23^d. 1785

Present

Mr Lewis Booker
Capⁿ. Matt^w. Anderson
M^r. Peter Kemp
M^r. W^m. Sears
M^r. Richd Taliaferro
M^r. Sterling Thornton
Col^l. Ja^s. Baytop

M^r. W^m. Duvall & Capⁿ. Charles Tomkies are Apointed Churchwardens for the time being

M^r. Benj^m Dabney & Capⁿ. Matt^w. Anderson are Chosen to attend the Convention the 18th day of Next Month

Rich^d. W Royston is Chosen Clerk of the Vestry for the time being

*Lewis Booker

It is ordered by a Majority of the whole Vestry to wit the Seven Members present that the Church Wardens do Sell the **whole** of the Bricks of the late Glebe House that was burnt in this Parish provided they can find a purchaser or purchasers that will take them on their being Valued by Three Honest reputable residents of S^d Parish giving twelve

---

*Note! This name has been scratched through with a pen in the MS.—C. G. C.

months Credit & taking bond with good Security for the Same & make return of their proceedings

Lewis Booker

[392]

At a Vestry held for Petsworth Parish y⁵ 5th day of Decemr. 1785

Present

Mr Lewis Booker   Mr Rich^d. Taliaferro
Mr Robert Yates   Mr Sterling Thornton
Mr Peter Kemp   Co^l James Baytop
M^r. W^m. Sears   Mr William Duvall

Petsworth Parish	D^r
To Rich^d W Royston as Cl^k of Church & Vestry and Sexton	3000^{lb} Tob^o
To Mrs West for keeping Danl. Haynes Child	500
To Mrs Busby for relief	300
To Mrs Puller for D^o	125
To Mr Pryer for Copy of List Tithes	20
To W^m. Haynes for relief	300
To Robt Nettles for D^o	150
To Elizth. Dickinson if she keeps Fra^s. Dunstons Child	500
To M^r. Richd Taliaferro for Bread & Wine for the Church	500
To John Bristow for keeping Elizth. Dudley	500
To the Church wardens for the Use of Elizth. Dudley	500
To Elizth. Coates for Relief	400
To the Collector for Collecting 6 ℔^r Cent	407
	7202
C^{rt}.	
By 826 Tithes a 9^{lb} Tob^o ℔ Tithe is	7434
	232 Depos^m.

Mr Benjn Dabney is Chosen Vestryman in the room of Mr John Wiatt who resigns

Richd W Royston is Appointed Collector for this year and that he receive 9lb Tobo of Each Tithe and pay the Paris Debt or 24/ ℔r hundred

It is the Opinion of this Vestry that Capn. Matt Anderson and Mr Benjn Dabney be Continued to meet in Convention at Richmond for the remaining Part of the three years

The Collector to Purchace a Tabl. Cloth and Napkins for the use of the Church & to have the Deposm.

         Chas. Tomkies
True Entry
 Richd W Royston C V   Wm DuVall

[393]

At Vestry held for Petsworth Parish June 28th 1786

      Present

Mr Lewis Booker	Col. James Baytop
Mr Robt Yates	Capn. Charles Tomkees
Capn. Mattw. Anderson	Mr. Wm. DuVall
Mr Richd. Taliaferro	Mr Thos. Booth
Mr Sterling Thornton	

Resolv'd a Committee be Appointed to Draw up a Petition to be presented to the next General Aſsemble Agreable to the Recommondation of the late Convention held at Richmond praying that the Act for incorporating the Protestant Episcopal Church may not be Repealed ———

Resolv'd that Mr Mattw. Anderson Mr Benjn Dabney Mr Robt. Yates Mr Jas. Baytop & Mr Chas. Tomkees be a Committee to Draw up the sd. petition ———

Resolv'd that the same Committee be Appointed to Attend to the Res⁸. of the Convention lately held at Richmond respecting a Return being made for the Minister &c and make a Report thereof

Resolv'd that the same Committee Draw up a petition & furnish each Vestryman with a Copy thereof for the purpose of Raising a fund to defray the Expences of Obtaining Consecration for a Bishop and for his Support after his Appointment &c

Resolv'd that Mʳ. Benjⁿ. Dabney be Appointed Treasurer to receive what ever may be Collected by the diffᵗ. Gentⁿ. of the Vestry Agreeable to the Above Resolution & for Other purposes

Resolv'd that the Clerk furnish the Gentⁿ. of the Committee Appointed for Diffᵗ. purposes with a Copy of the several Resolutions

Chaˢ. Tomkies
Wᵐ. DuVall

a true Copy
    Richᵈ W Royston Clk

[394]

[   ]ᵗʰ 1787 On this day met the Freeholders & [   ]eepers in Petsworth parish for the Electing of [   ]try for the said Parish agreeable to an ordinance [   ] convention for regulating & appointing of Vestrys & Trustees & for other purposes; due notice of the said Election to be held on this day at the Church of the said Parish being first given; the following & underwritten members were chosen viz.

Lewis Booker Senʳ	1
Richᵈ Taliaferro	2
Mattʷ. Anderson	3
Peter Kemp	4

James Baytop	5
Thoˢ. Booth	6
Ben Dabney	7
Sterling Thornton	8
William Du Vall	9
Christopher Garland	10
James Wyatt	11
Lewis Booker Ju.	12

Rich˄ W Royston C C

[395]
1787 July 14ᵗʰ. We the Subscribers being (on [   ] of last month) duly elected Vestrymen for the P[   ] Petsworth in Gloucester County, do profeſs our selves members of the Protestant Episcopal Church

*Lewis Booker
Rich˄. Taliaferro
M, Anderson
Petʳ Kemp
Jaˢ Baytop
Thoˢ. Booth
Ben Dabney
Sterling Thornton
Wᵐ Du'Val
Christopher Garland
James Wiatt
L Booker Jʳ
Meaux Thornton

*Note! The following are autograph signatures.—C. G. C.

[396]

[ ]estry held for Petsworth Parish July 14th. 1787

Present

[ ] Lewis Booker
[ ]'. Richd Taliaferro
[ ]pn Mattw. Anderson
[ ]r Peter Kemp
Coll. Jas. Baytop

Mr William Du Val
Mr Chrisr. Garland
Mr Jas. Wiatt
Capn. Lewis Booker

Mr Wm.. Du Val & Capn. Lewis Booker are Chosen Churchwardens ———

Richd W Royston is Chosen Clerk of Vestry Clerk of the Church &c ———

Mr Jas. Wiatt is Appointed Treasurer

Capn. Mattw Anderson Mr Richd Taliaferro Mr Peter Kemp & Mr Chrir. Garland are Appointed Collectors

Order'd that the Dift. Collectors proceed to Collect what Money they can and as soon as may be deposit the same in the hands of the Treasurer Subject to the Order of Vestry

Order'd that the late Churchwardens Settle up their Accts. and pay the Money due to the Parish at the Next Vestry

Lewis Booker

True Copy

Richd W Royston C V

[397]
At a Vestry held for Petsworth Parish Decr. 15th: 1787

                    Present
    Mr Lewis Booker   Mr Ja^s Baytop
    Mr Peter Kemp   Cap^n. Lewis Booker
    M^r W^m.. Du Val   Mr Thos. Booth
    Mr Chri^r. Garland

The present Vestry has Unanimusly agreed to Imploy the Rev^d. M^r Ja^s. Elliott as Minister of the Parish for the year 1788 and that he have the Benifit of the Gleeb

         Lewis Booker

True Entry   Rich^d W Royston C V

[398]
[   ]stry held for Petsworth Parish Decr. 10th. 1788

                    Present
    [ ]^r Lewis Booker   ⎫
    [ ]^r Richd Taliaferro ⎪ Mr Chri^r. Garland
    [ ]^1 Ja^s. Baytop   ⎬
        ap^n. Thos. Booth ⎪ M^r Ja^s. Wiatt
    Mr Sterling Thornton   ⎭ Cap^n. Lewis Booker

This day Mr Meaux Thornton is Chosen Vestryman in the Room of Mr Benjn Dabney who is Remove'd out of the Parish

M^r Ja^s. Wiatt is Appointed Churchwarden in the room of M^r W^m.. Duvall and to settle with the late Churchwarden for his proceading

        L Booker Ju^r C W

True Entry
  Rich^d W Royston C^k

[399]
April 5th. 1790 — On this day meet the Freeho[   ] Houſekeepers in Petsworth Parish for the Electing of a [   ] for the said Parish agreable to an Ordinance

of Conve[   ] for Regulating and Appointing Vestrys and Trustees and [   ] Other purposes, Due notice of the s⁴. Election to be held on [   ] Day at the Church of the s⁴. Parish be first given the follow[   ] and under Written members were Chosen Vz^t

*Lewis Booker   Ja⁵ Baytop
 Tho⁵ Booth   Willm Booth
 James Wiatt   Fra⁵. DuVal
 Christopher Garland   John Jones
 L Booker J^r   John Hughes
 Lewis Wood   Ja⁵ Bentley
                        Peter Wiatt

†March y⁵. 2: 1792   Meaux Thornton In place
                        of Lewis Booker Decſ⁴

Cap^n Tho⁵. Booth and Mr Chri^r Garland is appointed Churchwardens and M^r W^m.. Booth is appointed Treasurer for the time being

                                        Lewis Booker

[400 Blank]

[401]

At a Vestry Held for Petsworth Parish [   ] 5th day of February 1791

                    Present
Mr Lewis Booker   ⎫ Mr Lewis Wood
Cap Thomas Booth C W   ⎬ Mr James Wiatt
Maj^r John Hughes   ⎭ & Christo^r Garland C W
Mr William Booth

Ordered that the Churchwardens for the Time Being Commence Suits for all money that appears to be due for The Rents of the Glebe of this Parrish

---

*Note! The following thirteen names are autograph signatures.
—C. G. C.
†Note! See pages 384 and 385.—C. G. C.

M[r] Peter Wiatt is Chosen a Vestryman in the Place of Cap James Bentley dec[d]

John Lutwytch is Chosen in Clerk of the Church to attend Every Sunday Unleſs Prevented By Sickneſs or Other accidents Untill the 5th day of February 1792

Tho[s] Booth

[402]

[ ] Vestry Held for Petsworth Parrish on the [ ] day of April 1791

Present The Rev[d] M[r] Fontaine

M[r] Lewis Booker	M[r] Fran[s] Duval
Col[o] James Baytop	M[r] William Booth
Cap Tho[s] Booth	M[r] Lewis Wood
Cap Lewis Booker	Maj[r] John Hughes
M[r] James Wiatt	M[r] Peter Wiatt
M[r] John Jones	& Christo[r] Garland

This Vestry have Unanimously agreed to Continue The Rev[d] M[r] Fontaine as Lecturer of this Parrish *and For this year & that he have the Benefit of the Glebe This year of M[r] Fontaine' Services to *Commence End on the 11 April 1792

This Vestry have agreed that the Churchwardens for the Time Being Shall Four Times in the year apply to the Congregation in Church immediately after Sermon for Such Donations from Each person as they may think proper to Give—which money When Received Shall by the Wardens be paid into the Hands of the Treasurer Subject to the Future Order of Vestry

---

*Note! These words have been scratched through with a pen in the MS.—C. G. C.

This Vestry has Chosen Col James Baytop and Mʳ William Booth to attend the General Convention at Richmond in May Next

John Lutwytche is Chosen Clerk of the Vestry

Jnº Lutwyche Clk

Thoˢ Booth C W
Christoʳ Garland C W

[403]

At a Vestry Held for Petswor[   ] on the 17 November 1791

Gentlemen Present

Capt Thoˢ Booth   Mʳ James Wiat[ ]
Mʳ John Jones   Mayjʳ Jnº Hughes
Mʳ William Booth   Mʳ Lewis Wood
Mʳ Francis Duvall

Orderd That twenty Shillings *that *was part of the money that was Collected in the Church be reserv'd for the Use of the Sacrament

agreed by the Vestry that Jnº Hughes put in as many dead lights as his wanted for the church at eight pence half penny pr light which is to be paid out of the Money that was Collected in the Church

Order'd That Mʳ Meux Thornton †be is appointed a Vestryman in the room of the late Mʳ Lewis Booker Deceas'd

‡Thoˢ Booth C W   ‡Jnº Lutwyche
Clk

---

*Note! These words have been scratched through with a pen in the MS.—C. G. C.

†Note! This word has been scratched through with a pen in the MS.—C. G. C.

‡Note! These names have been scratched through with a pen in the MS.—C. G. C.

Orderd That the Church-wardens do settle with Major Jn° Hughes and draw an order on the Treasurer for pay-*for ment and also that the Church wardens do draw an order on the Treasurer for what money shall [404] [   ]ed for furnishing the Bread [   ]ine for the Sacrament out of [   ] Money appropriated for that purpose

           Jn° Lutwyche
Tho⁸ Booth C.W.   Clk

At A Vestry Held for Petsworth Parrish on the 2ᵈ March 1792

        Present

Col° James Baytop	M' Francis Duval
Cap Tho Booth	M' James Wiatt
Maj' John Hughes	M' Meaux Thornton
Cap Lewis Booker	& Christo' Garland C W

This Vestry has Unanimously Chosen Col°. Baytop and Cap Thomas Booth to attend the General Convention at Richmond in April Next

M' Thomas Hall is Chosen by this Vestry to Serve as Clerk of the Church *Who for one year his Time of Service Commences the 1ˢᵗ Sunday in March

M' Tho⁸ Hall is allso Chosen Clerk of the Vestry

        Booth & Garland C W

---

 *Note! This word has been scratched through with a pen in the MS.—C. G. C.

[405]

At a Vestry Held for Petsoe Parrish on t[   ]
May 1792

Present

The Rev⁴ M⁻ Fontaine
Col° James Baytop ⎫ M⁻ Peter Wiatt
Maj⁻ John Hughes ⎪ — Lewis Wood
M⁻ James Wiatt ⎬ — Meaux Thornton
— John Jones ⎪ — Christo⁻ Garland
Francis Duval ⎭

The Rev⁴ M⁻ Fontaine is Unanimously Chosen by This Vestry as Lecturer for Twelve Months Which Ends on the 11ᵗʰ of April next to attend the Church Once a Fortnight Unleſs prevented by Sickneſs Or Other accidents M⁻ Fontaine is *to at Liberty to attend the Church of Abingdon at Least Three Times in the year Allso He is to have the Benefit of the Glebe for the present year when it Can be Collected from the Tennant

Thoˢ Hall C V

[406]

[   ] Vestry Held For Petsoe Parrish on the [   ] Day of September 1792

Present

Cap Thoˢ Booth C W ⎫ M⁻ Francis Duval
Cap Lewis Booker ⎪ M⁻ Lewis Wood
Maj⁻ John Hughes ⎬ M⁻ Meaux Thornton
M⁻ James Wiatt ⎭ M⁻ Christo⁻ Garland C W

The Rev⁴ M⁻ Fontaine having Decline⁴ Attending as Lecturer of this Parrish this Vestry Has Thought Proper to Recommend M⁻ Thomas Hughes to the Right Rev⁴ Doctor James Maddison to Be Ordain⁴ a Minister of the Protestant

---

*Note! This word has been scratched through with a pen in the MS.—C. G. C.

Episcopal Church and it is Resolved by this Vestry to Receive him as their Minister Provided He Comes to act in Their Parrish Within One Month after his Ordination and Take Upon him the Cure of the Same and that he Be Endowed with all the Spiritualities & Temporalities Due to a Minister

Thos: Hall C V

*Francis *Du Val *his *Book

[407]
At a Vestry held for Petsworth paris[ ]
March 1793

Present
Thomas Booth C W John Hug[ ]
Francis Duval, Lewis Wood Meaux Tho[ ]
ton James Baytop John Jones Vestrymen

The Revd Thomas Hughes having produc[ ] satisfactory Testimonials of his having been ord[ ]ined a Deacon by the Right Rev^d. Bishop Madison, to this Vestry

ordered that the said Revd Thomas Hughes be and he is by this Vestry inducted as minister into this parish, agreeably to a Resolution of †this a Vestry held the 28th day o[ ] September 1792

I Thomas Hughes hereby acknowledg[ ] that I hold the parish of Petsworth su[ ] to be removed at any time by a Determin[ ]tion of any future Convention of the Clergy & Lay Deputies of this State   Witneſ[ ] my hand this 27th day of March 1793

Thos Hughes Cl

orderd that m^r Thomas Hall be appointed Clerk of the Church & Vestry

Tho: Hall

---

*Note! These words are evidently not a part of the record.
†Note! This word has been scratched through with a pen in the MS.—C. G. C.

[408]

[   ] *Vestry held for Petsworth parish [   ]hursday the 11th. of July 1793

Present. Mr. Thomas Booth, Mr. Lewis Booker, Mr. James Wiatt, Mr. Peter Wiatt, Mr. John Hughes, Mr. John Jones, Mr. Francis DuVal, Mr Lewis Wood, Mr. William Booth*

We The Subscribers having been elected on Easter Monday last past. being the 1st day [ ]f April, by the Members, of the protestant [ ]piscopal Church, in Petsworth parish, to [ ]ct & serve as Vestrymen, do hereby subscribe [ ] be conformable to the Worship Doctrin, and Disciplin of the protestant Episcopal Church,

Witneſs our hands this 11th. day of July 1793

†Jas. Baytop	Fras. Du Val
Thos Booth	John Hughes
Lewis Booker	Peter Wiatt
James Wiatt	Lewis Wood
John Jones	Meaux Thornton
Willm Booth	‡T Buckner

[409]

At a Vestry held for Petsworth [   ] 11th. day of July 1793

Present. James Baytop Mr. Thos: Booth, mr. Lew[   ] Booker, mr. James Wiatt, mr. John Jones, mr Wm: Booth, mr. Fras. Du[   ] mr. John Hughes, mr Peter Wiatt, m[ ] Lewis Wood, and mr. Meaux Thornton

---

*Note! The whole entry between the two asterisks has been scratched through with a pen in the MS.—C. G. C.

†Note! The twelve names following are autograph signatures. —C. G. C.

‡Note! This name is written in different ink from the rest, and the name itself is hard to make out. I may have read it incorrectly.—C. G. C.

ordered, that mʳ Thomas Hall be appoint[ ] clerk to this Vestry

Ordered, that Colº. James Baytop & mʳ Wood be appointed church Wardens

Ordered, that mʳ. William Booth be a[ ]pointed Treasurer to this Vestry

Ordered, that the churchwardens commen[ ] suit immediately against mʳ. William Fo[ ] junʳ for a Balance due from the Estat[ ] Henry Pointer decd, for the Rent of the Glebe

ordered, that the church Wardens settle wit[ ] the late church Wardens, and receive whateve[ ] money may be in their hands, upon any account whatever.

Thoˢ Booth

Teſᵗ. Thoˢ. Hall C V

*[410]

F. Duval

Records of the gude
Auld Chuch of
England

The gude auld Kirk's
notes of conduct 1719

John Jameſon

---

*Note! The official record stops with the signature of Thoˢ Hall C V on page 409. What is written on page 410 is evidently the idle scribbling of some would-be "funny-man."—C. G. C.

APPENDIX

CLERGYMEN

Th following list contains the names of the ministers (Incumbents of Petsworth Parish, temporary supply preachers, and other clergymen) mentioned in this volume. The numerals (in parentheses) preceding each clergyman's name indicate the number of the page on which the name first appears; the date (in parentheses) following the name indicates the year in which the clergyman is first mentioned in the Vestry Book.

(1)	Thomas Vicaris (1677)
(48)	Joseph Hoult (1697)
(48)	James Clack (1697)
(57)	George Young (1700)
(65)	Emanuel Jones (1700)
(257)	Robert Yates (1739)
(258)	John Reade (1739)
(258)	Bartholomew Yates (1739)
(261)	——— Ford (1741)
(313)	William Yates (1761)
(313)	Richard Hewit (1761)
(317)	Robert Reade (1762)
(320)	James Horrox (1763)
(320)	——— Fox (1763)
(323)	James Murra Fountain (1764)
(330)	Charles Mynns Thruston (1767)
(340)	Arthur Hamilton (1768)
(355)	Thomas Price (1775)
(381)	James Elliott (1787)
(383)	——— Fontaine (1791)
(386)	James Madison (1792)
(387)	Thomas Hughes (1793)

Notes

James Clack. In *The Vestry Book of Christ Church Parish, Middlesex County, Virginia* 1663-1767 we find on page 68, under the date Nov. 11, 1690, the following entry:

"Ordered to Mʳ John Vauſe 500ˡᵇ of Tobacco and Caske to be by him pʳsented (as being Ch warden for the Middle Pʳcqs of this Pʳish) to mʳ Clack with Kinde Thanks for his Trouble and paines in Comeing to give us a Sermon at the Great Church"

Emanuel Jones. In *The Vestry Book of Christ Church Parish, Middlesex County, Virginia,* 1663-1767 we find on page 245, under the date Nov. 23, 1736, the following entry:

"This Day the Vestry agreed with the Reverend Mʳ Emanuel Jones to Preach in This Pariſh Every Friday at Each Church in turn and to be paid after the rate of Sixteen Thousand pᵈˢ of Tob° pʳ year for the time he Serves."

Again on the same page, under the date Oct. 13, 1737, we find the following entry:

"The Revᵈ Mʳ Bartho: Yates being arrived this Vestry do unanimously choose him Minister of this Parish. And that the Church Wardens return the Revᵈ Mʳ Emanuel Jones thanks for his faithfull Service."

Robert Yates. In *The Vestry Book of Stratton Major Parish, King and Queen County, Virginia,* 1729-1783 we find on page 55, under the date Feb. 23, 1743, the following entry:

"It is Order'd and agree'd on by this Vestry that The Reverᵈ. Meſsʳˢ. Bartholomew & Robert Yates do Officiate in this Parish on Wednesday in Each week till the Parish is Supplied or the Vestry shall Order to the Contrary, and that they be Paid at the rate of 16000ˡᵇ. Tob°. ℔ Ann. for each Sarmon—to begin at the Lower Church on the 1ˢᵗ. Wednesday in March."

John Reade. In *The Vestry Book of Christ Church Parish, Middlesex County, Virginia,* 1663-1767, we find on page 238, under the date Nov. 11, 1734, the following entry:

"The Reverend Mʳ John Reade offering to officiate as Minister of this Pariſh until the arival of one of the Sons of our late worthy Minister Mʳ Bartho Yates for the Legal Salary .... This Vestry do agree to receive him upon the terms afore Sᵈ And accordingly Order That he be admitted as Minister of this Pariſh from this Day to the end of the term aforesaid Provided he can obtain the Governor's leave to remove himself into the Pariſh."

Again on page 244, under the date Nov. 23, 1736, we find the following entry:

"The Reverend Mʳ John Reade Informing the Vestry his Intention to leave the Pariſh, being Chosen Minister of Stratton major Pariſh in King & Queen It is Order'd that the Church-wardens write to Mʳ Bartho: Yates to deſire him immediately to come over."

In *The Vestry Book of Stratton Major Parish, King and Queen County, Virginia,* 1729-1783, we find on page 29, under the date Nov. 15, 1736, the following entry:

"The Gentlemen of this Vestry have Agreed to receive the Revᵈ: Jno Reade as Minister of this Parish."

Mr. Reade served as Minister of Stratton Major Parish until 1744.

Bartholomew Yates. On page 258 of this volume Mr. Yates is referred to simply as "the Revᵈ. Mʳ Yeats of Middleſex." That the Rev. Bartholomew Yates is meant is evident when it is recalled that the Rev. Bartholomew Yates became Minister of Christ Church Parish, Middlesex County on Oct. 13, 1737 and that he served continuously as Minister of the parish until 1767 or longer.

See Note above, under the heading *Robert Yates,* for entry recording the service of the Rev. Bartholomew Yates as supply preacher in Stratton Major Parish in 1743.

Robert Reade. In *The Vestry Book of Kingston Parish, Mathews County, Virginia,* 1679-1796, we find on page 110, under the date Feb. 6, 1778, the following entry:

"The Rev'd Mr Robert Read & the Rev'd William Dunlop offering Themselves as Candidates for this Pariſh .... and by a Majority of the Veſtry the Rev'd Mr R. Read was Choſen."

Whether the above Mr. Robert Read, of Kingston, and Mr. Robert Reade of Petsworth were one and the same man is a question. If they were, the Rev. Mr. Read (or Reade) must have been a bird of passage; for he appears never to have come to Petsworth Parish at all, and in Kingston Parish he seems to have served not more than six months.

Arthur Hamilton. On Dec. 19, 1770 the Rev. Arthur Hamilton presented himself, but unsuccessfully, as a Candidate for the Incumbency of Kingston Parish. (See *The Vestry Book of Kingston Parish, Mathews County, Virginia*, 1679-1796, page 94).

On Sep. 23, 1778 the Vestry of Stratton Major Parish "Ordered, that the Church Wardens make application to the rev^d. M^r. W^m: Dunlap, and the rev^d. M^r. Auther Hamilton about moving from the Glebe; and provided they refuse to move, the Church Wardens are hereby authorised to commence suit against them." (See *The Vestry Book of Stratton Major Parish, King and Queen County, Virginia*, 1729-1783, page 210) Under what circumstances Mr. Hamilton had settled himself at the Glebe, the Vestry Book does not say.

——————— *Fontaine.* In *The Vestry Book of Kingston Parish, Mathews County, Virginia*, 1679-1796, we find on page 118, between the dates Jan. 27, 1783 and Aug. 19, 1784 the following entry:

"Ordered that the Revd Mr Fontaine be requested to prea[ch] once a Month until a Minister resides in the Parish."

CLERKS OF THE VESTRY

The following list contains the names of the Clerks of the Vestry of Petsworth Parish between 1681 (possibly 1679) and 1793. The numerals (in parentheses) preceding each clerk's name indicate the number of the page on which the name first appears as that of the Clerk; the date (in parentheses) following the name indicates the year in which the Clerk began to officiate as such.

(11)	Phil. May (1679)
(34)	Richard Simco (1692)
(57)	Hugh Macktyer (1700)
(82)	Thomas Potts (1704)
(88)	Joseph Ledford (1706)
(115)	Thomas May (1712)
(143)	John Carter (1718)
(184)	Wm. Brooking (1725)
(269)	Daniel New (1744)
(303)	James Baker (1758)
(361)	Richard Wyatt Royston (1778)
(384)	John Lutwytche (1791)
(385)	Thomas Hall (1792)

PHYSICIANS AND SURGEONS

The following list contains the names of the physicians and surgeons mentioned in this volume.

(25)	William Crymes (1684)
(32)	———— Alexander (1691)
(32)	Thomas Green (1691)
(33)	Thomas Blake (1692)
(55)	Ralph Baker (1699)
(103)	Charles Tomkies (1710)
(155)	Richard Edwards (1720)

(159)	Edward Walford (1721)
(159)	James Boyd (1721)
(201)	Hugh Noden (1727)
(226)	———— Symmer (1731)
(240)	John Edward(s) (1736)
(260)	———— Stretchey (1740)
(262)	Alexander Mackenzie (1741)
(280)	Charles Leith (1749)
(298)	———— Read (1756)
(308)	———— Clayton (1760)
(309)	Alexander Dalglish (1760)
(349)	William Carter (1773)
(354)	Robert Spratt (1775)
(373)	Richard Jones (1784)

Notes

Ralph Baker. On Nov. 8, 1709 a Doctor Baker (first name not given) was allowed by the Vestry of Christ Church Parish, Middlesex County, 4000 pounds of tobacco for "curing" three persons. [*Vestry Book of Christ Church Parish,* page 115]

There are altogether four references to Dr. Baker in the Christ Church Vestry Book, the first and the last dates being Nov. 8, 1709 and Jan. 7, 1711.

Edward Walford. On Oct. 18, 1717 a Doctor Wallford (first name not given) was allowed by the Vestry of Christ Church Parish, Middlesex County, 500 pounds of tobacco for "Physick administered" [*Vestry Book of Christ Church Parish,* page 160]

There is one other similar entry referring to Doctor Wallford in the same book, the entry being dated Oct. 7, 1719.

James Boyd. On Oct. 9, 1730 "Docter James Boyd" was allowed by the Vestry of Christ Church Parish, Middlesex County, 1280 pounds of tobacco, the amount of his account against the parish. [*Vestry Book of Christ Church Parish*, page 223]

──────── *Symmer*. On Oct. 9, 1733 Doctor John Symmer was allowed 860 pounds of tobacco, the amount of his account, by the Vestry of Christ Church Parish, Middlesex County. [*Vestry Book of Christ Church Parish*, page 231.]

There are some eight references to Dr. (sometimes Dr. John) Symmer in the Christ Church Vestry Book.

On Oct. 12, 1743 Doctor Symmer was allowed 1794 pounds of tobacco, the amount of his account, by the Vestry of Kingston Parish, Mathews County [*Vestry Book of Kingston Parish*, page 29.]

There are altogether seven references to Dr. (sometimes Dr. John) Symmer in the Kingston Vestry Book.

──────── *Stretchey*. In the *Vestry Book of Christ Church Parish* there are two references (dated Oct. 12, 1744 and Oct. 1, 1747, respectively) to a Doctor John Strachey, and one reference (dated Oct. 4, 1752) to a "Doct^r Strachey"

In the *Vestry Book of Stratton Major Parish* there are twenty-one references to Dr. (sometimes Dr. John) Strachey, the first being dated Oct. 9, 1738 and the last dated July 26, 1755

Charles Leith. On Oct. 6, 1749 the Vestry of Stratton Major Parish allowed to "Doctor Charles Leith for Sallavat^s Isabell Whitsides" 800 pounds of tobacco. [*Vestry Book of Stratton Major Parish*, page 81]

──────── *Read*. There are several references in the *Vestry Book of Christ Church Parish,* to a Dr. Alexander Reade, the first of which (page 271), dated Oct. 1, 1747, records an item of 374 pounds of tobacco to be paid Dr Reade by the parish. The last of the items is dated Oct 1, 1760

──────── *Clayton*. In the *Vestry Book of Kingston Parish* there is a single reference, on page 90, dated Dec. 11, 1769, to a Doctor Tho⁸ Clayton, who was to be paid 508 pounds of tobacco "on acc' of Elizabeth Parrett"

Robert Spratt. On Oct. 21, 1765 the Vestry of Christ Church Parish, Middlesex County, ordered that Dr. Robert Spratt be paid £12||12||9 "by Account" [*Vestry Book of Christ Church Parish,* page 332] A similar item, under the date Dec. 1, 1767, occurs on page 341.

ERRATA

Page 138. "Margret *Losey*" should probably be "Margret *Lasey.*"

Page 172. "*Cradd* Allexanders Quarter" should probably be "*Madd* Allexanders Quarter."

Page 190. "*M^{rs}* Fra Easter" should probably be "*M^r* Fra Easter."

Page 269. "Edwd *Balston*" should probably be "Edwd *Batston.*"

Page 364. "*Chri^n* Garland should probably be *Chri^r* Garland."

Index of Names of Persons

Acre: Jno.—142
Adams (Addams): Ann Shepard —325, 328, 329; Mg^t—321; Mary —336; Rich^d—196, 198^3, 199
Adamson: Mary—236
Adderson (Aderson): Rich^d—328; Sarah—321
Alexander (Allexander, Allexsander): Capt.—114, 129, 132, 134, 149, 261, 264, 267, 272; Capt David—72^2, 76, 78, 80, 81, 83^2, 85, 86, 88, 90^2, 93, 94, 95, 101, 103^2, 105^2, 106, 107, 109, 110, 112, 114, 115, 116^2, 118, 120, 121, 123^2, 128^2, 131, 138, 141, 152, 257^3, 263, 269^2, 270, 272, 273, 275, 277, 282; David—46, 49, 54^2, 55, 56, 58, 59, 63, 64^2, 65, 66^2, 67, 68^3, 69, 70^2, 71, 72, 73, 74, 82, 111, 227, 228, 230^2, 231^2, 232^3, 233^3, 234^2, 235, 236, 237, 238, 240, 242, 243, 244, 245, 247, 248, 250, 251, 252, 253, 256, 258, 259; Doct^r—32^2, 33, 57, 86; Capt Jno.—180, 185, 188, 190, 194, 196, 206^3, 207, 208, 209, 211, 212, 217^2, 218; Jno—159, 166, 196, 198; Madam —172; Madam Ann—158, 164; M^r—34, 234; Mrs Ann—155
Allard:—245
Allen (Allin, Alling): Rich^d—58^2, 59^2, 60^4; Sarah—102, 103, 106, 107; Susanna—58, 59; W^m —34, 35
Amis (Amies):—263; Ja^s—130, 238, 256, 266; Jno—100, 101, 284^2, 295^2; M^r—260; Thos—197
Anderson: Capt Matthew—377^2, 380^2; M.—375^2, 379; Matt—349, 352; Matthew—354, 363, 375, 377, 378; W^m—25, 108, 116, 142, 146^4, 152
Arington (Arrington):—303; Rebecca—299; W^m—279
Arthur (Arther): Frances (Francus)—195, 204^3, 205; M^{rs}—231; Widow—225
Ashur (Arshur): Rich^d—232, 257

Ascough: Jno—3; M^r—6
Augur: Jno—11
Austin (Austine, Auston): Bartholomew—1, 5, 8; Jeff—41; Mary—346^2, 350; Rich^d—91^2; W^m—348

Badston (Batston):—271; Edwd—269, 271^2, 274, 278, 279, 285
Baker: Benj^a—170^4, 173, 180, 185, 189, 197, 200, 210, 224, 238, 249, 284, 295, 305, 319, 334; Doct^r (Backer, Baker, Beaker)—55, 97^4, 99^4, 130, 150^2; Elizth—362; Ja^s—303^2, 305, 306, 307, 308^2, 310^2, 311^2, 313^2, 314^2, 315^2, 318, 320^3, 322, 323^2, 324^2, 325^3, 326^2, 327, 328^2, 329^2, 330^3, 333, 334^2, 335, 337^2, 338^2, 339, 340^2, 342^2, 344^2, 346^2, 347^3, 348, 349, 350, 352^2, 353, 354, 355, 356^2, 357^2, 358, 359^2, 360^2, 361, 362, 364; Ralph (Baker, Beaker)—51, 99, 101; Doct^r Ralph—72, 73, 86; W^m J^r—325, 336
Ballard (once Ballerd): Jno—134; Mary—128^2; Thos—107, 118; Widow—137^2, 138
Bane (Bain): Jno—306, 309, 312, 315, 325
Barden: Sarah—288
Bardin: Jos.—224
Barnard (Barnet, Barnett, Bernard, Berrnard, Burnett):—94, 96; Capt—229; Ja^s—177, 178; Jno—176, 181, 182, 185^2, 186; M^r—2, 6, 17, 44; Rich^d—3, 4, 8, 10, 73; Saml—87; Thos—178, 179; W^m—43^2, 45, 46, 47, 49^3, 50^4, 51^4, 53, 54, 55, 56, 57, 58^5, 59^2, 60^3, 63^2, 64, 65^4, 68^2, 71, 72, 73^2, 74^5, 76^3, 77, 78, 80, 81, 87, 189
Barnes: Susana—205
Bayley (Bailey, Balye, Bayly): M^r—97, 100, 118^2; Maj^r Rich^d—105^2; Rich^d—46, 50, 53, 55, 74, 106
Baynton: Jno—21

Baytop (Batop):—339; Capt Thos—369; Col. Ja^s—367, 368, 376, 377, 380, 383, 384, 385, 386, 389; Ja^s—349, 366, 375^2, 377, 379^2, 381^2, 382, 387, 388^2; M^r—322; Thos—193

Beauford:—312

Bell: Humphry—89; Peter—226, 227

Bellfure (Belfeire, Belfure): Ja^s—104, 107, 124, 125; Sarah—93, 104

Bendixon: Marcus—205

Bennett: Rich^d—16, 18

Benson: Jane—41^2

Bentley: Capt Ja^s—383; Ja^s—306, 352, 357, 370, 382

Berry (once Berrey):—54; Ambrose—98, 100; Jno—38, 51^2, 136

Beverley (Beverly, Beverlye): Col.—108, 114, 132, 134, 152; Col. Peter—94, 120, 141; Maj^r—52, 76^2; Maj^r Peter—63, 73; Maj^r Robt—9

Bevis (once Beves): Ralph—135^3, 136

Blackman (once Blackburn): Grace—41, 43, 44, 49, 52

Blake: Doct^r Thos—33; Jno—208; W^m—366

Blan: Fr^s—349; Mr^s—350

Blancot:—73

Blasingame (Blasingan, Blasinghame, Blasingim, etc): Ja^s—328; Jno—6, 262, 264, 281, 288, 289, 290^2, 292, 294, 301, 307, 316, 333, 354; Judith—366, 367, 369, 372, 374; M^r—274; Mr^s—331; Mr^s Judith—360; Sarah—331

Bluefoot (Blueford):—286, 287, 288, 290, 291, 292; Elizth—300; Nancy—293

Boaden: Thos—234, 235

Bob:—301

Bolton (Boulton): Henry—62; Thos—120, 237, 259

Bond: Dorothy—291; Margaret—187, 191, 201, 205, 236; Widow—184, 223

Booker: Amy—285, 287, 289; Ja^s—162, 218, 220, 225^2, 228, 229, 230, 231, 233, 239, 240, 245, 248, 254, 259, 262, 263, 265, 267, 271, 274^2, 275, 277, 279, 281; Ja^s J^r—279; Lewis—284, 295, 304, 319, 331, 334, 335, 337, 338^2, 340^2, 342, 343^2, 344^2, 345, 346, 347^3, 351^2, 352, 353, 354, 355, 356^2, 358^2, 360^2, 361, 362, 363, 366, 367, 368, 369, 370, 373^2, 374, 375, 376^2, 377, 379, 380^2, 381^3, 382^4, 383, 384, 388^3; Capt Lewis—380^2, 381^2, 383, 385, 386; Lewis, J^r—379^2, 381, 382; Lewis, S^r—378; Thos—221, 280, 315, 321, 325

Booth:—385; George—295, 305, 306, 307, 308, 309, 310^2, 311^2, 312^2, 313, 314^2, 315, 317, 318, 319, 320, 322, 323^2, 324, 327^2, 328, 330, 333, 335, 337^2, 338, 340, 342, 344, 346^3, 347^2, 351, 353^2, 356, 358^2, 360^2, 361^3, 362, 363^2, 365, 366^3, 367, 368, 370^2, 372, 373, 374; Jno—6; M^r—232, 245, 326; Thos—222^2, 223, 224, 225, 226, 227, 228, 229^2, 230^3, 231, 232^2, 233, 234, 235, 236, 237, 238, 242^2, 244, 245, 247, 248, 250, 251, 252, 254, 257, 258, 375, 377, 379^2, 381^2, 382^2, 383, 384^2, 385, 387, 388^3, 389; Capt Thos—382, 383, 384, 385^2, 386; Thos J^r—127; W^m—382^3, 383, 384^2, 388^3, 389

Boswell: Thos—285

Bourk: Jeffry—205, 223

Bowen: Widow—236

Bowls (Bools, Bowells, Bowels):—316, 321; Peter—325, 328; Stubblefield—325, 328; W^m—106, 107, 115

Boyd: Doct^r Ja^s—159

Bradshaw: Rich^d—54

Bray: Ann—102; Henry—31, 32, 33, 35^2

Breemer: Jno—10^2

Bristow: Jno—376

Brock: Jno—31

Brooking (Brooken, Brookin, Brookins): Ann—339, 362, 365, 366; M^r—31; Robt—108; Saml—331, 334, 354, 364; Susanna (Susanne)—186, 205, 209; W—179, 185, 197, 198, 201, 208, 218, 220, 232, 235, 236, 237, 238, 239, 240, 243, 244, 247, 248^2, 250^2,

251, 253, 256, 257, 258, 259², 261, 265; W^m—49, 51, 52, 53, 54, 63, 68, 72, 73², 74², 130², 150², 173², 176, 177, 178³, 180, 184, 185², 186, 188, 189², 190, 192², 193, 194, 195², 197, 198, 199, 200², 202, 203, 204, 205, 206², 207, 209, 210, 211, 212, 213, 214, 215, 216, 217, 219, 220, 222, 223, 224, 225², 227, 228⁴, 229, 230, 231, 233², 238, 240, 241, 245, 252, 254, 256, 262², 263, 265, 266, 267, 269, 284, 316
Brooks: Ja^s—335, 341; Rebeckah —341
Brown: Alex^r—370; Ann—284; Daniell—91², 92³, 94; Eliz^a—205; Francis—196, 198², 199², 264; George—196, 198; Grace—198, 201, 202⁴; Jn°—51², 55, 316; Nicholas—118, 119, 133², 137, 138; W^m—239
Brumbly: Eliz^th—83
Buckner: Capt—152, 226², 229, 230, 245, 252, 265; Col.—277, 279², 280, 282, 290, 292, 297, 301², 305, 318²; Francis—218, 219; Jn°—1, 2, 3, 4, 8, 9, 10, 11, 12, 13, 14², 15, 17, 19, 24, 26, 27, 28, 31², 33², 38, 40, 308², 310³; Maj^r—261, 263², 265, 267², 269, 271, 272; M^r—1, 5, 15², 20, 24, 35, 44; Saml—127, 219³, 220; Capt Saml—221², 222², 225², 227², 228, 230, 231², 232, 233, 234, 235², 236, 237, 238, 239, 240, 242, 243, 245, 247, 248², 249, 250², 251, 253, 254², 257², 258, 259³, 264²; Col. Saml—274, 275, 277², 279, 281³, 283, 284, 285, 287, 289, 290, 292, 294, 295, 296, 298, 300, 302², 303, 304, 305, 307⁴, 308, 310, 311², 313², 314³, 317, 318, 319, 320, 323; Maj^r Saml—262, 270, 271, 272, 273²; T.—388; Thos—43², 45, 46, 47, 50⁴, 51³, 53³, 65, 82, 106, 110, 114, 118, 138, 139, 148, 155, 176; Capt Thos—54, 55, 56, 57, 58, 59, 63, 68², 71, 72, 76, 78, 80, 81, 83, 85, 86², 88², 90, 93², 95, 96, 105, 107, 109, 110, 112, 114, 115, 116², 117, 120, 121², 123, 133, 134, 136, 141, 143, 151, 153, 154, 157², 159, 162, 163², 166, 167, 168, 171, 175, 180, 181, 184, 188², 192
Bugg: Patrick—103
Burage (Buredge): Ann—336; Sarah—320
Burges: Sarah—326
Burk:—341; Arnold (Arnold Shumake)—343, 345, 346; Eliz^th— 349; Jn°—286; M^rs—345, 348²; Susan (Susanah)—331, 336, 339, 341², 343, 346, 350, 352, 359, 361²; Thos—285, 288, 291, 293, 296, 299, 300, 302, 306, 309, 311, 315, 320, 325, 331²
Burton: Henry—345, 352; Jn°—128²
Busby (once Buzbee): Mary—325; M^rs—376; Sarah—362, 365, 367, 369, 372, 374
Bushrod: M^rs—365
Butcher: Mildred—321
Butler: Ellianer—169²; Martin—26

Caley:—18, 20; Owen—14
Camel: Ja^s—283; Margret—283
Camp: Striplehill—293; W^m—273
Candel: Rich^d—89
Candill: Ja^s—141
Cant: Jn°—39
Carnill: Jn°—140
Carter: Benj^a—154; Chas—252, 253²; Col.—262; Doct^r W^m—349; Edwd—128, 144²; Eliz^th—67⁴, 72, 83; Henry—290; Ja^s—262, 264, 267, 277², 279, 281, 283, 285, 287³, 288, 289³, 290, 291, 292², 294, 297, 298², 300, 302, 305; Jn°—130, 143³, 144², 145, 146², 147⁴, 151, 152, 153², 154³, 156², 157, 158², 159², 160, 161², 162, 163³, 168², 169, 170², 175², 177², 178, 180, 181, 187, 194, 197, 214, 224, 227²; M^r—6, 13, 15, 25; Robt—4, 7, 10², 12, 14², 19, 22, 28², 29², 31, 32, 33, 37, 38, 40, 43, 46, 47, 49, 99, 101, 109, 111, 130, 150, 169, 173, 178, 179, 180, 185, 189, 194, 197, 206, 214, 224, 238; Sarah—146, 154, 159, 170; Widow—223

Carver: W^m—43, 44
Cary: Col. Wilson—347, 352; Mary—54; Wilson—335
Chapman: J^no—35
Chew: Larken (Larkin)—68, 69, 72
Cilligrue: Phillis—236
Clack: Ja^s (Reverend?)—48
Clare: Edwd—5
Clark:—288, 291, 325; Ja^s—10³; J^no—74, 83, 87, 171, 196, 285; Lucy—286, 315; Purcilla—325, 328
Clayton (Cleayton, Cleyton): Capt—233, 239, 240, 262, 263, 267, 271, 274, 276, 278, 279, 281, 285, 287, 290, 292, 296, 298, 300, 330; Capt J^no—181, 190, 200, 207, 221², 225, 228, 231, 306, 308², 311², 315, 320, 325², 328, 330, 335, 338, 341, 342, 344, 347; Doct^r—308; J^no—154, 160, 163, 176, 186, 245
Clunies: M^r—20
Cobson: J^no—38, 54
Cocke: Mary—7; Hannah—7
Cole (Coal):—335; Rich^d—294, 296, 297, 298, 300, 301, 302, 306, 308, 311, 315, 320, 325, 328, 330, 335², 338, 339, 341, 342, 343, 345, 347, 349², 352, 357, 359, 360
Coleman: Ann—107; J^no—46, 96³, 101, 102, 103; Joseph—73; Rich^d—372; Saml—213
Collawn (Collawne; *once* Collane): J^no—238, 256, 266; M^r—97, 99; W^m—9, 38, 99, 101, 110, 111, 131, 151, 174, 355
Colles: Capt—15, 20, 24; Capt Robt—18, 19, 22, 27; M^r—23³; Mr Robt—14⁴, 22, 24, 26
Collins: Anthony—244, 246, 249, 255, 260, 261
Conaway: Saml—6
Connor: Martin—256, 266
Cooke (Cook): Benj^a—237; Mordecai (spelled in various ways)—283, 295, 304, 318; M^rs—260; Rich^d—62, 253²; Thos—34, 37, 50, 51, 53, 54, 56, 63², 64², 65, 66², 67, 68³, 69, 70², 71, 72, 73³, 74, 76, 78, 80, 81, 82, 83, 85², 88²,

90. 93, 95, 101, 103, 105², 106², 107, 116², 118, 121, 131, 136, 139, 141, 142, 143, 147, 148, 152, 153, 154, 155, 156², 159, 160, 171, 184, 206, 224, 230, 237²; Thos J^r—197
Cooper: J^no—94; M^r—96
Cordle (Cordell):—Rich^d—76, 77
Cotes (Coates, Coats): Bridget—309, 312, 315², 321, 325, 336, 339; Eliz^th—376; George—362, 365
Cotten (Cottle): Ezra—85, 86²
Cox^- (*once* Coxe): Mary—231, 234; Rich^d—11
Crabbin: Catharine—350
Crimes (Crymes): Doct^r—25, 29, 130, 132, 150, 173; Doct^r W^m—86, 89; M^r—49; W^m—7³, 9, 19, 22², 24, 27, 28, 29, 37, 50, 53
Crittenden: Anne—262, 263; J^no—213; M^r—237; Rich^d—98, 101, 172, 197, 219, 224, 227², 229, 230², 256², 284,
Crockford: J^no—102, 103, 106, 107, 139, 142, 144³, 164²

Dabney: Benj^a—375², 377³, 378, 379², 381
Dalgleish (Dalgliesh, Dalglish, Delgleish): Alex^r — 301, 317², 318, 324, 326, 327; Doct^r—309; Doct^r Alex^r—311, 320, 322², 323², 327, 329
Danbee: Danl—184, 187
Dance:—286; Mary—286, 287, 290; Rich^d—164, 286, 291, 293, 297
Daniel (*once* Danel): Beverly—364; Maj^r Robt—331; Robt—305, 319, 334, 354
Darling (Darlin): Jeremiah—236, 249, 312
Darnal (Darnel, Darnill, Darnold): Jeremiah—41, 240, 241, 245, 254, 309, 349; Margery (Marget)—42, 43³, 325; Mary—299, 315, 321, 325, 328, 331; Widow—49², 50, 52
Davis (*once* Davyes): Antho—365; J^no—16; Rich^d—300; Saml—357, 359; Thos—134, 221; Widow—54
Dawkins: Thos—23
Dawson: J^no—41, 43

Day: Jno—71⁵, 72, 98, 101, 120, 142, 152; Lewis—5
Delawood: Jno—22
Denis: Ann—190
Dickenson: Daniel—201
Dickerson: David—345
Dickeson: Thos—97, 100
Dickinson: Daniel—4; David—315; Elizth—374, 376
Dickison: David—312
Dickson: Jno—89, 94³
Dillard: George—295
Dowling: Jane—198, 203²
Draper: Elizth—325; Robt—11
Driver: Mary—312, 315, 321, 325, 328; Thos—190, 207, 208
Drumond: Dun.—5
Dudley (Duddley, Dudly, *once* Doodley): Elizth—374, 376²; George—237, 256; Ja^s—22², 24, 28², 29², 31, 33, 35, 37, 38, 39², 43, 46, 47, 49, 50, 51, 57, 58, 63, 68, 72, 78, 80, 81, 83, 85, 86, 88, 90, 93, 95, 96, 103, 105², 106², 107, 110², 111, 112, 116², 118, 123, 130, 150, 152, 153, 169, 173, 178, 237, 244, 245, 256; Ja^s J^r—217; M^r—18, 20; M^{rs}—278; Mrs Sarah—279; Thos—9, 118, 238, 266
Duglace: W^m—144, 145²
Duninge: Saml—5², 7, 8
Dunlavy: M^r—294
Dunston: Fra^s—374², 376
Dutton: Ja^s—371
Duval (DuVal, Duvall): F.—389; Fra^s—178, 382, 383, 384, 385, 386², 387², 388³; M^r—274; M^{rs}—328; Saml—274, 278; W^m—249, 254, 326, 340², 342², 343, 344², 346, 347², 349, 351², 353², 355, 356³, 357, 358², 359, 360², 361, 362, 363, 366, 367, 368, 369, 371, 375², 376, 377², 378, 379², 380², 381²; W^m J^r—363, 364

Easter: Francis—155, 161, 162, 187, 190, 194, 197, 201, 221, 226², 234, 237, 245, 249, 256; Ja^s—226, 227; Jno—76; Thos—120, 177, 181², 184, 186, 190, 200, 207, 217², 226, 227

Eastwood: Jno—223; Joseph—280
Edwards: Eleanor (spelled in various ways)—231, 293, 296, 299, 300, 302, 306, 309, 311, 315, 320; Doct^r Jno—240; Doct^r Rich^d—155; Mrs Sarah—365; Widow—229; W^m—70
Elcock: Thos—33², 35
Elliott: Rev. Ja^s—381
Ellis: Ann—300; Mary—234; Sarah—300
Elton: Robt—31
Ennis (Ennies, Enies): Elizth—207, 217, 223; Robt—69², 70, 73², 76, 83²
Evans:—1; Hump.—6; Jno—12, 22³, 24, 27; M^r—23
Exon:—1

Fary (Ferry, Fery): George—164, 168, 176, 177, 178, 179⁴, 201, 224, 227, 231, 329
Faulkner (Falkner, Fallkoner): 11, 68, 74
Fergason (spelled in various ways): Mary—88, 90³, 94, 102; Widow—86
Fiffe: W^m—84⁶, 85
Figg: Mrs Ann—365; Thos—165
Finny (Finnie): W^m—322, 363
Fitsummuns:—303, 306
Fleming: Jno—153, 172, 190, 201; M^{rs}—279, 290, 292; Thos—234, 239; W^m—65², 90, 129, 256², 266, 275, 295, 333²
Fontaine (Fountain): Ja^s—317; M^r—318; Rev Ja^s Murra—323, 324; Rev M^r—383³, 386⁴
Ford: Rev M^r—261
Forgas: Margret—139²
Forsith: Ja^s—108
Fowler:—120, 132², 134; Elizth—102, 103, 108; M^r—49; Saml—69
Fox: Capt Jno—363, 369, 370; Jno—332, 337, 344, 346², 347³, 348, 349², 350², 353, 356, 368; M^r—348; Rev M^r—320; W^m J^r—389
Francklin: Nich.—9
Fuller: W^m—9

Galleman: Jno—184

GLOUCESTER COUNTY, VIRGINIA, 1677-1793   405

Gardner: George—222, 229, 239; Zac^h—354
Garland (*once* Garlant):—385; Christopher—354, 364, 371, 379^2, 380^2, 381^2, 382^3, 383, 384, 385, 386^2; Jno—197, 224, 238, 256; Robt—305, 319, 334, 341
Garnet: Thos—73
Gibson (*once* Gipson): Eli.—139; Eliz^a—152^3, 153, 154, 160, 164, 187, 190; Wm Liall—359
Gilbord: Jno—77
Good: Abra.—5
Goodwin: Abraham—75; Margrett—75^2, 76
Goosetree: David—25
Goram: Sarah—164
Gorgy (Goargy, Gorgi, Gorgit):—263; Dorothy—240, 245, 249, 254^2, 260, 262, 263^2
Goulder: Thos—229
Grabige: Edwd—2
Graves:—221
Green: Doct^r—33; Doct^r Thos—32; George—355; M^r—272; Ralph—4, 28; Ralph J^r—7, 10, 12, 14, 27, 38; Ralph Senr—4, 7, 10, 12, 17; Thos—28, 29^3, 30, 31^2, 33, 35, 38, 40, 41, 46, 47, 98, 100, 127, 129, 141, 154^3, 156^2, 157^2, 159, 160^3, 162, 163^2, 164, 166^2, 167, 168, 171, 175^2, 180^2, 181^2, 184^2, 186, 192, 194^2, 198, 200, 203, 205, 206^2, 207, 214^2, 217, 219^2, 220, 222, 223, 227, 228, 232^2, 233, 234, 235^2, 236, 237, 238, 239, 240^2, 242, 244, 245, 247, 248, 250, 252, 253, 257, 258, 259, 261^2, 263, 264, 265, 267, 268^2, 269^2, 270^2, 271, 272^2, 273, 274, 277
Greenley: Edwd—22
Greenwood:—271; H e n r y—190; Will—141
Gregory: Widow—70
Griffin (Griffing): Henry—225, 239, 240, 249; Thos—187, 191, 195, 201
Griffith: Edwd—128
Grindly (Grindley, *once* Grindlye): Thos—117, 141, 160, 164; Thos S^r—182

Grindy (Grindee): Christyan—231, 232; Thos—42, 176, 187, 190, 231, 232; Widow—231
Grinly: M^{rs}—31
Gront: Jno—32^2, 34
Grumly (Grumley, *once* Grumbley): Frances—331; Swan—364, 371; W^m—143, 154, 159, 163, 175, 181, 183, 186, 280, 285, 295
Grymes (Grimes): George—208; Jno—145, 176, 181, 182, 190; Capt Ludwell—304, 305, 306, 307, 308; Ludwell—292^3, 294, 296, 297^2, 298, 300, 302, 304, 310
Guthrie, Rich^d—283

Halcomb (*once* Holcomb): Rich^d—184, 187, 191, 201, 207, 219, 221, 223, 226, 231, 234; Simon—229, 236
Hall: Ann—303, 339; Robt—99, 101; Solomon—262, 325; Stephen (Steven)—30^3, 31^2, 33, 35^2, 38^2, 41; Thos—290, 366, 367, 369, 372, 373, 385^2, 386, 387^3, 389^2; W^m—342, 345^2, 347, 348, 350; W^m J^r—365
Hamilton: Rev Arthur (Rev M^r)—340^3, 342^2, 343, 344^2, 347, 349, 351^4, 353^2, 355, 356, 357, 358^2
Hansford (Hanford): Chas—116; Eliz—207; M^r—20, 23, 129^2, 149; W^m—3, 8, 10, 12^2, 14, 15, 16, 17, 19, 22, 86^3
Hardcastle: Jno—261
Harington (Harrington): — 287; Reb^o—265; W^m—240, 245, 249, 267, 269, 271, 276, 278, 282, 286, 288^2, 291, 292, 297
Harper: Jno—100, 101, 131
Harris: Thos—120
Hartwell: Margret—236, 239
Harwood: W^m—363
Hay: Timothy—87
Hayes (Hase): Ja^s—58^2, 59^2, 61^3, 62^5, 71
Haynes (Haines, Hains, Hayns):—216^3; Ann—207; Danl—376; Elizth—372, 374^2; George—150^2, 160, 164, 174, 221, 322; Ja^s—164, 326; Jane—252, 274, 299, 301, 302, 306, 320^2; Jean—309, 311,

315; Jn°—130, 366, 374; W^m—374, 376
Hester, Jn°—69
Hewit (Hueit): Rev. Rich^d—313, 316
Hide: Thos—1, 2², 4, 5, 8
Higgins: Ann—136
Hill: Mary—108, 114, 128, 137, 152, 155, 160, 164, 176, 181, 187, 191; Rich^d—66, 91, 102, 103; Widow—118, 138
Hilton:—259, 262, 263, 265, 268; Eliz^th—254, 262; Mary—249; Thos—254
Hobday:—372
Hogg: George—8, 13³
Hogsden (Hogsdon, Hoggsdone, Hogsdun): Ellenor—20, 24; Mary—41²; Robt—6, 18; Widow—29, 31, 32, 33, 35, 38, 41, 43, 44, 49
Hoile: Ed—9
Holloway: Jane—112, 113², 116; Rich^d—16
Hook: Mary—102
Hope: Africa—108, 114², 116, 120, 122³, 123, 131, 134, 139; Hanah—103; Rich^d—236; Saml—56, 59, 63²
Hopkins:—299; Job—34, 35, 51; Rich^d—164, 166
Hopwood: Ann—252
Horrox: Rev. Ja^s—320
Horsley (*once* Horsly): Mary—292, 297, 299, 300, 302, 306, 309, 312, 315, 316²; Rhode—316, 321, 325
Hoult: Rev Joseph—48³, 49, 51, 52³, 54², 55, 56², 63
Howard:—290; Ja^s—279; W^m J^r—10; W^m S^r—12
Howlit (Howlet, Houlett): Jn°—303, 338, 341, 345, 352, 367
Hubard: Capt Ja^s—330², 332, 333, 335, 338², 340², 341², 342, 344, 346, 347³, 349², 351, 352², 353, 356, 358², 360, 361, 362, 363², 367², 368, 369, 373; Capt Ja^s J^r—327, 330; Capt Jn°—341, 348, 349, 350, 351², 352, 353³, 354, 355³, 356², 357², 358², 359, 360, 361³, 362, 363²; J—264; Ja^s—252,
256, 257², 258, 259³, 260², 261, 262, 263², 264, 265², 267², 269, 270, 271², 274, 276, 277, 279², 281², 283, 285, 287², 289, 290, 292, 296, 299, 302, 303, 304, 306, 307, 308², 309, 310², 311², 313, 314², 318, 320, 324, 326, 327, 329, 330, 331, 333, 335², 337, 338², 339, 340, 341, 342, 344, 346, 347², 349, 352, 355; Jas J^r—324, 326; Ja^s S^r—327, 328; M^r—262, 267, 291, 301, 332, 333; M^r J^r—326; W^m—325
Hubbard: Henry—173, 224; Ja^s—233; Johanah—159; Margaret—332; Rich^d—6, 99, 101, 130, 150; W^m—332
Hudson: Mary—331
Hues:—132; Jn°—120, 134
Hughes: Jn°—382, 384, 387, 388²; Maj^r Jn°—382, 383, 384, 385²; 386; Rev. Thos—387²; Thos—386, 387²
Humphris: Robt—44
Humphryes: W^m—54
Hunley: Rich^d—145
Hunt: Jn°—354
Hunter: Daniel—236, 239², 240; Mary—280, 282, 286, 288, 291, 293, 336, 348; M^rs—271², 293, 296, 299
Hurst: W^m—6
Hurt: Abigall—83
Hutson (Hutsing): Flo^r—335, 336

Ireland (Ierland, *once* Eirland): Rich^d—6, 36², 50, 51, 52, 53, 54, 63, 69, 70, 73; Widow—76, 83, 86
Iremonger: Francis—21; M^r—25
Ivers: W^m—41²

Jackson: Eliz^th—268, 276; Thos—164, 223, 233, 236; Widow—267, 271, 274
Jameson: Jn°—389
Jenkins (*once* Jenkings): Ja^s—38, 39, 41; Rebecca—269, 276, 279, 286,
Johnson: Shep—6; S t e p h e n (Steven)—52, 114, 130, 131, 149, 151, 173, 174,
Jones: Ann—259, 265, 268²; Capt—289, 326, 348², 357; Capt Rich^d—

287², 292, 294, 295, 298, 304², 306, 310, 311, 313, 314³, 317, 318, 319, 320, 323³, 324², 327⁴, 328, 329³, 330, 332, 333, 335, 337, 338², 340², 342, 343, 344, 345, 346², 347², 349², 351, 352, 353², 355, 356², 358², 360³, 361, 362, 366, 367, 368, 369; Doct' Rich⁴—373; Rev Emanuel —65³, 68, 69, 71, 72², 73, 76, 77, 80, 81², 82, 83², 86², 88³, 90², 91, 93³, 95², 96², 101, 102, 103², 105², 106, 107³, 110, 112, 114³, 116³, 118, 120², 121⁴, 123², 128², 131², 132, 133, 134³, 136², 137², 138, 139³, 141³, 143, 148, 151, 152, 154³, 155, 156, 157², 159², 162, 163³, 166, 167, 168, 171, 175², 180, 181², 182², 184, 186², 188, 190², 191³, 192, 194, 196, 198, 200², 201², 205⁴, 206, 207⁴, 214, 217⁴, 218, 219², 220⁴, 221, 222, 223, 225³, 226², 227, 228², 229, 230², 232, 233³, 234, 235, 236, 237, 238², 240³, 242⁴, 244, 245³, 247, 248², 250, 251, 252, 253, 254³, 257, 258², 259; Jn°—382, 383, 384, 386, 387, 388³; Mʳ—117; Rich⁴—281, 282, 283, 284, 285², 287², 289², 308², 327, 335, 336, 339, 361; Thoˢ— 11, 16, 18, 240, 268, 270; Widow —271³

Jones & Scott, Messrs:—287
Jonson: Elizᵗʰ—267

Kallaham: Flurinah—329; Kilmon—326; Rhode—328
Karr (*once* Kar): David—313; Elizᵗʰ—187, 190
Keiningham: Jn°—371; Wᵐ—371
Kelley:—23
Kemp (*once* Cemp): Peter—238, 266, 280, 282, 283, 285³, 287², 289, 290², 292, 296, 298², 300², 302, 304, 305, 306, 308², 310, 311, 313², 314², 317, 318, 320, 323², 324, 327², 328, 329, 330, 333, 335, 337, 338, 340, 341, 344, 349, 351, 353², 355², 361, 366, 367, 368, 369, 370², 371, 372, 373³, 375², 376, 378, 379, 380², 381; Robᵗ—334; Thoˢ—188, 284, 296, 305, 319; Wᵐ—189

Keningham: Jn°—284, 295; Wᵐ— 266
Kilingham: Jn°—319
Killiham:—321; Kilmⁿ—321
Killingham: Jn°—305
King: Frances—316, 321
Kiningham: Jn°—334, 339, 344, 354; Mildred—271
Knight:—221
Knoles: Elizᵗʰ—229; Robᵗ—229; Widow—229; Wᵐ—229

Lacey: Margret—137, 138
Lagg: Catherine—106
Lamb: Mary—287, 290, 292, 300, 343, 345, 348, 349, 352, 355; Mʳˢ —345; Wᵐ—271
Lambarth: Mary—209
Lankford:—211
Laughlin, Jaˢ—364, 371; Thoˢ—226
Lawd: Peter—5
Lawrence: Elizⁿ—17; Thoˢ—6
Lawson: Jn°—309, 312, 315, 320, 325, 328
Ledford: Joseph—88³, 90, 93², 102, 103, 107, 108, 114², 115², 117, 134, 139, 141, 152
Lee: Francis—149, 238, 256, 266; Robᵗ—1, 2, 3, 4, 16², 18
Leigh: Rich⁴—370; Zach—235
Leith: Doct'—280, 288, 290, 294, 296; Doct' Chaˢ—282
Lennard: "old"—31³, 33
Levitt: Thoˢ—139
Lewis: Col.—8; Col. Jn°—131², 151², 175²; David—189, 190, 191; Edwᵈ—31; Elizᵗʰ—252, 269, 286, 288, 291, 292², 297, 299, 300, 302, 306, 309, 311; Jaˢ—58, 59, 61, 62⁴, 71², 72, 223, 233, 234, 236, 241, 249; Jn°—66, 69, 132; Majʳ —5; Nicholas—55, 56, 58, 60, 61², 63; Thoˢ—321², 326, 328; Widow —267
Lightfoot (Lightfoote): Capᵗ—35; Col.—15³, 23, 24; Col. Phil—21; LᵗCol.—14; Majʳ—11, 12²; Mʳ —1², 5, 6, 8, 9; Phil.—1, 3, 4, 8, 9, 28; Capᵗ Phil—29
Linford: Francis—21³
Litey (*once* Lighty): Jn°—20, 24, 29, 31

Littefeild: Robt—9
Levingston:—352
Livingston: Cornelius—320, 327; M^r—315
Lodge: Robt—254
Loe:—211; Frank—208
Loraigne: Thos—6
Lovel: Rich^d—249
Lutwyche (Lutwytch, Lutwytche): Jno—383, 384^3, 385
Luvel: Susana—372

Madison: Rt. Rev Ja^s—386, 387
Malton: Elizth—249
Mampus: Thos J^r—302^2; Thos S^r—30
Mann: M^r—18
Mansfild: Joseph—233
Marcy (Macy, Marcey): Eliz^a—195, 207, 217; Rich^d—299, 303
Mareye, Thos—160
Marvil (once Marvill): Jno—181, 187, 190, 192^2, 193^2; Watkinson—187
Mason:—287
Mastin: Saml—31, 32, 33
Mathis: Sarah—35
Matthews (once each Mathews, Mathewis):—104; Robt — 41; Thos—90, 94, 96, 102
May: Jane—123, 136, 141, 182, 184, 187, 191; Phil—11, 15, 18, 19^2, 21, 23, 24, 30, 31; Thos—46, 98, 101, 115^2, 116^2, 117, 118, 119^6, 120, 121, 122^2, 123^2, 124^2, 128, 131^2, 133, 134^2, 135^3, 138^2, 139
Maylin: Edwd—32
Meacham: Joseph—229
Mead: Jno—18
Mears: Joseph—276
Miller: Ann—190; M^r—5; Nich—53; Thos—3, 4, 8, 10, 14^2, 22, 24; W^m—50, 51^2, 53^3, 54^2, 56, 57, 59^2, 60^2, 61, 62, 63^2, 64, 66, 68, 69, 72, 74, 76, 78, 80, 81, 83, 85, 86^5, 93^2, 95, 96, 101, 103, 105^2, 106, 107, 109, 110, 111, 112, 114^2, 115, 116, 117^2, 118, 120, 121^3, 123^2, 128^3, 129, 130^2, 131, 132^2, 133^6, 134^2, 136, 138^2, 139, 141, 143, 147, 149^2, 151, 153, 154^2, 156, 157^2, 159, 162, 163^2, 166, 167, 168, 169^4, 171, 172, 175, 180, 181^2, 182, 183, 184^3, 186, 187, 188^2
Mills:—69; Eliz^a—285; Nathl—55, 63, 66^4, 69, 76, 83, 86, 89; Widow—86
Minor (Miner, Myner): Jane—144, 145^4; Rich^d—11, 38^2, 40, 41, 43, 50; Thos—255, 266, 283^2, 295, 304, 318^2, 333^2, 354^2, 363^2, 370, 372
Mitchell (once Michel): George—86; Sarah—106, 108
Monorgan: Daniel—9
Montague: M^r—223
Moodie: M^{rs}—1
Moore (Moor, More): — 268^2; Daniel—161, 162; Jno—190, 208, 219, 229, 238, 256, 263; Jno Gilbert—229, 231, 254, 265; Widow—6
Moreing: Michel—294
Morgan: M^{rs}—5
Morris (Morrish): Henry—56^3, 60, 61^3; W^m—316, 335
Mount: Mary—240, 245, 249
Murray: David—339
Musgrove: Edwd—107, 122

M^{c}claran: Daniel—235; Jno—235
McClare: Daniel—234
McClary:—239
M^{c}claron: Mary—240
Macdonald: Chr—268
Mackcartee: Celia—133
Mackentree (Mackendree, Macingtree, Macingdree, Macindree, M^{c}kindree, M^{c}ingdree): Humphry—284^2, 285, 287, 295, 305, 319, 334; Johanna—328, 331^2, 335, 336, 339, 341; M^{rs}—329
Mackenzie (Mackinsie, Mackensie, Mackinza, Mackensey, MacKenzey): Alex^r—270, 273; Doct^r Alex^r—276; Doct^r—262, 263, 265, 271, 274, 279
Macknele: Jane—159
Macktyer: Hugh—57, 58^2, 60, 61^2, 62, 63, 66, 68, 69, 70, 71, 73
Macrary: Guilb—12
McWilliams (Mackwilliams): Eliz^a—21; Isabella—21; Jno—10, 16,

17, 21³, 76, 120, 167², 176, 181, 187, 221; Thoˢ—345; Wᵐ—359

Neale (Neal, Neele, Nealle): Lewis—171, 226; Thoˢ—63, 73, 89, 102; Widow—236
Nelson: Thoˢ—352, 366
Nettles:—300; George—213³; Jnº—231; Mary—210, 211, 212⁴; Margaret—286; Mʳˢ—311; Robᵗ—64, 77, 84, 372, 374, 376; Sollomon—211³; Vicaris (Vicars, Vicares): 223, 236, 252, 276, 277, 279, 282, 286, 288², 290, 291, 293², 297, 299, 300, 302, 306, 309, 311, 312, 315; Wᵐ—210⁵
New: Daniel—261², 263, 265, 267, 269², 270², 271, 274, 275², 277², 278, 279, 280, 281², 282, 283, 285², 286, 287, 288, 289², 290, 291, 292, 293, 294, 296², 297³, 298², 299, 300², 301, 302², 303², 359; Daniel Jʳ—352, 357; Jnº—358²
Nicholson: Francis (Governor)—80, 81
Noden: Doctʳ Hugh—201
Northey: Edwᵈ (Sir)—79², 80
Norton: George—321

Oakes:—17; Jnº—5
Ocaine: Joseph—54
Oliver (once Olyvers): Isaac—37, 70, 72, 118, 119, 134, 137, 138; Nicholas—69; Widow—118, 119, 137, 138; Wᵐ—255

Page: Capᵗ—33; Col. Matthew—63; Mʳ—97², 100²
Pagget: Jnº—128
Paine: Mary—226
Panter: Richᵈ—31
Pass: Jnº—107
Pate (Paytt, once):—149, 150, 173²; Col—8², 9, 11², 13, 15², 17, 18, 97³, 98, 99²; Col. Thoˢ—8, 10, 12, 13, 14², 17, 24, 27, 37, 38; Jnº—53, 82, 87, 88, 90; Majʳ Thoˢ—1, 2, 3, 4, 6, 7; Mʳ—130²
Patrick (once Pattrick): Lawrence (spelled in various ways)—54, 63, 89, 90, 94, 102, 104

Peacock: Mary—91², 92⁴; Samˡ—247²; Sarah—86, 89, 90
Pearse: Richᵈ—12
Peirson: Alice—32; George—33, 35²
Pemberton: Wᵐ—16, 26
Perry: Micajah—72
Petsworth: George—135, 136
Philpots: Benjᵃ—342; Ocly—341
Pointer: Henry—389
Pollard: Mʳˢ—327; Thoˢ—341, 343; Wᵐ—305, 319, 334, 336, 339, 354, 364
Poole (Pool): Daniell—56; Thoˢ—226, 227, 231, 252
Porteus (Poortees, Portues, Portuse, Portegees, Pourtees, Pourtus): Mary—134; Capᵗ Robᵗ—109, 112; Col. Robᵗ—143; Edwᵈ—16², 17, 18, 22², 24², 27, 28, 29, 31, 32, 35, 37, 38, 40, 41²; Madᵐ—120; Madᵐ Margaret—89, 90, 131; Mʳ—19², 23, 24, 25, 136; Robᵗ—46, 53, 69, 82, 85², 88, 89, 90², 91, 93, 95, 102, 123³, 128², 131², 132², 134, 135, 136, 137³, 138, 139, 141, 153, 154, 181, 187, 283, 295, 304, 318
Potter: Jean—342
Potts: Thoˢ—72, 73, 76, 82², 83, 84, 85, 86
Powell: Thoˢ—10, 11, 29, 55²
Power: Jaˢ—297; Mildred—297, 299, 301, 302, 306, 309, 312, 315
Powers:—345, 346; Danˡ—336; Mʳ—265
Pratt: Jnº—94, 95, 96³, 105, 106, 108, 109, 112, 121, 123, 129, 137², 148, 171; J. W.—46
Price: Rev. Mʳ.—366, 368; Rev. Thoˢ—355, 368
Pritchett (Prichard, Pritchet): Jnº—54, 99, 101, 110, 111; Mʳ—5; Wᵐ—1, 4, 8
Procer (once Prosser): Elizᵗʰ—312, 315, 321; Jnº—325, 328; Sarah—325, 328
Pryor (Pryer, once Proyor): Arthur—139; Chrisⁿ—369, 374; Jnº—129³, 148, 149; Mʳ—372, 376; Robᵗ—41², 49, 52, 89, 90, 92, 94, 266

Puller (Pullar): Ann—328², 345; Eliz^th—350, 352, 357, 360, 362, 365, 367, 369, 372, 374; Ja^s—347; Ja^s J^r—321, 335, 336; Ja^s S^r—325; Joseph—345; M^rs—376

Punch:—139

Pursell (Purcel, Purcil, Purcill, Pursel, Pursill): Johanah—362; Henry—132, 134, 139, 149, 224, 256, 315, 319, 358, 364; Peter—369, 373

Purshur (Parssur, Purser, Pursur): Eliz^a—159, 160, 164², 176, 181, 187, 190

Quorrels (once Quarrills): Doyle—103, 104², 114

Ramsey: Capt—12; Capt Thos—3, 4, 10, 14, 17

Ran: W^m—242²

Reade (Read): Benj^a—132; Capt Thos—222, 230, 237, 240, 242, 244, 252; Doct^r—298; Gwyn—237, 238², 240, 242, 244; Jn°—123, 127, 131², 133, 136, 138, 141, 143, 148, 151, 153², 154², 156, 157, 159, 160⁴, 161³, 162, 163, 166, 167, 168, 171, 175, 180², 181, 184, 185, 186, 188, 190, 192², 197, 207, 210, 211⁴, 216, 217, 224, 227, 228, 284; M^r—120, 134; Rev Jn°—258, 259; Rev Robt—317³; Thos—151, 161, 166, 168, 176, 177, 181, 184, 186, 190², 194, 217, 219², 228, 233, 250; Thos J^r—163, 165, 166, 168, 175

Renolds (Rannalds, Reanalds, Rennalds): Ja^s—99, 101, 110, 111; M^r—176

Rice: Jacob—271

Richardson: W^m—25

Robbins: Capt Steven—187

Roberts (once Robberts): Mary—103, 107, 114

Robertson: Wil—80

Robin: Free—287

Robinson: Benj^a—364, 371; Jn°—354; Maj^r Jn°—370; W^m—196, 209⁴

Robottom (Rowbottom, Roboton): —217; Alex^r Young—215; Ruth—207²

Rock: Dorothy—152²; Eliz^th—147²

Roane (Roan, Rhoan, Rone, Royne): Alex^r—173, 189, 193, 197, 217, 220, 224, 225, 228, 230, 233, 238, 239, 240, 245, 248, 254, 256, 259; Chas—10, 12², 14², 24², 26, 27, 150, 219, 257, 259, 260³, 262, 263, 264, 267, 268; M^r—15; Warner—319; W^m—99, 101, 110, 111²

Rootes (Roots): Capt Jn°—312, 313, 314, 316, 323, 327, 328, 337; Jn°—310, 311, 322, 324, 327, 342; M^r—326

Rose: Jn°—31

Ross (Roos, Rosse): Christian—132, 134, 136³, 138, 139, 142, 196; Edwd Carter—196, 199, 200; Francis—320; Thos—186, 199, 212, 216

Rosum: Dorothy—33

Roundree: W^m—286

Routon: Jn°—221, 234

Row: Benj^a—337; Edwd—44; M^r—310

Royston (Roystone): Conquest—284, 295; Jn°—46, 74, 77, 82, 90, 93², 95², 96², 101, 103², 104, 105², 106³, 107, 110², 111, 112, 114², 116, 120, 121, 123, 124, 127, 128², 131, 133, 134, 136, 138, 139, 141, 143, 148, 151, 154², 156, 157², 159, 163², 166, 167, 168, 171, 175, 177, 180³, 181², 182³, 183, 184, 185, 188, 189, 190, 194, 196, 200², 205, 206², 207, 214, 217, 219², 220, 222, 223, 225, 227, 228, 230, 233, 235², 236, 237, 238, 239², 240, 241, 242, 243, 244, 245, 247, 248, 250, 251, 253, 254, 257², 258, 259², 261², 263, 264, 265, 267²,, 268, 271, 272, 273³, 274², 275, 277, 350; M^r—12, 41, 280; Rich^d—296; Richd Wyatt—303, 305, 334, 354, 361², 362², 363, 365², 366², 367, 368, 369, 370², 371, 372², 373⁴, 374², 375, 376, 377², 378, 380², 381²; Thos—1, 3, 8, 9, 10, 12, 14, 15, 19, 28, 29, 35, 37³, 38, 39, 40², 41, 42, 43², 44, 46, 47, 49, 51

Rumball:—1, 5, 8, 11, 15, 17, 20, 22, 24, 29, 49; Jn°—31, 33, 35, 38, 41, 43, 51, 54
Ryley: Jn°—239

Sadler: Elizth—292, 297, 299, 303, 306; Thos—279, 280, 282, 286
Sallis: Saml—9, 11
Salmon: Jn°—275
Sampson:—97, 98
Sanders: Edwd—316, 321^2; Elizth —194, 195^2; Sarah—196, 209^2
Sandiland: Masdrye—107
Sandling: Mary—142
Sarnderlens: Mary—146^2
Saunlings: Mary—116
Sawyer: Jn° Smith—171, 196, 223
Schools: George—164
Scott: Jn°—284^2, 292, 296^2, 298^2, 300, 302^2, 303^2, 304^2, 308^2, 310, 313^2, 314^3, 317, 318, 320, 323^4, 324, 327^2, 328, 330, 333, 335^2, 337, 338, 340, 344; M^r—326; Thos— 120^3, 147, 149, 172, 197, 202, 203, 214, 224, 332
Sears: W^m—334, 355^3, 356^2, 358^2, 359, 360^2, 362, 363, 368, 370, 373^2, 375, 376,
Seaton: Bayley (spelled in various ways)—127, 238, 242, 244^2, 248, 250, 251, 252^3, 253, 254^2, 255^2, 258, 260, 269, 284^2, 334, 355; Capt Bayley—270, 273^2, 277, 279, 281^2, 282, 296, 305, 320; M^r—140, 238, 262; Rich^d—110, 112, 123^2, 124, 125, 127, 128, 132^2, 133^2, 134^2, 136, 137, 138, 139, 140, 141, 143, 151^2, 157, 161
Shackelford (Shacleford): Jn°— 89, 90, 93; Line—349; M^r—12, 19; Roger—10, 14, 16, 17, 18, 19, 22, 24, 26^2, 27
Shanks: W^m—271
Shaw: Elizth—352, 355, 357, 359, 362; M^{rs}—357
Shedd:—Thos—6
Shepard (Sheapard, Shepherd, Shephard, Sheppard): Jn°—166, 286, 288, 291, 302, 306, 309, 348, 353, 360, 362, 365, 366
Sherard (Serrerd, Sherd, Shurrard, Shurrad, Shurred, Shurrud):

Mary—119, 137^2, 138, 152, 163, 176^4, 181, 183, 187, 190^2; Eliz^a— 163; Widow—118
Shermer: Jn°—266^2, 267, 268, 269, 270^3, 271, 272^2, 273^2, 274^2, 275, 277; M^r—272
Shillerd (Shillard, Shellard, Shellerd): Elianer (spelled in various ways)—119, 128^2, 141, 152; Widow—118, 137, 138
Shirley: W^m—9
Simco (Simcoe): Francess—170^2; Jn°—128, 133, 137, 138; R.—27; Rich^d—11, 15, 17, 19, 22, 24, 29, 30, 31^3, 33^2, 34, 35^2, 38, 41, 43, 49, 52, 54, 56; Sarah—123
Simkins: Widow—118, 119
Simmons (Simons, Simmonds, Semonds): Edwd—6, 37, 172, 198^2, 201; Frances—198, 202^5; M^r—97^3, 98, 99, 100
Sinar (Siner): Jn°—234^2; Widow —184, 233, 241
Singleton: Henry—120
Sins: Ja^s—280; W^m—280
Skelton (Skilton): Ja^s — 156^2, 157^2, 160, 161^2, 164, 166^2, 167, 168^4
Smith: Augustine—46, 100, 101, 106, 107^2, 108, 110, 112^2, 113, 114^2, 115, 117, 118^3, 119^6, 120, 121^2, 123^2, 128^3, 131^3, 132, 133, 134, 136, 138, 139^3, 141, 143, 148, 151^3, 154^2, 156, 157^2, 159, 162, 163^2, 166, 167, 168, 171, 174^2, 175, 176, 180, 181^2, 182^2, 183, 184, 185^3, 186^3, 187, 188^2, 190^2, 191^2, 192, 194, 196^2, 198, 199^3, 200^3, 205, 206, 207, 208, 217^2, 219^2, 220, 221, 223, 224, 225, 228^2, 230, 233, 234, 235, 236^4, 237, 238^2, 240, 241^3, 242, 243^5, 244^2, 245^2, 246^4, 247^2, 248, 249^2, 250, 251^2, 252, 254^2, 255, 256, 257, 260, 261^2, 264, 265^2, 267, 268, 269, 270, 271, 272^2, 273^3, 274^2, 275, 279, 283, 284^2, 285^2, 287, 289^4, 290, 291^2, 292, 296, 319, 323, 327, 328, 329, 330, 334, 337, 338; Capt—237; Capt Jn°—35, 37, 38, 40, 41^2, 42, 43^2, 44, 47, 49, 53, 109, 110, 235; Col. Jn°—6; Ezekiel—112, 113^3, 114, 116, 132,

134; Jane—235; Jn°—25, 27, 39, 42, 43, 46, 95, 115, 180, 184, 189, 196, 207, 213, 223, 224, 226, 305; Jn° (Sawyer)—171, 196, 223; Katherine—184; Lawrence (spelled in a variety of ways)—190, 192^2, 193^4; Madam—55; Madam Mary—63, 67, 70^2, 114, 120; M^r—115, 184; Mrs Mary — 51; Nicholas—43, 44, 50, 51^2, 53^3, 54, 56, 58, 59^2, 60^2, 61, 62, 63, 64^2, 66, 68^2, 72, 74, 76, 78, 80, 86, 88^2, 90, 93, 96, 101, 103, 105, 106, 109, 110, 111, 112, 116, 118, 120, 121^2, 123; Peter—50; Philip—67^6, 70^3, 109, 112, 123, 124^4, 125, 127, 128, 131, 133, 134, 135, 136^2, 137^3, 138, 139^2, 141^2, 142^2, 148, 151, 154^2, 157^2, 163; Sarah—201^2; Widow—54, 233, 234^2; W^m—34, 231

Smithing: Francis—4, 10

Soles: Jn°—316, 321, 325^2; M^{rs}—328; Mrs Mary—329

Spann: Mary—362; Mrs Mary—365

Spinke: Paul—9

Spotswood: Hugh—370

Spratt (Sprat):—279, 290; Ann—279; Christian—279, 280; Doct^r—364; Doct^r Robt—354; Jn°—233, 279^2; Mary—252, 262, 267, 268, 269, 274^2, 276

Stannum: W^m—9

Stanton (Stantton): Margrett—69^2

Staples: Jn°—122

Stark: Elizth—72

Starrs: Ellisabeth—69

Stears (Steers):—263^2, 278, 279, 286, 288, 291, 293^2, 296^2, 299; Fra^s — 268; Joseph—262, 263, 280^2, 281, 282, 300, 302, 306, 309, 310, 321, 325, 336, 339; Susanah—226^2, 234; Widow—221, 223, 226, 229^2, 231^2

Steer: Jn°—75^3, 76

Stendham: Thos—25

Steward: Margrit (Margery)—42^3, 43^2, 44, 49, 52, 55

Stichall (Stichalls, Stichal, Stichel, Stichell, Stickel, Stitchel, Stit-chell): George—89, 90, 94^2, 96, 102, 103, 106, 108^2, 116, 120, 132, 134, 139, 141, 152, 154, 159, 163, 175, 181, 182, 187, 190

Stretchey: Doct^r—260

Stripling-Powers: Jn° — 343; Ja^s—343

Stubblefield (Stublefield): Jn°—215^3, 216, 217, 223; Mary—325

Stubbs: Capt Jn°—277^2, 279, 283, 285, 287, 289, 290, 292^3, 293, 294^3, 295, 296, 298^2, 302, 304^2, 308; Francis—283, 290, 292^2, 294^2, 297^2, 298^2, 300^2, 301^2, 303, 304^2, 306, 307^3, 308, 310, 313^2, 314, 317, 318, 323^2, 327, 328, 332; Jn°—68, 87, 98, 101, 129, 149, 153, 281, 306, 323, 338; Jn° J^r—65, 74, 284, 293, 304; Jn°. S^r—65, 337, 370^2; M^r—267, 272; M^{rs}—187, 224, 237; Peter—295, 304, 364, 371; Thos—127, 225, 231, 233, 263, 266, 270, 271^2, 272^2, 273, 274, 275^2, 276^3, 277^2, 278^2, 281, 283, 285, 287, 288, 289, 290, 292, 294, 296, 298^2, 300, 302, 304, 306, 308^2, 310, 311, 313, 317, 333; W^m—331

Swabbsone: Jn°—4

Swan:—18

Swepson (Swepston): Jane—119, 128^2; Thos—100, 101, 120, 208; Widow—118, 137, 138

Symmer (Symer, Symers, Semors, Semer, Semers, Simmer, Simer): Doct^r—226, 231, 234, 240, 254, 260^2, 262, 263, 267, 270, 286^2, 288

Syms: George—75^6, 76

Taler: Mary—160

Taliaferro [spelled in a variety of ways]: Phillip—352, 357; Rich^d—319, 333^2, 337^2, 338, 340, 342^2, 343, 344, 346, 347, 353, 354, 363, 364, 366, 367, 368, 369, 370, 371, 372, 373^3, 374, 375^2, 376^2, 377, 378, 379, 380^2, 381

Taunton:—22; Thos—15, 17, 20, 21^2, 24, 26

Taylor: Chas—54

Terry: Easter—205; Widow—181, 184

Thomas (Tomas, Tommas): Margret—166, 244, 245, 249, 254²; Martha—141, 158, 159; Mary—299, 301, 302, 306, 309², 312², 315², 320², 325, 328²; Rowland—4

Thompson: Chaˢ—286

Thorne: Mʳ—172²; Mʳˢ—4

Thornton (Thorntone): Anne (Mʳˢ)—249, 251; Capᵗ—282, 285, 290; Capᵗ Wᵐ—277², 279, 280, 282, 283, 285, 290²; Francis—127, 129, 141, 148, 152, 154, 159, 161, 163, 164, 165, 171, 175², 177, 180, 181², 182, 183, 184, 188, 190, 192, 194, 196, 198, 205, 206, 207, 214, 215, 217², 219, 220, 222, 223, 225, 227, 228, 230, 232, 233, 235, 236, 237, 238, 240⁶, 241², 242, 243, 244, 245³, 246, 247, 251; Jnº—224, 237, 256, 266, 273, 275², 276², 277², 278², 279, 281, 283, 285, 287, 296; Mʳˢ Mary—259; Meaux—373, 379, 381, 382, 384, 385, 386², 387, 388²; Mʳ—12, 137, 149; Mʳ Jʳ—27, 30; Mʳˢ—1, 8; Presley—371; Seth—114, 148, 194³, 195, 196², 198, 200², 203, 205², 206, 207², 208, 214, 219², 222, 223, 225, 227, 228, 229, 230, 232, 235, 236, 238, 240, 242, 243, 244, 245, 246, 247, 248, 249, 250², 251², 252, 254², 255, 256, 258; Sterling (Starling)—354, 355, 356, 359, 363, 370, 372, 373², 375², 376, 377, 379², 381; Thoˢ—266; Wᵐ—1, 2, 4, 16, 29, 32, 46, 65, 71, 80, 81, 83², 85, 89, 93², 94, 95, 96, 101, 103, 105, 106, 110, 114², 116³, 118, 120, 123, 129, 132, 134, 139, 148, 171, 191, 237, 248, 249, 250, 253, 354, 255², 257, 258, 259, 260², 261, 262², 263, 266, 267, 269, 270, 278, 281², 283, 295², 318, 333, 337, 338², 342, 346², 347, 348; Wᵐ Jʳ—12, 14³, 17, 19, 28, 31, 33, 34, 36, 37, 38, 39, 40, 41, 46, 47, 49, 50, 51, 53², 55, 57, 58, 65, 68, 71, 76, 78, 84², 86³, 87, 88², 89, 90, 171, 197, 216³, 233, 247, 304; Wᵐ Sʳ—3, 8, 10, 14², 17, 19, 22, 27, 28, 31, 33, 35, 37, 38, 40, 47, 50, 53, 54, 56, 57, 58, 63, 68, 76, 88, 224; Wᵐ the Younger—256²

Thrift: Thoˢ—371; Wᵐ—364, 371

Throckmorton (Throcmorton): Albion—46, 97, 100, 105², 106³, 107, 108², 109, 112², 113, 114, 115, 123, 129, 138; Col.—288; Jnº—2, 3, 8, 12², 148, 163, 165, 166², 175, 176, 177, 180, 190, 194², 205, 206², 207, 214², 219², 220, 223, 225, 235, 295, 318; Mʳ—115, 143; Mʳˢ—15

Thruston: Capᵗ—311, 312; Chaˢ Mynns—310², 311, 312, 324, 327; Capᵗ Chaˢ Mynns—313², 314³, 315, 317², 318, 319, 322³, 323², 324; Col. Chaˢ M—370; Rev. Chaˢ Mynns—330³, 335², 337, 338², 340; Mʳ—326; Rev Mʳ—332, 333, 339

Thurston: Jnº—266; Capᵗ Robᵗ—;ł42; Seth—130², 150², 174, 180, 185; Wᵐ—84, 87

Timberlack: Richᵈ—104

Timberlick: Jnº—176

Titbery: Mary—274²

Tomkies (Tomkees): Chaˢ—83, 121, 132, 139, 346, 348², 349, 350, 353, 364, 374, 377², 378; Capᵗ Chaˢ—371, 372, 375, 377; Doctʳ Chaˢ—103, 104; Chaˢ Jʳ—364; Francis—322, 339, 353; Col. Francis—337, 341; Majʳ—298, 301, 303, 310, 313

Trivilion (Trivillion, Trivillon): Ann—262, 263, 265; Jnº—259

Tryplow (once Tryplowe): Ann—143, 152, 154, 159, 163, 175

Underwood: Mʳ—56

Upshaw: Wᵐ—46, 55, 65, 76, 77², 78, 80, 81, 86², 88, 90, 91, 92, 93², 94, 95², 96, 103, 105, 106, 107, 110, 111², 112, 116², 123, 132

Van Ittoon: Godfrey—72

Vicaris (Vicares): Rev. Thoˢ—1², 2, 3, 4², 5, 8², 10, 11², 12, 13, 14², 15³, 17³, 18², 19³, 20, 22², 23, 24², 25, 27², 29³, 30, 31², 32², 33³, 34, 35², 36, 37, 38², 39, 40, 41², 42, 43², 44, 46, 48, 49; Mʳˢ, Mʳˢ Dorothy—48², 49, 51

Vinson: Eliz^th—33

Walden: Lewis—350
Walford: Doct^r—173, 174, 181, 183; Doct^r Edwd—159³, 163², 164², 176², 190; Edwd—152²; M^r—130
Walker: Eliz^th—36
Waller: Jn°—199
Wallis (Walles, Wollis): Thos—231, 236, 239
Ward:—245; Ja^s—128; Jn°—231
Ware: Jn°—266
Warner: Col.—6, 18; Eliz^a—155, 159, 160, 164³, 176, 221; Jacob—9; Robt—1, 5, 6, 8
Washer: Cathrine—312, 315, 321, 325; Hurt—353, 360, 362, 366; Jn°—348; Nancy—329; Rich^d—350; Sarah—326, 329², 350, 352
Washington: Capt John—184, 186, 192², 196, 206, 214, 220, 222²; Jn°—143², 151, 157, 161, 162, 163², 164, 165, 166², 171, 175, 180, 188, 269, 270²; Maj^r—265, 267, 269; Maj^r Jn°—230, 235, 242, 244, 245, 247, 248, 251, 252, 253, 254, 257, 258, 259, 261, 269, 270, 273; M^r—326, 332, 333; Warner—275, 276, 277², 279, 280², 281, 287, 291, 294, 296, 298², 302, 304, 305, 306, 310, 311, 313, 314², 322, 323², 324, 327², 328, 330², 337, 340
Waters (Watters, Warters): Susanah—94³, 103, 108, 152; Thos—51, 54; Walter—46, 64, 90, 91², 92, 93
Watkins: Ja^s—158²
Wats: W^m—158³, 159
Watson: Maj^r Jonathan—344, 348, 349², 351², 352, 353², 355
Webb: W^m—176
West: Ann—297, 312, 315², 321, 331; Dianah—325, 328; Edwd—166, 184; M^rs—374, 376; Rich^d—175, 224; Susanah—201; Thos—138; Widow—205
Wethers: Eliz^th—195, 204²
White: Jn°—278, 279, 286, 288, 290, 293, 297, 299, 300, 306; Lawrance—374; Symon—231
Whitehead, Robt—83

Whitehorn (Whithorn): Edwd—198, 202, 203⁵; Jn°—139
Whiteseed (Whitseeds): Ellis—239; Saml—90, 122, 128, 134, 139, 152, 155², 160, 164², 176, 181
Whiting (Whiteing, Whitting): Fran—120; Henry—319, 327, 333, 335, 337², 338, 340, 344; Thos—180, 185, 197
Whitlock: Ja^s—36
Whitrence: Eliz^th—226, 227, 231
Whittamore: Jn°—16
Whitus (Whittus): Saml—231, 249
Whittew, Saml—223
Willcocks (Wilcocks): Jn°—132, 152, 154, 160, 163, 176, 181, 221; Sheriff—134
Willett: Ann—6
Willis: Capt Henry—138², 139, 143, 151, 154², 157, 161; Henry—127; Francis—323; Maj^r—189; Maj^r Henry—176, 181, 188, 189, 191, 192, 194; Michael—252; M^r—310; Widow—271
Willkins: Eleazer—354
Wills: Jn°—188
Wilson: Jn°—139
Wisdom (Wisdome, Wisdum): M^r—1; Thos—2, 6; Widow—54
With: M^iss—335
Wood: Charity—108, 122²; Jn°—319, 331, 334; Lewis—364, 371, 382², 383, 384, 386², 387, 388³; M^r—389; Rachel—357, 361; Robt—103, 114
Wooten: Thos—181
Wright (once Right):—296; Ann—325; Francis—84², 85³; Jn°—350; Mary—73; Rich^d—128, 354, 364; Thos—102, 279, 334; Widow—83; W^m—287, 293, 296, 299, 300, 302, 306, 309, 311, 315, 320
Wyatt (Wyat, Wiatt, Wiat): Capt—318²; Conquest—28, 33, 34, 35, 36, 38, 39, 40, 43, 46², 47, 51, 54², 55, 59, 60, 63, 72, 78, 80, 81, 83², 84², 85, 86², 87, 88, 89, 90, 91, 93², 94, 174, 189, 194³, 195, 196, 200², 205, 206², 207, 208⁴, 209, 211, 212⁴, 213, 214, 216, 217, 218², 219⁴, 220, 221², 222⁴, 223², 225,

226², 227, 240, 242, 244, 245, 252, 257, 259, 263, 265, 267, 269, 272, 273, 274, 284, 296, 309; Capt Conquest—275, 277; Edwd—210⁵, 212, 214, 224, 258², 260, 264², 265, 266, 270³; Francis—110, 111, 123¹⁰, 124⁵, 125, 127, 131¹⁵, 133⁵, 136⁵, 139⁵, 140⁵, 141⁷, 143, 151³, 153², 159, 171, 175, 180, 181, 184, 188, 190, 191, 192³, 194³, 195⁴, 196, 198, 200, 203, 207², 208, 222, 256; Ja^s—197, 206, 214, 224², 256, 371, 379², 380², 381², 382², 383, 384, 385, 386³, 388³; Jn°—175, 197, 284, 296², 297, 300, 303, 305, 318, 337, 338², 340², 341, 342², 344³, 345, 346, 347, 349², 351², 353², 355, 358, 360², 361, 362, 363, 366, 367, 369, 370, 371, 372, 373², 377; Capt Jn°—296, 298³, 300, 302, 304, 305, 308², 310, 311, 313², 314, 315, 317, 320, 323³, 324, 327², 328, 329, 331, 335, 337; Jn° S^r—334; M^r—35², 91, 221, 223, 267; Peter —320, 334, 355⁴, 356³, 357, 358, 359, 360³, 361, 366, 382, 383², 386, 388³; W^m—371

Yaman (Yeaman, Yannan): Sarah —154, 167, 175, 181
Yard: M^r—102; Robt—28, 29², 30, 31², 32², 33², 35, 37, 38, 39², 40, 41, 43, 46, 47, 49, 50, 53², 55, 56, 57, 59, 64, 65, 68, 74, 76, 80, 82, 86, 88, 90, 93
Yates (Yeats *once* Yats): Mary— 141, 159², 164³; Robt—363, 366², 367, 368³, 369², 370, 372, 373, 374, 376, 377²; Rev. Robt—257, 260, 263², 264, 265², 267², 269², 270, 271³, 272, 273², 274, 275², 276, 277², 279², 280, 281², 282², 283, 285², 286, 287, 288, 290, 291, 292, 293, 294, 296², 297, 298³, 299², 300², 301, 302², 303, 304, 306³, 308⁴, 311², 313²; Rev M^r (of Middlesex)—258, 259; Rev. W^m —313², 314, 315; Widow—314
Young: Rev. George—57², 58, 59, 62, 63

Geographic Index

Abingdon Church:—386
Alexanders's Quarter (Capt.):—129, 149; (Madam):—172
Attapotomoys (Attopotomoys) Swamp:—97, 98^2

Baker's (Doctor Baker's) Swamp:—130^2, 150^2
Bennitt's (Bennit's) Creek:—37^2, 96, 98^2, 171^2, 172
Branch between Mr. Hansford's and John Pryor's:—129, 148, 149
Bridge (i. e. Dragon Bridge):—130
Bridge over "ye Runn" (i. e. Dragon Run):—38
Brierry (Bryerry, Bryery) Branch:—37, 130, 149, 173
Bristol (England):—21, 26

Carolina:—139^2
Chiscak (Chiscake, Chistake) Mill:—97^2, 100^2
Christ Church Parish:—310
Claybank:—237
Claybank Creek:—96, 98

Dragon, The:—305, 319
Dragon Bridge:—37, 97, 99, 130, 150^2, 173, 174
Dragon Bridge Road:—37
Dragon (Draggon) Road:—97^4, 99^4, 130, 150
Dragon Swamp:—284, 295

Eastermas Creek:—37^2
England:—112, 187, 205, 284, 317, 318, 324, 326

Ferry, y^e:—37
Ferry Road:—97, 99

Gloucester County:—30, 59, 60, 61, 66, 67, 70, 81, 82, 84, 92, 113, 122, 124, 135, 144, 145, 146, 147, 157, 161, 169, 170, 178^2, 185, 193, 195, 198, 199, 202, 203, 204, 209, 210, 211, 212, 213, 215, 216, 374
Great Britain:—236, 258

James City:—57

James Town:—32
Jones Creek:—37^2, 97, 98^2

King and Queen County:—44, 52, 53, 56, 234, 235, 283
Kingston Parish:—290

Lewis' Mill (Coll. John):—131, 151, 174, 175
Lewis' Mill Swamp (Coll. John):—131, 151

Middlesex [County]—258
Mill on Jones Creek:—37
Morgan's Neck:—13

Neck, The:—129, 149, 172

Orange County:—268

Page's Quarter (Mr.):—97^2, 100
Parradice Bridge Swamp:—37^2
Pate's Mill (Coll.):—97^2, 98, 99
Pate's Mill Dam (Coll. Thos.):—38
Pate's (Pats, Patts, Paytt's) Mill Swamp (Coll., Mr.):—97^2, 98, 99, 130, 149, 150, 173^2
Pate's Quarter (Col. Thos.):—37
Peanketank River:—97^2, 99, 100
Poplar Spring:—1, 3, 4, 5, 7^3, 17, 20, 27, 45, 156^2, 157^2, 160, 166, 167, 208, 233, 242
Poplar Spring Branch:—37
Poplar Spring Church:—21, 40^2, 43, 47, 48^2, 50, 52, 53, 68, 168, 219, 247, 248, 258
Poplar Spring Road:—44
Poplar Spring Swamp:—129, 130, 149^2, 172^2
Poropotanck Creek:—354
Poropotank (Potopotank Swamp):—97, 99
Purton Church:—43

Richmond:—377^2, 378, 384, 385
Richland (Rich Land) Swamp:—97^3, 99^2, 100, 130, 131, 150, 151, 174^3

Richland (Richlans) Swamp Road: —37, 38
Road to the Dragon Bridge:—130, 150, 173, 174

Sampson's Quarter:—97, 98
Simmon's (Simons) Quarter (Mr.):—97³, 98, 99, 100
Stratton Major Parish:—48, 52, 56, 280, 281, 350

Thorne's Mill Swamp (Mr.):—172²

Thornton's Mill Swamp (Mr.):—129², 149²
Totopomoy Swamp:—122
Totopottomoy's Creek:—37²
Turck(s) Ferry:—44, 45
Turks Ferry Road:—97, 99

Virginia:—57

Walford's Swamp (Doctor):—173², 174
Ware (Wear) Parish:—45, 96, 97², 98³, 161, 163, 323
Williamsburg(h):—79, 80, 280, 287

Index of Topics

Abjuration, oath of:—124, 194
Act (for Incorporating Prot. Episc. Church):—377
 (of Assembly):—79, 179, 184, 189, 206, 214, 250, 258, 351, 358
 (of Parliament):—45, 53, 55
Acting Church Warden:—301
Addition to the Church:—72
Additional Tobacco Law:—123
Address to the Governor:—318, 324
Agents notes:—124
Agreement between Vestry and Contractor:—157
Allegiance, oath of:—45, 53, 55, 124, 194, 219
Altar piece:—247, 248, 252, 253
Anne, Queen:—84, 92, 113
Annual Meeting of Vestry:—29
"Antient & not able to labour":—188
Apprentice:—227
"Art of Coopery":—56, 61
"Art ____ of a bricklayer":—199
Articles, breach of:—26
 The Thirty Nine:—25
Assembly, Act of:—79, 179, 184, 189, 206, 214, 250, 258, 351, 358
 The General:—179, 250, 377

Bacon:—12^{13}, 13
Banns of matrimony:—14, 58
Barn at the Glebe:—338
"barr^{11}": corne to y^e Glasier":—120
Bastard (child, children):—1, 2, 4^2, 5, 7, 8, 17, 18, 20^2, 23^2, 30, 31, 32, 34, 35, 38^2, 51, 63, 86, 89^2, 90^2, 107, 141, 152, 155, 158, 159^2, 164, 166, 176, 187, 190, 192, 193, 199, 227, 231, 234, 279^2, 283, 286^2, 290, 300, 312, 315, 316, 321
Bedding for the Poor:—329
Beef:—13, 120, 329
Benches:—54, 89, 115, 217, 262, 285, 303
Bequests (of various sorts to the parish or to the poor):—10, 16, 53, 338

Better Support of Clergy, Act for the:—258
Bible, gift to the Church of a:—25
 reference to in indentures:—84, 113, 122, 124, 136, 144, 145, 146, 147, 158, 162, 169, 170, 178, 179, 186, 193, 195, 199, 200, 202, 203, 204, 209, 210, 211, 212, 213, 215, 216
"bigg with Child":—42
Bill for 500 lbs of Tobacco:—119
Bills of Exchange:—72
Binding out (children, poor children, orphan children, bastard children):—2, 7, 35, 56, 58, 60, 61, 66, 67, 71, 84, 91, 92, 93, 104, 142, 144, 145, 146, 147, 157, 161, 167, 169, 178^2, 192, 193, 194, 195, 196, 198^3, 199, 201, 202, 203, 204, 209, 210, 211, 212, 213, 215, 216, 227^2, 232^2, 235^3, 236, 268, 283, 300^2
Binding out Orphans, laws relating to:—113
Bishop, Consecration of a:—378
 of London:—81, 317, 324
Bonds with conditions to bind contractor:—156
Books (and other articles) for the Church:—5, 217, 342, 343
"Both churches":—10
Breach of Articles:—26
Bread and wine for the Communion:—234, 241, 265, 271, 274, 275, 277, 279, 281, 286, 288, 290, 292, 296, 298, 300, 302, 306, 308, 311, 315, 320, 325, 328, 330, 335, 338, 340, 342, 345, 347, 349, 352, 357, 359, 367, 372, 373, 376, 385
Brick Church:—39, 40
Bricklayer:—196, 198, 199
Brick wall (around the Church):—201, 208, 218, 219
Bricks of Glebe House:—375
"Bringing two women to bed":—331
Broom:—307
Brush:—307
Bucket for the Church:—343

Building the Church:—5²
  a New Church:—155
  wall around Church:—201, 208, 218, 219
Burying (poor people):—231, 233, 275, 294, 303, 316, 321, 328, 339

Caley's orphan:—15, 18
Canons of Church of England, Book of:—25
Care of the poor:—49, 51, 52
Carriage by oxen:—1
Carrying the chain:—120
Cart:—259
Carting:—49, 86, 357
Casements for Church windows:—69
Cast action:—1
Cedar posts:—1
Chain, carrying the:—120
Chairs and table for Vestry House:—332
Chapel, not to be built:—39
Cherubin, drawing the:—11
Chimney(s):—105, 114
Church, a new, to be built:—39
  addition to the:—72
  at Poplar Spring:—1, 3, 5, 27, 167
  Bible to be sent to England to be rebound:—205
  building the:—5, 155
  cleaning the:—181²
  gates:—335
  land:—142, 152
  new:—156², 157², 160, 161, 165, 166, 167², 168, 177
  of England:—82, 314, 317², 318, 324²
  of Petsworth:—236
  painting the:—11
  plate to be delivered by retiring Church Warden to successor:—355
  "rebuilding of yᵉ old":—41
  tarring the:—15
  to be repaired:—109
  yard, pailing the:—11, 118
Church Warden(s), as Collectors of Parish Levy:—2, 7, 9, 16, 18, 22, 23, 26, 28, 30, 32, 34, 36, 40, 42, 45, 50, 53, 56, 64, 70, 74, 77, 83, 87, 91, 95, 103, 105, 109, 117, 140, 142, 153, 155, 161, 165, 177, 183, 188, 192, 208, 218, 222, 227, 230, 232, 235, 239, 241, 246, 250, 255, 262, 264
  three for the parish:—3
  to serve term of two years:—4, 7
  to agree with workmen to do work on church:—4
  continued in office:—10
  to cover Church with shingles:—16
  (nearest) to be notified by Inhabitants wishing to entertain foreigners or persons of another parish:—19
  two (instead of three) appointed:—26
  to sign indentures binding out orphans:—56
  ordered to bind out children:—91, 93
  ordered to procure copies of laws about processioning and binding out orphans:—113
  ordered to bring suit to recover legacy to the poor:—118
  to make up accounts with the parish:—121
  give bonds to Vestry for payment of Agents Notes:—124
  to bind out bastard child:—158
  asks protection in execution of his office:—192
  to petition Court to relocate a road:—195
  to petition Court to move poor people back to their home parishes:—195
  empowered to make agreements relative to taking poor children off the parish:—330
"Clarrit":—107
Clearing away trash around Church:—167, 176
Clergy, Act for better support of:—258
Clergyman elected "Lecturer":—386
Clerke:—1, 5², 8, 11, 15, 17, 19, 35, 38, 54², 102, 103, 107
Clerk of the Church:—22, 24, 29, 31, 33, 58, 72, 73², 76, 139, 141,

143, 152, 154, 159, 163, 175, 181, 183, 186, 217, 220, 225, 228, 230, 233, 240, 245, 248, 254, 261^2, 263, 366, 367, 369, 372, 373^2, 380, 383
Clerk of the Church and Vestry:—
41, 43, 52, 56, 57, 63, 69, 83, 86, 88^2, 90, 93, 114, 116, 120, 131, 134, 186, 190, 200, 207, 217, 271, 274, 275, 277, 279, 281, 285, 287, 292, 296, 298, 300, 302, 303, 306, 308, 311, 315, 320, 325, 328, 330, 335, 338, 340, 342, 344, 347, 349, 352, 357, 359, 361, 376, 387
Clerk of the Council:—80
Clerk of the County:—228
Clerk of the Court:—338, 367
Clerk of Gloucester Court:—154, 160, 163
Clerk of the Parish:—25, 198, 211
Clerk of the Parish and Vestry:—49
Clerk of the Vestry:—18, 19^3, 21, 23, 24, 25^3, 29, 30, 31, 34, 35, 46, 54, 60, 61, 62, 70, 71, 88, 93, 107, 115, 117, 118, 123, 124, 128, 129, 133, 135, 137^3, 138^2, 139, 142^2, 143^2, 144, 145, 146, 148, 149^3, 150^3, 151^2, 152, 154, 156, 158, 159, 161, 163, 168, 169, 170, 175, 177, 181, 183, 193, 195, 199, 202, 203, 204, 209, 210, 212, 213, 215, 216, 220, 225, 228, 231, 233, 239, 240, 245, 248, 254, 259, 262, 263, 265, 267, 269, 360, 361, 362^2, 365, 366, 367, 369, 372, 373^2, 375, 380, 384, 385^2, 389
   to sign indentures:—30, 58, 117, 142, 144
   to enter the various Oaths in the Vestry Book:—124
   to record returns of processionings and of juries:—148, 171
   to provide bonds with conditions binding contactor:—156
   salary of:—183
   to be paid 5 shillings per pair of indentures made:—228
   to employ a lawyer to bring suit for recovery of money:—313
Clerk (or Reader) to be paid for publishing banns of matrimony:—14

Clerk's Fees:—20, 23, 24, 31, 33, 35, 52, 63, 73, 76, 89, 94, 120, 132, 186, 225
Clothing for the poor:—263, 287, 332, 336^3, 345, 353
Cloths for Communion Table:—9
Coffin:—83, 190^4, 231^2, 233, 239, 240, 249, 274, 328, 331, 336^2, 342, 349, 350, 366^2
Collector:—262, 264, 266, 268, 270, 272, 275, 276^2,, 277, 278, 281, 282^2, 287^2, 288^3, 289, 291^2, 292, 294^2, 297, 300, 302, 303, 307, 310, 312^2, 316^2, 322^2, 326, 327, 330^2, 332^3, 336^2, 337, 340^2, 342, 344, 346^3, 348^3, 350, 353^3, 358^2, 359, 361^3, 362, 363, 365, 366, 367, 368, 369^2, 370^2, 372, 374^2, 376, 377^2, 380
   resigns his office:—358
Column under the Gallery:—267
Committees for various purposes:—260, 377, 378^3
Common Prayer, Book of:—25, 69, 205
Communion, The:—262, 263
   Bread and wine:—221, 234, 241, 265, 271, 274, 275, 277, 279, 281, 286, 288, 290, 292, 296, 298, 300, 302, 306, 308, 311, 315, 320, 325, 328, 330, 335, 338, 340, 342, 345, 347, 349, 352, 357, 359, 367, 370, 373, 376
   table cushion and cloths:—9
   Wine:—1, 11^2, 15^2, 23, 24^2, 154, 160, 164, 187, 217^2, 226, 229, 231, 239, 246, 249, 255, 260
Complaint of being "Very Antient and past his Labour":—117, 118
Concealment of Tythables:—26
Consecration of a Bishop:—378
Constables:—3
Contract:—74, 75, 85, 168
Contractor:—167, 208, 219, 220
Convention:—378
   for Regulating and Appointing Vestries:—382
   General:—384, 385
   of Clergy and Lay Deputies:—387
   of Prot. Episcop. Church:—375, 377^2

Cooper, art and skill of a:—61
Coopery, art of:—56
Copy of list of tythables:—107
Corn (chiefly for the poor):—12⁸, 31, 114, 120, 132, 133, 155, 176, 181, 191, 229, 234, 331, 333, 336, 341, 348, 349, 350³, 357, 362¹⁰
"Cottin for the Negro Woman at the Work house":—332
Council, Clerk of the:—80
  held at Williamsburgh:—79
Counting tobacco plants:—180
County Court:—148
Court, order of:—11, 37, 196
Cow and calf for poor woman:—292
Creed, Lord's Prayer and Ten Commandments:—253
Crimson velvet cloth:—285
Cure (Curing) poor people:—89, 153, 160
Cushion (for Communion Table):—9, 284, 346
"Cutting Off Tho Fleming Arme":—234
Cypress heart boards:—168

Dairy on Glebe:—259
Deacon:—387
Dead lights:—384
"Decease of the Late Revr^d. Mr Emañuel Jones":—257
Deciding vote in Vestry cast by minister:—121
Deeds (to Glebe land):—351
Delinquents:—128, 207, 208, 221, 231²
Dial:—290
Digging grave:—274, 335
Disagreement in Vestry over question of who should pay cost of repairs on Glebe:—258
"Discharg'd from paying Parish Levy":—280
Doctor agreeing to take care of poor woman put under bond:—183
Donations from the congregation to be asked for four times a year:—383
Door, lock to church:—8
  mending the church:—155

"Draweing ye Cherubin":—11
Dried meat:—12²
Dyal (sun dial), to be set up at the church:—215, 217
  post:—190, 229

Easter—date for Church Wardens to go into office:—10
"easing ye Parrish of an olphan child":—63
Election, of Clerk of Church and Vestry:—56
  of "Lecturer":—386
  of Minister of the Parish:—65, 257
  of Vesry:—378, 381, 388
  of Vestrymen:—14, 355, 374
Enlargement of Poplar Spring Church:—68
Excellency, his:—80
  his in Council:—79, 80
Exon vs. Evans:—1
Expedition against Indians:—2

Fees:—5, 23, 24, 31, 33, 35, 52², 63, 73², 76, 77, 89², 94, 120, 132², 134², 186, 225, 287
"Ferrages":—262
"Finding the Negro Woman Cloths at the work house":—331
Finding a coffin and burying:—233
Fine(s):—36, 102, 106, 133, 136³, 137, 138, 184, 205, 219, 222, 252, 307, 309, 310, 313
  for servant:—11³
  for swearing:—136
  Ann Willitt's:—6
  maid's:—2
  servant's:—9
  woman's:—6, 25⁵
  woman servant's:—9, 27
  of ten shillings on Vestrymen failing to attend meetings:—77
  to the poor of the parish:—133
Fine money, given to the poor:—137, 184, 205, 219, 222, 223, 233, 236, 241, 252, 267, 269, 309
  belonging to the poor of the parish:—310, 313
First precinct, bounds of:—171
Food and clothing for the poor:—341

"Forreigner":—19
Foreigners in the parish, Vestry order concerning entertainment of:—42
Forms (i. e. benches?):—52, 134
"Four Duz: panes of London Duble Crownd Glass":—205
Frame for King's arms:—11
"free houlder, house Keeper or freeman":—64, 70, 74, 77, 84, 87
Freeholders and housekeepers:—378, 381
Freeholders and housekeepers to meet with Vestry to decide about building brick church:—40
Freeman, liberty to take one:—21
Frocks:—55

Gallery at Poplar Spring Church:—239, 241, 242, 267
Garden to be built at the Work House:—344
General Assembly:—179, 250, 377
General Convention:—384, 385
Gentlemen "summon^d to meat the Vestry":—95
George I, King:—122, 124, 125, 126, 135, 144, 145, 146, 147, 158, 161, 169, 170, 177, 178, 185, 193
George II, King:—198, 199, 201, 203, 204, 209, 213, 215^2, 216
George III, King:—351
"George ye Currier":—17
Gifts to the parish (of wine, silver flagon, bowls, and plates, books, etc):—9, 24, 25^2
Glasier:—8, 120
Glass:—5, 69, 114, 205, 217
Glazing Church windows:—274
Glebe:—69, 73, 76, 83, 117, 120, 272, 316, 345
  to be bought:—48, 72
  to be added to:—116
  barn at the:—338
  benefit of the:—381, 383, 386
  building of houses on to be advertised:—298
  buildings to be repaired:—220
  buildings on the:—298
  chimneys:—114, 139
  deeds to:—351
  lime for:—120^2
  mansion house on:—220
  mending windows at:—288
  new buildings to be erected on:—259
  out-houses on, to be repaired:—278
  "pailing a Garden at":—264
  rent of the:—322, 329, 369, 382, 389
  repairing the:—226, 242, 258, 259, 264, 272, 305, 314, 316, 339
  tenant of the:—386
  terrier of the:—351
  threshing floor at:—281, 346
  tobacco house on:—191, 281, 282, 337
  Vestry held at:—264
  work done on:—281, 286, 301, 307
Glebe house:—75, 86^2, 275
  and kitchen to be built:—85
  repairing the:—105, 118, 140, 142, 153, 225, 245
  plastering the:—120
  new, to be built:—273, 274
  burned:—375
Glebe land, quitrents of:—191^2, 201, 207, 217, 221, 226, 229, 230, 233, 239, 240, 245, 248, 254, 263, 267, 271, 274, 275, 277, 279, 281, 285, 287, 290, 292, 296, 298, 300, 302, 306, 308, 311, 315, 320, 325, 328, 330, 335, 338, 340, 342, 344, 347, 349, 352, 356, 358
  surveying the:—121
  tax for the:—300, 360
Gloucester (County) Court:—111^7, 112^4, 129^4, 130^3, 131^2, 148^3, 149^3, 150^2, 151^2, 171, 172^2, 173^2, 174^2, 175, 198^3, 203, 210, 211, 212, 213, 223, 230, 237, 283, 294, 304, 318, 333, 353, 363, 370
Gloucester Court, Clerk of:—154
  Order for dividing Petso parish into precincts:—96
  Sheriff of:—154
Gold leaf:—274, 253
Goods, payments to poor to be made in:—205
Goods to or for the poor:—160, 190, 249, 254^2, 259
Gout, the:—93

GLOUCESTER COUNTY, VIRGINIA, 1677-1793   421

Cooper, art and skill of a:—61
Coopery, art of:—56
Copy of list of tythables:—107
Corn (chiefly for the poor):—12^8, 31, 114, 120, 132, 133, 155, 176, 181, 191, 229, 234, 331, 333, 336, 341, 348, 349, 350^3, 357, 362^{10}
"Cottin for the Negro Woman at the Work house":—332
Council, Clerk of the:—80
 held at Williamsburgh:—79
Counting tobacco plants:—180
County Court:—148
Court, order of:—11, 37, 196
Cow and calf for poor woman:—292
Creed, Lord's Prayer and Ten Commandments:—253
Crimson velvet cloth:—285
Cure (Curing) poor people:—89, 153, 160
Cushion (for Communion Table):—9, 284, 346
"Cutting Off Tho Fleming Arme":—234
Cypress heart boards:—168

Dairy on Glebe:—259
Deacon:—387
Dead lights:—384
"Decease of the Late Revr^d. Mr Emañuel Jones":—257
Deciding vote in Vestry cast by minister:—121
Deeds (to Glebe land):—351
Delinquents:—128, 207, 208, 221, 231^2
Dial:—290
Digging grave:—274, 335
Disagreement in Vestry over question of who should pay cost of repairs on Glebe:—258
"Discharg'd from paying Parish Levy":—280
Doctor agreeing to take care of poor woman put under bond:—183
Donations from the congregation to be asked for four times a year:—383
Door, lock to church:—8
 mending the church:—155

"Draweing ye Cherubin":—11
Dried meat:—12^2
Dyal (sun dial), to be set up at the church:—215, 217
 post:—190, 229

Easter—date for Church Wardens to go into office:—10
"easing ye Parrish of an olphan child":—63
Election, of Clerk of Church and Vestry:—56
 of "Lecturer":—386
 of Minister of the Parish:—65, 257
 of Vesry:—378, 381, 388
 of Vestrymen:—14, 355, 374
Enlargement of Poplar Spring Church:—68
Excellency, his:—80
 his in Council:—79, 80
Exon vs. Evans:—1
Expedition against Indians:—2

Fees:—5, 23, 24, 31, 33, 35, 52^2, 63, 73^2, 76, 77, 89^2, 94, 120, 132^2, 134^2, 186, 225, 287
"Ferrages":—262
"Finding the Negro Woman Cloths at the work house":—331
Finding a coffin and burying:—233
Fine(s):—36, 102, 106, 133, 136^3, 137, 138, 184, 205, 219, 222, 252, 307, 309, 310, 313
 for servant:—11^3
 for swearing:—136
 Ann Willitt's:—6
 maid's:—2
 servant's:—9
 woman's:—6, 25^5
 woman servant's:—9, 27
 of ten shillings on Vestrymen failing to attend meetings:—77
 to the poor of the parish:—133
Fine money, given to the poor:—137, 184, 205, 219, 222, 223, 233, 236, 241, 252, 267, 269, 309
 belonging to the poor of the parish:—310, 313
First precinct, bounds of:—171
Food and clothing for the poor:—341

"Forreigner":—19
Foreigners in the parish, Vestry order concerning entertainment of:—42
Forms (i. e. benches?):—52, 134
"Four Duz: panes of London Duble Crownd Glass":—205
Frame for King's arms:—11
"free houlder, house Keeper or freeman":—64, 70, 74, 77, 84, 87
Freeholders and housekeepers:—378, 381
Freeholders and housekeepers to meet with Vestry to decide about building brick church:—40
Freeman, liberty to take one:—21
Frocks:—55

Gallery at Poplar Spring Church:—239, 241, 242, 267
Garden to be built at the Work House:—344
General Assembly:—179, 250, 377
General Convention:—384, 385
Gentlemen "summon^d to meat the Vestry":—95
George I, King:—122, 124, 125, 126, 135, 144, 145, 146, 147, 158, 161, 169, 170, 177, 178, 185, 193
George II, King:—198, 199, 201, 203, 204, 209, 213, 215^2, 216
George III, King:—351
"George ye Currier":—17
Gifts to the parish (of wine, silver flagon, bowls, and plates, books, etc):—9, 24, 25^2
Glasier:—8, 120
Glass:—5, 69, 114, 205, 217
Glazing Church windows:—274
Glebe:—69, 73, 76, 83, 117, 120, 272, 316, 345
  to be bought:—48, 72
  to be added to:—116
  barn at the:—338
  benefit of the:—381, 383, 386
  building of houses on to be advertised:—298
  buildings to be repaired:—220
  buildings on the:—298
  chimneys:—114, 139
  deeds to:—351
  lime for:—120^2
  mansion house on:—220
  mending windows at:—288
  new buildings to be erected on:—259
  out-houses on, to be repaired:—278
  "pailing a Garden at":—264
  rent of the:—322, 329, 369, 382, 389
  repairing the:—226, 242, 258, 259, 264, 272, 305, 314, 316, 339
  tenant of the:—386
  terrier of the:—351
  threshing floor at:—281, 346
  tobacco house on:—191, 281, 282, 337
  Vestry held at:—264
  work done on:—281, 286, 301, 307
Glebe house:—75, 86^2, 275
  and kitchen to be built:—85
  repairing the:—105, 118, 140, 142, 153, 225, 245
  plastering the:—120
  new, to be built:—273, 274
  burned:—375
Glebe land, quitrents of:—191^2, 201, 207, 217, 221, 226, 229, 230, 233, 239, 240, 245, 248, 254, 263, 267, 271, 274, 275, 277, 279, 281, 285, 287, 290, 292, 296, 298, 300, 302, 306, 308, 311, 315, 320, 325, 328, 330, 335, 338, 340, 342, 344, 347, 349, 352, 356, 358
  surveying the:—121
  tax for the:—300, 360
Gloucester (County) Court:—111^7, 112^4, 129^4, 130^3, 131^2, 148^3, 149^3, 150^2, 151^2, 171, 172^2, 173^2, 174^2, 175, 198^3, 203, 210, 211, 212, 213, 223, 230, 237, 283, 294, 304, 318, 333, 353, 363, 370
Gloucester Court, Clerk of:—154
  Order for dividing Petso parish into precincts:—96
  Sheriff of:—154
Gold leaf:—274, 253
Goods, payments to poor to be made in:—205
Goods to or for the poor:—160, 190, 249, 254^2, 259
Gout, the:—93

Governor, the :—25, 318, 324
Grand Jury :—230, 361
Great subscriptions made for organ: —236
"Green or Blue plains" :—332

Hair, 2½ bushels of :—120
"Half-thick & Canvis" :—332
Help to be no longer given to certain persons able to maintain themselves :—106
Henry, Lord Bishop of London :—57
Highways, to be cleared and amended :—38
  Surveyors of to be presented to court for neglect of :—50, 77
  Overseers or surveyors of :—4, 10, 38, 42, 44, 53, 55[2], 65[2], 68, 74, 87[2]
Hinges :—15, 343
Hire of Negroes :—308, 331, 335, 339, 349
His Excellency (the Governor) :—63, 79, 80[2]
Homilies, Book of :—25
Hooks :—15
Horse and man :—12[8], 15[8]
Horse block :—41, 54, 89, 108, 117, 155, 217, 221, 225, 234, 240, 249, 262, 287, 303, 343
"House for the poor" :—327
Housekeepers and freeholders to meet with Vestry to decide about building church :—40
Hubbard's Store (Mr. James) :—233

Indenture, taking by :—279[2]
  wording of :—59, 60, 61, 66[2], 70, 75, 84, 92, 113, 122, 124, 135, 144, 145, 146, 147, 158, 161, 169, 170, 177, 178, 185, 192, 195, 198, 199, 201, 202, 204, 209, 210, 211, 212, 213, 215, 216
Indentures, Clerk of Vestry to be paid 5 shillings for every pair made by him :—228
Indentures for binding out children—
  to be made by Clerk of Vestry :—56
  to be sealed and delivered by Clerk of Vestry :—30
  to be signed by Clerk of Vestry :—21, 117, 142
Indians, expedition against :—2
Indigent sick persons :—280
"Inducted as minister" :—387
Induction of ministers :—80
  Opinion of Sir Edw[d] Northey relative to :—77
Inhabitants, meet to make choice of Vestry (1690) :—28
  of the parish :—40
  to notify nearest Church Waden before entertaining "any Foreigner or persons of another pish" :—19
"Inlargening y[e] Church" :—69
Insolvents :—298, 307, 315, 320, 329, 330[2], 341, 348, 349, 353, 357
Inspector's notes :—227
Insured the danger of the seas, organ to be :—236
Interest due on Bond due to the parish :—370
Iron work :—11

James III (so called) King of England :—126
Joiner :—205
Joiner's inside work :—8
"journeys from James Town" :—32
Juries, returns of from the Court concerning processioning : — 129, 148, 171
Justices of Peace :—143

Key, mending the Church :—341
King George I :—45, 122, 124, 125, 126, 135, 144, 145, 146, 147, 158, 161, 169, 170, 177, 178, 185, 193
King George II :—198, 199, 201, 203, 204, 209, 213, 215[2], 216
King George III :—351
King William III :—45, 59, 60, 61, 66[2], 70
King's arms :—11
  highways :—44, 45

Land tax :—299
Lath, white wash, & plaister the Church :—7

Law book for the parish:—234
Laws relating to the "poor of the parish & vestry":—112
Lawsuit (parish):—26, 267, 268, 280, 290, 303, 310, 322, 323, 337, 338, 370², 382, 389
Lawyer:—264
"Laying a Thrashing Floor":—281
Lead on pediments of church:—166, 221
Leading the windows:—234
Leaf gold:—247, 253
Leak in the Church:—267
Leaves of leaf gold:—247
Lecturer of the parish:—383
Leg, care and cure of:—153, 176, 201, 244
Legacies to the parish and to the poor of the parish:—18, 54, 70, 118, 370
Letter from Governor Sir Francis Nicholson:—57, 80
Levy free:—59, 166
Lime made from oyster shells:—7
"for mending yᵉ Gleib Chimneys":—114
for the Church:—120
for the Glebe:—120²
List of Tythables to be gotten every year:—156, 190
Lock to Church door:—8
London, Bishop of:—57, 317, 324
"loss of weights in his tobaccoes":—89
Lower Church:—20, 39
Lower precinct:—123, 156, 161, 177, 184, 194, 218, 222, 226, 232, 240, 246, 247, 255, 265

Maid's fine:—2
"Making the Coffin & Diging the Grave":—231
Mansion house on Glebe:—220
Master, his:—253
Masters to be provided for two orphan boys:—270
Masters and mistresses must teach orphans to read:—183
Matrimony, fee for publishing banns of:—58
Meal:—12
Meat for the poor:—31, 349

Meat house on Glebe:—259
Medicine for the poor:—69, 152, 159², 263, 276, 298
Mending benches:—115
Church doors:—108, 155, 205
Church Key:—341
Church windows:—288, 367
the surplice:—327
Merchant at Mr. Thornton's:—137
Messrs Jones & Scott:—287
Minding the work house:—331, 335
Minister—appointed Parish Collector:—95
authorized to hire workman:—225
casts deciding vote in Vestry:—121
continued in parish "on likeing" etc:—14
election of:—65, 257
resigns parish:—340
to be paid by subscription:—368
to be secured to officiate temporarily:—326
to give public notice of processioning:—100
to make repairs on Glebe:—242
to officiate temporarily:—318
will resign living if forced to pay for repairs:—220
Ministers—induction of:—80
opinion of Attorney General Sir Edwᵈ Northey relative to induction of:—78
Mistress of the Work House (poor house):—328, 341, 342, 343, 345, 348, 349, 352, 355, 357, 359
Molasses:—120
Money—to the poor to be paid in goods:—223², 233, 241
that was collected in the Church:—384²
Montague's Store:—223
"Moved out of the Coliny":—355
Moving the poor:—288, 290, 349
Mulatto:—75, 135², 136
Mulatto bastard child:—33
Mulatto boy whose mother was a white woman:—75

Nails:—5, ११२², 23, 24, 38, 108, 134, 226, 297

Neat or neet (tobacco) :—282, 303, 306, 308, 311², 315, 320², 324, 325, 330², 335², 338², 339, 340², 342², 344³, 347², 349², 351, 352, 356, 357
Necessaries for the poor :—104, 231, 301
Necessary house on Glebe :—259
Negroes, hire of :—308, 331, 335, 339, 349
Negro woman at Work House, "cottin for the" :—332
New Church :—155, 156², 157², 160, 161, 165, 166, 167², 168, 177
New column under the Gallery :—267
New Glebe house to be built :—273
Nicholson, Letter from Governor Sir Francis :—57, 80, 81
Nursing a bastard :—231

Oak—lathes :—85
  chest :—285
Oaths (various forms of and references to) :—45, 47, 53², 55³, 96, 123², 124³, 125³, 127, 194, 219, 222, 250
Objection of vestryman to action of Vestry :—192
Old Church :—22, 23, 24, 47, 167, 176
Old and past their labors :—122
Opinion of Sir Edwd Northey :—78, 79, 80
Order of Court :—2, 11, 37, 96, 196
Order of Vestry—for building brick church, suspended :—40
  concerning the entertainment of Foreigners :—42
  relative to money subscribed for organ :—244
Orders of Vestry to be signed by two vestrymen :—261
Ordinance, The :—358²
Ordinance of Convention :—381
Ordination :—317, 324, 387
Ogan (various references to) :—236, 243, 245, 246, 247, 249², 260
Organ gallery :—242
Organ pipes :—249
Organist (various references to) : —244, 246², 247, 250, 255, 261

Ornaments for the Church :—287, 289, 291
Orphan, orphans :—14, 20, 21², 24, 63², 84, 113, 122, 124, 144, 145, 146, 147, 158, 161, 164, 169, 170, 177, 178, 182, 185, 194, 195², 196², 198³, 202, 203, 204, 209, 216, 226², 227, 232, 280, 345
Orphan children, bound out, to be taught to read by the time they are 13 years old :—183
Overseer(s) of Highways :—38, 42, 44³, 50, 53, 55², 65², 68, 87²
Oxen, carriage by :—1
Oyster shells for lime :—7

Paling the Church yard, Glebe etc : —11, 38, 54, 76, 120, 264
Painting :—11, 239, 247, 252, 253
Parish—agrees to indemnify Stratton Major Parish :—350
  divided into three parts for highway supervision :—4
  boy :—215
  child :—91, 93
  girl :—92, 94
  levies, excused from paying :—188, 189
  to institute lawsuit :—26
  woman :—45
Parliament—Act of :—45, 55
  Oaths enjoined by Act of :—53
Passage of pauper back to England :—21, 26, 187
Pediment(s) over doors, lead on the :—166, 221
Perry (Micajah) & Co. :—72
Personal charity of minister and vestrymen :—32
Petition (s) :—195², 250, 377
Petsworth—first occurrence of the word in the Vesty Book :—127
Parish Church :—285
Pews :—155
Physic :—49², 86, 94, 114, 134
"Plains" :—332
Plank(s) :—8, 108
Plantation :—21²
Plaster, Plasterer, Plastering :—7, 8, 29, 55, 113, 120³
Poor, care of the (various references to) :—26², 29, 32, 36, 53,

54, 55, 69, 70, 77, 112, 122, 128², 133, 136, 137³, 181, 184, 187, 189, 190, 205, 219, 222, 223³, 229, 233, 234, 236, 241², 249, 252, 254², 257, 259, 267, 269, 278, 280, 287, 288, 292, 298, 299, 301, 303, 309, 310, 313, 327, 329, 332, 336⁷, 341, 353, 362¹⁰, 369, 385²
Poor's house—Mistress of the :—328
  Provision & necessaries for :—329
Pope, the :—45
Porch to church :—17
Pork for the poor :—336
Pork and beef "for the youse of the Work House" :—333
Posting the Church :—23, 41
Posts for the Church :—42
Powder :—12
Precincts for processioning :—171, 172³, 173², 174², 175
Precinct, Lower :—156
Precincts, Totopomoy Swamp to be dividing line between upper and lower :—122
Present—of £5 to poor of the parish :—137
  to the parish made by Mr. Augustine Smith :—246
Presentation of living :—80
Presentment to Court for neglect in repairing highways :—77
Prices—tar and nails :—23
Prince of Wales :—126
Princess Sophia of Hannover :—126
"Priseing" tobacco" :—357
Processioner, processioners, processioning, processionings : — 100, 109, 110, 111, 112, 113, 129, 133, 148², 149, 150, 151, 153, 171
Processioning orders :—171, 172, 173, 174, 175, 196, 197, 223, 224, 227, 228, 237, 238, 255, 257, 266, 283, 284, 294, 295, 304, 305, 318, 319, 320, 333, 334, 354, 355, 363, 364, 365, 370
Protection in the execution of his office asked by Church Warden :—192
Protestant Episcopal Church :—386, 388

Provisions etc for the poor, the Poor's house, the Work House :—329, 332, 336, 348
Public Landing :—357
Publishing Banns of matrimony :—14
Pulling down the old Church :—176
Pulpit—to be on the north side of the Church :—163
  to send to England for a :—284
  cloth bequeathed to parish :—10
"purchasing of a gleeb" :—72

Queen Anne :—84, 92, 113
Quitrents :—191², 201, 207, 217, 221, 226, 229, 230, 233, 239, 240, 245, 248, 254, 263, 265, 267, 271, 274, 275, 777, 279, 281, 285, 287, 290, 292, 296, 298, 300, 302, 306, 308, 311, 315, 320, 325, 328, 330, 335, 338, 340, 342, 344, 347, 349, 352, 356, 358
Quoetus :—88
Quorum, three out of a committee of five to constitute a :—272

Read (well, or perfectly in) any Chapter in (or part of) the Bible :—84, 85, 113, 122, 124, 135, 144, 145, 146, 147, 158, 162, 169, 170, 178, 179, 186, 193, 195, 199, 200, 202, 203, 204, 209, 210, 211, 212, 213, 215, 216
Reader (or Clerk) to be paid for publishing banns of matrimony :—14
Rebuilding the old Church :—41, 47
Recommendation for ordination :—317, 324, 386
Record book for processioners' returns :—133, 148
Rector of Pettsoe :—81², 82², 88
Refusal to serve as vestryman :—273, 337
Regester, or register book (i. e. Vestry Book) :—25, 69
Rent—of the Glebe :—329, 369, 389
  of the Work House :—367, 369, 373
Repairs, of various sorts :—22, 30, 74, 83, 87, 105, 109, 113, 118, 139, 140, 142, 153, 220, 225, 226, 233,

234, 242, 245, 258, 259, 264, 272, 278, 301, 305, 314, 316, 339, 342
Resignation—of Collector :—358
  of Minister :—340
  of Vestryman :—95, 188, 230, 292
Returns (processioning) :—129, 133
Riv'd boards :—27
River (i. e. York River) :—63
Roads and bridges to be cleared and mended :—68
Rome, See of :—45
"Rouling Tobb" (i. e. tobacco) :—72, 73, 91
Rug :—41, 132
Rum :—120
"run away" :—140

Sacrament—of the Lord's Supper: —46
  use of the :—384
  bread and wine for the :—385
Salary—of Clerk of the Parish :—25
  of Clerk of the Vestry :—25
"Salivates" :—104
Salt :—329, 336
"Saudering the Organ pips" :—249
Sawen (sawed) Timber :—13
"Sawyer" (possibly a family name) :—196, 223
Sawyer's work :—8
Scaffolding :—253, 254
Schooling :—112, 116[2]
Seats for Church yard :—234
"Secretaries Note" :—282
Security :—2, 6, 92, 323, 346[2], 348, 350
"sedar pale 2: stooles a pewter bason" :—69
See of Rome :—45
Servant (man, woman) :—2, 7, 9, 17
Serving a writ :—285
Sexton :—4, 8, 10, 11, 15, 17, 19, 20, 22, 24[2], 29[2], 31, 33[2], 35[2], 38[2], 41[2], 43[2], 49, 50, 51, 52, 53, 54, 63, 69, 73, 76, 83, 86[2], 120, 139, 186, 190, 200, 207, 218, 220, 225, 228, 230, 233, 239, 240, 245, 248, 254, 259, 262, 263, 267, 271, 274, 275, 277, 279, 281, 285, 287, 289, 290, 292, 294, 296, 298, 300, 302, 306, 308, 311, 315, 320, 325, 328, 330, 335, 338, 341, 342, 345, 346, 347, 349, 352, 357, 359, 360, 366, 367, 369, 372, 373, 374, 376
Sexton, spade and hoe to be provided for :—346
Sextonis (woman sexton) :—88, 90, 94, 102, 103, 107, 114, 116, 131, 134, 141, 143, 152[2], 154, 159, 163, 175, 177, 181
"Sheat to bury Tho[s] Burk" :—331
Sheet & Coffin :—342
Sheriff :—20[3], 154, 160, 163, 176, 207, 221, 225, 226, 231, 233
Sheriff as Parish Collector :—20
Sheriff's fees :—20, 52, 73, 77, 89[2], 132
Sheriff's note :—348
Shingles :—16, 85, 132, 134, 248
Shingling the Church :—27, 90, 92, 134
Ship Captain :—187
"Shipping" :—14, 17, 80
Shirts :—55, 86
Shoes (and stockings) for poor people :—31, 164
Shot (3[lb]) :—128
Side-men :—26
Silver—Bowls :—25
  Flagon :—25
  Plates :—25
"Singing Psalms" :—56
"Siprus shingles :—85
Smith's work :—290
Soldiers' accounts :—12
  charge :—13, 15
Sophia, Electress of Hannover :—126
Spade and hoe for sexton :—346
Specifications :—3, 39, 75, 85
Stable (and Hen house) on Glebe: —259, 298
Standing rule of the Vestry :—261
Steps for the organ :—249
"Stop the leak in the Church" :—267
Store—Mr. James Hubbard's :—233
  Mr. Montague's :—223
Subscribers to Minister's salary :—368
Subscriptions — toward building church :—1
  toward Minister's salary :—368

Suit (law) :—1, 117, 264
Summoning witnesses :—288
Sundries for the poor :—385^2
Supplies for the Work House :—343
Supply minister for the parish :—313
Supremacy oath of :—222
Surplice (purchase, washing, mending of) :—24, 112, 134, 225, 229, 231, 276, 327
Surveyor(s) of Highways :—4^3, 10, 64, 74^2, 84
"Surveying ye Glieb land" :—121
"Sweareing," fine for :—136

Table Cloth (and Napkins) :—284, 377
Taking an (by) Indenture :—226, 229^3, 231^2, 234^2, 239, 279^2
Tar :—11, 23, 29, 33, 49^2, 166, 220, 248
"Tarring ye Church" :—15, 49, 249
Tax (Land) :—299, 300, 360
Tenant of the Glebe :—386
"Tending the Parish Cause against Stratonmajor Parish" :—281
Terrier of the Glebe :—351
Test—the :—47, 55, 96
 wording of the :—46, 127^2
Three years schooling :—59, 60, 61, 71, 91, 92^2, 124, 135, 144, 145, 146, 158, 162, 169, 170, 178, 179, 185, 193, 195, 198, 199, 202, 203, 204, 209, 210, 211, 212, 213, 215
Threshing floor in barn :—346
Timber :—5, 8, 13, 38
Tithables—number of in 1679 :—13
 number of in 1680 :—15
 concealment of :—26
 list of :—107, 240, 245, 263, 276, 279, 281, 285, 287, 290, 292, 296, 298, 300, 306, 308, 311, 315, 320, 325, 330, 335, 338, 341, 352, 360, 361, 366, 367, 369, 372, 374, 376
Tobacco—Act :—179, 184, 189, 206, 214
 Counters (or Tellers) :—184, 189, 194, 206, 214
 for the Poor :—369

house on Glebe :—191, 281, 282, 337
Law :—123
plants, counting :—180
Transubstantiation :—46
Treasurer :—380^2, 382, 383, 385^2, 389
 of Fund to defray expenses of Bishop :—378
Tub :—120
"Turn to Serve" as Church Warden :—222
Two years schooling :—66, 113

"Unleagally Sent into this Parish" :—257
Upper Church :—20
Upper Precinct(s) :—161^2, 177, 183, 191, 222, 226, 230, 235, 237, 241, 250, 252, 268, 276
"Use of the Hospitol" :—357
Use of the Work House :—352

Very Indigent & Dropsical :—189
Very Old & past his Labour :—133, 134, 138, 166
Vestry—agrees with minister of Stratton Major Parish to preach :—48, 52
 arranges to provide for passage of pauper to England :—21, 26
 chosen by "Inhabitants" in meeting (1690) :—28
 election of :—381, 388
 orders that two overseers of highways for upper part of the parish be appointed :—44
 orders that there shall be but one church in the parish :—47
 orders that notice be published of its desire to buy land for a Glebe :—48
 orders that two men be "presented to Next Court" for not sufficiently repairing highways :—77
 orders that no further financial help be given certain persons :—106
 standing rule of :—261
 suspends former order for building a brick church :—40

votes not to build a chapel:—39
votes to replace old church with a new one:—39
votes on question of allowing Cask:—121
Vestry and Inhabitants approve the life and conversation of their minister:—17
Vestry Book:—112, 119, 124
Vestry house:—195, 233, 234, 331
Vestryman—appointed to oversee the Work House:—356
wording of oaths taken by:—45, 47
objects to action of Vestry:—192
refuses to continue to serve:—192
refuses to serve:—337
released from office on ground of ill health:—93
resigns office:—95, 230
strikes his name out of Vestry Book:—192
Vestryman-elect refuses to qualify:—368
Vestrymen—election of:—14, 374
not coming to meetings to be fined:—77
oath of:—124
Visits and Medicines:—159
Vote in Vestry whether Cask should be allowed:—121

Wales, Prince of:—126
Wall, building the:—218
Walls of Poplar Spring Church:—74
Washing the surplice:—225, 229, 231
Wench:—18, 20
Wheat:—331

White oak sills:—85
Whitewash (whitewashing): — 7, 55, 120
William III, King:—59, 60, 61, 66^2, 70
Wills:—21^3
Windows, repairs to:—301, 342, 367
Wine:—132, 134^2, 139, 190, 201, 221^4
Wine for the Communion:—5, 11^2, 15^2, 23, 24^2, 154, 160, 164, 187, 217^2, 221, 226, 229, 231, 239, 246, 249, 255, 260
Wine, sugar and rum for poor man:—94
Woman—as sexton:—4, 8, 20
servant:—32, 33
Woman's fine:—6, 25^2
Woman servant's fine:—9, 11^2, 27
Wording of—Oath of Abjuration:—125
Oath of Allegiance:—125
Oath of a Vestryman:—127
Oath of Supremacy:—125
the Test:—127
Work House (various references to):—326, 329, 331^3, 332^2, 333^2, 335^2, 336^2, 339, 340, 341^2, 342, 343^3, 344, 345^2, 348^2, 349^3, 352^2, 355, 356, 357, 359, 367, 369, 373
Workman:—118^2
Worship, Doctrine, and Discipline of the Protestant Episcopal Church:—388
Writ, serving a:—285
"writing ye vers. on ye Guarder. in ye Church":—55

"Y^e old Church," mending:—34

www.ingramcontent.com/pod-product-compliance
Lightning Source LLC
Chambersburg PA
CBHW020054020526
44112CB00031B/125